HISTORY

OF THE

GERMAN SETTLEMENTS

AND OF THE

Lutheran Church

IN

NORTH AND SOUTH CAROLINA,

FROM THE EARLIEST PERIOD OF THE COLONIZATION
OF THE DUTCH, GERMAN AND SWISS SETTLERS
TO THE CLOSE OF THE FIRST HALF OF
THE PRESENT CENTURY.

BY

G. D. BERNHEIM,

PASTOR OF ST. PAUL'S EVANGELICAL LUTHERAN CHURCH, WILMINGTON, N. C.

"LOOK UNTO THE ROCK WHENCE YE ARE HEWN."
—ISAIAH 51:1.

PHILADELPHIA:
THE LUTHERAN BOOK STORE,
117 NORTH SIXTH STREET.
1872.

PHILADELPHIA:

SHERMAN & CO., PRINTERS.

TO

THE MEMORY

OF

REV. ERNEST LEWIS HAZELIUS, D.D.,

AND TO

REV. JOHN BACHMAN, D.D., LL.D.,

STILL LIVING,

TO WHOM THE LUTHERAN CHURCH IN THE CAROLINAS IS GREATLY INDEBTED FOR ITS PRESERVATION AND PROSPERITY,

THESE PAGES

ARE RESPECTFULLY DEDICATED,

BY

THE AUTHOR.

PREFACE.

An historical work requires no haste in its production,—it should be the creature of time, inasmuch as the arrangement of material, the weighing of testimony, and the search for missing links in the chain of narrative, all require time. That the historical contribution which is herewith offered to the public has not been hastily prepared, nor unadvisedly thrust upon the reader's notice, may be seen from the following statements.

In the year 1851, the Lutheran Synod of South Carolina, by resolution, made it the duty of the author to gather together a copy of all its printed minutes, have them properly bound, and place the bound volumes in the library of its Theological Seminary. In so doing, the author became interested in the records of Synod, provided a set of duplicate copies for himself, and arranged certain tables of statistics of that Synod, exhibiting the gradual increase of the Church, the date of each minister's licensure and ordination, &c., &c., and had these written statistics bound with his volumes of the Synod's minutes, merely for his own private use and future reference. A prominent minister of that Synod happening to overlook these statistics, suggested the propriety of their publication. To which the author replied, that it might be done, provided the minutes of the North Carolina Synod could also be procured, and similar statistical tables be arranged from them, when both could be published at the same time.

Not long afterwards, in 1858, the author was called to reside in North Carolina, when he commenced collecting the minutes of the Lutheran Synod of that State also, and found such a large amount of additional historical documents, that he became exceedingly interested in the search, and the labor has been to him a recreation and a pleasure rather than a wearisome toil. Public libraries were next visited; the records of the Secretaries of State in the Capitol buildings of North and South Carolina were examined; each colony of Germans in the two Carolinas was traced to its origin; missionary journals, discovered to have been sent from the first ministers in North Carolina to Germany and there published, but no longer known to have any existence, were sought after and obtained in Europe; all of which produced a collection of historical material greater than was at first believed to be possible.

During the years, from 1861 to 1864, the author published, from the material then on hand, seventy-two "Historical Sketches" in the columns of the "*Southern Lutheran*," which were received with so much favor, that unsolicited suggestions came from Rev. John Bachman, D.D., LL.D., and from editors of several Southern journals, to have these "Historical Sketches published in a more convenient and durable form;" besides, letters were received from private parties urging the same thing. On a visit to the North at the close of the war, these "Sketches" were exhibited to Rev. Dr. Hawks, of New York, author of the History of North Carolina, and to Rev. Dr. Krauth, of Philadelphia, and the same suggestion was repeated by both those learned gentlemen.

And now, believing that the information contained in this work is too valuable to be lost; believing also, that the ripe and scholarly judgment of others should not be disregarded; believing, that the labor of twenty-one years, the leisure time of which was mostly spent in gathering together the materials for this work, should not be spent in vain; and lastly, believing that some good towards the advancing of the interests of the Redeemer's kingdom will thereby be effected, and that a generous public will so regard this work, these pages are sent upon the world with the earnest hope that they may accomplish this their mission.

But probably the most important question is: Is this book a reliable historical work? To which the author replies, that it is as much so, as human labor and patient toil can make it. This work has been altogether a labor of love, hence no pains were spared to make it eminently correct and exact in dates, names, localities, &c. That it occasionally comes in conflict with other historical authorities could not be avoided, as the author felt assured that Church records, missionary reports, records of the Councils of State, minutes of Synod, private journals and the like sources of information, produced at the time when the events occurred, are all of them more reliable than the statements made by authors, who had not these records at their command, however highly those authors may otherwise be regarded.

Some of them were unacquainted with the German language, German characteristics, and the religion of the German settlers, hence originated the errors that are sometimes found in American histories in reference to the German colonists.

It was deemed unnecessary to furnish a list on one or more separate pages of the sources whence the materials for this work were derived; but, in order to remove all doubt concerning the reliability of this work, it was thought to be more serviceable to the reader to mention the names of authorities on the page where such authors and records are quoted.

There is a niche in the history of North and South Carolina that has never been filled. It is a well-known fact that these two Provinces were largely settled by German colonists, and yet their history has hitherto never been fully written. In the various histories of North Carolina we have extended accounts of the German settlements at Newberne and at Salem, but of the other German settlers, who located themselves in the central and western parts of the State, nothing is said, although they comprise more than three-fourths of the German population. South Carolina historians have been equally remiss; with the exception of the Purysburg and the Hard Labor Creek settlements, very little is said concerning those colonies from Germany and Switzerland, which were spread over a large portion of the interior of that Province. There can be but one solution of this apparent neglect, and that is, the records of these German settlements were couched in a language foreign to those historical writers. It is hoped that the omission has been, at least, largely supplied. A few more years, and the records of the history of our German forefathers would have passed beyond human reach. In view of this fact, how forcible are the remarks of Dr. Ramsay in the preface to his "History of South Carolina:" "Every day that minute local histories of these States are deferred is an injury to posterity, for, by means thereof, more of that knowledge which ought to be transmitted to them will be irrecoverably lost."

The author confesses to a few omissions in this work, and that this history has not been extended to the present time. His reason for the latter fact is, that occurrences so recent can scarcely be regarded as history, until they have been mellowed by age—have passed into perspective—when "distance lends enchantment to the view." At all events, the author prefers to close at a point, where he will not be obliged to record occurrences in which he was more or less personally interested.

The first *omission* consists in the want of an extended account of the ecclesiastical difficulty that arose in the year 1819, between the North Carolina Synod and the ministers, who afterwards formed the Tennessee Synod. In this the object was, not to open afresh those wounds which have been more than fifty years in healing. Let us by all means have a hopeful future, and let us throw no obstacles in the way of "the dead past burying its dead."

The second omission is a trifling one, namely, the passing in silence the efforts made in 1842 by the North and South Carolina Synods to celebrate the supposed centenary anniversary of the introduction of the Lutheran Church in America. To the South this celebration was peculiarly anachronistic. German Lutheranism was established in Pennsylvania in 1742, but it existed in the South eight years earlier, when Revs. Bolzius and Gronau commenced their labors in the German (Salzburg) colony at Ebenezer, Georgia, A.D. 1734, and in the Carolinas, five years sooner, when Rev. Giessendanner labored for the Germans in Orangeburg, S. C., in 1737.

The author is aware that this historical work, especially in its detailed ecclesiastical information, must be interesting chiefly to the members of the Lutheran Church in the Carolinas ; it is hoped, nevertheless, that the general reader will gather from it much information which is not to be obtained from any other source.

G. D. Bernheim.

Wilmington, N. C.,
June 10th, 1872.

CONTENTS.

CHAPTER I.

An Account of the Early Colonization of the Dutch, German and Swiss Settlers in the Carolinas.

CHAPTER II.

Condition and History of the German Colonies in the Carolinas to the close of the Revolutionary War.

CHAPTER III.

HISTORY OF THE LUTHERAN CHURCH IN THE CAROLINAS FROM THE CLOSE OF THE REVOLUTIONARY WAR, A.D. 1783, TO THE ORGANIZATION OF THE SYNOD OF NORTH CAROLINA, A.D. 1803, EMBRACING A PERIOD OF TWENTY YEARS.

CHAPTER IV.

HISTORY OF THE LUTHERAN CHURCH IN THE CAROLINAS CONTINUED, FROM THE ORGANIZATION OF THE NORTH CAROLINA SYNOD, A.D. 1803, TO THE FORMATION OF THE FIRST LUTHERAN GENERAL SYNOD IN AMERICA, A.D. 1820; EMBRACING A PERIOD OF SEVENTEEN YEARS.

CHAPTER V.

FROM THE ORGANIZATION OF THE TENNESSEE SYNOD TO THE ESTABLISHMENT OF THE THEOLOGICAL SEMINARY AT LEXINGTON, SOUTH CAROLINA, A.D. 1833.

CHAPTER VI.

History of the Lutheran Church in the Carolinas continued to the Close of the Year 1850.

HISTORY

OF THE

German Settlements and the Lutheran Church

IN

NORTH AND SOUTH CAROLINA.

CHAPTER I.

AN ACCOUNT OF THE EARLY COLONIZATION OF THE DUTCH, GERMAN, AND SWISS SETTLERS IN THE CAROLINAS.

Section 1. The causes, in general, which led to the colonization of America with European settlers.

THE memory of the early settlers of America should ever be regarded as sacred; it was their courageous hearts or conscientious convictions of duty that led them to venture upon the dangers of a long and tedious voyage across the Atlantic, and to endure the perils and hardships of an inhospitable wilderness, which greeted them upon their arrival in this country. To them America owes the debt of gratitude for having planted the "westward star of empire" on its shores; for having introduced the dawn of civilization on this continent, where brutal savages, always at war with themselves, and threatening each other's destruction, formerly roamed unrestrained over its wide and trackless forests; for having borne the standard of Christianity to this vast country, where once the curses of idolatry hung like a funeral pall over its future progress and prosperity. In such a wilderness, and under many adverse and dangerous circumstances, our adventurous or pious forefathers made their homes and reared their hardy families; well may those early settlers, in more senses than one, be denominated *the fathers of this—their adopted—country.*

The causes which induced the early settlers of America to leave their native homes and seek an abode in the Far West, across the wide Atlantic, which, on account of its dangers, and a long, tedious, and expensive voyage, severed them forever from all that they once held dear, were numerous and of great variety; but the principal of these causes of emigration shall be given and described in the following narrative.

Amid the over-abundant population of Europe, crowded within a small area of productive land, there always existed, for many centuries past, a large proportion of inhabitants of every class of society, whose pecuniary circumstances ever forbade them to arrive at the condition of competency and wealth in the ordinary pursuits of life; the titled nobleman, by misfortune or bad management, had become deprived of that affluence, which once gilded the coronet of his ancestral house; the unfortunate merchant, by unwise speculation, improper investments, want of success, or some other mismanagement in his commercial affairs, brought himself and family to the verge of ruin; the industrious artisan could scarcely maintain a large and increasing family on the small pittance which was his daily support, forbidding his industry ever to reach beyond that which was necessarily consumed in the maintenance of his esteemed wife and beloved children; whilst the tenant upon a lordly estate was so overburdened with tithes and gatherings, that he groaned over the profitless labor which he daily performed.

In addition to these classes, many young and unmarried men and women, who could see nothing before them but pre-occupied situations, closed avenues of industry; and servants, already too numerous, awaiting the rich man's bidding, felt but too keenly that the Old World had little employment to offer, and less bread to spare.

Thus necessity, as well as inclination, induced these worthy members of society to seek a fortune in America, or at least to improve their pecuniary condition, which was accomplished by engaging in remunerative agriculture, trading with the aborigines of the forests, or in the pursuit of such commercial enterprises as invited the settlers to the enjoyment of prospective wealth, luxury, and influence. Capital was necessary, connected with the ordinary commercial judgment and prudence, to build up a fortune for the enterprising merchant in the Old World, but in America, industry and economy accomplished astonishing results; opportunity was wanting to many an anxious aspirant in the Fatherland in all the various departments of industry, but in the New World, unoccupied situations presented themselves every day to all classes of honest and useful men, whilst the want of labor in the wilds of America was constantly felt. Lands, farms, and plantations were freely offered to every settler for a small amount of purchase-money, or for an annual quit-rent of a trifling character.

What an alluring prospect presented itself in this country to all the inhabitants of Europe, a country crowded for many centuries to its utmost capacity! What an outlet to the inhabitants thereof, groaning under the stringent civil laws necessary for such a superabundant population, which was at times somewhat reduced by the horrors of civil war! They came, like so many swarms of bees from their native hives, to seek subsistence and wealth in America, where good prospects and fine opportunities awaited them.

A large number of emigrants to this country were possessed of a romantic spirit, desiring to roam free and unrestrained through the primeval forests in search of adventure; their highest ambition was to hunt the wild deer, chase the fox and the buffalo, trap the beaver and the otter, or encounter other but more dangerous animals without the restraints of law or privilege of favoritism, which forbade their entering into European forests with the rifle, the huntsman's dog, and the horn; at that time even the Atlantic slope of our country afforded them ample opportunities and advantages to follow the bent of their inclinations; their wonderful narratives composed many of the winter-evening tales that were then published for the amusement and instruction of many a European family.

Another, and a very useful and valuable, class of colonists were the redemptioners, who came to America to escape the poverty and starvation that stared them in the face in their native country; bread for themselves, their wives, and their little ones, was all they asked and expected from the fruitful soil of their adopted country; too poor to pay their passage-money across the ocean, the father, and sometimes the mother also, were sold by the captain of the ship, as soon as the vessel arrived in port, and thus several years' labor of these poor emigrants were required to pay the expense of their passage to America. These settlers had a hard life of it; however, with strict economy and by honest industry they became qualified for future independence, which they had learned to appreciate well by a previous state of servitude. Others of the same class were aided by European philanthropists to settle themselves in the various colonies in America, having a debt of gratitude ever resting upon them and their children, for the kindness extended to them by their benefactors in the Fatherland.

Political refugees also found an asylum and a home in this country; some of these came from

Scotland, who had espoused the cause of the Pretender, Charles Edward, and were persecuted by the reigning house of Hanover in Great Britain; others came from Ireland, after the rebellion; and some again emigrated from other countries for the same reasons; many came from all parts of Germany, in order to escape the demands of their country upon them for military service; whilst not a few from all lands came to settle in America, having been fugitives from justice, and "left their country for their country's good."

Thus these early settlers came from every nation in Europe; they spoke every language of that country; they were possessed of every shade of idea; they differed in their manners, customs, and habits. In this way was America peopled; and these were the parents of that hardy and indomitable race which eventually broke the rule and power of the English crown in the colonies of America, during the bloody period of the Revolutionary War.

Section 2. The religious persecutions in Europe, as another effective cause of emigration to America.

What would finally have become of America with its heterogeneous mass of inhabitants, without the intermixture of a people possessed of an earnest and active Christianity, as "the salt of the earth," or "the leaven for the whole lump," is a fruitful subject for the pen of the speculative philosopher; happily, however, Providence furnished this precious leaven at the commencement of the colonization of America, by employing the fires of bloody persecutions in various parts of the Old World, and thus again was "the wrath of man made to praise God," whilst "the remainder of wrath He did restrain." We are familiar with the history of the Puritans of England, who sought and found a home on the barren rocks and shores of Plymouth, Massachusetts; but the story of the persecuted Huguenots of France, who settled themselves in the Carolinas; of the Non-conformists of Scotland; of the German Palatines (Pfalzer) from the Rhine; of the Salzburgers from the Alpine districts of Austria, is as yet but imperfectly known, and but partially understood.

It was religious persecution which caused a very large number of European inhabitants to emigrate, and to seek an asylum in America, and, in so doing, they sought not wealth nor fortune, but simply, "freedom to worship God;" here they found the asylum they sought; no hand of political or ecclesiastical power has ever *materially* disturbed the votaries of any religious tenet or worship in the enjoyment of this inalienable right. These noble colonists erected many a Plymouth monument of religious liberty on our Southern shores, and under circumstances much more interesting than those which attended the crossing of the noted Mayflower from Old to New England.

A cloud of persecution overshadowed the Protestant Christian on the continent of Europe, more fierce and unrelenting than that which ever oppressed the Puritans in their native country. The Church of Rome, which had long been schooled in the doctrine of "death to heretics," which had led a John Huss and a Jerome of Prague to a martyr's death, which had endeavored to exterminate with fire and sword the pious Piedmontese in their peaceful valleys and mountain fastnesses of Italy, which had inaugurated the horrors of St. Bartholomew's night, continued its savage orgies against the devoted Huguenots of France, by the revocation of the edict of Nantes in 1685, when France lost 750,000 of its most useful and industrious citizens, many of whom located themselves permanently in America.

The name "Huguenot" was a term of derision applied by the Romish Church to those Protestant Christians who had early embraced the doctrines of the Reformation, and is said to have originated from a certain locality near the city of Tours, where the first French Protestants usually assembled themselves for public worship.

Under the reign of Henry II, of France, the Huguenots increased rapidly, which so alarmed the Romanists, that they organized themselves into a party with the intention of exterminating all traces of Protestantism in the realm; yet in this they were not successful. Thus matters were continued during the short reign of Francis II, a young and imbecile prince; when at last his brother, Charles IX, surnamed the Bloody, ascended the throne. A civil war now broke out between the Romanists and Protestants, in which the former were in the main successful. Charles IX, instigated by his wicked mother, Catharine de' Medicis, introduced the awful horrors of St. Bartholomew's night, August 24th, 1572, when Admiral Coligni and thousands of his fellow-Protestants met with a treacherous and bloody death. "The massacre was continued in the city and throughout the kingdom for a week, and it is computed that from eighty to one hundred thousand were slain in France. The annals of the world are filled with narratives of crime and woe, but the massacre of St. Bartholomew stands, perhaps, without a parallel."

During the reign of Henry IV, the Protestants were treated with marked favor, and in 1598 he proclaimed an edict at the city of Nantes, granting to the Protestants the right of religious liberty. This celebrated Edict of Nantes continued in force for eighty-seven years, until the reign of Louis XIV, when, in 1685, it was revoked, and now again were the fires of persecution lighted anew, and the Huguenots, feeling themselves no longer secure in their own native land, and dreading a repetition of the horrors of former years, resolved to leave a country over which such a hostile government had unlimited sway. They fled to Switzerland, Germany, Holland, England, and America, and thus was France depopulated of thousands of her most useful, industrious, and wealthy citizens, who carried with them not only their religion, but likewise some of the finer and most useful arts of France. In America the Huguenots located themselves principally in the provinces of North and South Carolina, where we meet with their honored descendants at the present day.

The Non-conformists or Dissenters were those Calvinistic Christians in Scotland, who were unwilling to be connected with the established Church of England, and were persecuted on account of their religious faith. Some of these fled directly to America, others at first located themselves in the northern part of Ireland, and from thence they and their descendants removed to this country, hence they are called Scotch-Irish. They came flocking in large numbers to America, and their descendants may be traced in the bosom of the various branches of the Presbyterian Church in this country.

We must now turn our attention to our German forefathers. Soon after the revocation of the Edict of Nantes, Louis XIV, king of France, not content with persecuting his own subjects, spread desolation into Germany. The country named Alsace, formerly a French province, located along the banks of the beautiful Rhine; the Palatinate, a country no longer known in the geography of Europe, but known well in its history, these were the fields of bloody carnage for the grand and cruel Louis, who threatened the utter extermination not only of the strong men, who might oppose him in battle, but of the aged fathers, as well as of the helpless females and innocent children, whose only crime was, in his view, the sin of Protestantism. The persecution of the German Palatines

(Pfälzer) was occasioned by the war of the Spanish Succession, to which brief allusion is made in Dr. Hazelius' American Lutheran Church, page 23, an account of which shall be given in the next section of this history.

Another valuable accession of German settlers, who were driven to this country by the cruelties of religious intolerance, were the pious Salzburgers from the regions of the Noric Alps, in Upper Austria, and who were persecuted on account of their religion by Leopold, the Roman Catholic Archbishop of Salzburg.

Of these German colonists, who settled themselves in Ebenezer, Georgia, twenty-six miles northwest of Savannah, Bancroft, the historian, writes thus: "They were indeed a noble army of martyrs going forth in the strength of God, and triumphing in the faith of the Gospel under the severest hardships and the most rigorous persecutions. They were marshalled under no banners save that of the cross, and were preceded by no leaders save their spiritual teachers and the great Captain of their salvation." Sympathy had been so greatly enlisted in their behalf throughout all Protestant Europe, that their journey from the interior of Austria to the seaboard was like a constant ovation; the cities and towns, through which they passed, vied with each other to do them honor and bid them God-speed.

They travelled on foot, passing through Augsburg and Halle, until they reached Frankfort-on-the-Main, where they embarked in a vessel, and were soon floating on the bosom of the beautiful Rhine. "And as they passed," says Bancroft, "between the castled crags, the vineyards, and the white-walled towns that adorn its banks, their conversation, amid hymns and psalms, is of justification and sanctification."

It is not necessary to give an extended history of the Salzburgers, inasmuch as they were not settlers of North and South Carolina, though near neighbors to their brethren in those two provinces, and exerting great influence over them. However, should the reader desire to know more of their history, he is referred to "Strobel's History of the Salzburgers," or to "Urlsperger's Nachrichten der ersten Niederlassung der Salzburger Emigranten in Georgien," and "Das Americanische Ackerwerk Gottes," in five large quarto volumes of some 1200 pages each.

It will not be uninteresting to state, that though these Salzburg emigrants were Germans at the time of their departure from Austria, they are, nevertheless, the descendants of those noble Vallenses of Piedmont, Italy, who had fled from the persecutions of the Dukes of Savoy, following the mountain crags of the Alps until they arrived at a place of comparative safety in Austria, where for awhile they could worship their God unmolested by Papal intolerance. There they soon embraced the Lutheran faith, and educated their children in the pure doctrines and principles of the Reformation; and it is only to be regretted that such an able historian as Bancroft should, with "Urlsperger's Nachrichten" before him, although written in the German language, make all these Salzburgers *Moravians*, which error is, of course, copied by nearly all the minor historians who have written text-books for our common schools. Even Moravians smile at this Bancroftian error in history and geography, as no Moravians had ever a habitation in that portion of Austria where once the Salzburgers resided.

Section 3. The War of the Spanish Succession.

War is always the occasion of great upheavals in society; the anxiety, the feeling of insecurity, the ravages of a brutal soldiery passing through the country of a people whom they regard as their enemies, has the effect of dislodging many a peaceful citizen from his native home. In addition to that, the persecutions which generally follow the unsuccessful party after the conflict is over, makes many a one a fugitive from the land he once loved, to seek an asylum in some undisturbed country, where he may enjoy both the fruits of his labor and his religion unmolested.

Among the many wars which afflicted Europe during the period of American colonization, the War of the Spanish Succession stands prominent in history, as being the chief instrument in sending numerous settlers to the English colonies on this side of the Atlantic; and, inasmuch as the English government was also drawn into the vortex of this strife, the British queen, Anne, made large provision for the welfare of those Germans who were made unfortunate and homeless exiles from their native land by the effects of this useless war. Extensive grants of land were made for the benefit of these German Palatines in New York, North and South Carolina, by the benevolent Queen Anne, of which more shall be said in this history at the proper place.

Charles II, king of Spain, departed this life November 1st, 1700, without having been blessed with any heir in his own immediate family as a successor to his throne. He was the last scion of that branch of the Hapsburg family which bore the rule in Spain for nearly two hundred years. In Austria the house of Hapsburg has been the occupant of the throne from A.D. 1273 to the present day, a period of about six hundred years; and on account of its distant relationship with the ruling family of Spain, one of the sons of Leopold I, king of Austria, was the natural successor to the vacant throne.

This matter would have been thus adjudged by all Europe without any difficulty, had not Louis XIV, king of France, by intrigue and persuasion, induced Charles, shortly before his decease, to make a will, in which he nominated Philip, a grandson of Louis, to be his successor to the Spanish throne. This involved the question of the Spanish succession in a difficulty, which agitated all Europe at the commencement of the eighteenth century, as it became a question of state policy which threatened to disarrange the system of equilibrium of power in Europe. Should the Bourbon family become possessed of the thrones of France and Spain, a power would then have been established which could and would overawe all the kingdoms and minor states of Europe, to the destruction of their independence and, perhaps, of their religion. Hence it was that all the powers of Europe became interested in the proper settlement of this vexatious affair of state.

The vacant throne of Spain presented a most tempting object of desire to the two claimants, for at that time Spain was in the enjoyment of the zenith of her wealth and glory; her rule extended over the Netherlands, Naples, Sicily, Milan, and the larger portion of America—a handsome legacy indeed, of wealth, power, and regal glory for the fortunate successor of the deceased Charles. What a blessing it would have been for Europe for a court of law to have decided this matter, as is done in all other cases of disputed inheritance; or, if resort must have been had to a conflict of arms, the persons immediately interested to have fought it out among themselves, without dragging their unfortunate subjects and neighbors into the bloody strife.

In this manner originated this dreadful conflict, known in history as the "War of the Spanish Succession," which raged so fiercely in Europe for a period of thirteen years.

Leopold I, Emperor of Austria, had two sons, Joseph I, heir-apparent to his father's throne, and Archduke Charles, whom his father expected to wear the crown of Spain, as the legitimate successor of his kinsman, Charles II. The King of France, Louis XIV, had no son living, but his two grandsons became the object of his care and solicitude. Louis, the Dauphin, afterwards Louis XV, was heir-apparent to the throne of France, and Philip, Duke of Anjou, afterwards Philip V of Spain, was the person named in Charles's will as his successor.

The French king enlisted France, Spain, and the Electorates of Bavaria and Cologne on his side; whilst the Emperor of Austria induced the German States, the Netherlands, and England to declare themselves in favor of the house of Hapsburg. Denmark permitted herself to be subsidized by England, and arrayed herself also on the side of the allies against France. The countries, which felt the direful effects of the war most severely, were Italy, Spain, France, Germany, and the Netherlands, as all of these countries became the theatre for the bloody strife.

The war had lasted several years, when Leopold, Emperor of Austria, died, A.D. 1705, and his eldest son, Joseph I, ascended the imperial throne as his successor, but without producing any change in the progress of the war, which was waged on both sides as fiercely as ever, and in which the allied Austrian powers were in the main successful, and Louis XIV would soon have been so humbled as to withdraw his claim to the Spanish throne; however, the new Emperor of Austria, Joseph I, died in the year 1711, leaving no issue, when his brother, the Archduke Charles, succeeded to the vacant throne. This event so materially affected the question in dispute, that it promised a speedy return of peace.

The derangement of the State system of Europe of equilibrium of power was now more to be dreaded in the Hapsburg family, by uniting the crowns of Austria and Spain, as in the Bourbon family reigning in France; consequently, England and some of the other European States were prepared for terms of settlement; and Charles of Austria could have been no longer so anxious for the throne of Spain, since he had come into possession of the crowns of Austria, Hungary, and Bohemia.

A change of administration in England interrupted for a season the settlement of the difficulty; however, all matters were finally adjusted at the Congress of Utrecht and Rastadt, A.D. 1713 and 1714, when it was agreed that Philip V, Duke of Anjou, and grandson of Louis XIV, should succeed to the Spanish throne, with the proviso that France and Spain shall be, and forever remain, separate kingdoms; that the crowns of these two kingdoms shall never descend upon one head, in order that the equilibrium of State power in Europe should in no wise be disturbed; and thus has the Bourbon family, until recently, occupied the throne of Spain, except for the short time when Napoleon I disturbed the peace of all Europe at the commencement of the present century.

It is not necessary to give an account of the battles that were fought during this war, or to name the generals who became conspicuous in the strife, or to enumerate the principles, rights, privileges, towns, and fortresses which each nation secured or lost at the peace of Utrecht and Rastadt; our purposes will be served by turning our attention to Germany, and notice the dire effects of this cruel war upon its peaceful inhabitants.

In order to gain his end, and the sooner to secure his coveted prize, Louis XIV carried his war into all Germany, except Bavaria and Cologne, which countries belonged to his allies; besides, being a bigoted Romanist, and the inhabitants of Germany being nearly all Protestants, he had a twofold motive in carrying fire and sword, desolation and ruin, wherever he sent his army among our German forefathers, who were residing so peacefully and prosperously in those countries bordering on the beautiful Rhine, insomuch that a proverb arose among them, "We dread the French, as well as the Turks, as enemies of our holy religion."

The peaceful inhabitants of the Palatinate, plundered of all their earthly possessions, were driven in midwinter as exiles from their native land to seek an asylum in some safe and friendly country. They beheld their comfortable cottages and once amply-filled barns and storehouses smouldering in the flames behind them, whilst they and their helpless wives and children, ruined in worldly prosperity, naked, feeble, and in a starving condition, were wending their weary way over vast fields of snow and ice, leaving their bloody footprints in the frozen snow, seeking shelter and finding none. Numbers perished by the way, others dragged along their feeble bodies until at last they found safety in the Netherlands, and from thence they journeyed into England. This is no overdrawn picture. Says a distinguished writer:* "The ravages of Louis XIV in the beautiful valleys of the Rhine, were more fierce and cruel than even Mahometans could have had the heart to perpetrate. Private dwellings were razed to the ground, fields laid waste, cities burnt, churches demolished, and the fruits of industry wantonly and ruthlessly destroyed. But three days of grace were allowed to the wretched inhabitants to flee their country, and in a short time, the historian tells us, 'the roads were blackened by innumerable multitudes of men, women, and children, flying from their homes. Many died of cold and hunger; but enough survived to fill the streets of all the cities of Europe with lean and squalid beggars, who had once been thriving farmers and shopkeepers.'"

The cruel-hearted Louis exhibited no mercy to his own French-Protestant subjects at the revocation of the Edict of Nantes, but persecuted them with fire and sword, and drove them from his realm, though their loss would be greatly felt in France; would he then be less lenient to those foreigners whom he regarded both as his political enemies as well as his spiritual foes, inasmuch as

---

* Rev. Dr. Thornwell.

they were believers in the principles of the Reformation? Thus were these inhabitants of the Palatinate continually harassed by the French army, until they were safely landed in England. The good Queen Anne had invited them to her realm, and thither they flocked by thousands, where they were kindly treated and hospitably entertained.

It occurred to the benevolent Queen, that she could better provide for these poor Palatines by inducing them to become settlers in her American colonies, where all classes of useful citizens were greatly needed. Accordingly, some were settled in the Province of New York; others again were brought over by De Graffenreid and Mitchell to Newberne, North Carolina; and some found a home in various portions of the colony of South Carolina, principally in Charleston and along the banks of the Congaree, Saluda, and Broad Rivers; whilst others can be traced to have settled in Orangeburg District, and some along the Savannah River, occupying some of the most fertile valleys of that Province.

Thus they became at length happily, and, to all appearances, safely located. Every possible arrangement was made by the Queen to provide not only comfortable homes for these unfortunate refugees, but likewise extensive grants of land for churches, pastorates, glebes, and schools for the education of their children.

When these persecuted German Protestants journeyed to America, they brought with them their Bibles, hymn-books, catechisms, and other religious books for edification and instruction; and, what was still better, they brought with them the pearl of great price, their religion, their piety, and their habits of devotion, and thus they became, in a great measure, the salt of the earth to all around them where they were located.

Whilst it is true that the War of the Spanish Succession left its dire effects upon the face of the lovely countries along the Rhine, and that the peaceful inhabitants, who were innocent in bringing it about, were nevertheless the principal sufferers, whilst wicked and designing men were the agents of this dreadful scourge; yet God, for wise purposes, permitted them to afflict and humble his people; America stood in need of pious, industrious, and useful settlers, who might otherwise never have departed from their comfortable and happy homes in the Fatherland, but who now came flocking to the New World in great numbers, to build up Christ's kingdom in a rising and future prosperous country. Time, progress, and industry—the powerful healers of all national troubles—would eventually rectify the devastations, and rebuild the ruins which war had made in the Palatinate, whilst America became blessed in her policy of being the asylum for the oppressed of all nations.

It is, however, sad to reflect that these German refugees did not improve the advantages offered and granted them for churches and schools by the benevolent Queen of England; their glebes, pastorates, and school-tracts were suffered to remain unoccupied by themselves and their descendants, until these grants and privileges were forgotten, and the lands otherwise disposed of. A large body of land, now forming a county in South Carolina, and yet remembered by the name of "the Saxe-Gotha tract," situated along the banks of the Congaree River, which was once allotted by Queen Anne for this purpose, was finally lost to the Church, although the Germans made settlements in that vicinity at a later date. What an immense amount of wealth might have been preserved to the Lutheran Church, to advance religion and education among the descendants of these Palatines and other German settlers to their latest generation, in the different colonies of America, where these grants were located.

Section 4. The Mission Societies established in Europe for the benefit of the early settlers in America.

It is not to be supposed that the various colonists of America were soon forgotten by their friends and relatives in the old country, or were neglected by their former spiritual shepherds. We send missionaries, at the present time, to nations still benighted with heathenism, and not at all connected with us by the strong ties of consanguinity; how much more would the European Christians feel interested in the progress of evangelization in this Western world, where their own kindred resided, who were of the same household of faith, and from whom they occasionally received information by letters, beseeching them to send them ministers of the gospel to break the bread of eternal life to them.

Some of the colonists, like the Salzburgers, took their pastors with them to America; others were not so fortunate; and all had need of more ministers, in order that they might regularly enjoy the administration of all the means of grace. Consequently, various mission societies were formed in Europe among the Episcopalians, the Lutherans, the Moravians, and, perhaps, some other denominations, to meet this want. A society of this kind seems to have been first organized in England, called "The Society for Promoting the Knowledge of Christ in Foreign Parts," with which the Lutheran Church on the Continent must have been in some way connected, having her directors in that institution, such as, the Rev. Dr. Ziegenhagen, Lutheran chaplain at the Court of St. James, London; Rev. Dr. Urlsperger, pastor of St. Anna Lutheran Church of Augsburg; Rev. Dr. Francke, son of the founder of the Orphan House at Halle; this missionary institution is also noticed in many historical works under its Latin title, "Societas promovenda cognitione Christi," and was exceedingly effective in doing great good in this country; under its care the mission in Ebenezer, Georgia, was placed; it not only supported their pastors, but built their churches and endowed them by various investments.

These Ebenezer pastors were in duty bound to report minutely, extensively, and frequently to the missionary board in Europe, or Fathers (as they were then called); which reports were published by Dr. Urlsperger, of Augsburg, for the purpose of keeping up the interest in Germany in behalf of this mission in Georgia; they are still extant, and known by the name of "The Urlsperger Nachrichten."

The University of Halle organized a separate mission society, which was altogether under Lutheran management. It was this society that sent Rev. H. M. Muhlenberg, D.D., and other Lutheran ministers to the Province of Pennsylvania, who labored there among the German settlers. Their missionary reports were sent to the society in Halle, where they were likewise published, and are now known by the double name of "Die Hallische Nachrichten," or "Die Pennsylvänische Nachrichten," many copies of which are still preserved in the libraries of several Lutheran colleges in the United States, to which they were donated by a great-grandson of the Halle Society's first missionary, H. H. Muhlenberg, M.D., of Reading, Pa.

At a later period another mission society was organized in Germany by the professors of the Julius Charles University, located in Helmstaedt, Duchy of Brunswick. This society sent a number of laborers to North Carolina. Rev. Dr. Velthusen was the leading spirit of that organization, which provided for the support of Rev. Nussmann, and sent out Revs. Storch and Roschen to labor among the scattered and neglected Germans in North Carolina.

The reports of these missionaries were published from time to time, as soon as they reached the Society in Helmstaedt. Some of them have recently been brought to light, but others are still missing. They are interesting to the antiquarian, and though not voluminous, they supply an important link in the chain of narrative concerning the German settlers in North Carolina.

No documents can be more valuable to the historian than the reports of these missionaries, which were written by learned, conscientious and reliable men, who were themselves residents in the colonies, and were well acquainted with facts that transpired under their immediate observation. An insight into the difficulties, the customs, and the spirit of those times is thus furnished, which enables the writer of history to understand the more readily the events of a succeeding age, which are but imperfectly reported in isolated state documents.

Section 5. John Lederer's Explorations, A.D. 1670.

Having now furnished the reader with such historical facts of a general character, which must necessarily be known in order to understand correctly the history of the German colonies in the Carolinas, inasmuch as those facts likewise apply to these two provinces, and frequent allusion must be made to those events, it is time to confine our attention to the principal subject of this history, which is introduced by an account of John Lederer's explorations. This will afford us an insight into the condition of these two provinces before they were colonized to any extent. This narrative of Lederer's explorations will be none the less welcome to the reader, when it is remembered that this early explorer was of the same nation, whose history in the Carolinas is made the subject of this volume.

Thus the first German that set foot upon the soil of Carolina was John Lederer, who was sent on three different expeditions by Sir William Berkeley, Governor of the Colony of Virginia, to explore the lands lying south and west of the James River, during the years 1669 and 1670.

From his map of the country which he explored, as well as from his journal, we gather the fact that he passed through North Carolina, and proceeded as far into South Carolina as the Santee River. North and South Carolina were at that time one province, and had passed, but a few years previous, A. D. 1663, by a grant of Charles II, into the hands of several noblemen in England, who were styled "The Lords-Proprietors."

At the time when Lederer made his first exploring tour, South Carolina was destitute of any white settlers, whilst the eastern portion of North Carolina had been improved by only two small colonies, the one on Albemarle Sound, the other on Clarendon (now Cape Fear) River. The entire interior and western part of North Carolina, with the whole of the territory of South Carolina, constituted as yet the undisturbed home of the red man of the forest. However, the same year that

John Lederer reached the interior of South Carolina, the first English colony, under Colonel William Sayle as their Governor, arrived at Port Royal, near Beaufort, and a few months later located themselves, "for the convenience of pasturage and tillage," on the banks of the Ashley River, and near its mouth laid the foundation of Old Charlestown, A. D. 1670.

Lederer was a man of learning. His journal was written in the Latin language, his map indicates a knowledge of geographical calculation, considering the circumstances and advantages of those times, and the difficulties under which he labored. The translator of his journal, Sir William Talbot, Governor of Maryland, also speaks highly of his literary attainments.

Concerning his courageous and enterprising disposition and the success of his explorations, we must permit Rev. Dr. Hawks to speak, who informs us that "John Lederer was a learned German, who lived in Virginia during the administration of Sir William Berkeley. Little was then known of the mountainous part of that State, or of what was beyond. Berkeley commissioned Lederer to make explorations, and accordingly he went upon three several expeditions. The first was from the head of York River due west to the Appalachian Mountains. The second was from the falls of the James River west and southwest, which brought him into Carolina. The third was from the falls of the Rappahannock westward towards the mountains.

"Certain Englishmen were appointed by Berkeley to accompany him. These, however, forsook him, and turned back. Lederer proceeded notwithstanding alone, and on his return to Virginia, which, by the way, was never expected, met with insult and reproaches, instead of the cordial welcome to which he was entitled. For this he was indebted to his English companions who had forsaken him; and so active were they in creating a prejudice against him, that he was not safe among the people of Virginia, who had been told that the public taxes of that year had all been expended in his wanderings."

Thus it appears that, like Christopher Columbus, John Lederer never received that respect and gratitude which was due him by his fellow-citizens, though they were greatly benefited by his scientific and hazardous exploits. How frequently does it happen that to future generations it is left to award tribute of just praise to merit, which an ignorant and selfish populace could not appreciate, who persecute their contemporaries for having excelled their fellow-men in literature, science, or moral excellence.

The following brief extract from Lederer's journal will afford us a nearer acquaintance with the character and attainments of this worthy and scientific German.

"The 20th of May, 1670, one Major Harris and myself, with twenty Christian horse (horsemen) and five Indians, marched from the falls of the James River, in Virginia, towards the Monakins;

and on the 22d we were welcomed by them with volleys of shot. Near this village we observed a pyramid of stones piled up together, which their priests told us was the number of an Indian colony, drawn out by lot from a neighbor country over-peopled, and led hither by one Monack, from whom they take the name Monakin. Here, inquiring the way to the mountains, an ancient man described with a staff two paths on the ground, one pointing to the Mahocks, and the other to the Nahyssans. But my English companions, slighting the Indian's directions, shaped their course by the compass due west; and, therefore, it fell out with us as it does with those land-crabs, that, crawling backward in a direct line, avoid not the trees that stand in their way, but climbing over their very tops, come down again on the other side, and so after a day's labor gain not above two feet of ground. Thus we, obstinately pursuing a due west course, rode over steep and ragged cliffs, which beat our horses quite off the hoof. In these mountains we wandered from the 25th of May till the 3d of June, finding very little sustenance for man or horse, as these places are destitute both of grain and herbage.

"The 3d of June we came to the south branch of the James River, which Major Harris, observing to run northwardly, vainly imagined to be an arm of the lake of Canada, and was so transported with this fancy that he would have raised a pillar to the discovery if the fear of the Mahock Indians and want of food had permitted him to stay.

Here I moved to cross the river and march on, but the rest of the company were so weary of the enterprise that, crying out, one and all, they would have offered violence to me had I not been provided with a private commission from the Governor of Virginia to proceed though the rest of the company should abandon me, the sight of which laid their fury.

"The air in these parts was so moist that all our biscuits became mouldy and unfit to be eaten, so that some nicer stomachs, who at our setting out laughed at my provision of Indian corn meal parched, would gladly now have shared with me; but I being determined to go upon further discoveries, refused to part with any of that which was to be my most necessary sustenance. The 5th of June my company and I parted good friends, they back again, and I, with one Susquehannah Indian only, named Jackzetavon, in pursuit of my first enterprise, changing my course from west to southwest and by south, to avoid the mountains. Major Harris, in parting, gave me a gun, believing me a lost man, and given up as a prey to Indians or savage beasts, which made him the bolder to report strange things in his own praise and my disparagement, presuming I would never appear to disprove him. This, I suppose, and no other, was the cause that he did with so much industry procure me discredit and odium; but I have lost nothing by it but what I never studied to gain, which is popular applause."

Lederer had several narrow escapes among the

Indians; often was he in danger of losing his life, or of being taken captive; but at other times he was kindly treated by them, and, on one occasion, the daughter of one of their Indian kings was offered to him in marriage, which courtesy, however, he declined, and pursued his exploring journey to the close, ending it at Lake Ushery. This lake is supposed to be nothing more than a portion of the waters of Santee River in South Carolina, as we learn from the narrative of Col. Byrd, that the Indians who were living along the Santee River were called Usheries. Besides, if we presume that Lederer was in possession of the instruments necessary to make correct calculations of degrees of latitude, we are then warranted to conclude, from the fac-simile of his map, where the degrees of latitude are noted on the margin, that his travels extended as far south as 33⅓ degrees, north latitude, which would likewise fix the terminus of his journey on or near the banks of the Santee River, and the lake of which he speaks must have been one of those immense swamps with which this river abounds.

On his homeward journey he took another route, and arrived safely in Virginia, where he was reproached and insulted in such a manner that he went to Maryland, where he finally succeeded in obtaining a hearing from the Governor, Sir William Talbot, and in submitting his papers to him. The Governor, though at first much prejudiced against the man by the stories he had heard, yet found him, as he says, "a modest, ingenious person, and a pretty scholar;" and Lederer vindicated himself "with so convincing reason and circumstance," as Governor Talbot says, that he quite removed all unfavorable impressions, and the governor himself took the trouble to translate his journal from the Latin, and published Lederer's account of his explorations.

The influence that this German explorer exerted by his account of the country he visited must have had its effect in the speedy settling of the Carolinas, inducing many of our forefathers to emigrate to this country, and seek their fortunes in the wilds of America; it is certain that, but ten years later, in 1680, the tide of German emigration to America commenced its flow; doubtless such men as John Lederer, and later, Louis Mitchell, whose journals of explorations were published, contributed greatly towards producing this happy result, and in making America wealthy in the development of her agricultural resources, when the thrifty farmers of Germany tilled her virgin soil.

Section 6. The Dutch colony of Lutherans on James Island, South Carolina, A.D. 1674.

The only settlement in South Carolina at this period was Old Charlestown, located on the Ashley River, several miles distant from where the present Charleston now stands. The settlers, who had been located there but little over three years, struggled for a name and existence against famine and other adverse circumstances, when, fortunately, "during the time Sir John Yeamans was governor of Carolina, the colony received a great addition to its strength from the Dutch settlement of Nova Belgia," now New York, which province surrendered, as is well known, without any resistance, to the armament commanded by Sir Robert Carr, and became subject to the British crown.

"Charles II donated Nova Belgia to his brother, the Duke of York," after whom its name was changed to New York, "who governed it with the same arbitrary principles which afterwards rendered him so obnoxious to the English nation. After the conquest many of the Dutch colonists who were discontented with their situation, had formed resolutions of moving to other provinces. The proprietors of Carolina offered them lands and encouragement in their Palatinate, and sent their ships, Blessing and Phœnix, which brought a number of Dutch families to Charlestown.

"Stephen Bull, surveyor-general of the colony, had instruction to mark out lands on the south-west side of Ashley River, viz., on James Island, for their accommodation. There each of the Dutch emigrants drew lots for their property, and founded a town, which was called Jamestown. This was the first colony of Dutch who settled in Carolina, whose industry surmounted incredible hardships, and whose success induced many from ancient Belgia afterwards to follow them to the Western world." (*Hewatt's Hist. of S. C. and Geo.*, vol. i, p. 73.)

Whether these Dutch settlers had their pastor or not, history does not inform us; it is known, however, that they constituted a distinct class among those numerous dissenters, who protested against that unjust legislation of A.D. 1704, which established the Church of England in the two Carolinas as the Church of the State, and supported by the public treasury. A full account of this transaction may not be uninteresting, and appears to be necessary for the better understanding of all the facts and circumstances in the case; the following narrative is gathered from various historical works.

The two first acts of the Legislature, which have been found in the records of the Secretary's office, were but right and proper. They enjoined the observance of the Lord's day, commonly called Sunday, and prohibited sundry gross immoralities, particularly "idleness, drunkenness, and swearing;" thus far the Government aided religion in the colony. (*Ramsay's Hist. of S. C.*, vol. ii, p. 2.)

"Both parts of Carolina were in a deplorable state as to religion. Such of the inhabitants as were born, or had grown up to manhood, in Carolina, were almost utter strangers to any public worship of the Deity. Among the first emigrants some sense of religion had been, for a while, preserved; but the next generation, reared in a wilderness in which divine service was hardly ever performed, and where private devotions cannot be supposed to have been much attended to, were rather remarkable for loose, licentious principles, and the fundamental doctrines of the Christian religion were often treated with the ridicule of professed infidelity. The population of the colony was composed of individuals of different nations, and consequently of various sects: Scotch Presbyterians, *Dutch Lutherans*, French Calvinists, Irish Catholics, English Churchmen, Quakers, and Dissenters, emigrants from Bermuda and the West Indies, which, from their late settlements, could not be places remarkable for the education of young people in Christianity and morality." (*Martin's Hist. of N. C.*, vol. i, p. 218.)

"In the year 1698, one step farther was taken by an act of the Legislature 'to settle a maintenance on a minister of the Church of England in Charleston.' This excited neither suspicion nor alarm among the Dissenters, for the minister in whose favor the law operated was a worthy, good man; and the small sum allowed him was inadequate to his services. However, the precedent thus set by the Legislature, being acquiesced in by the people, paved the way for an ecclesiastical establishment. In the year 1704, when the white population of South Carolina was between five and six thousand, when the Episcopalians had only one church in the province, and the Dissenters had three in Charleston, and one in the country, the former were so far favored as to obtain a legal establishment. Most of the proprietors and public officers of the province, and particularly the Governor, Sir Nathaniel Johnson, were zealously attached to the Church of England.

Believing in the current creed of the times, that an established religion was essential to the support of civil government, they concerted measures for endowing the church of the mother country, and advancing it in Carolina to a legal pre-eminence." (*Ramsay*, vol. ii, p. 2.)

"Preparatory thereto Governor Johnson, assisted by the principal officers of the southern part of the province, exerted his influence with so much success, as to procure the election of a sufficient number of Episcopalians, who were disposed to forward his views. Notwithstanding the great opposition which the bill received, it passed into law. The southern part of Carolina was divided into ten parishes, and provision was made for the support of ministers, the erection of churches and glebes; and an act was passed requiring members of Assembly to conform to the religious worship in the province, according to the Church of England, and to receive the sacrament of the Lord's Supper according to the rites and usages of that Church." (*Martin*, vol. i, pp. 218, 219.)

"This act passed the lower house by a majority of only one vote. It virtually excluded from a seat in the Legislature all who were Dissenters, erected an aristocracy, and gave a monopoly of power to one sect, though far from being a majority of the inhabitants. In this way did Granville, one of the Lords-Proprietors, who had thus instructed the governors of Carolina, expect to effect his purposes of impious bigotry; he, however, found it very hard work in which he was engaged, to fuse by one act of human legislation all the various dissenting denominations into one lump of piety and orthodoxy. The usual consequences followed. Animosities took place and spread in every direction. Moderate men of the favored church considered the law impolitic and hostile to the prosperity of the province. Dissenters of all denominations, both in North and South Carolina, made a common cause in endeavoring to obtain its repeal. The inhabitants of Colleton, which was chiefly settled by Dissenters, drew up a statement of their sufferings by this oppressive act, which they transmitted by John Ashe, an influential character among them, to lay their grievances before the Lords-Proprietors.

"The Governor succeeded in preventing this gentleman's obtaining a passage to England in any of the ships in Charleston; he was therefore compelled to travel by land to Virginia, where he embarked. On his way he stopped in the county of Albemarle, where he was received with great respect and cordiality, and the people, feeling the same interest as his constituents in the object of his mission, prevailed on Edmund Porter to accompany him, in order to aid, by the representations of the people of the northern part of the province, the object which the people of Carolina had much at heart." (*Ramsay*, vol. ii, p. 3.)

When these commissioners from North and South Carolina arrived in England, the Palatine received them as "the emissaries of their lordships' vassals," with considerable coldness.

Mr. Ashe, unable to effect the object of his mission by his representations to the Lords-Proprietors, and finding the public sentiment in his favor, determined on raising it into action, by a candid representation of the grievances of his constituents; but death prevented the intended appeal. His papers fell into the hands of those who had an interest to suppress the expression of his sentiments. Thus was this first effort of the people to throw off a galling ecclesiastical yoke frustrated; it proved a failure for that time.

Sir Nathaniel Johnson, governor of Carolina, intent upon carrying the Palatine's views into execution, overcame every obstacle in his way. A corporation, composed of twenty individuals, was instituted, with power to exercise high ecclesiastical jurisdiction. Authority was given it to deprive ministers of their livings, and the acts of the Legislature, of which John Ashe had gone to procure the repeal, were executed with great zeal and rigor. Thus did Lord Granville, a bigoted member of the Church of England, who had instructed Governor Johnson to establish that church by legal enactment, effect his purpose.

The Dissenters of all denominations were exasperated; a migration to Pennsylvania was spoken of, but it was at last determined to send Joseph Boon to England, with a petition to the House of Lords. On the introduction to this petition, the House, on motion of Lord Granville, the Palatine of Carolina, heard counsel at its bar, in behalf of the Lords-Proprietors, and, after some debate, came to a resolution, "that the laws complained of were founded on falsity in matter of fact, repugnant to the laws of England, contrary to the charter of the Lords-Proprietors, an encouragement to atheism and irreligion, destructive to trade, and tended to the ruin and depopulation of the province."

The Lords next addressed the Queen, beseeching her to use the most effectual means to deliver the Province of Carolina from the "arbitrary oppression under which it lay, and to order the proprietors of it to be prosecuted according to law." The subject was referred to the Lords-Commissioners of Trade and Plantations, who reported that the facts stated in the petition were true; that the powers granted by the charter had been abused; that the grantees had incurred a forfeiture of it; and recommended that process might be ordered to issue accordingly against their lordships.

The Queen's law servants were thereupon directed to procure a writ of *quo warranto*, and to report what might more effectually be done, in order that the Queen might take the government of Carolina into her own hands. The matter was, however, abandoned, and no step was taken to annul the charter, or to relieve the people. (*Ramsay*, vol. ii, p. 3.)

From this narrative we learn that our Lutheran brethren, the Dutch colonists of South Carolina on James Island, likewise suffered severely by this impious act of human legislation, and that they were not attached to the principles and usages of the Church of England, otherwise they never would have been classed by all historians of the two Carolinas among the number of those who dissented from that Church, and protested against its establishment by law.

It may be asked, what reasons we have to conclude that the Dutch settlers on James Island were members of the Lutheran Church? To which we reply, that they are so denominated by all historians who have given us an account of the oppressive act instigated by Lord Granville, and carried into effect by Governor N. Johnson; consequently we conclude that these settlers from Nova Belgia (now New York) were mostly, if not all, Lutherans. However, should this doubt arise, that Englishmen were in the habit of denominating Germans as *Dutch*, thus confounding them with Hollanders, and that thus this mistake might very easily arise, we can safely meet this doubt with the fact, that at this early period, A. D. 1704, there were no other Lutheran Protestants, of either German or Swiss origin, in all the territory of the two Carolinas; the first German emigrants to these provinces were the Palatines, and they did not arrive at Newbern, N. C., until 1709, and in South Carolina about the same time. Every history of the two provinces, as well as the records in the office of the Secretary of the State, have been thoroughly examined, and no trace of any other

Lutheran colony could be found for this early period. The conclusion is, therefore, correct, that the Dutch Lutherans mentioned are none other than the Dutch settlers of James Island.

This opinion is confirmed by examining Rev. Dr. Schaeffer's Early History of the Lutheran Church in America, in which it will be seen, that in Holland there were Dutch Lutherans as well as Dutch Reformed, at this period, and that a great many of the Dutch settlers of Nova Belgia (now New York) were of the Lutheran faith, and were, on that very account, sorely persecuted by Governor Stuyvesant. Dr. Schaeffer states, p. 64: "The Lutherans had long been accustomed to meet in their own dwellings for purposes of social devotion. Against these meetings, called 'conventicles' in contempt, Stuyvesant published a fiery proclamation, showed that the Lutherans could expect no indulgence from him, encouraged the Dutch Reformed clergy in enforcing their baptismal formulary, so obnoxious to the Lutherans, and continued to punish by fines and imprisonment those who refused submission." Their first minister, the Rev. John Ernest Goetwater, who was sent to them by the Lutheran Consistory of Amsterdam, Holland, upon his arrival at New Amsterdam (New York), "was cited to appear before the civil tribunal, and forbidden to preach, or to hold any Lutheran 'conventicles;' in short, he was forthwith banished from New Amsterdam; and having spent some few weeks in sickness in the suburbs of the city, he embarked, in the month of October, and returned to Holland." (*Schaeffer*, p. 65.) Besides, if Rev. Dr. Howe is correct in dating the arrival of the Dutch settlers on James Island, S. C., as far back as December, 1671, then certainly these Dutch settlers must all, or nearly all, have been Lutherans, for that was the period when they suffered such fierce persecutions from Governor Stuyvesant, before the reins of his government had yet passed into the hands of the English, and the Dutch Lutherans were doubtless greatly rejoiced to have an opportunity of escaping religious intolerance, by removing to South Carolina in the proprietary government's ships, Blessing and Phœnix; all of which must of necessity stand opposed to the statement found in Dr. Howe's History of the Presbyterian Church in South Carolina, p. 86: "The Dutch settlers were of the Presbyterian Church of Holland."

History also informs us of the final fate of this Dutch colony as follows: "The Dutch inhabitants of Jamestown, on James Island, afterwards finding their situation too narrow and circumscribed, in process of time spread themselves through the country, where they soon lost their individuality by marriage with the other settlers, and their town was totally deserted." (*Hewatt*, vol. i, p. 73.)

We sometimes meet with traces of Dutch settlers in the Carolinas and Georgia at the present day; they may be supposed to be the descendants of this early Dutch colony on James Island; they themselves, as well as their surnames, inform us that they are descendants of Dutch ancestry, but they remember no longer their own colonial history, it being so remote that even tradition has left them no traces of the same. Many of these are still in full connection with the Lutheran Church, and retain a strong attachment to her doctrines and usages.

Section 7. The colony of Palatinate and Swiss Germans in New-Berne, North Carolina, A.D. 1710.

That lovely and picturesque portion of Germany, situated on both sides of the river Rhine, attached now to Bavaria and Baden, formed at one time the country known in history as "*The Palatinate.*" Its inhabitants were mostly Protestants, having early embraced the principles of the Reformation, but were compelled to suffer grievous persecutions on account of their religion. In 1622, Heidelberg, the principal city of the Palatinate, was laid in a heap of smouldering ruins by General Tilly, the leader of the Spanish army, during the thirty years' war between the Romanists and the Protestants. In the destruction of this city, the University of Heidelberg was plundered of its immense library, and presented to Pope Gregory XV. The city was afterwards rebuilt, and remained in peace for some time, though deprived of much of its former greatness, until a new source of tribulation arose, at the time when the Protestant Electoral house became extinct, and a bloody war with France ensued, which, in 1689, again reduced almost the entire city, with its beautiful palace and gardens, into a heap of ruins.

But the cup of calamity and sorrow was not yet full for the inhabitants of this unfortunate country. During the War of the Spanish Succession, a description of which is given in Section 3d, page 37, of this history, a large number of the inhabitants of the Palatinate, without shelter or home, were driven from their fatherland to seek an asylum in foreign countries. A knowledge of their sad condition reached England, and attracted the notice of that magnanimous and tender-hearted sovereign, Queen Anne, who invited thousands of these unfortunate people to the hospitable shores of her realm, where every provision which humanity could devise was made for their welfare. "Great sympathy," says Dr. Hawks, in his History of North Carolina, "was felt for these poor creatures, whose sin was Protestantism merely; the Queen of England, pitying their condition, by her proclamation in 1708, offered them protection in her dominions, and about twelve thousand of them went to England."

Numbers of these exiles, about four thousand at one time, were afterwards sent, with most liberal provisions, to the Province of New York, where the benevolent Queen made them large grants of land on the banks of the Hudson River, where the towns of Newburg and New Windsor now stand. Other grants were made, through the instrumentality of Queen Anne, by the Proprietary government, along the banks of the Congaree River, in South Carolina.

However, there were still many of these German Protestants remaining in England, too poor to help themselves, and living upon the charities of the Queen and her benevolent subjects, for whom there had as yet no provision been made for their emigration to America, when Providence opened another and a new way before them.

Baron Christopher de Graffenreid, a Swiss nobleman from Berne, induced a large number of his countrymen, about fifteen hundred souls, to migrate with him to America. They first landed in England, and whilst there the Baron met with Louis Mitchell in the city of London, who had been to America, had spent a number of years on that continent, and was well acquainted with the country; he had been sent over by the Canton of Berne as an exploring agent, in order to search for a large and vacant tract of land, suitable for a colony, either in Pennsylvania, Virginia, or Carolina. These two gentlemen, acting in concert, determined to accept of the fair proposals of the Lords-Proprietors, and settle their colony in Carolina. They accordingly purchased ten thousand acres from their lordships, which they were permitted to locate in one body, on or between the Neuse and Cape Fear Rivers, or any of their tributaries. They paid twenty shillings sterling for each hundred acres, and bound themselves to a quit-rent of the sum of sixpence yearly for every hundred. It was also agreed that instruction should be given to the surveyor-general to lay off in addition one hundred thousand acres, to be reserved for them twelve years. De Graffenreid was then made and declared a landgrave.

It now occurred to the good Queen of England that this would be a favorable opportunity to plant another colony of her adopted German Palatines in her transatlantic dominions, which plan was so satisfactory that it met with favor on all sides. On the one hand, the Queen was thereby relieving herself of the support of these poor Germans, for whom she had appointed commissioners to collect money, and thus provide speedily for their permanent settlement, besides increasing the strength of her American colonies. On the other hand, these Germans themselves, trained to habits of industry and economy, could but rejoice at the prospect of so soon occupying their own homes, and tilling their own fruitful lands, dependent no longer upon the charities of the benevolent. The Lords-Proprietors could, of course, make no objection, as it was their interest to have Carolina peopled with frugal and industrious citizens; and De Graffenreid and Mitchell were glad enough to obtain tenants for their lands, which could but enhance the value thereof; and, inasmuch as the Swiss emigrants were also Germans, speaking the same language with the Palatines, there could be no conflicting interests between them; and this addition of settlers could only increase the safety and prosperity of the new colony.

A negotiation, therefore, was entered into between the Queen's commissioners, the Swiss leaders of the colony, and the Lords-Proprietors. Their articles of agreement were soon written and signed, a copy of which may be seen in Hawks' History, from which we learn that the number of German Palatines who emigrated with De Graffenreid and Mitchell amounted to six hundred and fifty, filling two vessels; and that the most liberal provisions were made for them by their English friends, who bound their leaders to the most far-sighted pledges in the contract for their comfort and prosperity. Two hundred and fifty acres of land were to be given them for five years without remuneration, after which they were to pay an annual rent of two-pence per acre; besides, implements for agriculture and building were to be furnished them gratuitously by De Graffenreid and Mitchell; to be also supplied with cattle, hogs and sheep, which were not to be paid for until seven years after receiving them; and for twelve months after their arrival they were to be supplied with necessary food for themselves and families, which, likewise, was not to be paid for until the end of the second year after their arrival. "The commissioners, on their part, agreed to give each colonist, young and old, twenty shillings sterling in clothes and money, and to pay De Graffenreid and Mitchell £5 10*s.* sterling a head for transportation."

In the month of December, 1710, these Swiss and Palatine settlers, with their leaders, landed safely at the confluence of the Neuse and Trent Rivers in North Carolina, where they built a town, which they named New-Berne, after the capital city of Switzerland, of which De Graffenreid and

Mitchell and the majority of the colonists were natives. The troubles of a long and tedious voyage across the Atlantic were now over; these poor Germans had at last found a home, and here could they worship God according to the doctrines and usages of their own Protestant religion, thanking their Almighty Preserver that they were safely beyond the reach of all Roman Catholic sovereigns.

In the year 1711, not many months after the arrival of the De Graffenreid colony, a dreadful Indian war broke out, brought on by the agency of two miserable white men, Carey and John Porter, whose turbulent ambition did not permit them to submit to the authorized and lawful government of Hyde; Carey, having determined to take the rule out of the hands of Governor Hyde, and to act in that capacity himself, but being unsuccessful in his attempt, resorted with his friends to the base and fiendish measure of stirring up the Tuscarora Indians "to cut off all the inhabitants of that part of Carolina that adhered to Mr. Hyde." For this purpose Carey dispatched his friend, John Porter, to those Indians, numbering twelve hundred fencible men, promising them great rewards for the accomplishment of this bloody deed.

The white settlers had all this while lived on the most friendly terms with the Indians, and if any case of disturbance among individuals occurred occasionally, it was soon amicably settled by the law, to which both parties had recourse, and was equitable enough on both sides. The Indians were frequently employed by the whites as domestics, without any suspicion or alarm, they having ingress and egress to and from the dwellings of the whites. "At length the appointed day of slaughter came. Twelve hundred Tuscaroras, separated into numerous small divisions, entered on their secret march. No outward manifestations of hostility were to be seen; individuals were sent among the whites to reconnoitre, and, as usual, entered the houses of their doomed victims as friends. As night approached, large numbers appeared, as if seeking provisions; but still not in such quantities did they show themselves as to beget alarm.

"At the dawn of day they impatiently waited for sunrise, which was the preconcerted signal for the simultaneous butchery. As soon as it arrived, those in the houses of the whites, and scarce a habitation in any settlement of the province was at that moment without them, gave a whoop, which was instantly responded to by their companions lurking in the adjacent woods, and the frightful work of blood began.

"The slaughter was indiscriminate, and the wonder is that any white person escaped. Gray-haired age, and vigorous manhood, and childhood's helplessness, all fared alike. One hundred and thirty victims were butchered in the settlements on Roanoke. *The Swiss and Palatines around Newbern, to the number of sixty or more, were murdered.* The poor Huguenots of Bath and its vicinity, to what number we know not, fell under the knife or the tomahawk. Happy he who could hide himself, or escape from the scene of horror. But soon the torch was applied to the dwelling and storehouse alike, and the concealed were forced from their hiding-places.

"The incarnate fiends, with loud yells, then marched in their several divisions through the forests to a common centre previously designated, and, infuriated now by drunkenness, staggered on their bloody man-hunt for the few whites, who had escaped the desolation of their habitations. They formed new parties, and scoured the country north of Albemarle as far westward as the Chowan. The carnage lasted for three days, and terminated at last from the disability produced in the savage by the combined effect of drunkenness and fatigue. The few colonists who had escaped slaughter, availing themselves of the forced suspension of wholesale murder, gathered together as they could with their arms, and stunned by the blow they had received, attempted at first nothing more than to collect the women and children, and guard them night and day until time would enable them to concert other measures." (*Hawks' Hist. of N. C.*, vol. ii, pp. 530–532.)

A few days previous to this general massacre, Baron De Graffenreid and the surveyor-general, Lawson, with a negro servant belonging to the Baron, ascended the river Neuse in a boat for the purpose of inspecting the lands and make further explorations. Not dreaming of Indian hostilities they expected to spend the first night at an Indian village named Corutra; but finding that several Indians whom they had met were armed, they did not like the appearance of these things, and determined to sail up the river; but as they made for their boat they were seized by the Indians, and were led the next day to a council purposely convened; but might have been liberated, as the council was dissolved without any apparent decision, had not an Indian who understood a little English, and listened to their conversation, told a falsehood against them, which so exasperated the others that they at once executed the negro in a manner not known, and poor Lawson was inhumanly murdered by having sharp pine splinters inserted in his flesh, which were then set on fire. De Graffenreid escaped by stating he was King of the German Palatines, and demanded of them by what authority they could put a king to death, especially as he had committed no offence towards them. His life was accordingly spared, though he was still kept in custody.

This massacre, as a necessary consequence, led to a war with the Indians in North Carolina, in which the Palatines were obliged to remain neutral, as De Graffenreid had obtained his liberty by a treaty of neutrality with such of the savages who were in arms. The principal terms of the treaty were, that he and his Palatines on the one hand, and the Tuscarora and Core Indians on the other, should preserve friendship towards each other; that in the existing war with the English the Palatines should remain neutral, and that the Baron should take up no land without the consent of the Indians.

The Baron adhered strictly to the terms of this treaty, which was, of course, not agreeable to the whites in general, but which was, nevertheless, of great advantage to the province, "as it afforded him an opportunity, which he improved at the constant risk of his life, to discover and communicate to the whites all the Indians' plans." "This neutrality alone probably saved the remnant of the settlement at what is now Newberne from utter extermination. The danger of discovery, however, was so constant and so great, that the Baron would gladly have removed with his Palatines to Virginia." (*Hawks*, vol. ii, p. 536.)

Shortly afterwards the settlers received aid from South Carolina against these relentless savages. Colonel Barnwell, with a detachment of the militia and friendly Yemassee Indians, was sent to attack these hostile savages, who were so much reduced by the loss in killed, wounded, and prisoners, that they caused the whites but little trouble afterwards, and soon removed to other parts, when the colony began once more to flourish through the benign influence of peace.

Baron De Graffenreid having had a bitter experience of Indian treatment, in which his life was in constant jeopardy, resolved to return to his native country, Switzerland. He, however, left the German Palatines, who were already sufficiently impoverished by the Indian war, in a most destitute condition, by withholding their titles to their lands, and contrary to the stipulations of the contract made between himself and the London commissioners appointed by Queen Anne.

Williamson, in his History of North Carolina, states that these poor Germans were looked upon by the Swiss gentlemen as mere objects of speculation, and that De Graffenreid mortgaged their lands to Colonel Pollock in order to satisfy a debt which he had incurred. Dr. Hawks, however, frees Louis Mitchell from all blame in this matter, since the power of making titles was not vested in him. Whether the Baron ever returned to America, or permitted his family to remain here whilst he visited his native country, or whether after all his family had departed from America, some again sought a home in Carolina, is not related; but it is well known that his descendants are still residing in different portions of Carolina.

The last resource left to these German Palatines was to send a petition to the council, dated November 6th, 1714, in which they stated that they were "disappointed of their lands," &c., which were to be provided for them, and petitioned that each family might have permission to take up four hundred acres of land, and have two years' time of payment allowed them. The council granted their petition, and represented their case to the Lords-Proprietors, from whom they doubtless received every aid and encouragement which could be afforded them.

It would require very patient and toilsome research among the unpublished archives of Europe in order to answer the question positively, *to what religious denomination these Swiss and Palatinate Germans at Newberne professed themselves.* All the historians of North Carolina are silent on this subject. However, let us not overlook such authorities which are within our reach even in this country.

The present, as well as the former religious condition of Switzerland is well known. The population is divided into the Roman Catholic, the Reformed, and the Lutheran Churches. The emigrants from that country to Newberne were doubtless all Protestants, inasmuch as they were brought over by Protestant leaders, and soon after their arrival in North Carolina connected themselves with a Protestant Church. The majority of them were most likely members of the Reformed Church, so supposed, because the Reformed Church is the strongest Protestant denomination in Switzerland.

The German Palatines were *all Protestants*, inasmuch as, on account of this "*sin*," as Dr. Hawks ironically expresses it, they suffered such grievous persecutions, and were forced to flee from their native country to seek an asylum in England. That the greater number of Palatines were Lutherans may safely be presumed; from the extensive history of Lutheranism by Seckendorff, we learn that Lutheranism made rapid progress in the Palatinate at the time of the Reformation, and that it had greatly prevailed in that country during the seventeenth century, which was the time immediately preceding the departure of these settlers from their native country. Seckendorff wrote his history but twenty-four years previous to the last Protestant exodus from the Palatinate.

In connection with this fact we have the additional proof, that the most of those twelve thousand Palatine Germans, who fled to England to enjoy Queen Anne's protection, and who settled in New York and other provinces, were members of the Lutheran Church, and it is but reasonable to conclude that their brethren in North Carolina were of the same faith with themselves.

The story of their religion in their newly adopted country is soon told, which may be gathered from the correspondence between De Graffenreid and the Bishop of London, published in Hawks' History, and reads as follows:

"My Good and Excellent Lord:

"The misfortune I met with in all being unexpectedly hurried away from London to New Castle to meet my Swissers, in order to transport them into North Carolina after those six hundred and fifty Palatines I had sent before, which unlooked-for arrival of them so far north, gave me notice to pay my duty to your lordship, whom then, I was told, was neither in London nor at Fulham. I can assure your lordship no person of any rank is unacquainted with that great and good character your lordship has and merits. So I can make no excuse on that behalf, but heartily beg pardon, and at the same time humbly request your lordship *to accept of me and my people, and receive us into your Church under your lordship's patronage*, and we shall esteem ourselves happy sons of a better stock, and, I hope, shall always behave ourselves as becomes members of the Church of England, and dutiful children of so pious and indulgent a father as your lordship is to all under your care, in all obedience. Craving your lordship's blessing to me and my countrymen here, I make bold to subscribe,

"My lord, yours, &c.,

"C. DE GRAFFENREID."

The answer of the Bishop of London to this epistle is contained in a letter to the Secretary, an extract of which is furnished us by Dr. Hawks.

"FULHAM, 12th January, 1711–12.

"SIR:

"As to the letter of Baron Graffenreid, whereby you may perceive that they are all ready to conform to the Church of England: if the Society will be pleased to allow a stipend for a chaplain to read Common Prayers in High Dutch (German), I will endeavor to provide one so soon as I have their resolution, which I would willingly hear so soon as possible, that I may send him over with Mr. Rainsford.

"I am, sir, yours, &c.,

"H. LONDON."

It is presumed that the bishop was successful in sending to this German and Swiss colony a clergyman of the English Church, who could minister to them in their native language, and thus these German Protestants glided gradually into the Episcopal Church. They may have been induced to take this step from the following motives: they had no pastor of their own faith, and thus were destitute of the means of grace; they had been kindly treated by the English sovereign and her people, and a feeling of gratitude for their benefactors led them to think very favorably of the religious faith of the English people; and furthermore, the Church of England was the established religion in the Carolinas.

Some of the names of these Germans are still on record; in the list of jurymen, in Craven precinct, dated 1723, we find, among others, the following undoubted German names: Christian Eslar, Christian Slaver, John Lecher Miller, Jacob Miller, Matthew Rasenober, John Dipp, John Simons, Henry Perk, Henry Perlerbo, John Wixedell, Michael Resabel, and Martin Franke. "An old document, signed by the Palatines," says Dr. Hawks, "gives us the following German names, yet familiar in Craven and the adjacent counties: Eslar (now Isler), Grum (Croom), Rennege, Mohr (Moore), Eibach (Hypock), Morris," and a number of others. "Of the Swiss, we find Coxdaille (Cogdell), from whom, on the maternal side, descend the North Carolina branch of the families of Stanly and Badger."

Section 8. The German settlers in Charleston, S. C.

We will now direct our attention to one more German settlement along the seacoast, whose history must not be omitted, and then we will turn our faces inland. James Island, S. C., opposite Charleston, has had our attention; Newberne, N. C., came next; no settlement of any note was as yet established along the Cape Fear River, and Wilmington, N. C., had no existence at that early date; but *Charleston*, the principal seaport of the Carolinas, was a flourishing town, and commanded a considerable share of the emigration to America; and the Germans, who sought and found a habitation in so many parts of America, during the commencement of the eighteenth century, also found a home in this locality. We have a few facts upon which we can build a very safe conclusion as to the probable date of the arrival of German settlers in Charleston, but no direct testimony has as yet been discovered, in which the year and day of their landing is mentioned.

Queen Anne of England caused lands to be donated in the Province of South Carolina to the German refugees from the Palatinate, as Dr. Hazelius informs us in his History, p. 25; this must have been done before the 31st of July, 1714, when her majesty departed this life. And we ask, would this grant have been made if there were no German Palatines remaining in her realm, or expected soon to arrive, for whom this location was provided? Or, is it likely that none of these Palatine Germans came to the port of Charleston, when they were landed at the seaports of other provinces in America, especially as an abundance of land in the Province of South Carolina was provided for them, and in order to reach the locality of that grant they had to be landed in

Charleston, even though they did not occupy, *at that time*, the lands of that grant, as we are informed by Dr. Hazelius?

The colony of the pious Salzburgers, with their pastors, Bolzius and Gronau, landed first at Charleston in the early part of March, 1734, before their arrival at Ebenezer, Georgia; and in Rev. Bolzius' journal, found in Force's Collection of Historical Tracts, we have the following statement, dated "Charleston, March 7th, 1734:" "We found here some Germans, who were very glad of our arrival, and will come to us, in order to receive the sacrament."

Next comes the statement of Strobel's History of the Salzburgers, p. 59: "Remaining in Charleston a few days, the Salzburgers re-embarked on the 9th day of March."

In Urlsperger's Nachrichten, Rev. Bolzius gives us a lengthy account of his visit to Charleston, in company with Baron Von Reck, in the following May; he arrived there on the 23d of May, 1734, and left again for his home in Ebenezer, May 26th. Here we have the following record: "A certain glazier and his wife, *who are from the Palatinate*, went with us to the Holy Supper, and manifested great attention and earnestness; their love for the word of God and the holy sacraments is so great, that they are determined to remain no longer in Charleston, and have concluded to remove to Ebenezer as soon as possible. They have many children, which will enlarge our small school.

Both these parents will be very useful to us in our house arrangements."

The above records settle the matter conclusively, that there *were* Germans residing in Charleston previous to the early part of 1734; that they were then sufficiently numerous to have the word of God preached to them, and to enjoy a communion season; and that some of them were from the Palatinate.

But how far back we are to date their arrival in Charleston is uncertain; they could not have settled there before 1708, as the exodus of Palatinate refugees into England did not take place until that time, and after the Queen's proclamation, inviting them to the hospitalities of her realm; and they certainly were living there in 1734.

These Germans did not occupy the lands granted them along the Congaree River, and for a very good reason; those lands were located too far inland for that period of time, being about one hundred miles remote from Charleston; that location would have been an unsafe dwelling-place at the time, for even Orangeburg County was not much settled until 1735, and that locality is much nearer the seaboard than the Saxe-Gotha grant on the Congaree River. The presumption then is, that when the Palatine Germans arrived at Charleston, they remained there and in the vicinity.

A number of Germans having thus located themselves in Charleston, and their wants having become known to the pastors of the Salzburg colony as they passed through to Ebenezer, these holy men resolved to do something for the spiritual welfare of their beloved brethren of the same faith in this town. Accordingly, on the 23d of May, 1734, Rev. Bolzius accompanied Baron Von Reck, Lord Commissary of the Ebenezer colony, as far as Charleston, on his return to Europe, where they remained a few days; and from Rev. Bolzius' journal we quote the following account of the first communion administered there among the Germans.

"*May 23, 1734.*—We were informed in Savannah where we could best lodge in Charleston, and we likewise found very friendly people in the hotel, with many accommodations there for reasonable charges. Several Germans of our Evangelical Confession mentioned to me and our Commissary their desire to commune at the Lord's table, for which they have had a great longing for a long time. I therefore determined to remain here over Sunday, and prepare the people from the word of God for this solemn exercise.

"*May 25.*—Many persons of distinction in this place showed us great attention, and constrained us to dine and sup with them, which we would rather decline, as in so doing we would be subjected to many dissipations of mind and heart. To-day those persons came to me, who had notified their intention to commune, in order that I might hold some scriptural conversation with them; as far as time and opportunity permitted, I discoursed with them on the importance and benefit of the Holy Supper, as well as the requirements of true Christianity. We deemed it advisable that, as those persons would hear us but once or twice, to press home upon their hearts the most needful truths, and to instil upon their memory 'the order of salvation,' together with several important Scripture passages.

"*May 26.*—This day a fine opportunity presented itself for me to return, and arrive at Ebenezer in a few days, consequently, I was compelled to leave Charleston to-day. I therefore assembled the communicants early, at 5 A.M., when we all sang several hymns, and I discoursed upon some of the important and practical truths from the gospel of to-day. After sermon we all fell upon our knees, and the Lord Commissary prayed very fervently to God in the name of the whole congregation. After the absolution and the celebration of the Lord's Supper, I prepared myself for the homeward journey. It was very remarkable to me, that a certain German shoemaker had also notified himself as being desirous to commune, but he came to my room after the services were ended, because, as he remarked, the house where I lodged had been locked. Afterwards I learned that this very man was a drinking character, who associated himself with low company, but which I could neither discover in his outward appearance, nor from his conversation, and had presumed something good of him in my short intercourse with him; I was, therefore, rejoiced that he was prevented from coming to the table of the Lord. A certain glazier and his wife, who are from the Palatinate, went with us to the Holy Supper, and manifested great attention and earnestness; their love for the word of God and the holy sacraments is so great that they are determined to remain no longer in Charleston, and have concluded to remove to Ebenezer as soon as possible. They have many children, which will enlarge our small school. Both these persons will be very useful to us in our house arrangements."

In 1742 the Rev. Henry Melchior Muhlenberg, D.D., visited Charleston; he had been sent from the Mission Society of Halle, in Germany, to labor in Pennsylvania, but it was made his duty first to visit the colony at Ebenezer, Georgia, and landed at Charleston on 21st of September, where he remained but three days, and then proceeded to Ebenezer.

Rev. Dr. Muhlenberg did not remain long with the pastors of the Salzburg colony, and, as soon as he had somewhat refreshed and strengthened himself from the effects of his perilous and wearisome voyage to America, he returned to Charleston in company with Rev. Bolzius, who had intended to accompany him to Philadelphia, and there induct him into his office; however, as no vessel was expected to sail from Charleston to Philadelpha for several months, Rev. Bolzius, after having remained a few days, returned to his own field of labor in Ebenezer.

Rev. Muhlenberg was a man of no idle habits, and, from the time of this, his second arrival in

Charleston, October 20th, 1742, whilst waiting for an opportunity to reach his destined field of labor, to November 12th of the same year, when he set sail in a very small and frail vessel for Philadelphia, he employed himself in laboring for the spiritual welfare of the Germans in Charleston. During his stay he made his home in the family of a painter, named Theus, the brother of a German Reformed minister, who labored in Saxe-Gotha, South Carolina, along the Congaree River. On Sundays Dr. Muhlenberg preached to several German families that had congregated themselves in Mr. Theus' house, and during the other days of the week he catechized their children, who were thus instructed in all the principles of the Christian religion, according to this excellent and ancient custom.

Eleven years later, A.D. 1753, the Revs. Christian Rabenhorst and M. Gerock, A.M., arrived at Charleston, upon the same vessel, from Germany, on their way to their respective fields of labor; the former having been appointed by the Society for Promoting Christian Knowledge in Foreign Parts as the third pastor at Ebenezer, and the latter, as the Lutheran pastor in Lancaster, Penna.; both of these ministers labored a short time in Charleston whilst they tarried there.

Section 9. The Swiss colony at Purysburg, S. C., A.D. 1732.

In Beaufort County, S. C., some thirty miles inland from the seacoast, and situated on the east bank of the Savannah River, there was once a flourishing German town and colony, named Purysburg. The inhabitants came from Switzerland, and under circumstances very similar to those of the settlers of Newberne, N. C.; for, what De Graffenreid and Mitchell were to the colony on the confluence of the Neuse and Trent Rivers, that Purry, Richard, Meuron, and Raymond were to the Swiss settlers on the east side of the Savannah River.

In the year 1731, "John Peter Purry, of Neufchâtel, in Switzerland, formerly a Director-General of the French East-India Company, having formed the design of leaving his native country, paid a visit to Carolina in order to inform himself of the circumstances and situation of that province. After viewing the lands," and satisfying his own mind, by means of personal observation, of the fertility of the soil, eligibility as to climate and situation for a settlement of his countrymen, "he returned to Britain. The government there entered into a contract with him, and agreed to give him lands, and four hundred pounds sterling for every hundred effective men he could transport from Switzerland to Carolina." (*Mills' Statistics of South Carolina*, page 369.)

Whilst Mr. Purry was in Charleston, he drew up the following flattering account of the soil and climate of South Carolina, and of the excellency and freedom of the provincial government, and on his return to Switzerland published it among the people. It reads as follows:

"PROPOSALS BY MR. PETER PURRY, OF NEUFCHATEL, FOR THE ENCOURAGEMENT OF SUCH SWISS PROTESTANTS AS SHOULD AGREE TO ACCOMPANY HIM TO CAROLINA, TO SETTLE A NEW COLONY.

"There are only two methods, viz.: one for persons to go as servants, the other to settle on their own account.

"1. Those who are desirous to go as servants must be carpenters, vine-planters, husbandmen, or good laborers.

"2. They must be such as are not very poor, but in a condition to carry with them what is sufficient to support their common necessity.

"3. They must have at least three or four good shirts, and a suit of clothes each.

"4. They are to have each for their wages one hundred livres yearly, which make fifty crowns of the money of Neufchâtel, in Switzerland, but their wages are not to commence till the day of their arrival in Carolina.

"5. Expert carpenters shall have suitable encouragement.

"6. The time of their contract shall be three years, reckoning from the day of their arrival in that country.

"7. They shall be supplied in part of their wages with money to come from Switzerland, till they embark for Carolina.

"8. Their wages shall be paid them regularly at the end of every year; for security whereof they shall have the fruits of their labor, and generally all that can be procured for them, whether movables or immovables.

"9. Victuals and lodgings from the day of their embarkation shall not be put to their account, nor their passage by sea.

"10. They shall have what money they want advanced during the term of their service in part of their wages to buy linen, clothes, and all other necessaries.

"11. If they happen to fall sick, they shall be lodged and nourished gratis, but their wages shall not go on during their illness, or that they are not able to work.

"12. They shall serve, after recovery, the time they had lost during their sickness.

"13. What goes to pay physicians or surgeons shall be put to their account.

"As to those who go to settle on their own account, they must have at least fifty crowns each, because their passage by sea and victuals will cost them twenty to twenty-five crowns, and the rest of the money shall go to procure divers things which will be absolutely necessary for the voyage." (*Carroll's Collections*, vol. ii, pp. 121, *et seq.*)

Here follows also, from the same author:

"A DESCRIPTION OF THE PROVINCE OF SOUTH CAROLINA. DRAWN UP AT CHARLES-TOWN, IN SEPTEMBER, 1731.

"The King of Great Britain having about three years ago purchased this province of the Lords-Proprietors thereof, has since studied to make agriculture, commerce, and navigation flourish in it. His Majesty immediately nominated Colonel Johnson, a worthy gentleman, to be Governor thereof; who, at his departure for Carolina, received divers orders and instructions, &c. His Majesty further grants to every European servant, whether man or woman, fifty acres of land free of all rents for ten years, which shall be distributed to them after having served their master for the time agreed on.

"In consequence of these instructions, Mr. Purry was permitted to go and choose on the borders of the river Savannah land proper to build the town of Purysburg upon; and having found it such as he wished, the government made him a grant thereof under the great seal of the Province, dated 1st September, 1731, and at the same time published throughout the whole country a prohibition to all sorts of persons to go and settle on the said land, which is already called the *Swiss Quarter*.

"In order to facilitate the execution of this undertaking in the best manner, the Assembly granted to the said Mr. Purry four hundred pounds sterling, and provisions sufficient for the maintenance of three hundred persons for one year, provided they be all persons of good repute and Swiss Protestants, and that they come to Carolina within the space of two years.

"The river Savannah is one of the finest in all Carolina, the water good, and stored with excellent fish. It is about the largeness of the Rhine, and there are two forts already built upon it, which the Indians have never dared to attack.

"The town of Purysburg will be situated thirty miles from the sea, and about seven miles from the highest tide. The land about it is a most delightful plain, and the greatest part very good soil, especially for pasturage, and the rest proper enough for some productions. It was formerly called the great Yemassee Port, and is esteemed by the inhabitants of the Province the best place in all Carolina, although never yet possessed but by the Indians, who were driven from thence by the English several years ago, and have never dared to return thither. All sorts of trees and plants will grow there as well as can be wished, particularly vines, wheat, barley, oats, pease, beans, hemp, flax, cotton, tobacco, indigo, olives, orange trees, and citron trees, as also white mulberry trees for feeding of silk-worms.

"The lands will not be difficult to clear, because there is neither stones nor brambles, but only great trees, which do not grow very thick, so that more land may be cleared there in one week than could be done in Switzerland in a month. The custom of the country is, that after having cut down these great trees, they leave the stumps for four or five years to rot, and afterwards easily root them up in order to manure the land."

The remainder of Mr. Purry's description of South Carolina is of so general a character that it would add nothing to the interest of this sketch. He gave such a flattering account of the country that many Switzers were induced to emigrate with him to Carolina. This document published in pamphlet form was then signed by four gentlemen, and extensively distributed. The conclusion reads as follows:

"We, whose names are hereunto subscribed, do attest that all which is contained in this account of South Carolina is the real truth, having been eye-witnesses of the most part of the particulars therein mentioned.

"Done at Charlestown the 23d of September, 1731.

"JOHN PETER PURRY, of Neufchâtel,
"JAMES RICHARD, of Geneva,
"ABRAHAM MEURON, of St. Sulpy, in the county of Neufchâtel,
"HENRY RAYMOND, of St. Sulpy."

After Mr. Purry's return to Switzerland, and his proposals having become generally known, the people flocked to him without delay, and he soon made every preparation necessary for the safety and comfort of the colonists, who placed themselves under his charge. Mills, in his Statistics of South Carolina, page 369, states: "Immediately one hundred and seventy Switzers agreed to follow him, to be transported to the fertile and delightful province, as he described it," so that in a few months they were ready to enter upon their long voyage, which was doubtless a prosperous one; for they left England about the 1st of August, 1732, and arrived in Charleston during the following November.

The Governor of South Carolina, agreeably to instructions, allowed them forty thousand acres of land for their settlement, which was surveyed and located on the east side of the Savannah River, where a town was laid out for their accommodation, and named Purysburg, after the founder of the colony and the promoter of its settlement. The interest in favor of this new enterprise continued in Switzerland for some time. Not long afterwards some two hundred more settlers were added to the new colony, who likewise arrived safely in Carolina.

It was the intention of the Swiss settlers, in connection with the other more necessary articles of husbandry, to plant the vine, and also to give their attention to the rearing and manufacturing of silk, for which this Province appeared to be admirably adapted, as the climate was warm, and the soil very productive for the growing of a variety of grapes, and the planting of the white mulberry tree, on which the tender silk-worm feeds. The Governor and Council likewise were happy in the acquisition of such a force, who, by their knowledge of these various branches of industry, gave promise of great service to the Province. "They allotted to each of them a separate tract of land, and gave every encouragement in their power to the people. The Swiss emigrants began their labors of raising silk and planting the vine with uncommon zeal and energy, highly elevated with the idea of possessing landed estates." (*Mills*, p 370.)

Rev. Bolzius visited Purysburg on his way to Charleston, in May, 1734, not two years after its settlement, and speaks highly of it in his journal as follows: "This town is built upon the more elevated banks of the river, and, as many wealthy people reside here, it is hoped that in a short time it will become a considerable town. The inhabitants labor industriously in their gardens and fields, and persons can already procure here fresh meats, eggs, garden vegetables, even more than in Savannah. We were shown all kindness, and several of the inhabitants besought us to return soon again, and administer the communion."

The majority of these settlers were, doubtless, members of the Reformed Church of Switzerland before they came to America; they were all Protestants, as this faith was made one of the conditions for their becoming settlers of this colony; a few families were connected with the Lutheran Church, as Rev. Bolzius' journal informs us. The colony brought their own pastor with them, the Rev. Joseph Bügnion, "a Swiss minister," who, when he arrived in England, on his way to Carolina, was induced to have Episcopal ordination laid upon him by the Rev. Dr. Clagett, Bishop of St. David's. His motives were doubtless pure, thinking that the Church of England was the established religion in Carolina, and that he might accomplish as much good, with less opposition, "as a stranger in a strange land," if he would conform to the rules and worship of that Church. Whether the majority of the Swiss Protestants coincided with him is not stated; probably many of them did so, but others connected themselves with the Lutheran Church at Ebenezer, Georgia. Rev. Mr. Bügnion did not remain a great while among his countrymen at Purysburg; about the commencement of the year 1735 he removed to St. James, Santee.

"In 1744 the Rev. Henry Chiffelle arrived in the Province as the first missionary from '*The Society for the Propagation of the Gospel in Foreign Parts*' to this parish. He was a native of Switzerland, and was ordained," as a minister of the Church of England, "by Dr. Gibson, Bishop of London, July 14th and 21st, 1734." During his time of service in this charge, in February, 1746, this settlement was established as a separate parish by an act of the legislature, under the name and title of St. Peter's Parish. "The Act directed that the Church or Chapel, and the dwelling-house wherein the Rev. Mr. Chiffelle had preached and dwelt, should be the Parish Church and Parsonage-house of St. Peter's Parish. The Rector or minister was to be elected as in other parishes, and to receive a salary of £100. Proc. money. Mr. Chiffelle continued in this mission until his death in 1758, and was succeeded by the Rev. Abraham Imer, who arrived in the Province in 1760, and died in 1766." (*Dalcho's History of the Prot. Epis. Church in South Carolina*, pp. 385 and 386.)

In regard to the Lutheran element of this colony, we may add, that they appear to have always had a warm attachment to their own faith. Their contiguity to their Lutheran brethren of the Ebenezer colony on the other side of the Savannah River, as well as the zeal of the Salzburg pastors, who occasionally visited them, had the effect of keeping up the interest in their own Church for a long time. The following extract from the journal of Rev. Bolzius, as found in Force's Collection of Historical Tracts, abundantly proves this: "March 19th, Mr. Oglethorpe, going to Purysburg, took with him one of us, Rev. Mr. Gronau, and recommended him to preach to the Germans there, which he accordingly did. There are three families of our Lutheran confession in that place. Rev. Gronau having preached for them from Gal. 2 : 20, they were very glad, and resolved to come constantly to our settlement, which is but a few, three German, miles from Purysburg to hear the word of God, and to receive the sacrament. They reckon the Salzburgers very happy in having their own ministers, for at Purysburg they are now without a minister."

As far as can be ascertained, no Lutheran congregation was ever established in this place, as there were but few families of that faith in the colony, and these could occasionally attend divine worship at Ebenezer. Of the Episcopal Church established there, Dalcho further states: "There has been no incumbent since the Revolution. Divine service has occasionally been performed by visiting clergymen. No organized Episcopal congregation exists here at present." A.D. 1820.

The final history of the colony is hinted at by Mills, page 370, from which we can draw our own conclusions. He states that "in a short time they felt the many inconveniences attending a change of climate. Several of them sickened and died, and others found the hardships of the first state of colonization much greater than they expected. They became discontented. Smarting under the pressure of indigence and disappointment they not only blamed Purry for deceiving them, but repented leaving their native country." The colony lingered up to the period of the Revolutionary war. Mills informs us that "Purysburg was the first headquarters of the American army under Lincoln in the Revolution. It afterwards was in possession of the British under Prevost."

A large number of these Swiss settlers sought and found homes in other parts of Carolina, both before and after the Revolution, which left to Purysburg very little more than a name in history.

Section 10. The German and Swiss Colonists of Orangeburg, S. C., A.D. 1735.

The story of the settling of Orangeburg, South Carolina is a page in the history of that State which has never been fully written. The cause of this omission can scarcely be accounted for, as ample materials were within the reach of former historians. Certain outlines have been given, but nothing very satisfactory has been furnished.

"The first white inhabitant who settled in this section of country was named Henry Sterling; his occupation, it is supposed, was that of a trader. He located himself on Lyon's Creek in the year 1704, and obtained a grant of a tract of land, at present in the possession of Colonel Russel P. McCord." (*Mills*, p. 656.)

"The next settlers were some three or four individuals, who located themselves at the Cowpens, northwesterly of the low country white settlements; these, and the Cherokee and Catawba Indians were all the inhabitants who had preceded the Germans." (*Mills*, p. 657.)

The colonists of Orangeburg County and town were mostly German and Swiss, who came over from Europe in a large body, occupying several vessels, and even to the present day their descendants are easily recognized by their unmistakable German names, and are found to be the principal owners and occupants of the soil in this portion of South Carolina.

The principal facts concerning the early history of these colonists are mainly derived from the Journals of Council of the Province of South Carolina, as found in manuscript form in the office of the Secretary of State, as well as from the Church record-book, kept by their first pastors, the two Giessendanners, uncle and nephew, written in the German and English languages, which is still extant, and has been thoroughly examined by the writer; and as these additional facts are now presented for the first time, it is hoped that they may open new avenues, which will afford future historians of the State additional sources of research and information.

That the German element of the Orangeburg colonists came partly from Switzerland, we learn from the records of the Giessendanners' church-book, as it was the custom of the younger Giessendanner to mention the place of nativity of all the deceased, in his records of each funeral of the early settlers; and as this emigration from that country to Orangeburg occurred only two or three years subsequent to the emigration of a former Swiss colony to Purysburg, S. C., it certainly requires no great stretch of the imagination to explain the causes which induced such a large number of emigrants from that country to locate themselves upon the fertile lands of South Carolina, which were described so glowingly by John Peter Purry and his associates.

Let any one examine the pamphlets, as found in vol. ii of Carroll's Collections, which Mr. Purry published in reference to the Province of South Carolina, and which he freely distributed in his native country, in which the fertility of the soil, salubrity of the climate, excellency of government, safety of the colonists, opportunities of becoming wealthy, &c., &c., are so highly extolled, and corroborated by the testimony of so many witnesses, and he will easily comprehend what the Switzers must have fancied that province to be, viz.: the El Dorado of America,—the second Palestine of the world.

Mr. Purry's account of the excellency of South

Carolina for safe and remunerative settlement went round, from mouth to mouth, in many a hamlet and cottage of the little mountain-girt country, losing nothing by being told from one family to another; which, with the additional fact, that many had relatives and friends living in both the Carolinas, whom they possibly might meet again, soon fastened their affections upon that province, and induced them to leave the Fatherland, and make their future homes with some of their countrymen in America. Their little all of earthly goods or patrimony was soon disposed of; preparations for a long journey were quickly made, as advised by Mr. Purry in his pamphlet; the journey through North Germany towards some seaport was then undertaken; and, with other Germans added to their number, who joined their fortunes with them whilst passing through their country, they were soon rocked upon the bosom of the ocean, heading towards America, with the compass pointed to their expected haven, Charleston, South Carolina.

These German and Swiss settlers did not all arrive in Orangeburg at the same time; the first colony came during the year 1735; another company arrived a year later, and it was not until 1737 that their first pastor, Rev. John Ulrich Giessendanner, Senior, came among them with another reinforcement of settlers; whilst Mills informs us that emigrants from Germany arrived in Orangeburg District as late as 1769, only a few years before the Revolution.

Like most of the early German settlers of America, these colonists came to Carolina not as "gentlemen or traders," but as tillers of the soil, with the honest intention "to earn their bread by the sweat of the brow," and their lands soon gave evidence of thrift and plenty, and they, by their industry and frugality, not only secured a competency and independence for themselves and their children in this fertile portion of South Carolina, but many of them became blessed with abundance and wealth.

From the records of Rev. Giessendanner we learn that there were also a considerable number of mechanics, as well as planters and farmers, among these colonists; and the results of this German colonization were extremely favorable to Orangeburg District, inasmuch as they remained there as permanent settlers, whilst many of their countrymen in other localities, such as Purysburg, &c., were compelled to leave their first-selected homes, on account of the want of health and of that great success which they had at first expected, but the Orangeburg settlers became a well-established and successful colony.

It has been asserted that the German congregation established in Orangeburg among these settlers was Reformed, which is evidently a mistake, as any one may perceive from the following facts. On the one hand, it must be admitted that the Switzers came from the land where John Calvin labored, and where the Reformed religion prevails, but where there are also many Lutheran churches established. It is also admitted that the Giessendanners were natives of Switzerland, but it would be unsafe to conclude from these facts that the German congregation at Orangeburg, with all, or nearly all, of its members, and with their pastors, were Swiss Reformed or Calvinistic in their faith. On the other hand, although nothing positive is mentioned in the Record-book of the Church, concerning their distinctive religious belief, yet the presumptive evidence, even from this source of information, is sufficiently strong to conclude that this first religious society in Orangeburg was a Lutheran Church. The facts from which our conclusions are drawn are:

Firstly.—Because a very strong element from Germany was mixed with their Swiss brethren in the early settling of this county, which, by still later accession of German colonists, appears to have become the predominating population, who were mostly Lutherans, and the presumption becomes strong that their church-organization was likewise Lutheran.

Secondly.—It seems to have been a commonly admitted fact and the prevailing general impression of that time, when their second pastor had become an ordained minister of the Church of England.

Thirdly.—In examining their church records one will discover, through its entire pages, a recognition of the festivals of the Lutheran Church, as were commonly observed by the early Lutheran settlers.

Fourthly.—In Dalcho's History of the Prot. Epis. Church in S. C., published in 1820, at the time when the son of the younger Giessendanner was still living (*see Mills' Statistics*, p. 657, *published as late as* 1826), it is most positively stated concerning his father, that "he was a minister of the Lutheran Church." (*Dalcho*, p. 333, *footnote.*) How could Dr. Dalcho have been mistaken when he had the records of the Episcopal Church in South Carolina before him; and in that denomination this was the prevailing impression, as was, doubtless, so created from Giessendanner's own statements in the bosom of which Church he passed the latter days of his life.

Fifthly.—One of the churches which Giessendanner served before he became an Episcopal clergyman, located in Amelia Township, called St. Matthews, has never been any other than a Lutheran Church, and is still in connection with the Evangelical Lutheran Synod of South Carolina.

Sixthly.—The Orangeburg colonists, after their pastor departed from their faith, were served with Lutheran pastors entirely, numbering in all about seventeen ministers, and only for a short time a Reformed minister, Rev. Dr. Zübly, once labored there as a temporary supply.

Seventhly.—In Dr. Hazelius' History of the American Lutheran Church, p. 64, we have the following testimony, gathered from the journal of the Ebenezer pastors, Bolzius and Gronau, found in Urlsperger's Nachrichten: "Their journal of that time mentions among other things, that many

Lutherans were settled in and about Orangeburg in South Carolina, and that their preacher resided in the village of Orangeburg."

It is to be hoped that all this testomony is satisfactory to every candid inquirer, that the first established Church of Orangeburg, S. C., which was likewise the *first* organized Lutheran Church in both the Carolinas, was none other than a *Lutheran* Church; that those early settlers from Germany and Switzerland were mostly, if not all, of the same denomination, and that Dr. Dalcho has published no falsehood by asserting that "their pastor was a minister of the Lutheran Church."

The first colony of German and Swiss emigrants who settled in Orangeburg village and its vicinity in 1735, as well as those who selected their homes in Amelia Township along Four-hole swamp and creek, did not bring their pastor with them; the Rev. John Ulrich Giessendanner did not arrive until the year 1737; he was an ordained minister and a native of Switzerland, and was the first and, at the time, the only minister of the gospel in the village and District of Orangeburg; we infer this from Mills' Statistics, p. 657, stating that there were but four or five English settlers residing in the District before the Germans arrived, and these few would not likely have an English minister of their own to labor among them. We infer this, moreover, from the record of Giessendanner's marriages; the ceremony of one was performed in the English language during the first year of his ministry, with the following remark accompanying it: "Major Motte having read the ceremony in the English language," from which we conclude that at the time, October 24th, 1737, Rev. Giessendanner was still unacquainted with the English language, and that on this account he solicited the aid of Major Motte in the performance of a clerical duty. That there could have been no other minister of the gospel within reach of the parties, who did not reside in the village, otherwise they would not have employed Rev. G. to perform a ceremony under such embarrassing circumstances.

Rev. J. U. Giessendanner came to this country with the third transportation of German and Swiss settlers for this fertile portion of South Carolina. In the same vessel also journeyed his future partner in life, who had resided at his home in Europe as housekeeper for twenty-six years, and to whom, on the 15th of November, 1737, he was "quietly married, in the presence of many witnesses, by Major Motte;" doubtless by him, as no minister of the gospel was within their reach, to which record he piously adds: "May Jesus unite us closely in love, as well as all faithful married people, and cleanse and unite us with himself. Amen." By this union he had no children, since both himself and his partner were "well stricken in years."

The elder Giessendanner did not labor long among this people. Death soon ended his ministrations in Orangeburg, and we infer that he must have died about the close of the year 1738, since the records of his ministerial acts extend to the summer of that year, whilst those of his nephew commence with the close of the year 1739. Allowing the congregation time to make the necessary arrangement with the nephew, and he to have time to seek and obtain ordination, as we shall see hereafter, besides the inference drawn from the language of a certain petition, &c., we learn that during the fall of 1738, the Rev. John Ulrich Giessendanner, Sr., was called to his rest, and thus closed his earthly career.

The congregations in Orangeburg village and District now looked about them for another servant of the Lord to labor among them in holy things, but the prospect of being soon supplied was not very encouraging. The Ebenezer pastors were the only Lutheran ministers in the South at that time, and they could not be spared from their arduous work in Georgia, and to expect a pastor to be sent them again from the Fatherland was attended with many difficulties. Another plan presented itself to them. The nephew of their first pastor, who had prepared himself for the ministry, was induced to seek ordination at the hands of some Protestant denomination, and take upon himself the charge of these vacant congregations in the place of his departed uncle.

From the records of the Orangeburg Church we learn that their second pastor was also named John Ulrich Giessendanner, but he soon afterwards dropped his middle name, probably to distinguish him from his uncle, and so is he named in all the histories of South Carolina, which give any account of him.

Difficulties and sore trials soon attended Rev. John Giessendanner's ministry; the Urlsperger Reports state, in vol. iii, p. 1079, that the town of Orangeburg was then, A.D. 1741, in a worse condition than Purysburg; that the people were leading very sinful lives, manifesting no traces of piety, and that between pastor and hearers there were constant misunderstandings. It is also stated that their lands were fertile, but, as they were far removed from Charleston, and had no communication with that city by water, they could not convert their produce into money, and on this account very little or no money was found among them. Dr. Hazelius likewise gives an unfavorable account of the state of religion in that community. On p. 64, he remarks: "From one circumstance mentioned with particular reference to that congregation, we have to infer that the spiritual state of that church was by no means pleasing. A Mr. Kieffer, a Salzburg emigrant and member of the Ebenezer congregation, was living on the Carolina side of the Savannah River, whose mother-in-law resided at Orangeburg, whom he occasionally visited. On one occasion he remarked, after his return, to his minister, Pastor Bolzius, that the people at Orangeburg were manifesting no hunger and thirst after the word of God; he was therefore anxious that his mother-in-law should remove to his plantation, so that she might enjoy the opportunity of attending to the preaching of the word of God, which she greatly desired." All this testimony, though in the main correct, needs, however, some explanation, and by referring to the Journals of Council for this province, in the office of the Secretary of State, we will soon discover the cause of such a state of things. The people had been but sparingly supplied with the preached word, the discipline of the Church had not been properly administered, and when the younger Giessendanner took charge of these congregations, and attempted to regulate matters a little, whilst the majority of the people sustained him in his efforts, a minority, who were rude and godless, became his bitter enemies, and were constantly at variance with him.

This condition of Church affairs opened the way for the Zauberbühler difficulties, which are very minutely described in the Journals of Council of the Province of South Carolina, vol. 10, page 395, *et seq.*; the main facts of this troublesome affair were the following:

During the year 1743, a Swiss minister of the gospel, formerly located along the Savannah River, at New Windsor, Purysburg, and other places, named Bartholomew Zauberbühler, very adroitly attempted to displace the Rev. John Giessendanner from his charge in Orangeburg, and make himself the pastor of those churches. He supposed that by becoming an ordained minister of the Episcopal Church, at that time the established church in the Province, he would have rights superior to the humble Lutheran pastor in charge at Orangeburg, and, as he supposed, have the law on his side in thus becoming the pastor himself. The records of his evil designs, which have long slumbered in oblivion in manuscript form on the shelves of the Statehouse at Columbia, are now brought to view, and read as follows:

"Nov. 9th, 1742. Read the petition of Rev. B. Zauberbühler, showing that as there were a great many Germans at Orangeburg, Santee, and thereabouts, who are very desirous of having the word of God preached to them and their children, and who desire to be instructed in the true religion, humbly prays: That he may be sent to serve them and to be supported with a competent salary until he shall be able to take a voyage to England to be ordained by the Bishop of London, and at the same time proposes to bring over with him a number of Germans, which he thinks may be as great a number as ever were brought at any time into this province, it being a great encouragement to them when they find that they may have the Gospel, not only on their voyage, but also after their arrival in this province, preached to them, &c.

"Upon reading the said petition, it was the opinion of His Majesty's Council, that providing the petitioner do produce a certificate from the inhabitants of Orangeburg, as also a certificate from ye Ecclesiastical Commissary, Mr. Garden, of his qualifications to receive orders in the Church of England, and his engaging to go home to London to receive ordination, and after that to go to Germany to procure others of his countrymen to come over to settle in this province, that the sum of five hundred pounds currency be advanced him out of the township fund, in order to enable him to perform the same."

Journals of Council, vol. xi, pp. 74–76. Under date of Feb. 13th, 1743–44: "Reconsidered the petition of Rev. Mr. Zauberbühler, which had been exhibited at this Board on the 10th day of November, 1743, praying that in consideration of the earnest desire of the inhabitants of Orangeburg, Santee, to have a person to preach the gospel to them in their own language, he is willing to perform that pastoral duty, but being as yet unordained, desires to be supported with a competent salary until he shall be able to take a voyage to England to be ordained, at which time he proposes to bring over a number of foreign Protestants to settle in this province, who are unwilling to come over for want of having the gospel preached to them in their voyage here. Whereupon it appearing by a former minute of Council, of the 10th of November last, that provided the petitioner shall produce a certificate from the inhabitants of Orangeburg of their desire to receive him as a preacher amongst them, and also a certificate from the Rev. Mr. Garden of his qualifications to receive orders, that then the sum of £500 current money be advanced him out of the township fund, in order to enable him to perform his voyage, and bring on the Protestants to settle here as he mentions. Whereupon the petitioner produced the following certificate from the Rev. Mr. Commissary Garden:

"SOUTH CAROLINA.

"These are to certify whom it may concern, and in particular the Rt. Rev. the Lord Bishop of London, that the bearer, Bartholomew Zauberbühler, a native of Appenzell in Switzerland, appears to me on creditable testimony to have resided in this Province for the space of seven years last past, and during that time to have been of good life and behavior as becometh a candidate for holy orders, &c., &c.,

"Signed, ALEXANDER GARDEN.

"February 13th, 1743."

"On producing the said certificate his Excellency signed an order on the public Treasurer for the sum of £500, to be paid him on condition that the Treasurer take his written obligation to repay the said money upon his returning and settling in the Province, in case he does not bring over the Protestants he mentions."

The following counter-petition against Mr. Zauberbühler from the Orangeburg settlers is found in vol. xi of Journals of Council, pp. 139–143, and dated March 6th, 1743:

"Read the humble petition of the German and English inhabitants of Orangeburg and the adjoining plantations, showing to his Excellency, to whom it is directed, that the petitioners heartily congratulate his Excellency on his auspicious ascension to the government of this Province, hoping that by his judicious care and power not only their present grievances, but likewise all other misfortunes may evaporate and vanish. And ye said petitioners humbly beg leave to acquaint ye Excellency, that above five years ago, the German minister happening to die, Mr. John Giessendanner, by the consent and approbation of your said German petitioners, went to Charlestown with the intention to make his application to the Rev. Mr. Alexander Garden, Commissary, to admit him into holy orders, to preach in German in this township; and when the said Mr. John Giessendanner came to Charlestown aforesaid, he accidentally met with one Major Christian Motte, who acquainted him that he ought not to trouble the said Rev. Alexander Garden with the affair, but to go with him to some certain gentlemen, who, if they found him sufficient, would directly give him orders according to his desire; upon which the said Mr. John Giessendanner, being then a stranger to the English method of proceeding in such cases, accompanied the said Major Christian Motte, and was by him introduced to an assembly of the Presbytery, who, after examination, presented him with orders to preach, which he has since done in German constantly for the space of five years to the inexpressible satisfaction of the congregation at Orangeburg; and about two years ago your said English petitioners, being fully sixty miles from any other place of divine worship, some of whom had not been favored with an opportunity of hearing a sermon in the space of seven years, observing the said Mr. John Giessendanner to be a man of learning, piety, and knowledge in the Holy Scriptures, prevailed with him to officiate in preaching once every fortnight in English, which he hath since performed very articulate and intelligible to the entire satisfaction of ye said English petitioners, and always behaves himself with sobriety, honesty, and justice, encouraging virtue and reproving vice.

"And the said Mr. John Giessendanner lately observing great irregularities and disorders being committed almost every Sabbath day by some wicked persons in one part of the township, publicly reprimanded them for the same, which reproof so exasperated them that they threatened to kick the said Mr. John Giessendanner out of the church if he offered to preach there any more, and have lately sent for one Bartholemew Zauberbühler, a man who not long ago pretended to preach at Savannah town, but, as your said petitioners are informed, was soon obliged to leave that place and a very indecent character behind him. The last week he arrived at Orangeburg, and upon the last Sabbath, he, the said Bartholomew Zauberbühler and his wicked adherents associated together, and pretended that the said Bartholomew Zauberbühler had brought with him a power from the Hon. William Bull, Esq., late Lieutenant-Governor of this Province, his Majesty's Hon. Council, and the Rev. Mr. Alexander Garden, Commissary, an order to expel the said Mr. John Giessendanner from the church, and to preach there himself, and some of ye said petitioners demanded a sight of his said authority, but he refused to produce it, which occasioned great animosities and disorders in the congregation, and when the said Bartholomew Zauberbühler makes his second appearance at or near Orangeburg, which he declares shall be at ye expiration of three weeks, there will certainly be more disturbance and confusion than before, unless some powerful means be used to obstruct it.

"Whereupon your said petitioners most humbly beg that your Excellency will be pleased to interpose with your authority, and direct the said Mr. Alexander Garden, if he hath given or granted any such orders, to countermand them, and to permit the said Mr. John Giessendanner still to officiate for them in divine service, free from any further disturbance or molestation, &c.

"Signed by John Harn, and above fourscore more subscribers.

"Ordered by Council that the consideration of this affair, and of the above petition, and those of Mr. Zauberbühler, be deferred until Mr. Zauberbühler's return from England, and that ye Clerk acquaint them therewith in writing."

Fortunately, however, Mr. Zauberbühler had not yet departed on his journey to England as the Council had supposed, but had been lurking for awhile in Orangeburg District, and as soon as he returned to Charleston he once more made his appearance upon the floor of the Council chamber.

Journals of Council, Vol. XI, p. 143: "Bartholomew Zauberbühler, being returned from Orangeburg Township, attended his Excellency in Council, and laid before him two written certificates from justices of ye peace there in his favor, and which were read, representing his sobriety and good behavior, whereupon Mr. Zauberbühler was by his Excellency directed to wait again on Rev. Mr. Garden, and to learn if he has any objections to his receiving orders in England, and to report the same."

Journals of Council, Vol. XI, p. 152: "Bartholomew Zauberbühler attended his Excellency, the Governor, in Council, according to order, whom the Governor gave to understand that he had not acted well in the exhibiting a certificate from the Township of Orangeburg, read at this Board on November 13th, 1742, seeing that under the notion of having an invitation to the ministry by the majority of that Township, there was, on the contrary, a later memorial laid before the Board, signed by near ninety of the inhabitants, and by far the majority of the Township, praying that Mr. Giessendanner, their present minister, might be continued to preach among them, and that Mr. Zauberbühler's going to preach in the said Township, and his design to be settled there as a minister, was not by their desire, on the contrary, had occasioned no small disturbance in the said Township. That his proceedings with the Lieutenant-Governor and Council in ye said affair had not been with that candor that might have been expected from one who designed to take on him holy orders, and that, therefore, he ought to be contented with at least one-half of what had been paid him by ye Treasurer, and return the other £250, or, at any rate, to procure a joint security of one residing in Charlestown that he would return the money in case he did not bring over the foreign Protestants mentioned, but that if he did bring them over the whole £500 should be allowed him; whereupon Mr. Zauberbühler withdrew."

After this action of the Governor and Council we read nothing more of Mr. Zauberbühler in the Journals of Council, and the Rev. John Giessendanner was permitted to continue his labor as pastor in Orangeburg without further molestation.

The historical facts deduced from the above State papers are the following:

That the Rev. John Ulrich Giessendanner, Sr., who was the first pastor at Orangeburg, departed this life during the close of the year 1738, having labored there but little more than one year.

That his nephew, the Rev. John Giesendanner, became his successor some time during the year 1739, and that he was "a man of learning, piety, and knowledge in the Holy Scriptures;" he was probably educated for the ministry, but left Europe before he had been ordained; that, although a Lutheran in his religious persuasion, as we learn from other documents, he applied for ordination at the hands of any Protestant ministry who were empowered to impart the desired authority, there being at that time no Lutheran Synod in all the American colonies. That he was ordained by the Charleston Presbytery is certain, but that he was not a Presbyterian in faith is evident also, else he would not have endeavored first to obtain ordination at the hands of the Protestant Episcopal authority, and only changed his purpose of becoming Episcopally ordained at the suggestions of Major Christian Motte, and doubtless also to avoid an expensive and wearisome voyage to Europe, which he would have been obliged to undertake had he insisted upon obtaining the requisite authority to preach the gospel and administer the sacraments either in the Lutheran or Episcopal Church.

That the first Orangeburg Church must have been built some time before the above-mentioned petition was written, A.D. 1743, as it is therein spoken of, as being then in existence.

That Rev. John Giessendanner labored faithfully as a good servant of his Master, even bringing enmity upon himself for reproving vice; likewise, that he preached in the German and English languages.

That the country in the vicinity of Orangeburg must have been sadly deficient at that time in the enjoyment of the usual means of grace, as many persons were living sixty miles from any other church, some having not heard a sermon preached for seven years; need we wonder at the irregularities in faith and conduct manifested in those days.

That Rev. Giessendanner must have had a considerable congregation, inasmuch as the petition drawn up in his defence was signed by nearly ninety male persons, who were either all members of his congregation, or mostly so, and the remainder his friends and adherents.

That Rev. Bartholomew Zauberbühler must have sadly degenerated in the latter period of his ministerial life, as the Ebenezer pastors give us a very favorable account of him several years previous in the Urlsperger Reports, when he first came to this country.

Rev. Giessendanner was affectionately remembered by the Church in Europe. Rev. Bolzius, in the Urlsperger Reports, Vol. III, p. 875, states: "I also wrote a letter to-day to young Mr. Giessendanner, the present minister in Orangeburg, informing him that a donation of about nine guilders had been collected for him in Switzerland, of which a respectable merchant in Zurich writes, that as old Mr. Giessendanner had died, this amount should be paid over to his nephew. Also, that we will send him, as soon as possible, those books collected for him in Switzerland, which are sent in the chest for us, and which has not yet arrived.

"I would have been pleased to have sent him this money sooner had any safe opportunity presented itself. I entreated him, likewise, to write to me occasionally, and inform me of the transactions of the departed Giessendanner, which may be of great service to him."

The name of Rev. Giessendanner occurs in several other paragraphs of the same Reports, but only in connection with the books and money above-mentioned; but nothing further is said concerning himself and his ministry, or that of his predecessor. He was probably prevented from imparting the desired information on account of the want of communication between Ebenezer and Orangeburg.

Rev. John Giessendanner labored ten years as a Lutheran minister, after which, in 1749, he went to London to receive Episcopal ordination at the hands of Rev. Dr. Sherlock, Bishop of London. The reasons for making this change in his Church relationship are not known; however, it is presumable that, as he was then the only Lutheran pastor in South Carolina, he preferred to enjoy a more intimate connection with some ministerial organization than the one that was then afforded him in the bosom of his own Church; and although the Ebenezer pastors were also then laboring in the South, nevertheless they were somewhat distantly removed from him, and dwelling in another Province. He doubtless also had his fears that some other Zauberbühler difficulty might harass him again, and thus, by taking this step, he would have all legal preferences in his favor, as the Church of England was then virtually the established Church of the Province.

He was united in marriage to Miss Barbara Hug, and became the father of several children, one of whom, a son named Henry, born July 3d, 1742, was still living in 1826, as he is mentioned in "Mills' Statistics;" and his widow spent the close of her life with one of her children residing in Georgia.

Henry Giessendanner was married to Miss Elizabeth Rumpf, February 25th, 1767; he recorded the birth of but one child, Elizabeth, in his father's church-book, though he may have had more children, whose names were not entered there. This record-book likewise informs us that Rev. John Giessendanner had a brother and sister living in Orangeburg, named George and Elizabeth (afterwards married to a Mr. Krieh), and that the whole family were natives of Switzerland; hence also the money sent Rev. Giessendanner came from this country, as mentioned in the Urlsperger Reports. This concludes the history of the Giessendanner family, as far as it is necessary for our purpose, and until recently it was not known that these two pastors were the first Lutheran ministers that labored in South Carolina—even their very names had become almost obliterated in the annals of the Lutheran Church. Dr. Dalcho yet adds this information, that Rev. John Giessendanner departed this life during the year 1761.

The Orangeburg settlers at first clustered together near the banks of the Edisto River, and built their dwellings near each other in the form of a small town, supposing that the adjacent stream would be advantageous in forming an outlet for them to Charleston, in the transportation of lumber to market. A year later other German emigrants arrived, who located themselves on lands adjoining their predecessors, and thus this tide of immigration continued until the entire district became mostly colonized with German and Swiss emigrants. The present town of Orangeburg is located very near the spot where this original

German village once stood. In this village the first Lutheran church in the Carolinas was erected, and there also the first Lutheran pastor of this congregation lived and died; his nephew and successor, as is supposed by some of the present inhabitants, had his home several miles from the village, where he died and was buried.

Some half a mile from the centre of the present town of Orangeburg and towards the Edisto River there is a graveyard, which presents the appearance of having been a long time in use for the interment of the dead, and where the entombed generations of the present day are silently slumbering with those of the past. It is still styled "*the old graveyard*," although there are many new-made graves to be seen in it; and here, doubtless, repose the remains of the first Lutheran pastor in the Carolinas.

During the evening twilight of autumn the writer visited this hallowed spot, in order to commune with the dead; the seared and faded leaves of October overhanging his head or rustling beneath his feet; the peculiar sighing sound of the winds of autumn, passing through the foliage of the Southern long-leaved pine trees, produced Nature's sad and fitting requiem for the dead. He sought for records of the past upon some dilapidated tombstone, but his search was unavailing, and, like the fallen leaves of many years past, even these mementos of a former age were no longer visible.

What lessons of the vanity of all human greatness, namely: the power of wealth, the pride of family, the pleasures and gayeties of life! All end at last in the grave—all alike blend in one common dust.

Around this place, with the old church edifice very near it, the former village stood; they are both thus described by a correspondent: "The Orangeburg church was built of wood and clay, in much the same manner as chimneys are when made of clay; the old graveyard is still used as a burial-ground common to all; and the site of the church is still plainly seen—it is in the village, and was at that day in the centre of it. I have learned this likewise from an old gentleman who remembers hearing his father saying this as above. It fell to ruins at the time of the Revolution; but the spot has never been built upon since that day, and is now known as 'the old churchyard.' This church was the one used by the Rev. John Giessendanner as an Episcopal church, and no doubt used likewise by him at first as a Lutheran church; its dimensions were—say thirty by fifty feet."

The time when the old church edifice was erected is now no longer known, and can only be a matter of conjecture; however, it is possible that this event occurred during the elder Giessendanner's ministry—the records do not positively state this to have been the case, nevertheless several indications are given which make it very probable that this was the time.

It became changed into an Episcopal house of worship in 1749, when the pastor, the younger

Giessendanner, took orders in the Church of England, as he continued to labor there to the close of his life. At the time this change was effected, the congregation numbered 107 communicants, and on Whitsunday following 21 persons more were admitted to the Lord's Supper.

In concluding the history of this congregation, we would simply add, that after Rev. Giessendanner's death nothing further is known concerning it until 1768, when a new Episcopal chapel was ordered to be erected, and the Rev. Paul Turquand preached there in connection with another congregation.

During the Revolutionary War, Rev. Turquand was absent, and labored in the valley of the Mississippi, but returned in 1788, when he resumed his labors in Orangeburg, and died the following year; since then no trace is left of the history of the church and its congregation.

The present Episcopal Church in the town of Orangeburg is of recent organization, and their house of worship is comparatively new, indicating that the old church edifice, the still later erected chapel, and the former congregation have long since become entirely extinct.

The existing Lutheran church and congregation in Orangeburg are of a still more recent date; both the organization and church edifice have no historical connection with the past, made up of material in membership who have become citizens of the place not many years ago.

Section 11. The German Settlers of Saxe-Gotha Township, now Lexington County, S. C., A.D. 1737.

In Mills' Statistics of South Carolina, page 611, we have the following statement in reference to Lexington District (now County): "This District, when first settled, was merged in Orangeburg precincts. A parish and township were laid out in about the year 1750, and named Saxe-Gotha, in compliment to the first settlers of the country, who came from that part of Germany."

An entirely different statement may be found on pages 25 and 26 of Dr. Hazelius' History of the American Lutheran Church; from which we learn that the name Saxe-Gotha originated in Queen Anne's time, and that the first settlers of that county "came from the neighborhood of the Rhine, Baden, and Würtemberg," kingdoms considerably removed from Saxe-Gotha.

But from the Journals of Council, in the office of the Secretary of the State, the date of the settlement of Saxe-Gotha by Germans is unmistakably fixed to be 1737, and that few, if any, of the first settlers of that county came from Saxe-Gotha.

Council Journal, vol. viii, p. 69: "May 26th, 1742.—Petition of John Caspar Gallier and family, John Caspar Gieger and family, John Shalling and family, Abram Gieger and family, Jacob Liver and family, Julius Gredig and family, Caspar Fry and family, Conrad and Caspar Küntzler (now Kinsler), John Jacob Bieman and family, Herrman Gieger and family, Elizabeth

Shalling and family, showing that, as they arrived and settled in his Majesty's Township of Saxe-Gotha, even since the year 1737, and received his Majesty's most gracious bounty of provisions and warrants for lands in Saxe-Gotha Township, but that they could not find in what office they are, therefore they humbly pray his Honor, the Lieutenant-Governor, and his Majesty's honorable Council, that they would be pleased to order that search may be made," &c., &c.

Again, under date 1744, "John Jacob Gieger arrived seven years ago, is now married, and prays for one hundred acres of land over against Santee River, opposite Saxe-Gotha, where he has already begun to clear ground and almost finished a house. Granted." Subtract seven years from 1744, and we have again the date 1737, the time of the first settlement of that township by Germans.

From the above reliable source of information we evidently perceive that Mills' statement is entirely incorrect, and that Saxe-Gotha Township was laid out and received its name long before the year 1750, as it is spoken of in the Journals of Council as early as 1742, as being then a township and known by the name, Saxe-Gotha, and may have been so called, according to Dr. Hazelius' statement, during Queen Anne's time, previous to the year 1714, the time of her Majesty's death. However, the Council Journals likewise prove the Doctor to have been mistaken in stating that these lands were wrested from the *Germans*, for they settled there, and their descendants are there still, occupying the very lands which their forefathers had received by warrant from the king of England, showing conclusively that, inasmuch as their titles came directly to them from the first legal authority, these lands had not yet passed into other hands.

But it is possible that, as in the State of New York, the benevolent Queen Anne did make grants of land for church and school purposes in Saxe-Gotha Township, which, however, could not be occupied at the time, as the settlements in South Carolina had then not been extended so far inland; the Indians were still in possession of that portion of the province, and the grants and good intentions of the Queen were eventually lost sight of and forgotten. Afterwards, when the Germans did actually locate themselves in Saxe-Gotha, new warrants were issued and secured to them by the authority of the then ruling sovereign, his Majesty George II.

Independent of the actual accounts and dates of the settling of this township, we have before us the general rule that "Westward the star of empire takes its way," and that the farther westward or inland the settlements were made, the later will be the dates of such settlements. This is the result of natural causes, and admits of no exceptions to the well-known rule; the first settlers of America necessarily located themselves along the seashore, afterwards a little more inland, whilst the aborigines, living in the forest, gradually receded from the march of civilization; then further encroaches were made upon their territory, and so on, gradually, until the Appalachian chain of mountains was reached. After the Revolutionary War even the mountains formed no barrier to the settlements of the whites, and thus, in a short time, nearly all of America became populated, even beyond the valley of the Mississippi.

Orangeburg, South Carolina, was settled by Germans in 1735; Saxe-Gotha, further inland, of necessity was settled still later; hence common sense will admit of no date of permanent settlement earlier than, or even as early as, that period of time.

Saxe-Gotha comprised nearly all that portion of territory embraced at present in Lexington County; it is not many years since the name was changed, in honor of the battle of Lexington, Massachusetts, by an act of legislature, which was a most unfortunate exchange of names, being less euphonic, very inappropriate, and altogether unhistorical. Give us back the old name, and may the citizens of old Saxe-Gotha, in South Carolina, never be ashamed of their German names and German extraction.

How the name originated, as applied to this township, it is impossible to state. It certainly was not so called in compliment to the Germans who settled there, as they came from a different section of Germany; it is possible that the name, "Saxe-Gotha," was applied to this scope of territory during Queen Anne's reign, as intimated by Dr. Hazelius, and thus, even by name, it was to be distinguished as a future home for German emigrants.

The following record of this settlement is made in the Urlsperger Reports, vol. iii, p. 1791: "Wednesday, December 2d, 1741. We had heard nothing before of Saxe-Gotha in America, but we have just received the intelligence that such a town (township) is laid out in South Carolina, twenty-five German miles (100 English miles) from Charlestown, on the road which passes through Orangeburg, and settled with German people. Doubtless the majority of them were German Reformed, as they have a Reformed minister among them, with whose character we are not yet acquainted." This minister was the Rev. Christian Theus, of whom we shall say more hereafter. He commenced his labors in Saxe-Gotha as early as 1739.

The Geiger families and their neighbors were not compelled to remain a long time as isolated settlers in their new homes; the name Saxe-Gotha sounded so agreeably familiar to the ears of the Germans that they flocked in numbers to this Germany in America.

Besides, a certain German, named Hans Jacob Riemensperger, contracted with the government to bring over a number of Swiss settlers, many of whom he located in this township, as we learn from Urlsperger, vol. iii, p. 1808, and from the Journals of Council, on several different pages. In addition to these settlers, this same Riemensperger, in company with a Mr. Haeg, brought a number of orphan children to Saxe-Gotha, for which service to the province, as well as for the boarding of the children, they brought in their accounts to the Council for payment. Vol. viii, pp. 69 and 70.

Settlement of Redemptioners.

Some of our best and most useful settlers in the South were persons, who, too poor to pay their passage-money across the ocean, were sold by the captains of the vessels, that brought them to America, to any one of the settlers who felt inclined to secure their labor. The price for which they were sold in Carolina was usually from five to six pounds, sterling money, and both men and women were thus alike sold to service; and then, by hard labor, which extended over a period of from three to five years, they eventually redeemed themselves from this species of servitude.

The advantages of such an arrangement to them and to their adopted colony were, upon the whole, important and salutary.

1. Our infant colonies stood in need of a useful population which would prove a defence to the country in case of the execution of the continued threatenings of a Spanish invasion, and the sudden attack of hostile Indians.

2. Besides, labor was greatly needed for the cultivation of the virgin soil, and these poor Germans —many of them excellent farmers, some of them useful artisans, and all of them hard-working people—furnished this labor, and at very cheap rates.

3. The country also needed permanent settlers who would become habituated to the soil and climate, who would learn to love their adopted country, by being compelled to remain until they had fully tested all the advantages of the same; these the Redemptioners abundantly supplied in their own persons.

4. Nor were the advantages to *them* of slight importance. They had nothing to risk in the shape of property, as they possessed nothing of this world's goods, and thus they never became a prey to those landsharks which often despoil the less sagacious immigrants of much of the possessions which they brought with them to America.

5. Besides, they were the poorer class of people at home in Europe, and would always have remained in this condition, had such an arrangement not existed; but now they enjoyed the flattering prospect of receiving competency and wealth at some future day.

6. Then again, their servitude became their apprenticeship in America; in the meantime they learned the English language, they became acquainted with the laws and customs of the new country, they discovered by silent observation what would in future be to their advantage, and thus in every way did they become qualified by sagacity, industry, and economy, for their new and independent sphere of life.

Yet it must be confessed that they had to endure many hardships; often were they rigorously treated by their ship captains; ill and insufficiently fed on their voyage across the ocean, and on shore before they were purchased for their services; exposed publicly for sale as the African slave; often treated harshly by their masters who purchased them, and compelled to labor in the broiling sun of a southern climate, and many, by disease and death, frequently closed their short earthly career.

However, when our country had become sufficiently populated, the government interposed and put an end to this kind of servitude, on account of the severity of the lot of these unfortunate laborers, and thus abandoned this source of colonization. In confirmation of these facts, the following extracts will furnish abundant proof, and are herewith submitted:

Journals of Councils, vol. xiv, p. 37, January 24th, 1744: "Read the petition of a considerable number of Protestant Palatines, most humbly showing that the poor petitioners have been on board the St. Andrew's, Captain Brown commander, these twenty-six weeks past, and there is as yet no likelihood for them to get free of her, because there are none of us yet who have purchased their service; they therefore humbly pray his Excellency and Honors that they may find so much favor as to their passages that a sum equivalent to discharge the same be raised by the government, for which they promise to join in a bond to repay the same within the term of three years, with lawful interest; and that if any of them shall not be able to pay the above sum within that time, that the government in that case shall have full power to dispose of them and their families as they shall think proper, &c. Ordered to make investigations, and report."

Vol. xiv, pp. 62 and 63: "Several Protestant Palatines, who arrived hither on Captain Brown's ship, and whose services have not as yet been purchased, sent a complaint, by their interpreter, to the governor, that the said Captain Brown had often withheld their diet from them on board his ship, and that they had been several days without meat or drink; particularly that last Friday they were the whole day without any, the least, sustenance, and had been the like for several days before, and not only they, but all the rest of the Germans that still remain on board Captain Brown's ship.

"Captain Brown being sent for and interrogated whether he had used those foreigners in the manner they had represented, answered, that if they had asked him for food in their language he would not have understood them.

"His Excellency ordered the captain's steward to be sent for, who attended accordingly, and the original contract between Captain Brown and those Palatines in Holland was also sent for and laid before the Board, which being read and the particular species of diet that was allowed for every day of the week specified, his Excellency asked, in particular, if the said Germans had been fed last Friday in the manner contracted for?

"The steward replied that the Germans would sometimes reserve the taking of diet on certain days in order to have double allowance another.

But his Excellency gave Captain Brown to understand that as he was by virtue of his contract bound to maintain those foreigners till they were disposed of, if any should die for want while aboard his ship, he must answer for their lives; after which they withdrew."

The accounts of the trials and hardships of these persons, as narrated in the Urlsperger Reports, are entirely too numerous to be inserted in these pages; those who feel inclined to search for themselves are referred to the volume and page of those Reports, where they can find all they desire to know concerning the Redemptioners. Vol. i, p. 10; vol. ii, pp. 2472, 2482, 2508. How the Redemptioners conducted themselves can be learned from vol. ii, pp. 2193, 2200, 2213, 2221, 2404, 2413.

One account is here translated for the information of our readers. Vol. ii, p. 2472:

"The poor people which Captain Thomson brought over with him as servants for this colony are chiefly Palatines and Würtembergers, a whole vessel full of men, women, and children; these are to be sold for five years' service, but for which the inhabitants have neither money nor provisions. An adult person costs £6 5*s.*, sterling. After I had preached to these poor people from Rom. 8: 28, they thronged around me and besought me to take them to our place (Ebenezer, Georgia), but which was out of my power. An old widow of fifty years, who had lost her husband at sea, and who, on account of her age, was despised and neglected, have I besought General Oglethorpe to release, and sent her to our Orphan House."

This was the general condition of these poor persons in almost every seaport of America. The following extracts indicate that many such servants were sold and located in Saxe-Gotha, and after their legal discharge from servitude they obtained the king's bounty and tracts of land, the same as other settlers.

Journal of Council, vol. xi, p. 486: "Petition of John Wolfe and wife, natives of Berne, Switzerland, too poor to pay passage-money, entered into the service of Anthony Stack, of Saxe-Gotha, for three years, being now discharged from service, prays for his quota of land and bounty-money. Granted, on evidence of his written legal discharge."

Vol. xi, pp. 142 and 143: "Fullix Smid, of Switzerland, servant of David Hent, lately deceased, discharged by his executors, applied for and received 150 acres of land and bounty in Saxe-Gotha."

It is useless to multiply instances, which could easily be done; these extracts will fully show the correctness of all the foregoing statements, and that Saxe-Gotha, with many other settlements, received her full share of this class of useful settlers, who proved to have been upon the whole a great benefit to their adopted country.

During the period that intervened between the years 1744 and 1750, Saxe-Gotha received a large influx of population, and much of the available land of that township was then occupied. The vessel which bore them across the ocean was the ship St. Andrew, Captain Brown, commander, who doubtless treated his paying passengers well, although he acted so unfeelingly to those who were to be sold for their passage-money. Mention is likewise made of a Captain Ham, who brought other German settlers to South Carolina, but whose passengers chiefly located themselves in Orangeburg, whilst others settled in Saxe-Gotha.

All these German colonists came mostly from those provinces bordering on the Rhine, such as Switzerland, Baden, the Palatinate, and Würtemberg. They excelled as tillers of the soil, and were accustomed to the culture of the vine, and thus they constituted the very class of people which did become greatly serviceable to the prosperity of Carolina, but whose influence upon the physical welfare of their adopted country has been as yet little noticed by the various historians of the South.

The Saxe-Gothans were fortunate and blessed in obtaining the services of a pious and faithful pastor; all the records extant speak in the strongest terms of praise concerning him, but, at the same time, all agree in stating that he had a hard life of it, that he was not appreciated, that he was often persecuted for righteousness' sake, and this treatment he received at the hands of the very people for whose good he labored and prayed. Two years after the first settlers set foot upon the soil of Saxe-Gotha, the Rev. Christian Theus arrived and labored in their midst; and as these settlers were not neglected in the administration of the means of grace, which unfortunately was the case with many others of the early colonists, they really had no excuse for their conduct, and should have treated their pastor in the most friendly manner.

Dr. Muhlenberg's journal, published in the Evangelical Review, vol. i, p. 540, contains the following statement:

"October 22, 1774. This afternoon I had an acceptable visit from the Reformed minister, the Rev. Theus, of the Congaries (Congaree River), in South Carolina, 120 miles from Charleston. His brother Theus, a painter, lately deceased, received me as a stranger most kindly into his house when, thirty-two years ago, I travelled through here on my journey from Savannah to Philadelphia, and afforded me an opportunity to preach on Sunday to the then yet few German families. The Lord requite his love in eternity! The aforesaid pastor, Theus, came with his parents into this country from Switzerland as a *candidatus theologiæ*, was examined and ordained by the Reverend English Presbyterian Ministerium, and since 1739 has performed the duties of the ministerial office in the scattered country congregations among the German Reformed and Lutheran inhabitants, and has conducted himself with the propriety and fidelity due his station, according to the testimony of capable witnesses. We had agreeable conversation, and he promised me a written account of church matters in these country congregations, which, moreover, he is best able to furnish, having lived longest in this country, and being an erudite man."

It is to be regretted that this "*written account of church matters*," if Dr. Muhlenberg ever received it, has never been published; what interesting material it could now furnish the Church, which must forever be buried in oblivion!

The Doctor continues: "He also furnished me with a more detailed description of the sect mentioned October 5th, the members living near him. At a certain time he came unexpectedly into their meeting, and found Jacob Weber contending that he was God, and the said Smith Peter (or Peter Schmidt) insisting that he himself was Christ, and that the unconverted members must be healed through his stripes. Pastor Theus, opposing such blasphemy, the leaders became enraged and threatened his life, and counselled with the rabble whether to drown or hang him. He escaped, however, from their hands, fled to the river, and fortunately found a negro with his canoe at the shore, sprang into it, and was conveyed across."

Here we have the impartial testimony of Rev. Dr. Muhlenberg, gathered from "capable witnesses," of the parentage, ordination, date of ministry in Saxe-Gotha, piety and learning of the Rev. Christian Theus, up to the period immediately preceding the Revolution. This brief narrative, coming from such a source, is not only entitled to our entire credit, but speaks as much of that devoted man of God as though a volume were written to perpetuate his name and memory.

Rev. Theus lived to be an aged man, for we

discover his name in the list of members of the "*Corpus Evangelicum*," and present at every meeting of that body until the year 1789, the last meeting of which the records are still extant. How much longer he was spared to do good we know not; but from the dates which are in our possession, he had at that time been half a century in the ministry of his Savior.

His resting-place is still pointed out to the stranger, and is located in a field along the state road, between Columbia and Sandy Run, about eight miles from Columbia. It is the only grave that can still be seen there, and tradition says that his dwelling was located not far from that grave-yard. Mr. Abraham Geiger, now also in eternity, erected the tombstone, at his own expense, at the head of Rev. Theus' grave, to perpetuate his memory. Had Mr. Geiger not performed this labor of love, the Church and the world would never even have known where the first pastor of Saxe-Gotha, the contemporary of Geissendanner, Bolzius and Gronau, had been laid down to rest. The inscription is now much defaced by the hand of time, and can scarcely be deciphered; nevertheless, we are thankful for this much, and would wish that we could gather similar mementoes of the resting-places of all the first German ministers in the South. The inscription reads as follows:

"This stone points out where the remains of Rev. Christian Theus lie. This faithful divine labored through a long life as a faithful servant in his Master's vineyard, and the reward which he received from many for his labor was ingratitude."

Rev. J. B. Anthony, one of the late pastors of Sandy Run Lutheran Church, adds yet this information, published in the Lutheran Observer, A.D. 1858: "Among the octogenarians of this vicinity we have not been able to learn much more of Mr. Theus than the rude stone, now standing in a vast cotton-field, records. Few now living recollect to have seen him. No records of those early times are known to exist. The small schoolhouse, which is said to have stood near his grave, has long since disappeared. A few other graves are said to be here, but as no stones can be found in this sandy section to place at the head and foot, light-wood knots are frequently substituted by the poor, hence, when these decay, there is nothing left to mark the place."

The spiritual and moral condition of the Saxe-Gothans is not very highly extolled in the Urlsperger Reports. Rev. Bolzius, who gives us the account, may have been somewhat prejudiced, inasmuch as his Ebenezer colony had lost some runaway white servants, who probably concealed themselves in the neighborhood of the Congaree River, and in several pages of his diary he berates both the Saxe-Gothans and the government of South Carolina that they were not returned; thus, perhaps, his human feelings were too much enlisted on the side of prejudice and interest whilst speaking of these people. We insert the following extract:

Urlsperger Reports, vol. iv, p. 672: "Wednesday, April 25, 1750.—The German Evangelical Lutheran inhabitants of Congaree, in South Carolina, which new settlement has been named Saxe-Gotha, had besought me, several months ago, to come to them and preach for them, and administer the Lord's Supper. I sent them books suitable for the edification of adults and the instruction of children, and wrote them that my circumstances did not permit me to make so long a journey. Now I have received another letter, in which the former request is renewed, and in which they likewise beseech me to assist them in the erection of a church and in obtaining a pastor. They have a congregation of about 280 souls, who all could attend church if the house of worship were erected in the midst of their plantations.

"The Reformed have received 500 pounds, Carolina currency, from the government, which amounts to something more than 500 guilders, for the building of a church, but no one is interested for the Lutherans, unless I would do something in their behalf. They live with the Reformed in great disunion, at which I showed my displeasure in my former letter. A few families have removed from this place among them, who might have supported themselves very well here; afterwards three adult youths were persuaded to leave their service here, and two (white) servants ran away, all of whom are harbored in the Congaree settlement. The citizens themselves, as a Carolina minister once wrote me, lived disorderly among each other, and estimate their Reformed minister very low. I have no heart for this people. If they were truly concerned about God's word, then so many unworthy people would not have located in their midst, as there are other places where good land and subsistence may be obtained.

"In this very letter they inform me that they have built both a saw-mill and a grist-mill, and expect to build more of the kind. Why then should they be unable to erect a house of worship if they were sincerely in earnest?"

The above record in Bolzius' diary, published in the Urlsperger Reports, is in strict accordance with the testimony of Dr. Hazelius on the Weberites—which sect arose some ten years later,—with Dr. Muhlenberg's account, with the inscription on the tombstone on Rev. Theus, and with several living witnesses, who were contemporaries with many old citizens of a former day, whose narratives they still well remember.

Whilst many of the Saxe-Gothans were not devoid of blame, and deserved censure in those days, there were others whose life and conduct were praiseworthy, and others who were devotedly pious, and who were anxious to enjoy the blessings of the means of grace, and it is sad that Rev. Bolzius permitted his feelings of interest for his own colony to cause him to act so unfriendly toward this people, and to send no kind word of encouragement to them, when they besought him to visit them and break to their hungry souls the bread of life. Who knows what good he might have accomplished by a friendly visit? Who knows what future evil, *e. g.*, that Weber heresy, he might have been the instrument of preventing? Besides all this, he, as a minister of the Gospel and of like persuasion with these people, had no right to withhold his influence and sympathy from *two hundred and eighty souls*, (we are surprised at so large a number) who extended such a Macedonian call to him, and besought him twice to interest himself in their behalf in procuring a minister for them, who were almost as sheep without a shepherd. Who could calculate the influence the Lutheran Church would have exerted in those regions, had this large congregation been properly cared for, and supplied with the means of grace? Besides, had Rev. Bolzius been instrumental in securing a pious and efficient pastor for them at that early period, and this pastor, laboring side by side with Rev. Theus, how much that faithful servant's hands would have been strengthened, and how much good seed might have been sown, springing up to everlasting life, which would have entirely changed the spiritual and moral condition of this people. Deprive men of the Gospel and the Sacraments, take away or refuse to give them the benign influences of Christianity, and we need not be astonished at "disorderly living" and heresy in doctrine.

Another Lutheran minister in South Carolina at this time, A.D. 1750, and one of the right character, Rev. Giessendanner being then in Orangeburg, who, in that event, might have remained in the Lutheran Church, with the three Ebenezer pastors in Georgia, these five might have formed the nucleus for a Lutheran Synod in the South, almost as old as the Pennsylvania Synod, which could have instructed and ordained other pious men for the Gospel ministry. At a later date the pastors of other established Lutheran congregations would have connected themselves with this Synod; their synodical reports sent to the city of Augsburg, in Germany, would have made the Urlsperger Reports as interesting in its records of Church affairs, as the Halle reports are now, filled, as they are, with general accounts of Church matters in the entire Province of Pennsylvania, and not simply the detailed accounts of daily occurrences in a single settlement. What short-sighted people even the most pious ministers of the Gospel sometimes are!

The present citizens of old Saxe-Gotha, now Lexington County, are an entirely different people; their forefathers could not prevent unworthy settlers from locating themselves among them. Many of those depraved men met an untimely death in the war with the Cherokees; a few perished miserably at the hand of administrative justice; others were cut off by disease and an early death; whilst a number moved to other parts of the country. It is exceedingly doubtful whether many of those reprobates left their descendants behind them in Saxe-Gotha, as all traces of Weber and Schmidt have entirely disappeared.

We have seen that Rev. Theus came to the Congaree settlement in the year 1739. In what building he first preached is unknown, but arrangements were soon made for the erection of a church. As early as 1744–5 John Jacob Riemensperger petitioned the government of South Carolina to do something toward the erection of churches and school-houses for the German settlers in various localities; otherwise they would continue to do what many had done heretofore, move with their families to Pennsylvania, where all these advantages could be enjoyed. That the government entered into such an arrangement we have already seen from the Urlsperger Reports, for five hundred pounds currency was donated for the building of a German Reformed Church, which, we presume, had been completed at that time, A.D. 1750, and the people were enjoying the means of grace in their new house of worship. Tradition informs us that this German church stood near the spot where the remains of Rev. Theus are deposited, but it has long since been no more. We now turn to an ancient map of South Carolina, originally published in 1771 and 1775, and recently reprinted in "Carroll's Collections." Near the Congaree River, a short distance below the confluence of the Saluda and Broad Rivers, and in the township of Saxe-Gotha, a church is laid down, bearing the name St. John's. This substantiates all the above-mentioned records and traditions, gives us the exact locality of that church, which, in the proper proportion of distances, would be the very spot where the grave of Rev. Theus can still be seen, and furnishes, furthermore, the name by which that church was known. This house of God must have been destroyed during the Revolutionary War, as all traces of the same after that period appear to have been lost; it is not mentioned in the general act of incorporation of all the German churches, passed by the legislature of South Carolina in 1788.

During the years 1759 and 1760, the people of Saxe-Gotha suffered greatly from the ravages of the Cherokee war. During the time that the French and English were at war with each other in the colonies of America, which however did not reach as far south as the Carolinas; the French instigated the Cherokee Indians to make war upon the peaceful settlers of the two Carolinas, who murdered the white inhabitants at midnight, whilst they were wrapped in their peaceful slumbers, and committed atrocities at which humanity shudders. The Congaree and Fork settlements were then mostly exposed to the fearful inroads of the savages, as but few settlers were living further in the interior than the Germans were at that time. Bolzius informs us, that many were compelled to take refuge among the Germans at Ebenezer and Savannah, whilst others fled for safety to Charleston, Purysburg, and other places, until those Indian hostilities were ended, and peace and security was again restored.

Section 12. The German Settlers from Pennsylvania in Central North Carolina, A.D. 1750.

Had a traveller from Pennsylvania visited, about forty or fifty years ago, portions of the present counties of Alamance, Guilford, Davidson, Rowan, Cabarrus, Stanly, Iredell, Catawba, Lincoln and some others in the State of North Carolina, he might have believed himself to have unexpectedly come upon some part of the old Keystone State. His ear would have been greeted with sounds of the peculiar dialect of the Pennsylvania-German language, familiarly known as "Pennsylvänisch-Deutsch," a language made up of the dialects used in the ancient Palatinate, Würtemberg and other countries bordering along the Rhine, intermixed with English words, which plainly indicate that many of their forefathers were some of those Protestant refugees, who fled from the persecutions of Louis XIV, king of France, and were brought to America under the kind and fostering care of Queen Anne of England.

This language, however, has almost become extinct in North Carolina; a few aged persons may still be found, who are fond of conversing in that kind of German with those who are acquainted with it, but in a few more years the last vestige of Pennsylvania-German will be sought for in vain in this State, where once even many of the negro slaves of these Germans spoke no other language.

Family names are to be met with in this section of North Carolina, which are familiar in Montgomery, Berks, Lehigh and Northampton Counties of Pennsylvania, such as the Propsts, the Bostians, the Kleins (Cline), the Trexlers, the Schloughs, the Seitzs (Sides), the Reinhardts, the Bibers (Beaver), the Kohlmans (Coleman), the Derrs (Dry), the Bergers (Barrier), the Behringers (Barringer), and many others still abounding both in Pennsylvania and North Carolina.

Our supposed traveller might have worshiped on Sundays in churches, where the services were still conducted entirely in the German language, in which both the Lutheran and German Reformed had equal rights and privileges, and each denomination alternately worshiped therein, as is still the case in many parts of Pennsylvania. The ever-present "Gemainshaftliches Gesangbuch" (union hymn-book) suited to the taste, at that time, of both denominations, would have been found in general use; and, at the centre of one of the long sides of the church, there would have stood the high and goblet-shaped pulpit, with a sounding-board suspended overhead of the officiating minister; a few such shaped pulpits may be seen in this State to the present day, but they will soon be numbered with the past.

The farm-yard of these Germans still abounds with fine and well-fed horses, and the old Pennsylvania four-horse wagon securely housed in the shed between two corn-cribs, with the bow-shaped body suspended above it upon chains, ready to be let down in its position on the wagon, whenever it should be needed.

In the dwelling-house, and behind a cheerful wood-fire, during the winter season, one might still notice a heavy iron plate placed upon the hearth to protect the back of the chimney, having singular devices cast upon its face, such as no ironworks of modern times are known to mould, with German sentences and "Redting Furniss" (Reading Furnace) standing out in relief, indicating that they were cast in the city of Reading, Berks County, at a time when those extensive iron manufactories of Pennsylvania were yet in their infancy, and perhaps brought along to North Carolina with the emigrants from the Keystone State.

On the blank pages of the old German Bibles of those first German settlers of North Carolina, we may frequently find the story of their colonization, stating that they were born in Pennsylvania at such a date, and that they emigrated to North Carolina and settled in such a county of that Province. Besides, all the aged citizens of that section, where the German descendants are located, will tell you that their ancestors came originally from Pennsylvania, and here and there you may meet a family, like the Heilig family, who still keep up a friendly intercourse with some of their relatives in Pennsylvania.

The conclusion then evidently is, in the absence of all State documents on that subject, and the silence of all historians of North Carolina, that the Province of Pennsylvania, and not Germany, furnished North Carolina with the most of her numerous German settlers, located in the central and western part of the State.

The cause of their migration from Pennsylvania to North Carolina may be found recorded in Williamson's History of North Carolina, vol. ii, p. 71, which, however, he applies only to their neighbors, the Scotch-Irish settlers: "Land could not be obtained in Pennsylvania without much difficulty, for the proprietors of that Province purchased the soil by small parcels from the natives, and those lands were soon taken up;" and at that early period no one ventured to cross the Alleghany Mountains for the purpose of settling there, so the seekers after new homes went southward instead of westward, and kept to the east of the range of the Alleghanies, until they found unoccupied lands where they could make their settlements. Williamson informs us, vol. ii, p. 71, that "Lord Carteret's land in Carolina, where the soil was cheap, presented a tempting residence to people of every denomination."

The eastern portion of North Carolina having been settled at an early date by various colonies of English, Swiss, and German Palatines at Newberne, French Huguenots, and Scotch refugees, and these colonies having, in process of time, located their descendants as far inland as Hillsboro on the northern side of the Province, and the Pedee River on the southern side, with a number of Quakers and Scotch-Irish among them; an entirely new class of colonists, the Germans from the Province of Pennsylvania, as above described, arranged themselves on vacant lands to the eastward and westward of the Yadkin River, whilst the Scotch-Irish from the same Province, who had always lived on friendly terms with their German neighbors in Pennsylvania, soon followed them southward, and occupied vacant lands mostly to the westward of the German settlers, along both sides of the Catawba River; these again, Germans and Scotch-Irish, at a later day, formed settlements of their descendants in the western part of the State. This is the brief story of the settling of North Carolina; the different European nationalities from which these settlers originated, occupying strips of land across the State mostly in a southwesterly direction, like so many strata of a geological formation.

The Pennsylvania Germans journeyed in much the same manner as did the later colonists to the Western States, before railroads afforded a cheaper, safer and more speedy mode of transportation; every available article for house and farm use, capable of being stowed away in their capacious wagons, was taken with them; and then the cavalcade moved on, every able-bodied person on foot, women and children on bedding in the wagons, and cattle, sheep, and hogs driven before them; they travelled by easy stages, upon the roads of the picturesque Cumberland and Shenandoah Valleys, crossing the Blue Ridge Mountains in some part of Virginia, until they reached the land of their hopes and promise.

It is impossible to date precisely the arrival of

all those German colonists from Pennsylvania, as they all depended upon themselves for leaving home and journeying southward; they arrived continuously for a number of years in succession, usually leaving home in the fall season, after all the harvesting was over and the proceeds of the year's labor could be disposed of; they arrived at their places of settlement just before the commencement of the winter season. The first arrival of the pioneer train may have occurred about the year 1745, but the large body of these German colonists did not commence to settle in North Carolina until about the year 1750; this may be gathered partly from tradition, partly from old family records in their German Bibles, but mostly from the title-deeds of their lands, which were always dated some years after their actual settlement, affording them time to decide upon a permanent location, and to make some other necessary arrangement, having to run no risk in losing their titles by the delay of a few years.

These German settlers were all industrious, economical, and thrifty farmers, not afraid nor ashamed of hard labor, and were soon blessed with an abundance of everything, which the fertile soil and temperate climate of that portion of North Carolina could furnish them. As they were all agriculturists, they generally avoided settling themselves in towns; uninformed in the ways of the world, ignorant of the English language, and unacquainted with the shrewdness necessary for merchandising, yet well informed in their own language, and well read in their Bibles and other devotional German books, they remained at their own country homes, and enriched themselves with the productions of the soil; hence we witness the fact, that very few Lutheran and German Reformed churches were erected in the towns of North Carolina at that early day; and when, in process of time, it did become necessary to build churches in the villages and towns of the State, it was found exceedingly difficult to get the members from the country to become accustomed to the new arrangement.

Inasmuch as these settlers located themselves so gradually, as before stated, besides being divided into two denominations, it was some time before they were sufficiently numerous to have a pastor located and permanently settled among them; sermons and prayers were usually read on Sunday by their German school-teacher, and whenever they were permitted to enjoy the regular administration of the preached word and sacraments, which was but seldom, it was afforded them by some self-appointed missionary, whilst their school-teacher usually buried their dead with an appropriate ceremony from the German liturgy, and, in case of urgent necessity, baptized their children.

Section 13. The Moravians at Salem, N. C., A.D. 1753.

The first colony of Moravians settled in Georgia in the year 1735, under the leadership of Rt. Rev. A.

G. Spangenberg, a bishop in the Moravian Church, or "Unitas Fratrum," as that Church is sometimes called. This new colony came one year later than the first arrival of the Lutheran Salzburgers at Ebenezer, Georgia, and located itself between Savannah and Ebenezer. The Moravians, however, did not remain long in Georgia; in 1737 a war broke out between the English colonies and the Spaniards, who believed themselves aggrieved by the colonization of Georgia under English government, and regarded it as an encroachment upon their territory; this war was renewed in 1739, and the Moravians, who were conscientiously opposed to taking up arms, were nevertheless compelled to do so, contrary to the promise made them, that they should be exempt from military service; hence they believed themselves necessitated to abandon houses and lands in Georgia, and removed to Pennsylvania, in 1738 and 1740, the peaceful government of the Quakers in that Province being well suited to their conscientious scruples against war. Here the Moravians now began their settlements at Bethlehem and Nazareth, and likewise their missions among the Indians in different parts of Pennsylvania and New York.

In the year 1751, the Moravians were induced to purchase one hundred thousand acres of land in North Carolina, from Lord Granville, President of the Privy Council of the government of Great Britain; Bishop Spangenberg was commissioned to locate and survey this large tract of land, and journeyed with some friends, during the month of

August, from Bethlehem, Pennsylvania, to Edenton, North Carolina, where he was accompanied by the surveyor-general, and at first attempted to locate the tract towards the head-waters of the Catawba, New and Yadkin Rivers, but suffered so much from sickness, cold and hunger, that they retraced their steps, and located the tract farther eastward, in the present county of Forsyth, to the east of the Yadkin River. The general deed for the whole tract, containing 98,985 acres, was signed and sealed August 7th, 1753, and received the name of "*The Wachovia Tract*," in honor of one of the titles of Count Zinzendorf, who was lord of the Wachau Valley in Austria, and the founder and head of the Moravian Society under its present new organization.

The sources whence the above information is principally derived are the Urlsperger Reports, Life of Bishop Spangenberg, and Martin's History of North Carolina, but the following continued narrative is copied from Martin's History, Vol. I, pp. 28–30, *et seq.*, of the Appendix.

"In order to facilitate the improvement of the land, to furnish a part of the purchase-money, and to defray the expenses of transportation, journey, &c., of the first colonists, a society was formed, under the name of *The Wachovia Society*, consisting of members of the Brethren's church and other friends. The directors of it were Bishop Spangenberg and Cornelius Van Laer, a gentleman residing in Holland. The members of it, who were about twenty, received in consideration for the money which they advanced, two thousand acres of the land. This society was again dissolved in 1763, having proved very beneficial and answered the intended purpose.

"In the autumn of the year 1753, the first colonists, twelve single brethren or unmarried men, came from Bethlehem to settle upon the land. They had a wagon, six horses, cattle, and the necessary household furniture and utensils for husbandry with them. After a very tedious and fatiguing journey, by way of Winchester, Evan's Gap, and Upper Sauratown, on which they spent six weeks, they arrived on the land the 17th of November, 1753, and took possession of it. A small deserted cabin, which they found near the mill creek, served them for a shelter or dwelling-house the first winter. On the spot where this cabin stood, a monument was erected in the year 1806, with the inscription, *Wachovia Settlement, begun the* 17*th November*, 1753. They immediately began to clear some acres of land, and to sow it with wheat. In the year 1754, seven new colonists, likewise single brethren, came from Bethlehem. It was resolved, that on the same spot where the first settlers had made already a small improvement, a town should be built, which was named *Bethabara* (the house of passage), as it was meant only for a place of sojourning for a time, till the principal town in the middle of the whole tract could be built at a convenient time. Bishop Bohler, who was here on a visit from Bethlehem, laid, on the 26th of November, the corner-stone for the first house in this town, which was appointed for a church and dwelling-house of the single brethren, with prayer and supplication to our Lord that he might prosper the work. He likewise examined more accurately the greatest part of the Wachovia tract, divided it into proper parts for improvement, and gave names to several creeks, which are yet sometimes used, and are to be found in deeds and public records.

"In May, 1755, Bishop David Nitschmann came on a visit from Bethlehem, and on the 11th of the same month the first meeting-house was consecrated, which solemn transaction was attended with a gracious feeling of the divine presence. Many travellers and neighbors have heard afterwards, in this house, the word of life with joy and gratitude.

"In the year 1758, the Cherokees and Catawbas, who went to war against the Indians on the Ohio, often marched through Bethabara in large companies, sometimes several hundreds at once, and the Brethren were obliged to find them quarters and provisions for several days. The Cherokees were much pleased with the treatment they received, and gave to their nation the following description of Bethabara: *The Dutch fort, where there are good people and much bread.*

"In 1759, the town of Bethany was laid out, three miles north of Bethabara, on Muddy Creek, and divided into thirty lots; and at the end of the year 1765, the number of inhabitants in Bethabara was eighty-eight, and in Bethany seventy-eight.

"In the year 1766, the beginning was made to build Salem, the principal settlement of the *Unitas Fratrum* in North Carolina, five miles to the south-east from Bethabara. Hitherto, all the brethren and sisters who settled in North Carolina came from Pennsylvania, but in this year the first company, consisting of ten persons, came from Germany by way of London and Charleston. Salem was laid out the year previous by Frederick William von Marshall, senior civilis of the Unitas Fratrum. It was resolved that Salem should be built in the same manner and have the same regulations as Herrnhut, Niesky, Bethlehem, and other settlements of the United Brethren, wherein the unmarried men and boys, and the unmarried women and girls live in separate houses by themselves. The house for the unmarried men or single brethren was built in the years 1768 and 1769."

Two other settlements were made on the Wachovia Tract, named *Friedburg* and *Friedland*, during the years 1769 and 1770, each having their own meeting-house and school, which received a considerable number of settlers from Germany and from that part of Massachusetts which is now the State of Maine. Another settlement received its name, *Hope*, and was made in 1772, by colonists from Frederick County, Maryland.

During the Revolutionary War, the Moravians again suffered severely on account of their peculiar principles not to take up arms personally, and were obliged at times to pay large amounts of money for substitutes for all those who were drafted as recruits for the American army, but were, at last, exempted from military service by taking the oath of allegiance and fidelity to the State of Carolina and the United States, and pay a triple tax, which they accordingly did, and remained unmolested.

"About eight miles above the Hope meeting-house, and ten miles from Salem, on the west side of Muddy Creek, a meeting-house was built in 1782, by a German Lutheran and Reformed congregation, wherein, since the year 1797, divine service is held by one of the ministers of the Brethren's church, every fourth Sunday, in the German language."

In the year 1804, the well-known Salem Female Academy was founded. The building was commenced the year previous, and has educated a large proportion of the matrons and daughters of the Southern States. "From the beginning of the institution, in May, 1804, to the end of the year 1807, about one hundred and twenty young ladies, from North and South Carolina, Virginia, Kentucky, Tennessee, and Georgia, received their education in it, of whom, at the end of 1807, forty-one remained in the Seminary."

This narrative of the Moravian settlement in and around Salem, North Carolina, has been included in this history, because it is also a *German* settlement, and was established by a religious denomination near akin to the Lutheran Church, with the Augsburg Confession as the basis of their faith. Besides two of the ministers, connected with the Lutheran Synod of North Carolina, came from this settlement of Moravians: the Rev. Gottlieb Shober, ordained by the Lutheran Synod of North Carolina in 1810, and who labored in some Lutheran churches in the vicinity of Salem, N. C., but who also retained in some way his connection with the Moravians, residing all his life in Salem; and the Rev. S. Rothrock, still living and doing good service in the North Carolina Synod.

Section 14. The German Lutheran Colony at Hard Labor Creek, Abbeville County, South Carolina, A.D. 1763 and 1764.

A few years before the Revolutionary War, there occurred a most interesting instance of German colonization, which added greatly to the growth and strength of the Province of South Carolina, and which, likewise, ought to have contributed much to the *permanent* establishment of one or more Lutheran churches in that vicinity; however, the facts, as taken from Hewatt's History of South Carolina and Georgia, vol. ii, pp. 269–272, will speak for themselves.

"Not long after this, during the years 1763 and 1764, a remarkable affair happened in Germany, by which Carolina received a great acquisition. One Stümpel, who had been an officer in the king of Prussia's service (Frederick the Great) being reduced at the peace (after the close of the Seven Years' War) applied to the British ministry for a tract of land in America, and, having received some encouragement, returned to Germany, where by deceitful promises, he seduced between five or six hundred ignorant people from their native country.

"When these poor Palatines arrived in England, the officer, finding himself unable to perform his promises, fled, leaving them in a strange land without money, without friends, exposed in the open fields, and ready to perish through want. While they were in this starving condition, and knew no person to whom they could apply for relief, a humane clergyman, who came from the same country, took compassion on them, and published their deplorable case in the newspapers. He pleaded for the mercy and protection of government to them, until an opportunity might offer of transporting them to some of the British colonies, where he hoped they would prove to be useful subjects, and, in time, give their benefactors ample proofs of their gratitude and affection.

"No sooner did their unhappy situation reach the ears of a great personage, than he immediately set an example to his subjects, which served both to warm their hearts and open their hands for the relief of their distressed fellow-creatures. A bounty of three hundred pounds sterling was allowed them; tents were ordered from the Tower for the accommodation of such as had paid their passage and been permitted to come ashore; money was sent for the relief of those that were confined on board.

"The public-spirited citizens of London, famous for acts of beneficence and charity, associated, and chose a committee on purpose to raise money for the relief of these poor Palatines. A physician, a surgeon, and a man-midwife, generously undertook to attend the sick gratis. From different quarters benefactions were sent to the committee, and in a few days those unfortunate strangers, from the depths of indigence and distress, were raised to comfortable circumstances. The committee, finding the money received more than sufficient to relieve their present distress, applied to his Majesty (George III), to know his royal pleasure with respect to the future disposal of the German Protestants. His Majesty, sensible that his Colony of South Carolina had not its proportion of white inhabitants, and having expressed a particular attachment to it, signified his desire of transporting them to that Province. Another motive for sending them to Carolina, was the bounty allowed to foreign Protestants by the Provincial Assembly, so that when their source of relief from England should be exhausted, another would open after their arrival in that Province, which would help them to surmount the difficulties attending the first state of cultivation.

"Accordingly, preparations were made for sending the Germans to South Carolina. When the news was communicated to them, they rejoiced, not only because they were to go to one of the most fertile and flourishing Provinces on the continent, but also because many of them had friends and countrymen there before them. Two ships, of two hundred tons each, were provided for their accommodation, and provisions of all kinds laid in for the voyage. An hundred and fifty stand of arms were ordered from the Tower, and given them by his Majesty for their defence after their arrival in America; all of which deserves to be recorded for the honor of the British nation, which has at different times set before the world many noble examples of benevolence. Everything being ready for their embarkation, the Palatines broke up their camp in the fields behind White Chapel, and proceeded to the ships, attended by several of their benefactors; of whom they took their leave with songs of praise to God in their mouths, and tears of gratitude in their eyes.

"In the month of April, 1764, they arrived at Charleston, and presented a letter from the Lords-Commissioners for Trade and Plantations to Governor Boone, acquainting him that his Majesty had been pleased to take the poor Palatines under his royal care and protection, and, as many of them were versed in the culture of silks and vines, had ordered that a settlement be provided for them in Carolina, in a situation most proper for these purposes. Though this settlement met with some obstruction from a dispute subsisting at that time between the Governor and Assembly, about certain privileges of the house, yet the latter could not help considering themselves as laid under the strongest obligations to make provision for so many useful settlers. Accordingly, in imitation of the noble example set before them in London, they voted five hundred pounds sterling to be distributed among the Palatines, according to the directions of the Lieutenant-Governor, and their necessities. That they might be settled in a body, one of the two townships, called Londonderry, was allotted for them, and divided in the most equitable manner, into small tracts, for the accommodation of each family. Captain Calhoun, with a detachment of the Rangers, had orders to meet them by the way, and conduct them to the place where their town was to be built, and all possible assistance was given towards promoting their speedy and comfortable settlement."

In the State Library at Raleigh, North Carolina, to which the writer had access by invitation of the late Governor Ellis, he found an old map of South Carolina, and discovered that Londonderry Township is the exact locality answering to that of Hard Labor Creek in Abbeville County, at which place, as is well known, a settlement of Germans was made, and a Lutheran church and congregation once existed; so that this fact, in connection with corresponding dates, besides they having been met by Captain Calhoun, which family settled and resided in Abbeville District, and various other circumstances, prove beyond a doubt that this interesting account, given by Hewatt, is the story of the colonization of our German Lutheran brethren at Hard Labor Creek.

Dr. Hazelius' history informs us (p. 120) that formerly there existed among them a Lutheran church and congregation, as it was incorporated by the legislature, February, 1788, under the name and title of "St. George, on Hard Labor Creek," and a few years ago, whilst on a visit to Abbeville, the writer was informed that the old church edifice was still standing.

These settlers had also their own pastor, for at the time when the above-mentioned visit was made there were persons still living who had heard him preach in St. George's Church.

The last account we have of this congregation may be found in the journal of Rev. R. J. Miller's missionary tour, published in the minutes of the Spring Session of the North Carolina Synod, of 1812, an extract of which is here given:

"Saturday, November 9th, 1811. I arrived in the evening, after having crossed Saluda River, at a Mr. Robert Smith's, on Hard Labor Creek, where my appointments were to commence. Sunday, the 10th, I preached in a German meeting-house; here was formerly a Lutheran congregation, but no remains of them (Lutherans) are now to be found; here the Methodists and Baptists have pulled each other out of the pulpit. Every person seemed very attentive. Here is a full proof of the necessity of missionary preaching. Brothers Dreher, Meetze, and Fulmar, from the congregation on Saluda, met me here."

The period of time when the above reported visit of Rev. R. J. Miller was made, and even before that time, was the trying period of the Lutheran Church in the South; the want of ministers to feed the flock was felt everywhere; the people lived as sheep without a shepherd, and soon became a prey to ravening wolves; and this congregation in Abbeville District, being somewhat isolated and remote from the present flourishing churches in the central and southern part of the State, and having become vacant, could not be easily visited by the few Lutheran ministers then laboring in South Carolina, they having their hands full and their time occupied in laboring among the other churches committed to their charge, and so the Lutheran congregation on Hard Labor Creek very naturally became extinct, and thus an interesting page in the history of our Lutheran Church in the South is practically lost to us.

Section 15. Other German Settlements, particularly in South Carolina.

It is impossible to give a correct account of all the smaller settlements of Germans in the two Carolinas, inasmuch as no records concerning them have been preserved, either in the colonial annals of these two States, or in the various other published or unpublished historical reports, from which reliable information might be obtained. In North Carolina the German emigrants from Pennsylvania, that scattered themselves over the central and western part of the State, located themselves in companies wherever they found vacant lands to be occupied, and continued to arrive almost every year from 1740 to the breaking out of the Revolutionary War. In addition to these yearly arrivals, the older settlements in the State began likewise to send out new colonies farther westward in this State, and in this manner were new settlements of Germans formed east and west of the Catawba River.

In South Carolina a number of other German settlements were made, which have not yet been noticed; the one in Barnwell County was doubtless formed by the breaking up of the Dutch colony on James Island, the gradual absorption of the unsuccessful German and Swiss colony at Purysburg, and the influx of other German settlers from Orangeburg County. In much the same manner were German settlements made along the boundary line of Richland and Fairfield Counties, on Cedar and Dutchman's Creeks. The most of these colonists doubtless came from adjoining older settlements; as the one at Saxe-Gotha Township, Lexington County, was nearest to Richland and Fairfield, it may have supplied the German element residing there. On Cedar Creek there was once a German church, which bore the name of "German Protestant Church of Apii-Forum," and was incorporated by legislative enactment in 1788. From the best accounts that we can gather at this late date, this congregation, having been so long neglected by our Lutheran and German Reformed ministers, became at last absorbed by and into a Methodist congregation in the vicinity. The Newberry County Germans were mostly all descendants from the original German settlers in Saxe-Gotha Township, with an occasional addition from the German settlements of North Carolina and Virginia.

In the southern part of Edgefield County, along the Savannah River, and opposite the city of Augusta, Georgia, there was a township laid out at an early date, bearing the name of New Windsor; here a number of German emigrants were located, that were brought over to America by the Rev. Bartholomew Zauberbühler of Orangeburg notoriety, or came over to South Carolina under his influence; at a later date an addition of German emigrants was made to this new colony, who were brought there by John Jacob Riemensperger, who appears to have been commissioned so to do by the provincial government of South Carolina; it is possible that the German descendants, now residing in the central part of Edgefield County, came originally from this settlement and Saxe-Gotha Township. This supposition is strengthened by the fact that Riemensperger brought colonists also to Saxe-Gotha, which may have induced both settlements to locate a colony on lands lying about midway between them.

Rev. Dr. Muhlenberg speaks of meeting a certain Philip Eisenman in Charleston during his visit there in 1774; this Eisenman informed him that he was a resident "of Old Indian Swamp, fifty miles in the country, who arranged his barn for public worship, and they (he and his neighbors) have accepted as preacher a young man lately arrived from Germany, and who might answer for a schoolmaster." The Doctor does not mention his name, nor does he speak very highly of his attainments. A church, bearing the name of "The German Protestant Church of St. George on Indian Field Swamp," was incorporated by the legislature in 1788. Taking these facts together, it is proper to conclude that a German settlement was made fifty miles from Charleston, that these Germans had a church of their own, which was doubtless unitedly Lutheran and Reformed, as it bore the name "German Protestant," but where to locate the church is now a matter of impossibility, as the afore-mentioned swamp is not shown on any of the old or modern maps of South Carolina; it is probable, however, that it had its position in Barnwell County, where there are Lutheran Churches at the present time.

About the year 1750, a German colony from the Palatinate arrived in South Carolina, and "after some delay, settled in" what was then called "Anson County," North Carolina, along the boundary line between the two provinces, on lands that are now located in Union County, North Carolina, and Lancaster and Chesterfield Counties, South Carolina, many of whose descendants are still living, and are gathered in Lutheran congregations belonging to the Tennessee Synod.

In company with this colony came the Rev. John Nicholas Martin, one of the first pastors of St. John's Lutheran Church, Charleston, South Carolina, but at that time a layman, and the father of a family "with several children." According to Rev. Dr. Muhlenberg's statement, he was a self-taught man, and was said to have been ordained afterwards by the Lutheran pastors at Ebenezer, Georgia. He did not remain long in Anson County, North Carolina, but, in company "with the larger portion of" his fellow-colonists, removed to the fork of Saluda and Broad Rivers, in South Carolina, where they found permanent homes, and where afterwards they were also served in spiritual things by Rev. Martin, after having been pastor in Charleston from 1763 to 1767, but who finally located himself permanently in that city.

Section 16. Hessian Deserters during the Revolution.

The period of the Revolutionary War was one of sore trial to all the American colonies, and the German settlers underwent an amount of suffering no less than that of other citizens; the thirteen Provinces numbered at that time three millions of inhabitants, and these had established their homes with but few exceptions, east of the Alleghany Mountains. It was a severe trial for them to take up arms and send ablebodied men into the battlefield, when they were needed at home in developing the resources of their country, which had been but partially reclaimed from its primeval condition. Thousands left home and enlisted for the war, who never again returned, but whose bodies filled the honored graves of the patriot soldier; thousands of widows and orphans lamented their irreparable loss, and a void was created in the heart and a vacancy at the fireside, which in most cases was never again filled.

England supplied her depleted ranks in the army from the overcrowded population of other European countries, whose military service she procured by large subsidies to the sovereigns of these people, and bounty money to the purchased soldier, thinking to gain thereby a two-fold advantage, that of saving her British subjects, who went reluctantly to fight against their own flesh and blood, for so were the American colonists regarded, and that of preventing desertion to the American army and cause of liberty and independence. It was confidently supposed that the German soldiers, mostly Hessians, numbering "a little over seventeen thousand men," ignorant of the English language, generally spoken in America, would be proof against the seductive representations made by the Americans; and to make this fancied security doubly sure, the most incredible stories concerning the character of the Americans were freely circulated among the Hessians.

However, one thing the British government had entirely overlooked, namely, that numbers of the American citizens were Germans and German descendants, still bearing German names, possessed of German characteristics, and speaking the German language. No sooner did the Hessian soldiers come in contact with these German-American citizens, than they deserted the ranks of the British army whenever they found a safe opportunity for so doing, and fled to the German settlements, to be delivered from the dangers and hardships of a war in which they had no interest.

In these settlements the identity of the Hessian deserters soon became lost to the British, and the German farmers were only too happy to have the Hessians in their midst as laborers ever to betray them to the British, who were their own enemies as well as they were dangerous foes to the Hessian deserters. The Hessians discovered that these American-Germans were both civilized and christianized, contrary to the slanderous tales circulated by the British leaders; and though they were not originally from the same German province, yet they spake the German language, and were generally of the same faith with themselves. Besides, they discovered that land was cheap and labor scarce, and that better prospects were before them in America, than they could ever hope to find on their return to Germany after the termination of the war.

In this manner were the German settlements at the North, where the Hessians first landed, supplied with a valuable addition to their strength; and farther south, particularly in the Carolinas, many honest, industrious, and useful German settlers came in good time to supply the loss that had been caused by the war. These did not, and of necessity could not, form separate settlements, as that would most certainly have endangered their safety as long as the war continued, but they located themselves among the German farmers, who had already been established in this country.

Among these Hessian deserters was one who afterwards became a Lutheran minister in South Carolina, named John Yost Mütze, known better as Rev. J. Y. Meetze, and whose history was obtained from one of his sons. He deserted near Charleston at the time the British army was besieging that city from the other side of Ashley River; he was pursued some thirty miles, but finally made his escape over Bacon's bridge, where he was safe within the American lines. He located himself in Saxe-Gotha Township, now Lexington County, six miles above the present county-seat, and became the forefather of a large and influential family in that section of the country. The following tablet inscription marks the spot where his remains now repose:

"Sacred to the memory of the Rev. J. Y. Meetze, who departed this life May 7th, 1833, aged 76 years, 5 months, and 5 days."

CHAPTER II.

CONDITION AND HISTORY OF THE GERMAN COLONIES IN THE CAROLINAS TO THE CLOSE OF THE REVOLUTIONARY WAR.

Section 1. A Brief Review of the Planting of the different German Colonies in North and South Carolina.

"THE child is the father of the man;" this is a trite but true saying, and is the key that unlocks many of the peculiar mysteries of habit, manners and customs, as well as the moral, intellectual and religious life of any community. The condition of an infant colony has much to do with its future development; one age of the world succeeds another as naturally, and adjusts itself to the preceding age as appropriately as do the several pieces of mosaic in making a grand whole—a perfect picture; and, inasmuch as there can be no effect without a cause, it is always necessary to study the character and condition of the early colonies, if we desire to understand fully their peculiarities of the present time.

It is not to be supposed that the German settlements in the Carolinas would form the only exception to this general rule. With these truths before us, and kept always in view, the peculiar differences, that still mark the North and South Carolina German descendants at the present day, can be easily understood. Local and State governments have had something to do with the forming of these peculiar characteristics, but when we reflect that these governments are the creatures of the settlers of each county, then we are again thrown back upon the original condition of the first colonies.

Again, it is not to be supposed that the German forefathers, coming directly from various parts of Germany or from the Province of Pennsylvania, would leave their German peculiarities at home, and be ready to adopt the manners and customs of the settlers who preceded them and among whom they lived, or be moulded into their religious belief and peculiar ecclesiastical usages. This doubtless was the case with those German settlers, who were isolated and cut off from all intercourse with their brethren, and where other elements of colonization predominated, but not until after process of time, when a generation or two had passed away.

The Dutch were the first Lutheran settlers in the Carolinas, and history has informed us how strenuously they, with others, resisted the encroachments of the Church of England upon their faith, and how they struggled against the efforts of the Proprietary government of South Carolina to make Episcopalians of them and their children;

whilst the German and Swiss colony at Newberne, North Carolina, in course of time, submitted to the arrangement of a change of their faith, when made in a more conciliatory spirit and manner. However, as both these colonies became practically lost to the faith of their early founders, it is unnecessary to follow them any farther, as on this wise their original identity was lost; although a number of the Dutch settlers found congenial homes, and preserved their original faith among German settlers in other parts of South Carolina.

Charleston, Purysburg, Barnwell, Orangeburg, Saxe-Gotha, Edgefield and Newberry received their Teutonic element previous to the year 1740, and inasmuch as, with the exception of Purysburg, the descendants of these settlers are still to be met there, and the Lutheran Church is firmly established among them, it is proper to examine the condition of these early settlements to understand their peculiar characteristics manifest at the present day. They received their principal strength from several German nationalities; natives of Switzerland, the Palatinate, Austria, Würtemberg, Holland and the Hessian States, located themselves principally in those parts of South Carolina, and all, of course, brought their peculiar national characteristics with them, and were so far beneficial to each other as to increase their intellectual and practical acquirements in almost every department of life, for they could communicate to each other the ideas and information which they received in their different mental and religious trainings, as well as what was customary and advantageous in the useful arts in their native countries. Besides, the Swiss element largely predominated over any one of the other German nationalities, and these Switzers, coming from the land of William Tell, were born and cradled in a republic, lived in an adopted country which had overthrown the Proprietary government in 1719, because of its oppressive rule in that province;—need any one then be astonished at their love of liberty, and the prompt assertion of their inalienable rights?

Their peculiar ecclesiastical condition is likewise the result of their early colonial training; in the interior of South Carolina the Lutherans and German Reformed did not continue long as two separate denominations, owing to the neglect of the German Reformed Church in taking care of their congregations so far south, and failing to supply them with ministers of the gospel after the older ministers there had all died. This, no doubt, the German Reformed Church in America could not avoid, and thus the members of that Church in those settlements soon lost their ecclesiastical identity, many having connected themselves with the Lutheran Church; whilst others, who were again necessarily neglected by the Lutherans, were absorbed by other denominations. In Charleston the ecclesiastical union of Germans extended still farther, and embraced even those who were attached to the Roman Catholic faith, of which the Rev. Dr. Velthusen, of Helmstaedt, Germany, reports in his preface to the North Carolina Catechism, as follows: "We have likewise the assurance from other parts of America, that our books of instruction are suitable to their wants. Besides, various of these books have been also introduced in Charleston, by the approval and support of the congregation, for the instruction of their youth. This congregation may be looked upon as an example of Christian harmony, *for it is composed of a union of Lutherans, German Reformed and Catholics*, all of whom live, according to the testimony of their pastor, the Rev. Mr. Faber, very peaceably together, although they are educated in different principles of religion. They visit the house of God faithfully, and contribute equally for the support of divine worship." Thus were these different elements united, communicating to each other their peculiar faith and church usages, retaining, however, the Lutheran name up to the present time.

The only other extensive settlement of Germans in South Carolina was the one in Abbeville County, on Hard Labor Creek, which remained Lutheran for a number of years, but, owing to neglect on the part of the Lutheran Church in supplying those people with the much-needed means of grace, they became, in course of time, lost to the Lutheran faith entirely.

In North Carolina there existed an entirely different state of things; all the German settlers, with the exception of those who were located at Newberne, came mostly from Pennsylvania during a period of twenty-five or thirty years before the Revolutionary War; even the Moravians at Salem and vicinity came originally and mostly from that Province; consequently, one will find Pennsylvania ideas, habits, manners and customs prevailing among the German descendants in North Carolina, and here and there the Pennsylvania-German dialect still spoken among the aged. In addition to that, the Lutherans, German Reformed and Moravians have always preserved their ecclesiastical identity, and although the Lutherans and Reformed built many joint-churches for themselves, in which both these denominations worshiped alternately, that arrangement has not materially interfered with their respective faith and ecclesiastical usages.

Again, these North Carolina German settlements have been mostly made in the country, as those colonists from Pennsylvania were principally farmers, and continued to follow their peaceful and unambitious pursuits for many years, and until recently, they cared to make but little progress in intellectual pursuits beyond that which their forefathers enjoyed, they continued their German schools and German worship for a long time, and but few of their descendants engaged in mercantile pursuits, or sought distinction and prominence in the arena of political life; and, as a general thing, they also adhered all the more closely to the faith and church usages of their forefathers. Besides, with the exception of the German and Swiss settlers at Newberne, the three

German denominations of North Carolina have lost but very little by the proselyting encroachments of other denominations, compared with the German settlements of almost every other State in the Union.

This is doubtless owing to various circumstances: *firstly*, they were more strongly attached to their own peculiar faith; *secondly*, they remained more closely together in their own settlements, and when they did colonize, it was generally done in such a manner as to have a number of German families locate in the same new settlement; *thirdly*, they were more regularly supplied with the means of grace in their own churches, although there were some exceptions to this condition of things in certain localities; *fourthly*, the German colonies were established in North Carolina at a later date, when the parent Churches in Europe had become fully awakened to the importance of taking care of their interests in America.

Section 2. Trials and Difficulties of the Early Settlers.

The trials of strangers in a strange land under the most favorable circumstances, when the necessaries and comforts of life are at their command, are sufficiently numerous and hard in themselves; the feeling of loneliness, the separation from affectionate relatives and friends, the sighings ("Ach und Weh") produced by home-sickness, especially such as the Swiss emigrant must have felt, when he contrasted the grandeur of the Alpine scenery in his native land with his surroundings in the Carolinas, located, as he was, upon the level and sandy plains, which extend there along the Atlantic coast. In the same manner, doubtless, were also the German Palatines affected, although war had driven them from their peaceful homes, when they remembered the beautiful banks along the Rhine and its vine-clad hills, which they had left behind them—never to behold again; all of which tended to make the heart sink within them in mental anguish and despondency. Wise indeed, as well as kind, was the divine injunction given to the children of Israel, Deut. 10 : 19: "Love ye, therefore, the stranger: for ye were strangers in the land of Egypt."

Yet how much greater must have been the anguish and suffering of the early colonists, who either willingly or necessarily abandoned home without the most distant prospect of return, to dwell in a land that could give them no shelter, until the log-cabin was erected by their own industry, and no necessary supplies of life, until they could cultivate these themselves; and all that they possessed to sustain life was often nothing more than what they brought with them from the vessel that conveyed them to America. The first English colony, located on Roanoke Island in North Carolina, actually perished from want, and was swept away entirely; not a soul was left to tell the tale of its woes and sufferings, of which Dr. Hawks speaks: "It was subjected to the horrors of famine; time and experience would probably have corrected the other evils we have named, but for starvation there was no remedy; and so, after the toil and suffering of years, the expenditure of much precious treasure, and the loss of still more precious life, the waves of Albemarle rolled, as of old, their ripples up the deserted island beach, and the only voice heard was that of the fitful winds, as they sighed through the forests of Roanoke, and broke upon the stillness of nature's rough repose. The white man was there no longer."

And then came also the exposure to all kinds of weather and the inhospitality of climate, to which the early settlers were as yet unaccustomed, which, with the ignorance in regard to the peculiarities of the new country, often locating themselves near streams of water, the malaria of which superinduced sickness, frequently brought the strongest constitutioned person to an early grave; whilst others were so enfeebled by sickness, that all their native strength and energy, brought with them from the Fatherland, was necessarily prostrated. It was some time before they became acquainted with the peculiarities of the country and climate, and discovered the healthy localities, where they would be free from the attacks of malignant fevers, and their physical constitution would adapt itself to the climate of their new homes.

But the greatest hardship of the early settlers was the occasional outbreak of hostility from the

Indians; this was a never-failing cause of apprehension and alarm. Whilst the Indians remained near them, they never felt themselves perfectly safe; war often broke out upon them quite unawares; the strong man, the helpless woman and the innocent child were not unfrequently murdered in cold blood. In this manner did many of the poor Palatines and Swiss, in and around Newberne, lose their lives during the Tuscarora and Core Indian war, as already related in chapter i, section 7, of this history, containing an extract from Dr. Hawks' History of North Carolina. Whenever the early colonists were pursuing their daily avocations, at home or in the field, at church or elsewhere, the trusty rifle had always to accompany them, so that they might be prepared for any sudden attack.

The sparseness of population was another great inconvenience to the early settlers, both in the matter of defence against the hostile attacks of the Indians, as well as in the procuring of most of the necessary articles of husbandry and domestic life. There were but few mechanics and still fewer trading-places, where the supplies of commerce could be obtained, so that nearly all the settlers were obliged to live and labor without those things which are now regarded as necessaries of life. This, of course, compelled each family to manufacture their own articles of clothing and implements of husbandry; the loom, the anvil, the tannery and the shoe-shop became necessary adjuncts to almost every household, whilst all the inmates of the family had to content themselves to live and be clad in the most primitive style; useful industry became every member of society at that time, and the hum of the spinning-wheel resounded in almost every dwelling.

Section 3. Character, Occupation and Condition of the German Settlers in the Carolinas.

Wherever the Germans have located themselves, they have usually manifested certain traits of character, which are upon the whole very commendable. Whilst they are generally retiring and peaceful in their intercourse with man, opposed to riot and contention, and will patiently suffer wrong for a long time, they are nevertheless unwilling to submit to oppression when persistently brought to bear down upon them; they may be led, their minds are open to conviction, but they cannot be driven, and will determinately resist all attempts to deprive them of their inalienable rights.

The Germans are the most industrious settlers that have ever come to America; they are willing to endure any amount of toil to secure a permanent home, or an establishment over which they may have entire control; they never shrink from labor that promises to be remunerative; everything around them must be well and profitably arranged, hence their farms usually present the appearance of order, thrift and comfort; all work must be well done, ere it can be made satisfactory to them. Besides, they also love home and its comforts, and are usually slow to leave the place which they have once secured as their own; there are plantations and farms at the present day in possession among the German descendants in both the Carolinas, that have never passed out of the family, being still held by virtue of the original grant or deed made in colonial times. They generally persevere in all their undertakings, even when the immediate prospects are not encouraging, and manage all their affairs with the strictest economy, often carrying their frugality to such an extreme as to become a fault, when such frugality is no longer needed. Honesty and uprightness are also marked characteristics of the Germans; they shrink from debt, and are unhappy as long as all their liabilities are not cancelled, and when once a promise has been made by them, it can generally be relied on, for their word is usually as good as their bond; there are, of course, exceptions to this general trait of character, yet not so many as materially to impair the confidence which is usually reposed in the Germans and their immediate descendants everywhere. They are slow in making changes, and often tenaciously adhere for a long time to the practices and conduct of their forefathers; this has been frequently attributed to them as a fault, inasmuch as they appear so unwilling to make progress and keep pace with modern advancement; yet whilst this may be true, it can also be said that they do not advance so readily in the vices, immoralities and fraudulent dealings of our progressive age.

The Germans appear to have been specially fitted in all their characteristics to make the wilds of America to blossom and bloom as the rose; their patient toil, together with their excellent and economical management, has made the soil of this country to produce abundantly, thereby enhancing its material prosperity.

The early German colonists were slow in abandoning their native language, especially where they lived in settlements of their own, and did not come much in contact with other people, as was the case in agricultural districts; this was one of the causes of their having retained their peculiar traits of character for so long a time, having had its influence also upon their educational, religious, social and moral condition. They established parochial schools in all their settlements, wherever it could possibly be done, and a teacher could be secured, an arrangement to which they had always been accustomed in their Fatherland, in which the catechism was taught, as well as the other branches of rudimental knowledge; neither was the Bible excluded from the school, and generally constituted the text-book in the reading classes; by this means a vast amount of religious intelligence was diffused among the German settlers and their descendants.

Their divine service was conducted for a long period of time in the German language, and when, at length, it did become absolutely necessary to introduce the English language occasionally in their churches, because some of their descendants and some English settlers among them could not understand the German very well, the minister or pastor in charge, who conscientiously favored or proposed this new arrangement, often met with a storm of opposition that generally impaired his usefulness, and obliged him to seek for another field of labor. His successor, however, then found the way prepared before him, and could officiate in English without much opposition, the storm having spent itself upon the pastor who first proposed the change. This same German characteristic, namely, opposition to all innovations, or firm adherence to the ways of their forefathers, had another deleterious effect: it sometimes became necessary to have a church located in town, in order to preserve its prosperity, when a number of the members had removed there, and the town became the central point of the congregation, then animosities would sometimes arise, which either defeated the proposed measure, or necessitated the removal of the pastor. The long use of the German language, whilst it exerted a deleterious influence upon the Church in retarding its progress, in many instances also preserved it from the encroachments of error and the inroads of proselytism, especially in the rural districts; whilst in cities and towns it had the opposite effect, and caused numbers of the German descendants to connect themselves with other denominations, who would gladly have remained in the church of their fathers.

Many of the Germans in the Province of South Carolina were brought there with the design of establishing the production of silk and the cultivation of the grape-vine, with which the Swiss and Palatines were well acquainted, as it was thought that the soil and climate were admirably adapted thereto; but it did not promise much success, owing chiefly to the little demand for those articles of luxury at the time, and the more profitable employment of labor in other and more necessary articles; besides, the cost of producing silk and wine was greater than in Europe. Wine could be made, as the grape-vine bears plentifully, but the wine produced in South Carolina cannot be long preserved in so warm a climate without admixture of other ingredients, especially in the lowlands, where the first German settlers were located. Planting, farming and the useful arts constituted the principal employment of the Germans and their descendants in the Carolinas: merchandizing, especially in towns and cities, eventually claimed their attention also, but only to a limited extent. Their mode of living, their industrious habits, and their simplicity of manners, to all of which they had been accustomed in their Fatherland, were well adapted to the condition of the country in its early period of colonization, of which Captain John Smith, though Governor of another Province, the Virginia Colony of Jamestown, very appropriately remarks: "When you send again, I entreat you, rather send but thirty carpenters, husbandmen, gardeners, fishermen, blacksmiths, masons and diggers up of trees' roots, well provided, than a thousand such as we have; for except we be able to lodge them and feed them, the most will consume with want of necessaries before they can be made good for any thing." (*Smith's History of Virginia*, vol. i, p. 202.)

The purity of morals of the early German settlers likewise contrasts very favorably with some of the English colonists, who came to Carolina to seek a change of fortune, and of whom Rev. Dr. Hawks writes: "The outcasts of London prisons and the sweepings of London kennels, then, as now, doubtless could furnish their quota to every shipload of adventurers. The dissipated scions of respectable families were gladly sent off, lest they should finally tarnish ancestral honors by a felon's fate at home: the inmates of the vile slums and alleys of the metropolis were but too glad to escape the grasp of violated law; to leave a country where they had nothing to gain and everything to lose, because they had reached an infamy and attained to a notoriety in guilt, which left them no further hope of committing crime with impunity. In short, we may not doubt, that some of the earliest colonists belonged to that class which the poet has described as 'the cankers of a long peace, and a calm world.'" (*Hawks' History of North Carolina*, vol. i, p. 253.)

Section 4. Great want of the Means of Grace among the early German colonists in the Carolinas.

"The harvest truly is plenteous, but the laborers are few," has been the cry for more than eighteen centuries, and the want of ministers of the gospel is continued to be felt up to the present time, but at no time and among no people to a more alarming extent than among the early German settlers in the Carolinas. The Dutch colony on James Island, South Carolina, the Swiss and Palatine settlers in Newberne, North Carolina, the German and Swiss colonists in Purysburg, South Carolina, never did have a minister of the gospel of their own faith among them, and were consequently lost entirely to the Church of their fathers; whilst all the other German settlements in these two Provinces suffered more or less, and some for a long time, for the want of the regular administration of the means of grace; and when German ministers did eventually come to labor among their brethren of the same faith with themselves, the enemy had already sown his tares among the wheat, which caused great spiritual degeneracy. From A.D. 1674 to 1737, that is to say, from the settlement of the Dutch colonists to the arrival of the first German minister in Orangeburg, South Carolina, embracing a period of sixty-three years, during which time a number of important German settlements had been made, not a single minister of the gospel of their own faith labored among these settlers in that entire territory; and after that time their pastors were so few in number that comparatively little good could be effected.

In some localities temporary houses of worship were erected, and grants of land were secured for that purpose; or in the absence of these, school-houses and barns were used for divine service, generally conducted by some pious layman or the school-teacher, who read a sermon or devotional essay from such books as constituted the library of the early settlers. Great desire was at first awakened to enjoy the preaching of the Word and the administration of the sacraments, which want was occasionally supplied by very unworthy men, who were generally denominated "straggling preachers," of whom Dr. E. W. Caruthers, in his "Life of Rev. David Caldwell, D.D.," speaks as follows: "Hardly any of these (preachers) were calculated to advance the interests of vital piety, or to elevate the character of the people. Some of them had no kind of authority to preach, and no claims on the confidence of the churches on the score of piety; but came out here, either from the Northern States or from Germany, pretending to be preachers; exercised an assumed authority, and acted as self-constituted pastors of the churches, or went from place to place, imposing on the people who knew no better, or were glad to meet with any one who came to them as a minister of Christ."

The effect of such great want of the means of grace, or the improper administration of them, can be readily imagined; it occasioned at first much sorrow and regret among the better class of settlers, who became greatly dissatisfied with their new homes on account of this deficiency; and, as in Saxe-Gotha, South Carolina, gave intimation that they would likewise remove from their present location to the Province of Pennsylvania, where they could enjoy these spiritual advantages, as many had heretofore done. In Purysburg, Charleston and elsewhere, a number of German settlers did leave for this very reason, and located themselves among the Salzburgers of Ebenezer, Georgia, who were supplied with two efficient and pious pastors, the Revs. Bolzius and Gronau. Others again grew cold and indifferent to their spiritual interests and welfare, whilst not a few abandoned themselves to the dictates of their own corrupt natures, and fell from that grace and those pious principles of which they were once possessed; permitting their children to grow up without a proper knowledge of God, of their duty, and of the way of salvation.

In one locality a singular heresy made its appearance among a number of settlers, which terminated in a very tragical affair, as found related in the succeeding section, and may readily be understood as a very natural consequence of the want of the means of grace administered in the regularly-appointed and divinely-ordered way.

In Charleston, South Carolina, the German settlers fared somewhat better; it being the centre of commerce in that Province, and having more intercourse with the European world, ministers of the gospel, who first landed there on their way to their respective fields of labor in other parts of America, occasionally supplied the German citizens there with the preaching of the gospel and the administration of the holy sacraments; Rev. Bolzius visited them in 1734, and accomplished much good in preaching and administering the communion to them for the first time; Rev. Dr. Muhlenberg, who had been sent by the Mission Society of Halle to labor in Pennsylvania, landed in Charleston, September 21, 1742, and whilst tarrying there he preached the gospel and catechized the children; Revs. Rabenhorst and Gerock, the one on his way to Ebenezer, Georgia, and the other destined for Pennsylvania, likewise visited the German citizens of Charleston, and labored a short time for their spiritual welfare, A.D. 1753; in this manner was the flame of true religion preserved from becoming entirely extinguished among them, until they secured the services of a regular pastor in 1755. But in the rural districts of South Carolina, the spiritual condition of the German settlers was most deplorable, inasmuch as, previous to the year 1737, not a single German pastor labored among them.

The Lutherans in Saxe-Gotha Township, numbering two hundred and eighty souls, wrote to the Ebenezer pastors, in 1750, for a minister of their own faith; but their urgent plea was not regarded, which greatly discouraged them. Need any one be astonished at the legitimate effects of so deplorable a want of the means of grace as was witnessed at that time in the Province of South Carolina. The settlements of Germans from Pennsylvania in the interior of North Carolina were not commenced until about this time, therefore they do not now claim our attention; but the Newberne colony of Swiss and Germans in 1710, as has been stated before, was entirely neglected, and became, as a necessary consequence, also entirely lost to the Church of their fathers.

Section 5. An Account of the Weber (Weaver) Heresy.

In Saxe-Gotha Township, Lexington County, South Carolina, and "in the neighborhood of what is now called Younginer's Ferry," there originated a sect among the Swiss and German settlers, who were called Weberites. Their heresy was of so revolting a nature, that it would be desirable to pass it by in silence, if it could be done without doing injustice to a faithful and correct narration of historical facts.

Rev. Dr. Hazelius gives us a brief sketch of the doings of these Weberites in his American Lutheran Church, p. 103; and the Rev. Dr. Muhlenberg has also furnished us a more extended account of them in his journal, translated and published in vol. i of the Evangelical Review, dating their transactions as having occurred in the year 1760; nevertheless, the origin of this sect must have taken place some time before, as that is the date of the culmination of their heresy into the crime, which brought their leader to suffer the just penalty of the law.

Dr. Muhlenberg's account is as follows: "Mr. Strobel, the son-in-law of Rev. Mr. Martin, a wealthy tanner, sent for me in a chaise, to convey me out of town to dine with him. He told me, among other things, a remarkable history of an abominable sect, which had arisen among the Germans in South Carolina, A.D. 1760–1, and had some similarity with Knipperdolling and Jan Van Leiden. They committed murders, on which account one of them, named Jacob Weber, who called himself a god, and slew a person, was hanged. Their founder is said to have been Peter Schmidt. The sect originated at Saluda Fork, about one hundred miles from Charleston (125 or 130 miles).

"Jacob Weber was a Swiss. He first became an exhorter, then he advanced himself still farther, but before his end he came to his senses, and saw his error.

"The people in the country, in general, grew up without schools and instruction. Occasionally a self-taught (auto-didacter) minister may labor for awhile amongst them, yet it continues only a short time. The people are wild, and continue to grow wilder, for what does it profit them to hear a sermon every four, six, or twelve weeks, if in early youth the foundation of Divine Truth had not been laid? The aforesaid sect had so far obtained the supremacy that several families united with it for fear of their lives; numbers of both sexes went about uncovered and naked, and practiced the most abominable wantonness. One of them pretended to be God the Father, another the Son, and a third the Holy Spirit; and the pretended Father, having quarrelled with the Son, repudiated the pretended Son, chained him in the forest, declared him to be Satan, and finally gathered his gang, who beat and trampled on the poor man until he died; he is reported also to have killed the pretended Holy Ghost in bed. A report of these circumstances having reached the authorities in Charleston, the militia were ordered to arrest the pretended deity, when he was tried, condemned, and executed upon the gallows.

"The English inhabitants scoffed about it, and said the Germans had nothing to fear, their Devil having been killed, and their God having been hanged. Such are the fruits of not inculcating the doctrine of Divine Truth early in youth, and of leaving man to himself. Rom. 1 : 21–32. This sect spread from South to North Carolina, thence to Maryland and Virginia, among the German and English population, and has likewise left some seed of this heresy in Charleston. Upon this gross Satanic tragedy a more subtle temptation followed. Quakers, Anabaptists, &c., spread themselves in the country regions around, and appear to be better suited to the circumstances of the land at this time.

"October 9th. To-day I received the original copy of a letter dictated by Jacob Weber in prison before his death, for the benefit of his children, which reads as follows:

"'*Jacob Weber's Confession.*

"'April 16th, 1761, being imprisoned and ironed, it occurred to me and the jailor to transmit to my beloved children a sketch of my mournful life. I, Jacob Weber, was born in Switzerland, in Canton Zurich, in the county of Knomauer, in the parish of Stifferschweil, and was raised and educated in the Reformed Church. In the fourteenth year of my age I journeyed with my brother to South Carolina, leaving my parents; and soon after my arrival I lost my brother by death. Thus I was forsaken of man, and without father or mother. But God had compassion on me amid much trouble and sorrow. He planted the fear of the Lord in my heart, so that I had more pleasure in the Lord, in godliness, and the Word of God, than in the world. I was often troubled about my salvation when I reflected how strict an account God would require, that I must enter into judgment, and know not how it would result. Although God drew me with his grace, I found also the reverse in my corrupt nature, which was excited with the love of the world, viz., of riches, honors, and an easy life.

"'Mankind love a social life, and as the Lord drew me back in many wonderful ways, I came, therefore, nearer to him; notwithstanding I always attended to my religious services and prayer, but with a heart cold and averted from God. Through such exercises of the heart I arrived at a knowledge of my sins, and learned how awfully the human race had fallen from God, and how low all mankind, without exception, are sunken in depravity. As soon as I experienced this, I earnestly besought God day and night for forgiveness, for the Holy Spirit, for a pure heart, and for saving faith, and I felt the necessity of retirement to restrain my thoughts, and to prevent the Divine work from being hindered in me. In this retirement I forgot the turmoil of the world. In this light I regarded all vain desires and thoughts and all human works as by nature damnable in the sight of God. Fear and sorrow now seized upon my poor soul, and I thought, what shall I do to be saved? It was shown me that nothing would suffice but being born again of water and of the Spirit. Realizing that I could not be saved in any other way, I prayed still more earnestly, and it was shown me still more plainly by the Holy Ghost in my heart how sinful I was (Rom. 7), so that I stood there before the judgment of God; but the judgment of God became manifest in me, so that I judged myself, and confessed that I had deserved a thousand-fold to be cast from the presence of God, and wondered that the forbearance of the Lord had not long since hurled me, poor and condemned wretch, into the lowest pit of destruction; and then too, I saw the whole world lay in sin. Feeling myself so lost, I cast myself entirely upon the mercy of God to lead me according to his holy will and pleasure, whether unto life or death, if he would only be gracious unto my poor soul for Christ's sake, and pardon my sin, and purify my heart from all uncleanness. Thus I lay at the feet of Jesus with all my heart in submission, sighing and praying night and day for his grace, and so continued for several days, until I had passed from death unto life. Then Jesus revealed himself unto my soul. Then there was great joy in heaven over me, a returning sinner. Then all my sins were forgiven me, and I was full of the Holy Ghost, and rejoiced with a joy unspeakably great. This occurred, or I experienced this joy, A.D. 1756, in the month of May. This grace caused me to despise the joy of the world, and to disregard its reproach, and kept me, thenceforth, continually with my surety, Jesus, amid many temptations not now to be mentioned, until finally I found rest for my soul. This peace and communion with God I possessed about two years, under every burden of affliction, for I had the grace to enable me, under all circumstances, to submit my will to the mercy of God. Through the grace which was in me I could govern temporal goods without danger to my soul. Upon this followed the great misery and awful fall into sin, already, alas! too well known. The devil bringing me into a greater temptation and fall than was ever known, of which Peter Schmidt was the origin and instrument. After this, by the providence of God, I was captured and cast into prison, that I might recover my reason, come to a knowledge of my great sins, and confess them before God, that thus it might awaken great wretchedness in my soul, humble me before God and man, yea, beneath all creatures, yea, that I might account myself as the poorest worm. I often thought each and every person too good to speak to me, and interest himself in me. Nevertheless I sought cordially the forgiveness of my sins in the blood of the Lamb of God, my Redeemer, who loved me and died for all my sins, and for his righteousness' sake arose, all which I heartily believe, because I experience again the witness of the Holy Spirit, which testifies unto my spirit that I am a child of God. And now, my children, beloved in the Lord, I must leave this world, and, perhaps, behold your face no more in this life. I commend you, therefore, to the protection and mercy of God! Pray without ceasing, learn and read; injure no one willingly and wilfully while you live; labor industriously and faithfully according to your ability; then, if we should meet no more in this world, we may hope to meet each other in heaven, in the world to come; which may the triune God, Father, Son, and Holy Ghost, grant to you for the sake of the crucified Jesus, Amen. Such cunning and celerity does Satan possess as to cause so great a schism and injury even among the children of God, and to lead them astray, and make them fall so suddenly against their knowledge and consent. May God preserve all persons from so great a fall, and trample Satan under foot, for Christ's sake, Amen. The grace of our Lord Jesus Christ be with you and all persons, Amen. And I beseech all persons who have been injured by me to forgive me, for Christ's sake.

"'Written or dictated by

"'JACOB WAEBER.

"'April 16th, 1761.'"

Dr. Hazelius' account of this tragic affair is as follows:

"It was about this time that a number of our (German) people, living on the banks of the Saluda River, in South Carolina, being destitute of ministerial instruction, agreed to assemble from time to time for singing, prayer, the reading of the Scriptures, and mutual edification. This was as it should be, but the enemy soon sowed tares among the wheat, by introducing spiritual pride among the small flock. One man, by the name of Weaver, personated Christ, another the Holy Spirit, a certain woman, the wife of Weaver, the Virgin Mary, and one poor fellow was doomed to represent Satan. The curiosity of the people became highly excited by the strange proceedings on Saluda River, in the neighborhood of what is now called Younginer's Ferry. Excess followed excess, until at length Weaver, representing either Christ or God, ordered, in virtue of his dignity, that Satan should be chained in a subterranean hole, and finally that he should be destroyed. For this purpose they met, placed the unfortunate man in a bed, covered him with pillows, on which some seated themselves, while others stamped with their feet on the bed until the life of the man had become extinct. The corpse was then taken out of bed, and thrown into a burning pile of wood, to be consumed to ashes. The perpetrators of this crime were taken to Charleston and tried. Weaver was found guilty, and suffered the penalty of the law on the gallows. His wife was pardoned."

The Rev. Christian Theus furnished Dr. Muhlenberg with a more detailed description of this sect of Weberites, as he was well acquainted with their doings, having lived about twenty-five miles from the place where the murder occurred. At a certain time he came unexpectedly into their meeting, and found Jacob Weber contending that he was God, and the said Peter Schmidt insisting that he himself was Christ, and that the unconverted members must be healed through his stripes.

Pastor Theus opposing such blasphemy, the leaders became enraged, and threatened his life, and counselled with their rabble whether to drown or hang him. He escaped, however, from their hands, fled to the river, and fortunately found a negro with his canoe at the shore, sprang into it, was conveyed across, and thus saved his life.

All traces of this abominable heresy have long since been obliterated; neither are there even any descendants of Jacob Weber and Peter Schmidt to be found in the Saluda Fork. To what region of country they emigrated, or what was their subsequent history, is not known. The object of history in preserving the record of such deeds is that it might serve as a warning to all not to depart from the truth as revealed in God's word, even in their religion. The Bible is given as a "lamp to our feet and a light to our path," and the promise is there that the wayfaring man, though a fool, need not err therein; but whosoever despises the revealed light will soon glide into very grievous and dangerous errors. Sincerity is no proof of the purity of faith, and no guide to man's actions. That Weber was sincere, his confession, which he made with eternity in view, fully proves; notwithstanding his sincerity, so great was his deception in spiritual things, that he became guilty of the most horrid blasphemy and of the greatest crime known to the law.

This narrative also demonstrates the value of an evangelical, educated and faithful ministry of the Gospel, an institution which has been divinely appointed, through whose ministrations God is pleased to bless mankind and keep them in the way of truth and peace. In such occurrences as these, the infidel is rebuked in his opposition to the preaching of the Gospel; man soon degenerates and becomes capable of committing all manner of excesses, where he is not restrained by the influence of the Gospel. In this locality, where the Weberites had their origin, and about that period of time, A.D. 1758, according to the import of Weber's confession, the Gospel was but seldom preached, and the effects of such neglect soon manifested themselves; the people generally gave a loose rein to their passions, rioted in their wantonness, and actually believed that in doing so they were rendering service to God. If in the commencement of this settlement the people would have been blessed with the faithful labors of an evangelical and intelligent pastor, doubtless such extravagance in religion and morals never would have been manifested there, as is sufficiently proved by the condition of those settlements where religious advantages were enjoyed; so likewise, where the young are well trained and indoctrinated, departures from the principles of a pure faith and correct morals are not likely to occur. Occasional ministrations of the word and the sacraments are not sufficient in any community; orthodox churches should be established in reach of every family, and a pastor should labor continually among his people, both at the fireside and upon the pulpit, if he expects to accomplish permanent good, for it appears that the want of such constant ministrations had a serious effect upon this community, at the time these criminal occurrences took place.

Section 6. History of St. John's Lutheran Church, Charleston, South Carolina, to the close of the Revolutionary War.

At the period of time when the first Lutheran Church in Charleston was established, so far as the records now extant appear to indicate, there was no longer a single Lutheran congregation nor Lutheran minister in the Province of South Carolina. The Rev. John Giessendanner, of Orangeburg, having become discouraged, and dreading further annoyance from such straggling preachers as Zauberbühler, connected himself and his congregation with the established Church of England in 1749; and the Rev. Christian Theus labored as a German Reformed minister in Saxe-Gotha Township, near the Congaree River.

The early records of the Charleston Lutheran Church are mainly derived from the journal of Rev. H. M. Muhlenberg, D.D., who labored in Pennsylvania, and who was sent, A.D. 1774, by the "Society for Propagating the Gospel" on a second visit to the South to adjust certain difficulties, which had arisen in the congregation at Ebenezer, Georgia; and on his way thither he spent some time in Charleston, and took notes of the principal occurrences in the Lutheran Church in that city, as well as of the German churches generally, located in South Carolina. Dr. Muhlenberg's journal was translated and published in the Evangelical Review in 1850, by a descendant of his, the Rev. J. W. Richards, D.D., then Lutheran pastor at Easton, Pennsylvania.

Dr. Ramsay, in the second volume of his "History of South Carolina," reprinted edition, p. 23, states: "Their first minister, the Rev. Mr. Luft, arrived in 1752." How much credit is to be given to this statement, the writer is not prepared to say; but it appears singular that Dr. Muhlenberg, who examined the records of this Lutheran Church in Charleston thirty-four years before Ramsay, and associated freely with its members for five weeks, arranging their church affairs, should not have mentioned the Rev. Mr. Luft's name in his journal. However, if the Rev. Mr. Luft was the first pastor of this people, they certainly had no house of worship of their own at the time, and very probably no regularly organized congregation, for even Ramsay states: "In the year 1759 they began to build a house of worship themselves," and that event took place during Rev. Friederichs' ministry in Charleston.

Rev. John George Friederichs arrived in Charleston, South Carolina, about the year 1755 or 6, and gathered the Germans residing there into a congregation, which he afterwards served for several years; he may, therefore, justly be regarded as the founder of the first Lutheran Church in Charleston. The elders of the French (Huguenot) congregation kindly offered and granted the use of their church for divine service to our German brethren, when not needed for their own worship; they likewise extended the right of sepulture to the Germans in their own graveyard, all of which was accepted with gratitude.

"Rev. Friederichs labored hard, and, together with the elders and wardens, exerted himself so as to procure a place in the town for a German Lutheran church and graveyard. He was acquainted among the English and beloved by them, and collected among them towards the erection of a house of worship. He desired the church to be built of brick, which would have been best, but several elders and members outvoted him, and caused it to be built of wood." The enterprise so far succeeded as to have the corner-stone of the new edifice laid on the 17th of December, 1759. Soon after this event, Rev. Friederichs resigned, and took charge of several congregations in the country, locating himself in Amelia Township, Orangeburg District, South Carolina.

After the removal of Rev. J. G. Friederichs the congregation secured the services of a Rev. Mr. Wartman, who was a highly educated divine, and is said to have been an animated preacher, yet his usefulness was very much injured, on account of his having been possessed of a very fiery and choleric disposition, which unhappy temperament had been the cause of his short stay in several congregations in Pennsylvania and Virginia, where he had frequently exposed his temper, and exhausted both himself and his people. This was also the reason of his short stay in Charleston, where he might have been exceedingly useful, as he was possessed of the other necessary qualifications of a pastor, had he been enabled to control his unhappy disposition. He remained but two years and then took up his residence in the country.

The fourth pastor of this congregation was the Rev. John Nicholas Martin, a self-taught man, who is said to have been ordained by the Salzburg pastors in Georgia, and who enjoyed the reputation of having been a sensible and industrious laborer in Christ's vineyard. He took charge of St. John's Church, November 24th, 1763, and served it for three years and three months; during his ministry the new church edifice was completed, which had been in course of construction over four years, and was dedicated on the 24th of June, 1764, John the Baptist's day. The officiating clergymen on this occasion were Rev. J. G. Friederichs, the founder of this congregation, and the Rev. J. N. Martin, the pastor in charge. The dedication sermon was preached from the text, Luke 1 : 68–70: "Blessed be the Lord God of Israel; for he hath visited and redeemed his people, and hath raised up a horn of salvation for us in the house of his servant David; as he spake by the mouth of his holy prophets, which have been since the world began." This church was a small wooden building, situated in the rear of where the present church stands, and "was an antiquated building of a peculiar construction, resembling some of the old churches in the rural districts of Germany;" a representation of it is still preserved, "suspended in the vestry-room of the present church; and for uniqueness of architecture, as well as for its value as a relic of the past, excites no little notice."

During the ministry of Rev. Martin in this congregation, a large number of worthy Germans organized themselves into a "German Benevolent Society," now known as the "German Friendly Society," which appears to have been in a most flourishing condition from its commencement to the present time. Rev. Dr. Muhlenberg gives a glowing description of this praiseworthy society, and informs us, that it was founded January 15th, 1766, and had increased in a little more than eight years to "upwards of eighty members, living in the town and country, of whom upwards of fifty are still living." During those years their funded capital had accumulated to £400 sterling, the interest of which is to be "applied for the relief of every such poor member, or of his widow and orphans, as shall have been connected seven years with the Society, and have paid their contributions. This commendable Society is, in a measure, the flower and crown of the German nation in this place."

By special invitation of the "heads of this Society," and escorted to their place of meeting by the Vice-President and Treasurer, Rev. Dr. Muhlenberg dined with the members, and thus became acquainted with the most influential Germans in the place. He speaks also very highly of their manner of conducting the business of this Society, and gives the names of the members present at that meeting.

Early in the year 1767, Rev. J. N. Martin took leave of this congregation, and labored in the Fork of the Saluda and Broad Rivers, where it is known that he still labored some seven years later, in 1774, as his name is incidentally mentioned in that connection in Dr. M.'s journal, and the presumption is, that he became the Lutheran pastor of the congregations in the Fork soon after his departure from Charleston.

The elders and wardens of St. John's Church now applied to Rev. Dr. Wachsell, in London, beseeching him to send them a regular teacher and pastor, and obtained through his instrumentality the Rev. John Severin Hahnbaum, to whom a call was extended on the 28th of January, 1767. He arrived with his family, and took charge of the church on the 12th of June of the same year; unfortunately, however, he was either in infirm health when he arrived in Charleston, or the climate there disagreed with him, for he was often indisposed, and lived only a few years. During the first year of his ministry, "the following persons were the elders or vestrymen of the church: Messrs. Johannes Swint, Melchior Werley, Philip Mensing, Abraham Speidel, Martin Müller, J. Shutterling, Jacob Breidell, John Kirchner, and Michael Kalteisen. One year later four wardens were elected, viz., Messrs. Joseph Kimmel, Henry Lindauer, Godman, and Jury.

"In 1768 the Hon. John Paul Grimpke presented the church with a silver plate of the weight of one pound, which was appropriated by the council for gathering the collections every Sunday. So also did Capt. Alexander Gillon, who had recently arrived from Germany, present to the church a pair of beautiful candlesticks, which were ordered to be placed on each side of the pulpit. He had also collected, whilst in Germany, £275 currency for the benefit of the church, which he offered to pay over, but the council requested him to retain it in his possession, and pay it out for the repairs and improvements of a house recently purchased by the congregation."

This fact, in connection with the additional one, that no charge was to be made to the pastor for house-rent, and the statement of Dr. Muhlenberg, indicate that the congregation possessed a parsonage at that time, which was rented out for the good of the church, when not in use by the pastor.

"In 1769 the officers made a contract with Mr. Speisseggir for a new organ, but no statement is given as to its cost."

A short time previous to Rev. Hahnbaum's death, a certain Master of Arts, Mr. Frederick Daser, who was yet very young, arrived in Charleston from the Duchy of Würtemberg, without credentials, without clothes or money, his trunk containing said articles, according to his declaration, having been stolen from him in Holland. A good-hearted elder of this congregation had compassion on him, paid his passage-money, and procured him respectable clothing suitable to his profession.

Pastor Hahnbaum having been sick a long time received this Artis Magister, with the consent of the vestry, as his vicar. He examined him, had him ordained, and afterwards also installed through two elders, and married him on his sick-bed, before his decease, to one of his own daughters, besides giving him the necessary books and skeletons of sermons.

After the death of Rev. Hahnbaum, which occurred February 10th, 1770, the vestry gave Magister Daser a conditional call for one year, with the hope that through "prayer, study, and temptation" (oratione, meditatione et tentatione), which was Luther's celebrated recipe for the making of a preacher, a theologian might yet be formed of him; but his young wife likewise conducted herself in a manner unbecoming a pastor's wife, besides being ignorant of housewifery, and destitute of the true ornament of a woman—1 Pet. 3:4; and he himself was light of body, light in spirit, and heavy in self-will and inordinate passions and affections; consequently, the fruits of such dispositions soon manifested themselves. The year having now expired, and having no other alternative, the congregation contracted with him to serve them three years longer.

The following account of this transaction, as gathered from the church records of this congregation by Mr. Jacob F. Schirmer, does not exactly agree with what is related above by Dr. Muhlenberg, but may, therefore, because taken from the records of the church, be all the more correct:

"The congregation appointed a committee to wait upon the pastor, and inquire upon what terms and what length of time he would be willing to serve them, and whether he would promise to be faithful, industrious, and conscientious in his walk and conversation, and to serve the flock as a faithful shepherd. Such questions, propounded to Rev. Daser after he had labored one year as pastor of that church, do not argue much in his favor, and yet the committee at the next meeting reported that the congregation appear to be perfectly satisfied with Pastor Daser, and that he on his part promises to discharge his duties faithfully, but he thought it unbecoming to enter into a regular contract between pastor and people, but was willing to serve them for three years at a quarterly payment of £500 currency. This was submitted to the congregation, and they finally agreed to engage Mr. Daser for two years, and that he receive £420 currency quarterly, still reserving to themselves the right, that if his conduct did not meet with their approbation, they were at liberty to discharge him, by giving him three months' notice. This arrangement was first objected to by the minister, but he finally agreed to it, and signed the agreement. He now requested his people to present him with a gown, which was accordingly ordered, and was made by Mr. Timrod.

"In 1773 Pastor Daser lodged a complaint against one of the members for his improper conduct towards him, and hopes he would treat him with more kindness, and not judge him so severely."

Dr. Muhlenberg states further: "However, as Rev. Daser had always discharged the duties of his office as a secondary business, and both he and his wife had digressed in several things, had frequented too much company, and became deeply involved in debt, &c., the vestry discharged him before the end of the third year. He had, however, a party of his own kind, who were offended at the vestry on account of his discharge, and who regarded his extravagance either as trifling or praiseworthy; yet they were far too weak to raise his salary without the aid of the elders and other well-disposed members." The vestry then wrote to the Reverend Consistorium of the Electorate of Hanover, supplicating that ecclesiastical body for a regular minister, but were informed that they could not be supplied from that source. Afterwards the elders and wardens addressed Dr. Muhlenberg, and besought him to send them an educated and exemplary pastor of the Pennsylvania Ministerium. The adherents of Mr. Daser also wrote to him anonymously at the same time, accusing the vestry, stating that Parson Daser had been a good preacher for them, and that the vestry had discharged him without the will and knowledge of the congregation, without cause and from motives of personal hatred, &c.

Dr. Muhlenberg answered both communications, informing them that, "God willing, he would make a journey to Ebenezer, in Georgia, in the fall, and would then also come to Charleston on his way to Georgia, and there personally investigate their affairs."

Accordingly Rev. Dr. Muhlenberg set sail for Charleston, South Carolina, August 27th, 1774, and arrived September 8th following. He was received and welcomed with the utmost kindness by the principal German families, as well as by many English inhabitants, and whilst there he exerted himself, as far as he could, to heal the unhappy division then existing in the German Lutheran congregation, caused by the irregularities of Pastor Daser, in which, as he was well adapted for this undertaking, and was frequently and justly entitled *the peacemaker*, he was quite successful.

In the mean time, which elapsed between Dr. Muhlenberg's answer to both parties in the congregation and his arrival in Charleston, Rev. Daser had procured a recommendation from the Lord Lieutenant-Governor of South Carolina, residing in Charleston, and also from the resident English Episcopal clergymen, to the Lord Bishop of London for Episcopal ordination, and afterwards to receive "a competent living in some country congregation, and thus become a dead weight in the English Established Church." However, before he had completed his arrangements for his contemplated visit to London, Rev. Dr. Muhlenberg arrived in Charleston; and then he hoped and expected, through the venerable Doctor's intercession, to be called by the vestry of St. John's Lutheran Church for life, and to receive an annual salary of £100 sterling.

But as soon as the Doctor had learned all the circumstances of Daser's own and his wife's conduct "from sensible and impartial persons," he could not conscientiously interest himself in Rev. Daser's behalf; "for," says the Doctor, "when a minister makes himself familiar with drunkards, flourishes with his sword at night along the streets, throws stones at windows, &c., and his wife frequents the theatre at night, leads in the dance at weddings, &c., we can easily imagine what impressions this must make upon well-meaning members! O Lord of Heaven, do Thou have mercy upon such a state of things!"

For the purpose of carrying out his design, Rev. Daser sailed in a vessel from Charleston to London, in order to obtain Episcopal ordination; many well-disposed persons subscribed liberally to the support of his wife and two small children during his absence; but a violent storm arose whilst the vessel was out at sea, and so injured her that she was obliged to return to Charleston. This providential occurrence had the effect of changing Rev. Daser's purpose, and may have induced him to become a wiser and better man, for his after-life appears to have been considerably changed.

It is also recorded of him, that during his absence at sea, the members of St. John's Church discovered that he had cut thirty-two leaves out of their church-record book, for which they took him to task immediately after his return, and he acknowledged that he had cut out and burned two leaves only. This accounts for the mutilation in that church-book as mentioned by Mr. Schirmer in his "Reminiscences of the Past."

Rev. Dr. Muhlenberg had no small difficulty in healing the dissensions of the congregation. He listened to all parties and heard their tale of grievances patiently, preached to them faithfully in the church every Sunday during his stay among them, called congregational meetings, and on the fourth Sunday of his visit administered the communion, and yet apparently with very little effect; for some still wanted Rev. Daser to be recalled, others desired the Rev. Mr. Martin, who now labored in the Saluda Fork, to return and be their pastor; whilst Dr. Muhlenberg, with many others, believed it to be the best policy to call an entire stranger from Germany or elsewhere, who could exert much more influence, and heal all divisions, than one who was already well known to the congregation. Acting upon this belief, and as a last resort, the Doctor drew up a petition to be sent to the "Society for Promoting Christian Knowledge," requesting it to send a pastor to this congregation, which reads as follows:

"We, the subscribers, for the time being, wardens, vestrymen, and contributing members of the German Lutheran St. John's Church and congregation in and about Charleston, in South Carolina, His Brittanick Majesty King George III's loyal and dutiful subjects, do send greeting to the most worthy and reverend fathers in God, Frederick Ziegenhagen, His Majesty's Chaplain in the German Chapel at St. James, Anastasius Freylinghäusen, Louis Schultz, D.D., and to the Directors of the East and West India Missions at Halle, Gustavus Burgmann of the Savoy, Rector, and William Pasche, Assistant in His Majesty's German Chapel, all worthy members of the venerable Society for Promoting Christian Knowledge; and do humbly request that," &c., &c. (here follows a description of the kind of minister that was desired, adding also this important clause), "who is able and willing to propagate the Gospel according to the foundations of the holy Apostles and

Prophets, whereof Christ Jesus is the Cornerstone, and to administer the holy sacraments, agreeably to the articles of our unaltered Augustan (Augsburg) Confession." (Then follow an enumeration of the other pastoral duties, salary promised, use of the parsonage rent free, precautionary promises against further divisions in the congregation, &c., concluding the whole with): "In witness whereof, we have hereunto interchangeably set our hands and seals at Charleston, in South Carolina, this 25th day of October, in the sixteenth year of His Majesty's reign, Anno Domini one thousand seven hundred and seventy-four." Evangelical Review, vol. i, pp. 401 and 402.

Dr. Muhlenberg had the satisfaction to see this petition signed by nearly all the members of the congregation. It was carried around to each one privately by several of the vestrymen, who by their personal influence, and the great desire for peace at last, enabled them thus to heal up the unhappy divisions then existing in the congregation.

As a matter of course, this petition terminated all hopes of Rev. F. Daser's ministrations in this congregation for that time; how he returned and served this people again, and under what circumstances, will also be made apparent.

The letter containing the petition of the congregation to the "reverend Fathers" in Europe for a pastor was sent to Rev. William Pasche in London; a merchant in Charleston, Mr. Mey, took it in charge, and forwarded it to Europe by the first opportunity.

The vestry also sent another letter to the Rev. J. N. Martin, beseeching him to serve the congregation once more until the new pastor would arrive, provided they should be successful in obtaining one from the Society in Europe. Rev. Martin consented to their request, as Dr. Muhlenberg states: "To-day an elder of the congregation showed me an answer from Rev. Mr. Martin, in which he states, that in compliance with the desire of the vestry, he will serve the Evangelical Congregation of this place one and a half years, and, Deo volente, will take charge the first Sunday in Advent. Thus, it appears, this object is gained, that the congregation will be supplied in the meanwhile, until it can be seen what will result from the critical strife between the Colonies and their angry mother, and whether the intended call to our reverend Fathers for an ordained minister will meet with the desired effect."

Under date of October 15, Dr. Muhlenberg states: "To-day I sent for the church records of this congregation, and recorded the actus ministeriales that occurred during my five weeks' sojourn in this place."

On the 26th of October, Dr. Muhlenberg took affectionate leave of this people, after having satisfactorily settled all the difficulties in the congregation. Many of his cherished friends attended him to the vessel which was to take him, together with his wife and daughter, who accompanied him, to

Savannah. The good that he had effected in Charleston was long remembered by many grateful hearts.

The church council agreed to pay Rev. J. N. Martin half of his travelling expenses to Charleston, and give him a fixed salary of £130 quarterly, which was accepted, and he returned once more to them as their pastor early in December, 1774, and labored faithfully among his people, beloved by all, and in harmony with the various opposing parties that had previously existed. About this time the German Friendly Society presented the church with a clock.

The time of engagement with Rev. Martin as pastor among the Lutherans in Charleston was now drawing to a close, and no hope as yet presented itself of obtaining a pastor from the Society for the Promotion of Christian Knowledge. Troubles of a more serious nature were gathering thick and fast. The high price of the necessaries of life, the struggles of the American Revolution which had caused it, the irregularity and final cessation of all commercial intercourse with Europe, made it now a matter of impossibility to obtain ministerial help from abroad; all of which induced the congregation in 1776 to enter into a new agreement with Rev. Martin, engaging him for two years longer, inasmuch also as they were well pleased with him as their pastor.

From an anniversary sermon, delivered by Rev. John Bachman, D.D., a glowing picture of the state of this church at that time is furnished us.

The Doctor informs us, that "during the stormy season of the Revolution, the Germans of this city had been the strenuous advocates and defenders of the rights of their adopted country. The German Füsilier Company was formed out of the original members of this congregation. They participated in the dangers and sufferings of the Revolution, and their captain fell at the siege of Savannah. Their pastor, the Rev. Mr. Martin, many of whose descendants are still living among us, on his refusal to pray for the king, was driven from his church and his property was confiscated. He was for a time placed under an arrest, and was afterwards compelled to leave the city, to which he did not return until the close of the war. In the meantime, the church was partially supplied by two other ministers, who were less exceptionable to our foreign rulers."

The two ministers, alluded to by Dr. Bachman, were the Rev. Christian Streitt, and Rev. Frederick Daser; however, it is not to be supposed that the former was a Tory in principle. In the memoir of Rev. Mr. Streitt, published in the Evangelical Review, vol. ix, p. 379, we are informed, that "during our Revolutionary struggle, Rev. Streitt was appointed Chaplain in the army, and was, for a season, in the service of the Third Virginia regiment. Afterwards he was settled as pastor of a congregation in Charleston, South Carolina. During the sacking of the city in 1780, he was taken prisoner by the British, and retained as such until exchanged. The cause of his capture was, undoubtedly, his unwavering patriotism and firm attachment to the principles of the American Revolution. It is a source of congratulation to the Lutheran Church, that those who ministered at her altars during that memorable and trying period, with scarcely an exception, were the devoted friends of their country."

The two pastors appear to have labored in friendly connection with each other, as the signatures of both are occasionally affixed to the records of the proceedings of the vestry, whilst at other times the signature of only one of them appears. This may have been permitted by Pastor Streitt and the vestry, from motives of respect to Rev. Daser, and for the purpose of conciliating him and his party.

Rev. Streitt entered upon the duties of his office in 1778. During the month of April of that year he preached several trial sermons, when he, soon afterwards, became the pastor. He was engaged to serve three years in this charge, but was taken away before the expiration of that term as a prisoner of war by the British. It was Rev. Mr. Streitt, says Ramsay, vol. ii, p. 23, who "first introduced divine service in the English language, so as to have one service in English every second or third Sunday." In July, 1782, he took charge of New Hanover Church, in Pennsylvania, and in 1785 he commenced his labors in Winchester, Virginia, where he remained to the close of his life.

An enormous rate of charges for ministerial duties appears to have been established by the vestry of St. John's Lutheran Church, in Charleston, in 1779, whilst the Rev. Mr. Streitt was the pastor. This was done on account of the very high price of provisions consequent upon the war, and was to remain in force only so long as such a state of things existed. They were as follows: For attending a funeral, £10; for preaching a funeral sermon, £30; and £50 for a marriage fee; of course, all in Carolina currency.

In the year 1781, Rev. F. Daser seems to have had sole charge of this church once more. This was the period of British rule in Charleston, and it is probable that he was the person who was "less exceptionable to our foreign rulers," as stated by Rev. Dr. Bachman. At all events he continued in office during the whole of that period, and resigned his charge of St. John's Church some time after peace was declared, viz., in July, 1786, when he removed to Orangeburg District, South Carolina.

Section 7. The Lutheran Church in Amelia Township, Orangeburg District (County), South Carolina.

In addition to the settlement of Germans and Swiss in and around Orangeburg village, which received the name of Orangeburg Township, so great was the influx of German emigrants there, that another township was soon laid out, northeast of Orangeburg, and adjoining it, which was named Amelia Township, where a Lutheran congregation was organized and a house of worship erected, that received the name St. Matthew's Church, and which has survived all the vicissitudes and encroachments of more than a century of time.

When it was organized and who was instrumental in effecting its organization can now be only a matter of conjecture. From the church-record book, kept by Rev. John Geissendanner, and still preserved by his descendants, we learn that he often visited the German settlers in Amelia Township, and performed ministerial acts among them; it is not improbable that he also occasionally preached there, but nothing is stated concerning a church-edifice and congregation having existed in Amelia Township during the first years of his ministry, and there is strong reason to believe that such was not the case, inasmuch as he, at that time, connected the records of baptisms, marriages, &c., of these people with those of the Orangeburg congregation. Nevertheless, as he must have labored there some nine years before any other German minister arrived, he may have been instrumental in organizing St. Matthew's Lutheran Church.

In the year 1747, the Rev. Joachim Zübly, D.D., removed from Frederica on St. Simon's Island, in Georgia, and labored in this community. He was a German Reformed minister, and is spoken of in the highest terms in Dr. Muhlenberg's journal, as follows: "Oct. 28. According to invitation, I and my family dined with Rev. Dr. Zübly, and I spent the afternoon very pleasantly with him in his library and study. He is an experienced, influential, learned, prudent, and very industrious man, of a sanguine temperament. He has a larger collection of fine books than any I have seen in America. The external appearance of his library and study is not surpassed by the most superior in Germany. All the books appear like trees that lose their fruit in autumn, so that innumerable printed leaves, whole and half tracts, manuscripts, &c., are scattered on the floor. It reminded me of the polyhistorian Markosius, and our venerable Bogatzky, whose studies are said to appear in such good order, that the most noted housewife dare not venture to arrange anything in them, lest she should put them in disorder. January 9th. Towards evening Rev. Dr. Zübly arrived here, who communicated to us in the evening his manuscript Latin dissertation, 'Pro gradu doctoris,' which will shortly be printed. January 10th. Towards evening Rev. Dr. Zübly returned from Purysburg, where he had preached in English, and refreshed us during the evening with Christian conversation."

During the ministrations of Dr. Zübly in Amelia Township, he doubtless was instrumental in effecting the organization of "The German Calvinistic Church of St. John on the Fourhole," which was incorporated by that name by the State Legislature in 1788, but is now no longer in existence, and its members and their descendants have long since been mostly absorbed by the Lutheran churches in the vicinity. Fourhole is the name of a creek in Amelia Township, which with the fact that this (St. John's) Church is clustered together with the two Lutheran churches located in Orangeburg District (County), in one and the same bill of incorporation, locates that church in Amelia Township, or immediately below it, in Orangeburg County, which encompasses all that territory.

Rev. Dr. Zübly afterwards removed to Savannah, Georgia; where Dr. Muhlenberg met him on his way to Ebenezer.

In the year 1760, the Rev. John George Friederichs, the founder of the first Lutheran church in Charleston, commenced to labor in Amelia Township, and remained in this pastorate for a long time, being still at that post of duty on October 15th, 1774, when Rev. Dr. Muhlenberg gives the following account of him:

"I received an agreeable letter from Rev. John George Friederichs, Lutheran minister in Amelia Township, one hundred miles in the country, dated October 15th, 1774, in which he states, that he learned of my arrival in Charleston, first from Rev. Hochheimer, who traveled through here, and was assured of it by letter of September 20th ult., which afforded him very great pleasure, and induced him to prepare for a journey to Charleston, but that he was prevented by sickness and the fear of not meeting me here, especially as I had intimated in my letter that I intended, God willing, to continue my journey to Georgia in October. But that he would request my host, Mr. Kimmel, to inform him when I returned to Charleston, and then, if we lived, visit me, &c., &c. The person bringing the letter returning to-morrow, I answered his letter and sought to encourage him to fight the good fight, to keep the faith, and to finish the course, &c. He sustains a good character for sound doctrine and exemplary conduct among informed persons; he has no family, and is satisfied with the necessaries of life.

"A laborer, standing thus alone in the wilderness among rude people, must be much encouraged when he receives unexpectedly a few lines of comfort from a fellow-suffering and tempted cross-bearer, as is manifest from his answer to my first letter. It is written, 'Woe to him that is alone.'"

How long afterwards Rev. Friederichs labored in this charge cannot be ascertained, but it is presumed that he remained there in the faithful discharge of his duty to the close of his life. Perhaps he did not live long after Dr. M.'s visit to Charleston, for nothing is further recorded of him, and his name does not appear among the list of ministers in South Carolina, who formed the Corpus Evangelicum in 1787; and in 1786 another minister had taken charge of the pastorate in Amelia Township.

It was during the ministry of Rev. J. G. Friederichs in this community, that a colony of Germans came from Maine and settled in Orangeburg District, accompanied by their pastor, the Rev. Mr. Cilley or Silly; but, inasmuch as the records of this colonization of Germans do not harmonize with each other, they are inserted here without comment, leaving the reader to form his own conclusions.

J. C. Hope, Esq., speaking of the Lutheran settlers in Orangeburg District, says: "In 1763 a colony of German Lutherans came from Maine, accompanying their pastor Silly, and joined their brethren in South Carolina; but in time the most of these returned."

Rev. Dr. Hazelius' statement is: "Rev. Mr. Cilley arrived in South Carolina with a colony of German emigrants from Maine, in the year 1773. But of his labors and success no accounts can be found."

The statement in "The Javelin," pp. 170 and 171, is as follows: "The disappointment and suffering which they were presently made to endure in consequence of the deceptions practiced upon them, were trying in the extreme. And to all their other troubles, the Indians fell upon them also, and destroyed many lives and much substance. Ill-treated, robbed, wronged and disappointed, many of them, under the guidance of a Moravian clergyman, left Muscungus (Maine), and emigrated to Carolina, in 1773."

Section 8. The Lutheran Churches in Saxe-Gotha Township, Lexington District (County), South Carolina.

Saxe-Gotha Township having been settled as early as 1737, principally by Germans and Swiss, who continued to arrive there for several years following, soon became well populated by these colonists, considering the difficulties of emigration and state of the country at that time. The German Reformed settlers, as already stated, were supplied with a pastor, who labored among them from the year 1739 to the close of his life, a period of more than fifty years, for he was still living in

1789. The Lutherans were not so fortunate as their German Reformed brethren, in being thus early supplied with the regular means of grace. At the time of Dr. Muhlenberg's visit to Charleston, in 1774, there were two Lutheran ministers laboring in Saxe-Gotha, the Rev. Lewis Hochheimer, at Sandy Run, and the Rev. J. N. Martin, in the Saluda Fork, and it is safely presumed that they were the first Lutheran ministers who labored in that township; at all events, it is an ascertained fact, recorded in the Urlsperger Reports, that no Lutheran minister had labored there previous to the year 1750, when a petition was sent to the pastors of Ebenezer, Georgia, signed by two hundred and eighty Lutherans, beseeching those pastors to send them a minister; yet their petition was not regarded, and they were left without a pastor of their own faith. How long they continued in this spiritually destitute condition is not known, but it is more than probable, judging from the condition of the colony and of the Church at the time of the criminal conduct of the Weberites, in 1760, that the Lutherans of Saxe-Gotha were then still destitute of the means of grace. Seven years later Rev. Martin removed from Charleston and commenced his labors in the Saluda Fork, but no records inform us at what time Rev. Hochheimer commenced his ministry in the Sandy Run Church.

The members of the Lutheran Church of that portion of Saxe-Gotha bordering on the Congaree River, known better as the Sandy Run settlement, although privileged to hear the Gospel in their native language from the lips of the German Reformed minister, Rev. Christian Theus, still felt it their duty to build a church for themselves, where they could worship God according to the principles of their own faith; but at what time they took the proper steps to secure this object, although so much discouraged by Rev. Bolzius, is not known. Nevertheless, as the Urlsperger Reports, which gives us the Church news generally, does not mention this fact up to the year 1760 (the latest date of the Ebenezer pastors' diary), and as the Cherokee War would naturally interfere with all ecclesiastical enterprises, it can be safely inferred, that the building of the Lutheran church at Sandy Run, probably the earliest erected Lutheran Church in Saxe-Gotha, was not commenced before the year 1765.

Nine years later we have a brief record from Dr. Muhlenberg's journal, as follows: "A visit from Rev. Lewis Hochheimer, 120 miles from here, at Sandy Run, who related to me the events of his life, and offered to assist me in preaching next Sunday." "Sunday, September 18th. In the afternoon I went again to church and heard Rev. Hochheimer preach from Psalm 50 : 21: 'These things hast thou done and I kept silence,' quite edifying and systematic." "Monday, September 19th. Rev. Hochheimer took leave, and promised to give me a correct description of some Lutheran congregations in this neighborhood." These records indicate that a Lutheran church existed at Sandy Run at that time, and that the congregation had a pastor, the Rev. Lewis Hochheimer.

The early settlers along the Congaree River selected their lands and erected their dwellings very near the river banks, where they could obtain the richest lands, and enjoy all the advantages of water transportation, fishing, &c.; but where they, on the other hand, suffered much from the effects of the miasma arising from the river and its numerous swamps. Nevertheless, they clung to their original settlements and homes until disease had made repeated inroads upon their robust constitutions, and death had greatly diminished their original number.

Wherever they had located their houses and homes, there likewise did they erect their church, about three miles from the present situation of Salem Church, Sandy Run. The old graveyard, which was not far removed from the church, is still pointed out under the appellation of "The Church Field;" and it is stated that so swampy or spongy is the condition of the land, that many a coffin was lowered in its grave which had become half filled with water, so that the coffin became quite covered with that element; and all efforts to remedy the evil at that place were unavailing. Yet it did not occur to the members of the church until a long time afterwards, to remove the church and graveyard to a more elevated situation.

It is to be lamented that we know so little of Rev. Hochheimer's history; when he became pastor, how long he remained at Sandy Run, what the condition of the church was during the Revolution, who succeeded Rev. Hochheimer, when and where he died and was buried? all these are questions which, it is feared, will never be answered, and these answers, with other interesting facts connected with them, may lie forever buried in the oblivion of the past.

Three Lutheran congregations composed at one time the Saluda charge: Zion's or Mount Zion, on Twelve-mile Creek, St. Peter's, on Eighteen-mile Creek, and Bethel, on High Hill Creek. They are always spoken of in the old records of their church-books as having formed one pastorate; but how far back this arrangement extended cannot now be ascertained. Salem Church, on Hollow Creek, was added to this pastorate at a much later date, probably some time at the beginning of the present century.

In the year 1767 the Rev. John Nicholas Martin commenced to labor in the Fork of the Saluda and Broad Rivers, and remained there until the close of the year 1774, when he was recalled to Charleston, as temporary pastor of St. John's Lutheran Church.

During the Revolutionary War, it is probable that these churches were vacant, as no Lutheran minister was residing then in that part of South Carolina, unless, perhaps, the Rev. Lewis Hochheimer of Sandy Run was still living, and occasionally visited them.

Section 9. Other German Churches in South Carolina.

Newberry District (County) was only partially settled by Germans, and at a period succeeding the colonization of Saxe-Gotha. A number of German churches existed there in 1788, which were incorporated at that time by legislative enactment, the names of which were: "The German Lutheran Church of Bethlehem, on Forest's (Fust's) Ford;" "The German Lutheran Church of St. Jacob, on Wateree Creek;" "The German Protestant Church of Bethany, on Green Creek;" and "The German Lutheran Church of St. Martin." The last one mentioned was not organized until after the Revolutionary War. (See minutes of Corpus Evangelicum.) When these congregations were organized, and whether they had a pastor previous to the Revolutionary period, is not known, and the probability is that no minister labored there at that time. The first pastor ministering there, of whom we have any knowledge, was the Rev. Frederick Joseph Wallern, whose name occurs in the first minutes of the Corpus Evangelicum, in 1787, but of the date of his arrival in Newberry nothing is said.

At Hard Labor Creek, Abbeville District (County), there was also a Lutheran Church, likewise incorporated in 1788, and named St. George; but unless the German settlers brought their pastor with them from Germany, of which nothing is said in the records of their colonization, it is exceedingly doubtful whether they were supplied with the means of grace in the German language previous to the Revolution, inasmuch as this German settlement was only made in

1764, eleven years before the breaking out of the war.

Concerning the other settlements of Germans in South Carolina very little can be said during this period, except that which has already been stated; the one on Indian Field Swamp, fifty miles from Charleston, had no minister for some time: they were supplied with the labors of a German preacher in 1774, whether Lutheran or Reformed is not stated, and even his name is not mentioned; the congregation worshiped in a barn belonging to Philip Eisenman.

Dr. Muhlenberg speaks of the condition of this German settlement as follows: "My kind host received a visit to-day from an intimate German family of our denomination from old Indian Swamp, fifty miles in the country. The man is named Philip Eisenman, has a farm of his own, but no negroes. He and his wife cultivate the place themselves, in the sweat of their brows. They lamented the want of schools and churches in their neighborhood. He has arranged his barn for public worship, and they have accepted as preacher a young man lately arrived from Germany, and who might answer for a schoolmaster. He writes his sermon through the week, and reads it on Sunday, and even reads with it the Lord's prayer also, being yet young, and excusing himself with: 'The Lord not having gifted him with a retentive memory.' The credentials brought by him from Germany are — a black suit of clothes. The remaining fragments, to wit, band, &c., he obtained from his countryman, Rev. Daser. The two honest old people complained that his preaching was so meagre and dry, and left the heart entirely unaffected, and they wanted something, therefore, more to awaken and nourish the heart."

It is not known at what time these people succeeded in building their church, but it is not very probable that they accomplished this undertaking until after the Revolutionary War, inasmuch as they had no church at the time of Dr. Muhlenberg's visit, which was only a few months previous to the battle of Lexington, Mass. In 1788 this settlement had a church organization and a house of worship, incorporated under the name of "The German Protestant Church of St. George, on Indian Field Swamp."

The German Protestant congregation in Richland District (County), near the Fairfield line, incorporated at the same time by the name of "The German Protestant Church of Appii Forum, on Cedar Creek," was established during this period. Mills, in his Statistics, p. 722, says: "The Presbyterians were the first religious society established in the (Richland) District; they erected a church on the banks of Cedar Creek anterior to the Revolution." Dr. Howe, in his "History of the Presbyterian Church in South Carolina," p. 494, says: "It must have been of the German Reformed connection, and was ministered to by Rev. William Dubard, who died of the small-pox in the city of Charleston, near the close of the Revolutionary

War." Dr. Howe thinks it probable that this was the church which became incorporated by legislative enactment, in 1788, under the name of "The German Protestant Church of Appii Forum, on Cedar Creek."

From the memoranda furnished Dr. Howe, p. 495, by A. F. Dubard, of Cedar Creek, Richland, we learn that "the traditions of the neighborhood speak of it as having continued in existence into the next century, the successors of Mr. Dubard being a clergyman by the name of Penegar, another by the name of Houck, and another by the name of Loutz. The house of worship was built of logs, with an earth floor."

"Our informant speaks of Mr. Loutz as a man of education and influence, who visited this church from North Carolina, where his residence was. The communion seasons were to his mind, in his youth, scenes of great solemnity. The communicants, approaching the table one after another, received the elements of bread and wine in a standing posture, and passed away from the table with clasped hands and uplifted eyes."

"This church had occasional preaching by others, but became extinct as a Presbyterian church of the German Reformed order, and the neighborhood became the seat of a Methodist church and congregation. No traces of this church now remain."

The Rev. Mr. Houck, or Hauck, is mentioned in the minutes of the Lutheran Synod of North Carolina, A.D. 1812, p. 7, as a candidate for the ministry, who desired to be ordained by that body as a minister of the German Reformed Church; "but this Synod, after due consideration, concluded that they could not consistently do anything in this matter."

Dr. Muhlenberg mentions the name of a Rev. Mr. Hausile as having preached twice in the German Lutheran Church of Charleston "a few years ago," but whether he became permanently located in South Carolina, and where he labored is not known.

The following is a list of all the German ministers who were laboring in South Carolina immediately preceding the Revolutionary War, as far as the records in the writer's possession appear to indicate, namely: 1. Rev. John N. Martin, pastor of the Lutheran church in Charleston; 2. Rev. F. Daser, no charge, but still residing in Charleston; 3. Rev. ——, preacher at Indian Field Swamp; 4. Rev. John G. Friederichs, pastor of the Lutheran churches in Amelia Township, Orangeburg District; 5. Rev. Lewis Hochheimer, pastor of Salem Lutheran Church, Sandy Run; 6. Rev. Christian Theus, German Reformed pastor in Saxe-Gotha Township; 7. Rev. Christian Streit, pastor, for a short time during the Revolution, of the Lutheran church in Charleston; and although the names of Revs. Cilley and Hausile are also mentioned, nothing special is known concerning them; 8. Rev. William Dubard, German Reformed pastor at Cedar Creek Church, Richland District.

Section 10. Early History of St. John's Lutheran Church, Salisbury, N. C.

It is a cheerful task for the writer of historical narrative to enter upon a field where the earliest records are abundant, carefully made, and well preserved. This is the case in regard to nearly all the churches in North Carolina, whose original church record-books and titles to church property are still extant, and the reports of whose pastors' labors, like those of the Pennsylvania and Georgia ministers, had been sent to Germany, and were published there.

St. John's Lutheran Church, in Salisbury, North Carolina, is first brought to view, and was doubtless the first Lutheran congregation organized in that Province, under the following circumstances:

The German citizens of that place organized themselves into a congregation in the days of King George III, and several years before the Revolution, when Salisbury was as yet denominated "a township," containing but few dwellings and a small number of inhabitants. One of the wealthy citizens residing there, John Lewis Beard, a member of the Lutheran Church, was bereaved by death of a beloved daughter. Whether the township of Salisbury could then boast of a regular "God's acre" is not known, and the probability is that the mortal remains of departed ones were, at that early period, deposited without many religious services in the grounds of each landholder in whose family or family connection the death occurred, a custom thus early established from the force of circumstances, and still reverently observed by many in various parts of this country.

In the same manner was the body of Mr. Beard's daughter laid in the silent tomb, opened on her father's town property, in a lot containing nearly an acre, and well selected for the quiet repose of the dead. However, the question then naturally arose, Shall that hallowed spot, consecrated by the repose of the dead and the tears of fond survivors, ever be disturbed by the march of civilization?

To prevent such an occurrence, the forefather of the Beard family in Salisbury made and executed the following land title, donating the grounds upon which his daughter slept the quiet slumber of the dead, to the German Lutheran Church, —— the Church of his choice. The original title is still preserved, and enables us to glance at the peculiar customs of that day in making conveyance of property, as well as to learn the condition of the Church at that time.

Leaving out all useless and redundant matter, it reads as follows:

"This indenture, made September 9, 1768, between John Lewis Beard, of Salisbury, in the County of Rowan, and Province of North Carolina (butcher), of the one part, and Michael Brown, Michael More, Caspar Guenther, and Peter Reeb, Trustees of the Evangelical Lutheran congregation in the township of Salisbury, of the county and province aforesaid, of the other part, *Witnesseth*, that for and in consideration of the sum of five shillings, &c., &c., and for other good causes, him thereunto moving, hath granted, &c., &c., unto the said trustees of the said congregation aforesaid, and to their successors in office forever" (here follows the boundaries and description of the lot, containing 144 square poles), "unto the German Lutheran congregation in and about Salisbury, for to erect and build thereon a church, for the only proper use and behoof of the said German Lutheran congregation forever" (here follows a long description of the manner the vacancies in the trustees' office are to be filled, granting also the use of the church to) "the High Church of England, and to the Reformed Calvin ministers at such time as the said Lutheran minister doth not want to perform divine service in said church," &c., &c. Signed and sealed by John Lewis Beard, in presence of John Braly, Andreas Betz, and Valentine Mauny.

The historical facts derived from this conveyance and from other sources are the following: In the year 1768, Salisbury had as yet no house of worship of any kind within its precincts; ministers of the Gospel may have often or occasionally preached in the private or public houses of the place, and persons may have worshiped in other churches in the country, but no church existed in Salisbury at that early period.

Although trustees had been elected for the Lutheran congregation there, indicating that some kind of organization had been effected, yet regular worship could not have been held among the members, as no Lutheran minister was then laboring in all North Carolina; all these arrangements were made preparatory to, and anticipating the regular administration of the means of grace.

The Lutheran church in Salisbury is the oldest church established in the place, and from other sources we learn that the congregation had a log church edifice erected on the lot granted by Mr. Beard, in order that they might secure the land to the congregation as stipulated by the grantor, in which he also rendered them every assistance in his power. This log church was built soon after the lot of land was granted.

This deed seems to have answered the threefold purpose of a title to the land, a charter, conferring upon the congregation certain rights and privileges, and a code of by-laws for its government, and thus has the appearance of a very peculiar legal document.

The first pastor of this church was the Rev. Adolph Nussmann, a ripe and thorough scholar, and, what is still better, a devoted, self-sacrificing, and pious Christian. He came from Germany in 1773 under circumstances related in Section 13, succeeding, but did not labor long in this congregation. He removed to Dutch Buffalo Creek Church, now better known as St. John's Lutheran Church, Cabarrus County. He was succeeded by Rev. Godfrey Arndt, who had charge of Organ Church at the same time, but soon removed to the west side of the Catawba River.

The Lutherans at Salisbury were energetic participators in the Revolutionary struggle, arraying themselves on the side of liberty and independence, as can be seen by referring to Wheeler's History of North Carolina, where the names of Beard, Barringer, Beekman, Mull and others, frequently occur in connection with those who labored and fought for their country's welfare and honor.

During this trying period the Lutheran church in Salisbury was vacant for a few years, but was visited by Revs. Nussmann and Arndt as often as the circumstances of the country would admit.

Section 11. Early History of Organ Church, Rowan County, N. C.

The proper name of this congregation is "Zion's Church," but there are few persons, even among its members, who are acquainted with its true name. The fact that it was, until recently, the only Lutheran church in North Carolina which was possessed of such an instrument of music, has given it this sobriquet, by which it is generally known and so called in all the records of the Lutheran Church in the State. The old organ—a relic of the past—is still there, but its voice is no longer heard in the worship of the congregation; like the voices of its contemporaries, who are now mouldering in the adjoining graveyard, its spirit of music is fled, and the external remains, encompassing a number of broken and disarranged pipes, are all that is left to remind us of a former age, a former congregation, and of a master whom it once honored. How forcibly, under such circumstances, do the following lines of Moore's Melodies strike the mind!

> "The harp that once, through Tara's halls,
> The soul of music shed,
> Now hangs as mute on Tara's walls,
> As if that soul were fled."

The history of this congregation is gathered from the old German church-book, which is still carefully preserved, and the historic records are made therein by one of the first pastors, Rev. C. A. G. Storch, from which a correct idea may be obtained of the past transactions of the people who worshiped there.

The first German settlers of that portion of Rowan County, along Second Creek, came from Pennsylvania, and were members of the Lutheran and German Reformed Churches, but in numbers far too few to erect a church for the sole use of either denomination; hence they concluded to build a temporary house of worship to be owned by themselves jointly, and which was called "The Hickory Church." According to the statement of the late Rev. J. A. Linn, this church occupied the site on which St. Peter's Lutheran Church now stands, and was built by permission on the land of Mr. Fullenwider, who, however, never gave the two congregations a title for this spot of ground, as the church was considered a temporary building only, to be occupied alternately by both these denominations, each of which expected to erect their own house of worship at a later period. The term

"Hickory Church" also indicates of what perishable material this house of worship was built, and was in keeping with the original idea. It was soon left unoccupied, and in course of a few years it crumbled into ruins. More than half a century later a want for a church to be built on this same site was again felt, when St. Peter's Lutheran Church was organized, and a more durable building was erected.

As was the case with all the first German settlers in North Carolina, who did not bring their pastor with them, so likewise were the Lutheran members of the Hickory Church destitute of the means of grace for some length of time, and as no other hope of obtaining a regularly ordained minister of the Gospel presented itself, the members were resolved to send to Germany for a pastor. In this manner they secured the services of Rev. Adolph Nussmann as their pastor, and Gottfried Arndt as their schoolteacher.

The new pastor preached but one year in the Hickory Church to both denominations, after which some dissension arose, and a majority of the Lutherans then resolved to build a church for themselves, and in this manner originated Zion's Church, better known as Organ Church. The members of the German Reformed Church soon followed the example of their Lutheran brethren, and likewise built a new church on another location, which they named Grace Church, but is more frequently called "The Lower Stone Church," on account of its position lower down the stream above mentioned, and built of the same material as Organ Church.

Before the building of Organ Church was quite completed, Rev. A. Nussmann left this congregation, and went as pastor to Buffalo Creek Church, in Cabarrus County.

The congregation, which now had a church but no pastor, sent their schoolteacher, Gottfried Arndt, to be ordained to the office of the ministry, in the year 1775. He served them through the trying period of the Revolution, until 1786, when he moved to the Catawba River, residing in Lincoln County, and labored in that field to the close of his life.

Section 12. Early History of St. John's Church, Cabarrus County, N. C.

Cabarrus County is known in the early records as Mecklenburg County, in which it was included, but was formed into a separate county in the year 1792. The eastern portion of it was settled entirely by Germans, the most of whom came from Pennsylvania.

During the Revolutionary War, a number of Hessian soldiers deserted from the British army at Savannah, after the siege of that place, and found their way to the German settlement on Dutch Buffalo Creek, intermarried with these settlers, and were thus permanently located there. They, in a measure, supplied the loss of so many young men in that settlement, who had sacrificed their lives in the service of their country. This colony suffered severely during that dark and bloody period. Although no regular army assailed these Germans, or passed through their settlement, yet they had to contend much with the Tories, whilst many of their young men enlisted as soldiers in the American army. One family, named Schwartzwälder (Blackwelder), had seven sons, four of whom were in the battle of Camden, South Carolina, and two or three of them found soldiers' graves upon that battlefield, having lost their lives in the service of their country. Others shared the same fate, whilst those at home had several skirmishes with the Tories. The following account of the action, which one of these early settlers took in the war for independence, is given by one of his grandsons, and may not be uninteresting:

"John Paul Barringer, who took an active part in all public matters, was known as Captain Barringer long before the Revolution, and during this war, though too old for regular service, took the lead against the Tories in his section, and so odious did he become to them from his efficient and unceasing efforts against them, that they surprised him in his bed at night, and posted him off as a prisoner to Camden, where he remained in confinement several months, if not during the remainder of the war. In the meantime the Tories stole and destroyed most of his property, and left his family, then afflicted with small-pox, in a most helpless and distressing condition."

In this manner did the greater number of these

German settlers suffer, inasmuch as a special hatred was manifested towards them by their enemies during the war, since they were residents of that patriotic county, whose citizens had first declared their sentiments of independence in the Mecklenburg Declaration, May 20th, 1775. Some one or two German names from this section of that county may be distinguished as signers of that Declaration.

Governor Tryon, who came to this part of North Carolina on a visit, with the view of again conciliating matters in favor of the existing government, some few years before the Revolution, when the Regulators had enlivened the minds of the people against the tyrannical authorities of the Province, arrived in the settlement on Dutch Buffalo Creek, and lodged with Captain Barringer, who was well known for his influence and hospitality.

"The story is," continues his grandson, "that the Governor appeared in full uniform, with a cocked hat and sword, drank freely of the Captain's rich wine, which was always kept on hand, condescended to try his skill in mowing the green meadows of Dutch Buffalo, and left fully persuaded, so kind and generous was the entertainment, that he had not a stancher friend in all the country as 'the gallant Dutchman.' But in this he was, of course, sadly disappointed."

In the old church record-book, and in the old minutes of the North Carolina Synod, the congregation of St. John's is known as "Dutch Buffalo

Creek Church," because its members were principally located along that stream of water, and because their first place of worship and their first graveyard had its location near the same creek, three miles distant from its present situation. The first church edifice was, of course, exceedingly plain, made of unhewn logs, and served the people the double purpose of a schoolhouse and place of worship. Both the German Reformed and Lutherans worshiped in the same building for a certain period of time, after which a more commodious building was erected for the united worship of the two denominations, about half a mile removed from the location of the present church edifice. This second building, in point of architectural style, was but little better than the former, except that it was somewhat larger, and fitted for the exclusive use of Divine worship.

About the year 1771, the members of the Lutheran Church, at the suggestion of Captain John Paul Barringer, separated themselves from their German Reformed brethren, and built their own church on the site of the upper portion of the present graveyard. The work was undertaken by Daniel Jarrett, whilst Captain Barringer acted as the building committee. This church was built chiefly at his own expense, and out of gratitude to him the congregation had a pew constructed for the special benefit of himself and family, which was somewhat raised above the others, located in a prominent place in the church, and inclosed. He was a true-hearted and thorough Lutheran, devotedly attached to his church, and seemed to have been a defender of the rights of the German settlers there, and a leading man among them.

It was not until the year 1774, that the congregation obtained their first pastor, who had been laboring about a year and some months at Organ Church and in Salisbury, and who had been brought to America by a deputation sent from Organ and St. John's Churches to Germany, in 1773. He located himself about one and a half miles east of St. John's Church, on a tract of land of his own entry or purchase, and labored faithfully all the remaining days of his life among this people. The congregation also secured about the same time the services of a Mr. Friesland as their schoolteacher.

On the 22d of October, 1782, three benevolent members of the church council, Jacob Fegert, Marx Haus, and Jacob Thieme, paid the sum of fifty shillings, the accustomed rate, for one hundred acres of government land, on a portion of which the church had already been built, and entered it "in trust for the congregation of Dutch Buffalo Meeting-House." This wise procedure manifested considerable forethought in those first members of the church, for the land is now valuable, and has been of much service to the congregation.

A short time before the close of the war, which had already so sadly affected all the peaceful pursuits of life, and disarranged much of the affairs of the church, when the prospect of peace and prosperity reanimated all hearts, a constitution was adopted for the government of this congregation. It is written in the German language, and in Pastor Nussmann's handwriting, inscribed in the antiquated church-book, still carefully preserved.

This constitution was compiled, as stated by Rev. Nussmann, from the "Kirchenordnung of our Evangelical brethren in Smyrna, and the one used in England and Holland, but made suitable to the circumstances of our country." From this constitution, which is exceedingly strict, both in doctrine and discipline, the following facts are gathered:

1. That the church was placed under the supervision of the Consistory of Hanover and the University of Göttingen, and that, whenever the congregation should be in want of a pastor, application was to be made to that Consistory or University. However, in case of war or other untoward circumstances, when correspondence would necessarily be interrupted, the congregation was then to apply to the ministry in connection with the Pennsylvania Synod.

2. That the pastor was *bound to confess himself with heart and mouth to the symbolical books of our Evangelical Church.*

3. That the pastor was to be in regular correspondence with the brethren of the same faith in Europe; that he was to send them minute reports of church matters every six weeks, asking aid and counsel whenever the circumstances required it, as soon as the long-wished-for peace would once

more open conveniences for correspondence between Europe and America.

4. A regular support for the pastor and schoolteacher was expected from the members, and before they could engage the services of either, it was made binding upon them to state the positive annual amount of salary for their support in the written call. A portion of the schoolteacher's salary consisted in the use of a certain amount of good land, which the members were to cultivate for him, and also to gather the grain, hay, &c., into his barn, when the proper season arrived.

5. Provision was also made for orphan children and such other persons, as were in needy circumstances.

6. All marriages had to be proclaimed, according to the custom of the country, three Sundays in succession before the marriage could take place, and none except the minister was allowed to perform the ceremony.

7. The church council were usually designated, according to the recommendation of this constitution, as adjunct executors in all wills and testaments, for the purpose of taking special care of the children of the deceased in their religious education.

8. The following order of service for public worship in the sanctuary was established:

a. A hymn of praise.

b. A collect, or the epistle for the day.

c. The principal hymn.

d. Reading of the Scriptures.

e. The creed, or a short Sunday hymn.

f. The sermon.

g. The singing of a few verses.

h. A short catechetical exercise.

i. A long prayer, suitable either to the catechization, sermon, or other circumstances.

k. The benediction.

l. The concluding verse of the principal hymn.

9. The liturgy adopted by this congregation was the one used in the German Lutheran Court Chapel of St. James, in London; and the Marburg hymn-book, which was reprinted for the use of the churches in Germantown and Philadelphia, was also introduced in the worship of this congregation.

Section 13. The Delegation sent from North Carolina to Europe for Pastors and Teachers, and the subsequent organization of the Helmstaedt Mission Society.

The German settlements in the interior of North Carolina, although commenced in the year 1750, were of very gradual growth, owing to the peculiar manner in which they were made. They were not favored with shiploads of emigrants direct from Germany; their increase of colonists depended on the overland route, made in wagons and on foot, from the Province of Pennsylvania. It took all of fifteen or twenty years before these settlers were sufficiently numerous to form themselves into congregations, but after these congregations were organized, the urgent want of the regular administration of the word and sacraments was also felt. The slow but gradual increase of these German settlements will account for the apparent tardiness which these settlers manifested in sending for ministers of the Gospel, and the manner in which they journeyed to North Carolina made it almost impossible for them to take their pastors with them. But after the harvest was ripe for the sickle, where to obtain pastors for their newly organized congregations, that was a question not easily answered. The Synod of Pennsylvania had no ministers to spare, for even in that favored Province the want of ministers was greatly felt, having to apply constantly to the Church in Germany to supply the wants of their ever-increasing German population and churches, and to go farther South for ministerial help was utterly useless, for there the want and scarcity was still greater.

In view of this great want, felt everywhere among the Germans in America at this time, Dr. Muhlenberg expresses himself as follows (Evang. Review, vol. i, p. 414): "True, enough teachers and false apostles may be found, who pervert the word of God, and manufacture the most baneful sects with it! O how necessary, useful, and consolatory would it not be, if we were able to erect a long-wished-for institution, in which Catechets could be trained who would be capable and willing to teach school during the week, and to deliver a discourse (Vortrag) on the Lord's day. It would not be necessary to torment such subjects many years with foreign languages; it would be sufficient if they possessed mother wit, a compendious knowledge and experience of the marrow and sap of theology, could write a tolerable hand, understood their vernacular (German) and the English tongues, and the elements of Latin. They should also possess a robust bodily constitution, able to endure every kind of food and weather, and especially have a heart that sincerely loves Jesus and his lambs.

"In America there are schools, gymnasiums, academies, and universities enough (and their number is multiplying with the increased taste) for lawyers, notaries, physicians, philosophers, candidates for benefices, critics, orators, sea captains, merchants, artists, &c., &c., but who helps the half-dead man that has fallen among thieves, and lies bleeding? Priests and Levites pass by on the other side, for their law forbids them to touch anything unclean. And if occasionally some be found who profess themselves Samaritans, they have, notwithstanding, ofttimes unrighteous objects; bind up, it is true, the wounds of the helpless sufferer, and set him on their own beast, but, at the same time, expect as a recompense to own him entirely and to lead him to their sectarian inn, when the proverb is verified, 'The remedy is worse than the disease,' as can be shown by many examples. This matter belongs to the *pia desideria* (pious desires), which are more easily accomplished in theory than in practice."

The newly organized Lutheran congregations in North Carolina had only one other resource remaining, and that was—to send to Europe for pastors and teachers for this new and promising field of labor among the Germans in this Province; and these congregations were not slow in making this resource available, as may be seen by examining the records of the old church-book belonging to Organ Church. They well knew that to send letters or petitions to Europe for pastors and teachers would accomplish but little, hence they resolved to send a delegation, who could make personal appeals to the hearts of their brethren of the same faith, describe the wants of the churches in North Carolina, and answer any question relative to the country in which they resided, support of the pastor, &c. Accordingly, in the year 1772, Christopher Rintelmann, from Organ Church, in Rowan County, and Christopher Layrle, from St. John's Church, in Mecklenburg County, were sent as a delegation to Europe, for the purpose of applying to the Consistory Council (Consistorialrath) of Hanover, in Germany, for a supply of ministers of the gospel and school-teachers, for the various Lutheran congregations then organized in North Carolina. The reason is also stated, why the delegation were instructed to apply to the proper authorities in Hanover in preference to any other place or kingdom: "Because at that time North Carolina, as well as all the other free American States, was under the jurisdiction of the king of England, who was at the same time elector of Hanover."

These commissioners traveled first to London, and from thence they journeyed to Hanover, and there, in accordance with their instructions, to bring at least one pastor and a schoolteacher with them, and through the kind efforts of "the late Consistory counsellor, Götten," they obtained the Rev. Adolph Nussmann as their pastor, and Mr. Gottfried Arndt as schoolteacher; both of whom arrived safely in North Carolina in 1773.

But this was not all the good which these commissioners effected, for by their faithful representations of the condition and want of the churches, the Lutheran congregations in North Carolina, as already seen from the constitution of St. John's Church, were placed under the supervision of the Consistory of Hanover and the University of Göttingen, from which they were promised and expected both pecuniary assistance and a further supply of ministers and teachers; and had it not been that the Revolutionary War broke out shortly afterwards, which stopped all communication with Europe for a period of nearly eight years, there is no calculating how much the Lutheran Church in the Carolinas would have been benefited by the arrangement made with the parent Church in Hanover. Even after the war ended, as will be seen in the next chapter, the money that had been collected in Hanover for St. John's Church, which was feared to have been lost or forfeited on account of the action which the Germans in North

Carolina took in the war, was nevertheless paid over to that congregation, according to the original intent of the donors.

One effect, however, the Revolutionary War did have upon the Consistory of Hanover and the University of Göttingen, although the cause or reason is not stated; the supervision of the Lutheran Church in North Carolina was placed in the hands of the professors of the Julius Charles University of Helmstaedt, in the Duchy of Brunswick. Doubtless the parent Church in Hanover became indifferent to the wants of the Lutheran congregations in North Carolina, because the revolt of the American Colonies was against the reigning house of Hanover, who was, as already seen, at the same time king of Great Britain, which may have occasioned the transfer of the care of the North Carolina mission field to the Duchy of Brunswick.

Rev. John Caspar Velthusen, D.D., theological professor of the Julius Charles University, in Helmstaedt, and abbot of the cloister of Marienthal, became the leading spirit of this newly-formed mission society, organized for the supervision and care of the Lutheran churches in North Carolina; with him were associated the Rev. Prof. Henke, and the Professors Crell, Klügel, and Bruns. The labors of this society, if formed before the close of the Revolutionary War, were interrupted during that stormy period, when all communication between Europe and America ceased, but became exceedingly efficient for the welfare of the North Carolina mission field soon after peace was again established, and to this Helmstaedt mission society is all the honor due, for having saved the Lutheran Church in North Carolina from sinking into decay, if not from total annihilation. It commenced, or recommenced, its labors for the North Carolina mission field on the 14th of October, 1786.

Section 14. The Labors of Revs. Nussman and Arndt in North Carolina.

The Lutheran Church in North Carolina was peculiarly fortunate in obtaining the services of so learned, devoted and self-sacrificing a Christian minister as was its first pastor, the Rev. Adolph Nussmann. His praise was in all the churches; men did him honor who had never known him, but heard of his influence and successful labors among the German settlers. Rev. Dr. Caruthers, a Presbyterian minister, speaks of him in the highest terms of praise. Rev. Dr. Velthusen in Germany does the same. Nussmann was indeed a man who might have filled with honor the highest position in any Church or literary institution, but was content to labor for the cause of Christ, and to sacrifice himself among the unambitious but honest German agriculturists of North Carolina.

He located himself at first in Rowan County, near Second Creek, and served Organ and Salisbury Churches, whilst the newly arrived teacher,

J. G. Arndt, occupied himself in giving instruction to the children and youth.

After having taken a survey of the field of ministerial labor in the interior of the Province, Rev. Nussmann perceived that it was already ripe for the harvest, and that he could effect but little by himself; the demands upon his time and energy would be far too great, were he to endeavor to supply all the Lutheran churches, then existing in that Province, with the appointed means of grace, and to labor simply as a missionary, organizing congregations, preaching and administering the sacraments among and in all of them, would effect but little good, unless these churches could be soon supplied with pastors: a number of congregations were already organized, and were hungering after the bread of life.

His only alternative was to have the teacher Arndt ordained, who indeed had received an excellent education in Germany, where much is required of a teacher, and make him a co-laborer in this hopeful field; so, after having properly arranged all Church affairs in Rowan County, he resigned the charge into the hands of Rev. Arndt, and removed to St. John's Church, in Mecklenburg County, where he labored industriously and faithfully all the remaining years of his life. He also made a number of missionating tours to Davidson, Guilford, Orange, Stokes and Forsythe Counties, "strengthening the things that remained," organizing Lutheran congregations, and serving them occasionally, particularly in the two last-mentioned counties.

Rev. Arndt's labors were chiefly confined to Rowan County until after the close of the Revolutionary War, when, in 1786, he removed to Lincoln County, and became the acknowledged founder of the Lutheran Church west of the Catawba River.

It must not be supposed that Nussmann's labors, confined to the wants of St. John's Church, would be comparatively light, except when he made missionary visits to other counties—nothing is farther from the truth. It was the custom in those colonial times, when the population was sparse, to have but one church centrally located in a county or district, and the people would come from a great distance to attend divine service, and attach themselves to the congregation, the bounds of which often embraced a territory within the radius of fifty miles, except where it came near to another church of the same faith in an adjoining county. This was the case with St. John's Church, out of which sprang a number of other congregations, located now in the same and different counties, all of which were faithfully and regularly supplied with the word and sacraments by Pastor Nussmann, until after his death the necessity arose for organizing new and separate churches. The same may likewise be said of the labors of Rev. Arndt, inasmuch as Rowan County embraced at that time all the territory of Davie, Iredell, and Davidson Counties.

Fifteen years did these two faithful servants of God labor alone, under many difficulties and privations, and through all the stormy period of the Revolution, before any additional laborers were sent to their assistance; however, they succeeded, by the blessing of God, in preserving life among those congregations that were remotely located from them, and in building up those of which they were the regular pastors.

Dr. Caruthers states, that in connection with the occasional labors of Rev. Nussmann among the German settlers of Guilford and Orange, the Rev. Mr. Beuthahn, a German Reformed minister, organized congregations in that territory, and preached for them, but supported himself principally by teaching a German school in the southeast corner of Guilford County. Many of these congregations held the church property jointly with the Lutherans, and each denomination had alternate use of these churches.

Section 15. Character of the Lutheran ministry in the Carolinas previous to the Revolutionary War; their piety, learning, firm adherence to the Confessions of their Church, faithfulness in the discharge of their ministerial duties; liturgical worship, &c.

The testimony of all the ancient records of the ante-revolutionary period, concerning the character of the early Lutheran ministry in the Carolinas, is so excellent and so impartially written, even by those who were in no way connected with the Lutheran Church, that it is refreshing to read them; God be praised, that, in the period of the founding of our Church in these two provinces, so excellent a beginning was made, the best and the most competent men were sent by the parent Church in Europe to labor in this field; and whilst the great want of ministers at that time did bring into the field some, who were not so distinguished for their learning, and others, like Revs. Wartman and Daser, who were possessed of characteristics calculated to interfere with their usefulness, nevertheless, the majority of the Lutheran ministers of that period, and who may be regarded as the early fathers of their Church, and certainly the best entitled to that distinction, were men of the noblest traits of character, and efficient in accomplishing a vast amount of good. Their faith and piety were made manifest without seeking public notoriety, and the noblest monument reared to their memory are the works which followed them, which still speak to their praise, though many of them now slumber in unknown graves.

They were men of learning, and might have filled positions of honor and usefulness in their native country; but, possessed of the true missionary spirit, they sacrificed all temporal advantages, in order that they might labor for the welfare of the souls of their neglected brethren in America, and build up the Church in that section of the country to which they had been sent. And when they arrived, great were the privations and hardships which they had to endure, and which can never be fully estimated without contemplating all the circumstances of colonial times; they not only felt the absence of relatives, friends of their youth, college and university associates, but also the want of frequent intercourse with ministerial brethren, of men of learning and refinement, of the literature of the day, of the comforts of advanced civilization, and even of good roads and conveniences for travelling. They were isolated and, so to speak, walled-in by the primeval forests, and were subjected to the constant intercourse with persons who, whilst they respected, esteemed and loved their ministers, never could enter into their feelings of refinement, nor appreciate any intellectual conversation.

The early records also indicate, that the Lutheran ministers of that period were firm believers in the doctrines of their Church, and unconditional adherents to the manner in which these doctrines were set forth in the Symbolical books. For proof of this we are directed first to the Urlsperger Reports. Rev. Bolzius makes the following record in his journal, under date, May 15, 1734: "This morning we returned to Habercorn, where we administered the Lord's Supper to two sick persons, who rejoiced that their souls were refreshed with the eating and drinking the body and blood of Christ. We held a short preparatory discourse on the words: 'Whosoever will come unto me, I will in no wise cast out,' to which they attentively listened with tears of contrition," &c. Although the Symbolical Books are not mentioned in this extract of Rev. Bolzius' diary, yet the distinctive belief of the Lutheran Church in reference to the Lord's Supper is set forth, plainly indicating the faith of these Ebenezer pastors. It is also admitted that Rev. Bolzius did not reside in Carolina, but at that time he occasionally visited Charleston and Purysburg, and labored among the Germans residing there; and the extract, as above given, occurs in his diary of a journey made to Charleston for this very purpose.

The next testimony on this subject is given in the journal of Rev. Dr. Muhlenberg. During his visit to Charleston, a petition of the members of the vacant Lutheran congregation in that city for a pastor was sent to Europe, in which they describe the kind of pastor they were desirous to obtain, and in which description the following clause occurs: "Who is able and willing to administer the Holy Sacraments agreeably to the articles of our unaltered Augsburg Confession." Whilst it is admitted that the Rev. Dr. Muhlenberg is the author of that petition, it was nevertheless undersigned by all, or nearly all, of the members of St. John's Lutheran Church in Charleston, South Carolina. After the Revolutionary War this congregation formed a union with Roman Catholics and German Reformed, as reported by Rev. Dr. Velthusen, "but from the beginning it was not so."

Another decided testimony is furnished from the first constitution of St. John's Church, Mecklenburg (Cabarrus) County, North Carolina, written by the founder of the Lutheran Church in that Province, Rev. Adolph Nussmann, which reads as follows: "Every pastor of this church is bound to confess himself with heart and mouth to the Symbolical Books of our Evangelical Church." From the same constitution we also learn that the worship in that congregation was liturgical, as it was, indeed, in all the Lutheran churches in the Carolinas at that early period, conforming very closely to the usages of the Lutheran Church in Germany.

The early fathers of the Lutheran Church in the Carolinas were conscientious and faithful in the discharge of their ministerial duties, performing labors for the welfare of the Church even outside of their own congregations, and were always ready in word and doctrine to lead souls to Christ. They generally devoted all their time to the work committed to their charge. Some of them had a very meagre support, especially in the rural districts, where the salary consisted principally in the productions of the soil, which the members of their congregations brought to them, and where this was insufficient for the support of themselves and families, they labored with their own hands on their farms, or on lands belonging to their churches.

Section 16. Gradual Improvement of the Condition of the German Colonies and of their Churches in the Carolinas, and bright Prospects for the Future.

The German colonies of North and South Carolina were now firmly established. The people had nothing more to fear from the incursions of the Indians, who had mostly been driven beyond the Alleghany Mountains; the whole Atlantic slope, from New England to Georgia, was in the possession of the white settlers, who could quietly and safely remain at home, and enrich themselves by the cultivation of the soil.

The peculiar adaptation of the German colonists to agricultural pursuits was soon rewarded by thrift and abundance. They became attached to their new homes, and their children intermarrying with each other, bound the settlers together in bonds of relationship, as well as of friendship. Their love for their former homes beyond the sea and in other American provinces was lost, in course of time, in the feeling of general prosperity, whilst those, who were "to the manor born," knew and loved no country so well, as the one in which they resided. The trials, want and hardships of early colonization were at an end, and bright prospects for the future appeared to greet every settler, who was willing to labor, and to manage his affairs prudently.

The Lutheran Church in the Carolinas likewise presented hopeful prospects for the future at this period immediately preceding the Revolutionary War. Congregations were being organized, and churches were erected wherever the number of settlers was sufficiently large to warrant them in taking these steps; often they did not always wait for the aid of ministerial counsel, but took the necessary steps themselves. The scarcity of ministerial labor was still greatly felt, yet the German settlers who had no pastors, were occasionally visited by the pastors of their own faith in more fortunate congregations; besides, the parent Church in the Fatherland had now become interested in their spiritually destitute condition, and the prospect was good that all the churches would shortly be supplied with either pastors or missionaries. This hope, or rather this dependence, whilst it promised the Germans in the Carolinas a speedy supply of the means of grace, exerted, nevertheless, an unwholesome influence upon them. No effort was made to organize a synod for the purpose of regulating their Church affairs; some of their ministers labored in an independent and isolated sphere, whilst others were under the control of the parent Church in Germany, to which they reported regularly, and from which they received aid, direction and counsel. Nor did they feel the necessity of establishing an institution of learning to educate ministers of their own in America, and thus be enabled to fill the vacant churches with pastors, which, if properly managed, could have been done with but little outlay of money in those days of economy and thrift, had they not had the prospect of receiving more ministers from Europe.

Rev. Dr. Muhlenberg foresaw this evil and its consequent effects, but whilst he lamented the want of such a literary institution, he made no personal effort to accomplish the good work, or was prevented from so doing by the indifference of the Church in regard to this matter. Not long after that time the Revolutionary War commenced, when it was too late to make the attempt, for the mind, heart and wants of the colonists were set in another direction.

Section 17. The Effect of the Revolutionary War upon the German Settlements and their Churches.

War is one of the most destructive calamities with which any people can be afflicted, bearing many evils in its train, and seriously affecting all the affairs and interests of civil, social and ecclesiastical life. Especially was this the case with the Revolutionary War in its effect upon the American people, who had but recently emerged from all the evils and hardships of early colonization, and who had as yet no independent national existence, no regular army and navy; and although the war was not altogether an unexpected event, yet when it did break out, it found the Colonies but little prepared for it, and consequently must have been productive of much suffering and many evils.

The effect of the war upon the German settlements was the same as on all the other Colonies.

It arrested all progress, it interrupted the pursuit of every peaceful art, except that which was necessary to support life. Many a plowshare rusted away in its unfinished furrow, many a field lay fallow for a long time, little improvement was made anywhere. The strength of manhood, which was needed at home for the development of the resources of the country, was more urgently required to fill up the rank and file of the army; and the women of that period were obliged to perform, to a certain extent, the hard labor that was needed to cultivate the soil, and to gather and prepare its productions for home consumption, whilst the long winter evenings were spent in making articles of clothing for the family and for the relatives in the army.

War had its sad effect also upon the faith and morals of the people. When it frequently occurs that brother is arrayed against brother, and one neighborhood known to be in open hostility to the other, when it was lawful for the adherents of royalty, called Tories, to rob and plunder, and even to destroy human life at pleasure, and reprisals on the American or Whig side were likewise not wanting, it can be readily imagined what the state of piety and morals must have been at such times of almost general anarchy. When law and order, in times of peace, can scarcely restrain the passions of men, what must have been the condition of society during the prevalence of a war for the establishment of a new government, which afflicted our country for so long a time, and concerning which, to a large extent, the opinions and feelings of the people were divided!

Upon the different churches the war had a most deleterious effect; it greatly reduced their number of membership; it caused those who remained at home to become careless and indifferent about their spiritual welfare; many of the churches in the cities were used as hospitals for the sick and wounded, and the congregations were more or less scattered to where the people were less exposed to the devastations of the hostile army; whilst in the country the danger of being robbed and plundered during absence from home, in attendance upon divine service, almost emptied the various churches of worshipers; all that the minister of the gospel could then do was to visit his flock as often as time and opportunity permitted, laboring only in hope of the dawn of a better day, and the speedy return of peace and prosperity. No congregations could think of making improvements on their churches and schools, or of building new houses of worship; it was even more than could be accomplished to hold their own, and "to strengthen the things which remained, that were ready to die." The close of the war witnessed churches in ruins, congregations dispersed; some of them so effectually died out that they were never again resuscitated, whilst others were so weakened and had grown so indifferent, that with the greatest difficulty they were revived into a new though lingering life. This was particularly the case with the Lutheran

Church in the Carolinas; it had suffered much in the days of its early planting, but it suffered still more during the dark period of the Revolutionary War, and approached very near to becoming entirely extinct.

The ministers themselves were often harassed, persecuted, and at times in danger of their lives. Rev. Christian Streitt, pastor of St. John's Lutheran Church, Charleston, South Carolina, was taken prisoner by the British soldiers, and was never again permitted to return, but found a field of labor elsewhere at the close of the war. "Rev. Mr. Martin, many of whose descendants are still living, on his refusal to pray for the king, was driven from his church, and his property was confiscated. He was for a time placed under arrest, and was afterwards compelled to leave the city, to which he did not return until the close of the war." "His house," writes his great-granddaughter, "had twice, during the Revolutionary War, been burned by our own troops, fearing that the dwelling might furnish a cover to the enemy's approach." This was doubtless done before the British succeeded in occupying the city. Rev. Nussmann in North Carolina fared no better, although no regular army passed through the country where he resided; but he was pursued by Tories, who threatened to take his life. Aged and defenceless as he was, he could do nothing better than to seek refuge in fleeing to a retreat near his home, where he was hid from their view, and thus escaped. During all this dark period of time the German ministers struggled single-handed and alone, but all were as faithful in the discharge of their duties, as the times and circumstances would permit. God also wonderfully preserved their lives, for it is not positively known that a single Lutheran minister in the Carolinas died during the war. Rev. J. G. Friederichs passed from the stage of action some time shortly previous to, or during the Revolution, but it is not certainly known when God took him to his rest; and Rev. L. Hochheimer's name also disappears from the records of that period.

Another sad effect of the war upon the churches in the Carolinas was the impossibility of having any correspondence with the parent Church in Europe, owing to the interruption of all commercial intercourse with foreign nations. This deprived the congregations of the sympathy and aid of their brethren in the Fatherland, and terminated the supply of ministers, books and donations in money for the good of the Church in these two Provinces as long as the war lasted. In short, the removals, the deaths, the changes and the sufferings that were caused by this war of England with her colonies in America can never be fully described, and will never be known, in all their details, by any human being this side of eternity.

CHAPTER III.

HISTORY OF THE LUTHERAN CHURCH IN THE CAROLINAS FROM THE CLOSE OF THE REVOLUTIONARY WAR, A.D. 1783, TO THE ORGANIZATION OF THE SYNOD OF NORTH CAROLINA, A.D. 1803, EMBRACING A PERIOD OF TWENTY YEARS.

Section 1. State of the German Colonies and of the Lutheran Church at the Close of the Revolution.

THE conflict of arms had ceased; the smoke and din of battle were seen and heard no more; peace again spread its benign influence over our long-afflicted country; the independence of the American Colonies was at last achieved—acknowledged even by England, and civil and religious liberty was the well-earned reward of the people, who had patiently struggled and suffered for eight long years. Prosperity again commenced to dawn upon the land, when all the energies of the people were directed to the development of its resources, and industry and economy soon restored the healthy financial condition of its inhabitants.

But there is another side to that picture which is generally overlooked. War had left its deep traces of evil upon the virtues and morals of the people, who had become more or less degenerated by the evil influences which a long war and a change of government generally exert upon mankind. The German people, especially in the rural districts, were not so greatly affected by these influences of the war as were others, owing to their isolated condition on account of language, and their temperate and industrious habits kept them more closely confined to their homes; nevertheless, a general indifference to all matters of religion prevailed almost everywhere, for the people were no longer hungry for the bread of life, but regarded the acquisition of wealth, or the repair of their former condition of competency, as of primary importance.

Old landmarks of government had been entirely overthrown, and the people were for five years politically unsettled in mind, ere a solid and stable government was formed and established. State governments existed, without which the whole land would have been subjected to all the terrors of anarchy; but one can easily imagine how little restraint these governments could enforce, and what protection they could warrant, as long as every political arrangement was regarded as merely provisional.

Foreign immigration, particularly into the Southern States, was, for a time, almost entirely arrested.

But the worst consequences of the success of the Revolutionary War were the almost deification of Liberty and the rapid rise of infidelity, rationalism and religious indifference. A prophecy was made by one of the wisest statesmen of that time or shortly afterwards, that in fifty years there would not a single copy of the Bible be found in this country. Nor was the influence of the success of the Revolution confined to America. France soon became dissatisfied with its monarchical government, and ran wild in its demands for liberty. It had its desire, but its reign of terror, which followed close upon the heels of American independence, became warning enough to all, that liberty, however excellent it is, when properly restrained by the virtue of its possessors and wholesome laws, becomes a dangerous plaything in the hands of incompetent, selfish and wicked men. How significant is the cry of one of the victims under the guillotine: "O Liberty, Liberty, how many crimes are committed in thy name!"

With this period we may also date the beginning of rationalism in the Lutheran Church in America; old landmarks of the Lutheran faith were set aside, or formally confessed with a mental reservation, church discipline was not generally, properly and impartially enforced, ancient church usages were abandoned; our Church, thus despoiled of her glory and strength, was made to correspond with the spirit of American liberty, and to assimilate itself to other denominations, and an anxious seeking after temporal advantage became manifest even among some of those, who were the acknowledged shepherds of the flock.

The spirit of the age was skeptical, selfish, and prone to deify a virtue and morality entirely disconnected from the religion of our Savior. Priestcraft, under which reproachful term the gospel ministry of all denominations was understood, was so generally dreaded and so frequently denounced, that it is a matter of surprise that ministers of the gospel could effect any good at all. But one extreme is usually followed by another, and generally by its opposite. The revival of 1800, which swept over the entire land, no doubt accomplished good in checking the growing evil of infidelity and religious unconcern, for it taught men that there is a future retribution; but its spirit was legal, and it became the parent of much fanaticism and Pharisaism, establishing an ethical kind of religion, which cut off some of the most tender cords of faith and love, that draw the human heart near to the Savior. An emotional religion became prevalent; religious experience exchanged places with Christ, and a subjective faith was substituted for the objective; but as a more extended account of this great revival will be furnished in another section of this chapter, it is unnecessary to enlarge here.

The Lutheran ministers in the Carolinas, who survived all the vicissitudes of the Revolutionary War, as far as can be ascertained, were Revs. Nussmann and Arndt in North Carolina, and Revs. Martin and Daser in South Carolina; concérning Revs. Friederichs and Hochheimer nothing is known positively; their names do not occur in any of the extant records of that period; what became of them, and when they died, must now remain, as it is feared, a matter of mere conjecture. Rev. Theus, the German Reformed minister in South Carolina, still lived, and continued to labor faithfully in his Master's vineyard. The names of four other German ministers in South Carolina appear in view four or five years later, but it is probable that they began to labor in that field only after peace was restored.

Section 2. Reorganization of Ecclesiastical affairs in the Lutheran Church in the Carolinas.

On the 26th of March, 1784, St. John's Lutheran Church in Charleston, upon the application of its members, made in 1783, obtained a charter of incorporation, under the changed name and title of "The Lutheran Church of German Protestants," from the State legislature, which then held its sessions in Charleston. This appears to have been the first effort that was made at reorganization of ecclesiastical affairs in the Lutheran Church under the new form of civil government in the Carolinas.

Rev. Frederick Daser was still the pastor, and continued in charge of that congregation until July, 1786; there is undoubted testimony on that point, firstly, from the extract of the records of the church-book, published by Mr. Jacob F. Schirmer, who states: "We find the name of Mr. F. Daser as pastor up to July, 1786, when he resigned his office;" secondly, from the Helmstaedt Reports, in which the author mentions having received a letter from Rev. Daser, and states: "We learn from his letter of the 20th of June, 1787, that he has now left Charleston since August, 1786, and has moved to another congregation, composed of English and German people, in Orangeburg District, seventy miles further inland."

Rev. John Nicholas Martin was again recalled, and became the pastor of this church for the third time, but labored only one year, until the new minister from Germany arrived, when, on account of the infirmities of age, he withdrew from the active duties of the ministry. The family memoir, furnished by one of his descendants, states: "Although aged, and having lost his former physical vigor, his congregation still clung to him with warm affection. They urged him in 1783 (1786) to resume his pastoral relations, until a stated minister could be procured from Germany. Upon the arrival of his successor, Rev. John C. Faber, he was released from further service, with a vote of thanks from the church for the fidelity with which he had ministered to their spiritual interests. He lived several years, after his withdrawal from the active duties of the ministry, on the little farm with which there were so many associations connected." This farm was situated about a mile from Charleston, on which the revolutionary incidents occurred, which were noticed in one of the preceding sections.

Concerning the other Lutheran congregations

in the interior of South Carolina, very little is known until 1787, excepting that the Orangeburg District charge was fortunate enough to have received Rev. F. Daser for their pastor in August, 1786, and who, doubtless, remained there to the close of his life.

In Rev. A. Nussmann's principal congregation, St. John's, Mecklenburg (Cabarrus) County, N. C., the want of a better house of worship was felt after the war, when the congregation had again become thoroughly organized. On the 6th of November, 1784, a beginning was made "for the purpose of rebuilding St. John's Church." It was resolved to erect the new church on the same site where the old one stood, in the inclosure of the present graveyard, near the upper part of it. The subscription list, taken in the currency of English money, and ranging from ten pounds to three shillings, is prefaced by the following pious wish: "May the good God help us, so that our undertaking may succeed well in peace and unanimity, and that every man may do his part as he would wish others to do towards himself." The whole subscription amounted to about £172½.

The church edifice was completed the following year, and was solemnly dedicated to the service of the triune God on the fourth of July, 1785, but with what ceremonies is not stated. Soon after another subscription was taken, for the purpose of purchasing a large gilt silver goblet from their pastor for communion service, which is still used for the same purpose.

In the Organ and Salisbury Churches matters remained unimproved, and those congregations became vacant soon after the restoration of peace, by the removal of Rev. J. G. Arndt to Lincoln County, where a new and promising field awaited him, and where he accomplished much good. Concerning the other German Lutheran settlements in North Carolina nothing much can be said, inasmuch as they never enjoyed the regular services of their own pastor until 1788, but were visited by Revs. Nussmann and Arndt as frequently as the attendance upon the wants of their own regular congregations would permit them.

Section 3. Arrival of Rev. John Charles Faber—Reunion of the North Carolina Churches with the Parent Church in Germany—The North Carolina Catechism, published by Rev. Dr. Velthusen, and Rev. Daser's Report to the Helmstaedt Fathers.

In the year 1787, the Rev. John Charles Faber, having received and accepted a call from the Lutheran Church in Charleston, South Carolina, "arrived from Germany and took charge of the church." He continued to labor there for thirteen years, when, during the year 1800, his health failed him, and he resigned his office as pastor of that congregation. "The Rev. Mr. Pogson," an Episcopal clergyman, "officiated on Sundays for a short time, and on his retiring Mr. Faber consented to serve the church as far as his strength would allow."

According to the testimony of Rev. Dr. Velthusen, in his preface to the North Carolina Catechism, Rev. J. C. Faber must have labored with great acceptance and success in Charleston, inducing many of the Germans of other religious persuasions to unite with the Lutherans in building up their church. Dr. V. says, "This congregation may be looked upon as an example of Christian harmony, for it is composed of a union of Lutherans, German Reformed and Catholics, all of whom live, according to the testimony of their pastor, the Rev. Mr. Faber, very peaceably together, although they are educated in different principles of religion. They visit the house of God faithfully, and contribute equally for the support of divine worship."

A strong effort was made at this time by Rev. Nussmann to place the Lutheran Church in North Carolina once more in connection with the parent Church in Germany, and this time he accomplished his purpose. His object was threefold: his congregation, St. John's, had money on deposit in Europe, which had been collected for its benefit previous to the breaking out of the Revolutionary War, and the amount, £90 sterling, was certainly worth the attempt to secure for the benefit of that congregation; besides, devotional books and German school-books were greatly needed everywhere, and, in order to obtain a supply of them, application was made to the Mission Society at Helmstaedt, Duchy of Brunswick, to send books in exchange for the money that was coming to that church, which could then be sold among the Germans in North Carolina, and more than the same amount of money realized from their sale. But the greatest necessity of all was a supply of German Lutheran ministers; accordingly, as is stated in Rev. C. A. G. Storch's journal, a call for several Lutheran ministers to labor in North Carolina was sent by Rev. Nussmann to Rev. Dr. Velthusen, in Helmstaedt, Germany, and by this means Rev. N. endeavored to preserve the Lutheran Church in this State from becoming entirely extinct, for in all human probability this would have been eventually its fate, if help, in the supply of ministers, had been delayed several years longer, when Revs. Nussmann and Arndt were called to their long rest.

For the purpose of taking these matters into consideration, particularly those bearing upon the welfare of St. John's Church, a meeting of the church-council was called on the 30th of September, 1787, which convened at the pastor's house, and the following business was transacted:

As before stated, many charitable persons in Europe had safely deposited a considerable amount of money in London, some time before the Revolution, for the benefit of "the congregation at Dutch Buffalo Creek, Mecklenburg County," which had been appropriated in part for the welfare of that church, and of which £90, sterling, were still remaining on deposit in that city, and which, it was feared, this congregation had forfeited, on account of the action of its members in the Revolution; it was, therefore,

"*Resolved*, That if those benefactors would still have the kindness to permit this amount to be appropriated to the welfare of this congregation, as was at first intended, that the money should always be considered as a fund belonging solely to the church.

"*Resolved*, That from the interest of this fund the yearly salary of the pastor shall be supplemented.

"*Resolved*, That no part of the principal shall be touched without the consent of the donors."

This fund had accumulated in 1843 to fifteen hundred dollars, and was then all consumed, contrary to this resolution, in erecting the present church edifice, in which the members of St. John's Church now worship.

"*Resolved*, That this amount of funds shall not be sent in money, but, as the congregation is desirous of obtaining books, especially those published by those five learned philanthropists in Helmstaedt, Revs. Abbots Velthusen and Henke, and the Professors Crell, Klügel and Bruns, for the benefit of the Christian religion in America; it is ordered that a part be printed by St. Michael's Day, and the other part by next Easter Day, and it is requested that the first four numbers be purchased, and strongly but not expensively bound, and then be sent over to us.

"*Resolved*, That the whole Society, or a part of the members by order of the Society, be permitted to appropriate the whole or a part of this money in the purchase of those expected books, which are to be sent to us.

"*Resolved*, That these resolutions be inscribed in the church-book.

"*Resolved*, That the chest, in which these books are to be sent, shall be directed M. C. D. B. C.," supposed to signify Mecklenburg County, Dutch Buffalo Creek.

This abstract of the proceedings of St. John's church council, held at the time and place above-mentioned, is taken from the old church-book, still extant and written in the German language.

The efforts of Rev. Nussmann and his congregation were crowned with success; the money was secured, the needed books were sent, and in compliance with the request of Rev. Nussmann, a second edition of one of those books, named at first "The Helmstaedt Catechism," was published, and received the title "North Carolina Catechism." A copy of its title-page is inserted here in its original language, for the benefit of all those who understand the German:

"Nordcarolinischer Katechismus, oder Christlicher Religionsunterricht nach Einleitung der heiligen Schrift, entworfen von Johann Caspar Velthusen, Doctor und ordentlichem Lehrer der Theologie, erstem Prediger in Helmstaedt, und General Superintend; auch Abte des Klosters Marienthal."

It is a book containing 254 pages, published in 1788, in the city of Leipzig, by Siegfried Lebrecht

Crusius, and also incloses Luther's smaller catechism in its pages. It informs us of the degree of interest which the Church in the Fatherland took in our ecclesiastical affairs in this section of our country. Its chief importance at this time is its historical value, giving us an insight in the manner in which the practical affairs of our churches in the Carolinas were conducted at the time of its publication. This is furnished us in its preface, in which Dr. Velthusen reports some interesting facts concerning the Lutheran Church in North Carolina and Charleston, informing us of the departure of Rev. C. A. G. Storch (Stork) from Helmstaedt to his future field of labor in North Carolina.

The preface to this "North Carolina Catechism" reads as follows: "This second edition corresponds verbatim with the first, which I then denominated the Helmstaedt Catechism, because it is likewise necessary for the use of the Catechetical Institute of this place.

"In the meantime two very strong congregations in North Carolina have most feelingly declared themselves willing to accept with gladness the preachers which we expect to send out to them. Rev. Mr. Storch is already upon the sea on his way thither."

"We have also the assurance from other portions of America, that the choice of our books of instruction are suitable to their wants. Besides, various of these books have also been introduced in Charleston, by the approval and support of the congregation, for the instruction of their youth." (Here follows the description of the condition of the Lutheran Church in Charleston, already quoted on another page.) "I have, therefore, given the above title to this Catechism from motives of love and regard to my friend, Rev. Nussmann, as such has been his desire from the beginning. May God bless the use of this book, my dear brethren, for your and your children's everlasting salvation.

"HELMSTAEDT, May 1st, 1788."

From one of the Helmstaedt Reports we are informed how these books and letters intended for Rev. Nussmann were sent to him. Dr. Velthusen says: "We had formerly sent everything which was intended to reach Rev. Mr. Nussmann, as we were requested, to the address of Rev. Mr. Daser, but who has now left Charleston, and has moved to Orangeburg District, where he must await such opportunities as the country market-wagons afford, before Rev. Nussmann could receive our letters, sent over through the kindness of friends in London, Amsterdam, Copenhagen, Hamburg, Altona and Bremen."

Rev. Mr. Daser also mentions a fact in his letter, which is worthy of notice, and assists us in obtaining an insight into the condition of the Lutheran Church in the interior of South Carolina at that time.

Dr. Velthusen states: "Rev. Mr. Daser mentions two congregations in South Carolina that are in search of a pastor, but the assurances were not sufficiently distinct and satisfactory to propose this call to one, whose welfare at the present time is even dearer to us than our own, or even to permit any one to make a journey upon such an uncertainty; for we have determined upon the principle, never to send any one as a preacher to America, except under such circumstances which would induce each one of us cheerfully to make this journey ourselves, if our individual circumstances would permit, in dependence upon God and upon the good cause; for we despise, with all our hearts, every uncalled-for emigration from the Fatherland, and all wandering about in the world as adventurers."

These two vacant churches in South Carolina must have been the one in Barnwell District, and Salem Church at Sandy Run, Lexington District, so supposed from the fact that all the other charges in that State appear to have been supplied with pastors that same year, when the Corpus Evangelicum was organized; and also, that Rev. Daser, residing in Orangeburg District at the time he wrote, was nearest to these two congregations, and was doubtless specially interested in their welfare.

Section 4. The Corpus Evangelicum, or Unio Ecclesiastica in South Carolina, and the Ordination of Rev. J. G. Bamberg.

We have now arrived at that period in the history of the Lutheran Church in the Carolinas, when the first attempt was made, in connection with the German Reformed ministers, to organize some kind of ecclesiastical body, that should have the supervision of all the German churches in the interior of the State of South Carolina.

This body was organized in Zion's Church, Lexington District (County), November 13th, 1787, and consisted of Lutheran and German Reformed ministers, together with lay deputies from the churches belonging to both denominations. It had the double name of Corpus Evangelicum and Unio Ecclesiastica, doubtless so given with the view that neither denomination could have occasion to object to the title and to its undenominational character. Its principal object was to make special arrangement for the proper incorporation of all the German churches by legislative enactment, which were located in the interior of the State; the Lutheran church in the city of Charleston having already secured its charter of incorporation. The ordination of a candidate to the office of the ministry indicated that the performance of this duty seemed to be also one of its objects; and the general oversight and welfare of all the churches in its connection, as was manifested by the presence of lay delegates, claimed a large share of the attention of that body.

The Lutheran congregation in Charleston never connected itself with that body; neither did the two Lutheran ministers, Revs. Faber and Martin, who resided there; but for what reason is not stated.

The Corpus Evangelicum was short-lived, as might have been expected, and as all such mixed ecclesiastical bodies must necessarily be. A union of denominations cannot be otherwise than false, where the united parties are not agreed either in doctrine or practice, for each party feels that it is not laboring specially for the upbuilding of its own denomination, and thus zeal and energy are paralyzed, and the heart grows weak. Such a union becomes the parent of indifferentism.

It is a Utopian dream ever to expect a union of all orthodox Christian denominations in this world, and every attempt to effect a union of this kind must finally become inoperative. Royal edicts, as in Prussia, may for a long time keep two or more denominations in an organized ecclesiastical connection, and galvanize such a union into a certain kind of life; but no sooner are such edicts revoked, than the former state of things is restored, with, perhaps, the forming of a third denomination where once but two existed, thus making the division still greater.

It is admitted that this is taking but a philosophical view of the case. The question, Is it right in the sight of God? is quite another matter, which need not now be discussed, as we have at present to deal only with historical facts. It is well known that such an ecclesiastical union was formed in South Carolina—an account of which may be found in Rev. Dr. Hazelius' History of the American Lutheran Church, pp. 118–121, which, however, is not here inserted, because the constitution and report of the proceedings of that body are preferred, as translated by Dr. Hazelius, and inscribed in the church-book of St. Peter's congregation, near Lexington Court House, South Carolina, in which church-book the orginal German copy was found.

Constitution of the Corpus Evangelicum.

Whereas our legislature, in virtue of a petition, has incorporated the major part of our Evangelical Zion in this free State, consisting of fifteen congregations, as a lawful society, with full power to constitute and make such by-laws, orders, and regulations as they may deem proper for the welfare of such a society, and to administer a salutary church discipline; therefore, the undersigned met on the 12th day of August, 1788, in the Lutheran Salem's Church, Sandy Run, and resolved that the following articles shall be signed and sealed by us, and be kept inviolably by every member of the fifteen evangelical churches, as a general Church discipline, and that every person, who is desirous of becoming a member of this Church, shall sign and observe these regulations, as follows:

ARTICLE I. All the Christian congregations, incorporated as aforesaid, shall form one corpus evangelicorum under the title: Unio Ecclesiastica of the German Protestant Churches in the State of South Carolina. Each and every congregation is depending on this *corpus*, by which all things concerning Church and religion shall be managed and directed, and the free course of the gospel be promoted within its bounds.

ARTICLE II. Whereas it would be highly detrimental, if members of the Lutheran and Reformed Confessions, who in this State live near each other, and attend the same churches, should be separated, therefore we have agreed to this ecclesiastical union, by which, however, it is not to be understood that any member of either confession should forsake his confession, but that both Lutheran and Reformed, who are members of one or the other incorporated churches, and who have hitherto united in the attendance on worship, shall continue to enjoy the same rights and privileges, without the least reproaches in consequence of their respective confessions.

ARTICLE III. Each of the united evangelical congregations agrees herewith, in accordance to the design expressed in their petition to the legislature, to establish and preserve among them a Directory of their churches as long as a majority of the fifteen churches agree to the same, which Directory shall consist of the ministers of said congregations and two delegates, suitable lay-members of each of these churches. Under the general superintendence of this Directory all affairs relating to churches shall be judged and regulated; as for instance, the reception and dismission of preachers, their election, examination, ordination, and induction, the establishment and regulation of churches and schools, where there are none at present, the improvement of such as are in existence, the manner of Divine service, so that uniformity may exist in this matter, the collections in churches, and the proposition in what manner a fund may be collected gradually for several necessary expenses, and, in general, whatever may be of importance for the furtherance and welfare of the whole body, as well as of each individual church.

ARTICLE IV. The officers of this Ecclesiastical Directory consist of a president, chosen from the ministers, a church council, selected from the deputies of the respective congregations, a secretary, and a warden; which officers are to be chosen yearly, on the second Wednesday of January, by the plurality of the votes of the whole Directory; and the place of meeting may be changed, provided it is a convenient and central situation.

ARTICLE V. Whenever a member of these incorporated churches should be cited before this Directory, such member promises to appear before the same, unless prevented by some extraordinary hindrance; and any member chosen to fill an office in the Directory engages to accept the office and to perform its duties, unless very special circumstances should prevent him from so doing.

ARTICLE VI. Every congregation is to reply in writing to the Directory, and to give an account of the state of their church. In all cases of importance seek advice from the Directory; but each incorporate church elects yearly on Easter Monday the necessary church officers, viz.: two elders, four wardens, a secretary, and a church treasurer. The officers of the last year are to give an account of the state of the church property to the newly-elected officers, and deliver to them all and every part thereof. And it is herewith agreed that all the church officers shall take an oath before a magistrate, that they will faithfully and honestly administer the property of the church.

ARTICLE VII. The Directory is to keep a book of record of all its regulations and ordinances. But each congregation shall keep its own minutes and church register through the medium of their ministers and secretaries, and it shall be the duty of the latter to register all the regulations concerning the temporalities of the church made by the vestry and ministry concerning the same. The books, which are to be kept by the minister, shall be mentioned below.

ARTICLE VIII. Wherever the major part of the members of a congregation should belong to the Reformed Church, such a liturgy, formula, and catechism are to be used as the Reformed Church in the Palatinate or Switzerland make use of; but where the divine service has hitherto been performed according to the ceremonies of the Lutheran Church, the Würtemberg or Halle formula shall be adopted. The Marburg Hymnbook, in its second edition, remains in use in our churches of both confessions.

ARTICLE IX. Every congregation has the undoubted right to elect, call, and to approve of its own minister; but whenever a parish is vacant, it shall be the duty of its officers to apply to the Directory in this case, as in all cases of importance, to propose a suitable candidate, and being approved by the congregation, and they promise to give him a support, it shall be the duty of the Directory to deputize two ordained ministers to install the new preacher in his parish.

Article X. Every congregation promises herewith, and obligates itself, to make up a salary by subscription, according to its ability, and regularly to pay the same; likewise to treat its minister with respect, and not to dismiss him from its service without a proper cause. Nevertheless, the minister shall have the right and privilege to accept a call from any other congregation, if Providence should so direct. Each congregation, likewise, fixes the contingent fees of the minister according to their respective abilities.

Article XI. The preacher, in any of these incorporated congregations, promises on his part, and binds himself before God and the Church, to administer his holy office, to adorn it by an unimpeachable walk and conversation. In the discharge of the duties of his holy office, whether public or private, he shall appear in his ministerial dress, which is to be provided by the congregation. He shall preach every Lord's day an evangelical and edifying sermon, and afterwards catechize the youth, except when baptism, communion, or a marriage is to be celebrated, or in case that he has to visit the sick. He shall yearly keep a fast and prayer day in his congregation, preach a harvest sermon, and celebrate in his church the high festivals of Easter Sunday and Monday, Pentecost Sunday and Monday, Ascension Day and Christmas Day, and other festivals of the Christian Church, such as Good Friday, New Year, &c. He likewise promises to continue his theological studies, and not to depart from the principles of our holy religion, and to warn his hearers against the sects which divide the Church, and to endeavor to prevent the growing evil. He shall also admonish his household and children to walk in the fear of God, and in every respect is he bound as a faithful steward of God to act conscientiously in his public and private vocation. Unless it is absolutely necessary, he shall not absent himself too far from his congregation, and shall submit to every regulation which either has been made or may be made by the Directory.

He shall, at least once every year, make a statement to the Directory of his parochial duties, according to a formula which he is to receive. He shall frequently visit the schools, and seriously admonish the parents to educate their children in the nurture and admonition of the Lord. He shall be diligent in exposing, and warning against, the vices and immoralities which may creep or prevail in congregations. In regard to marriages, and everything connected with the same, he is to act with circumspection, and he shall endeavor to preserve good morals, peace, and harmony, both in the Church and families.

Every quarter he shall call a meeting of the church officers, to counsel with them concerning the temporal and spiritual state of the congregation, examine the account of the church treasurer, and keep an exact account of these proceedings in his own book, as the secretary has to preserve a similar account in his. If hitherto no register of baptisms, communicants, confirmations, marriages, and deaths has been kept in a congregation, the minister is to make diligent search in his congregation, whether any records of former times may be discovered, and if not, he shall henceforth keep such a record, a model of which shall be sent to them by the president. Every minister, who is cited to appear before the Directory to answer to any accusation which may be brought against him, is bound to appear before the same, and to submit to the decision thereof.

ARTICLE XII. A copy of this act and church discipline shall be made and deposited in each of our united and incorporated congregations; this copy shall be subscribed and sealed by each member, and it shall frequently be read to the congregation. Whosoever desires to become a member of the church or Directory has to subscribe and seal this discipline before he can be admitted to a vote in any election held by the church.

ARTICLE XIII. We herewith agree to keep a box in every church, into which every attendant on divine worship may cast his contribution, according to his ability and good will. The amount of these contributions shall yearly be declared before the Directory. This money is to be applied for the purchase of baptismal and communion vessels; ministerial gowns, however, are to be provided by private collections in the congregation.

ARTICLE XIV. We will make application by letter to our brethren in the faith in Europe to consider our weak state, and especially to supply us with ministers and schoolmasters.

ARTICLE XV. As far as it is possible we will aid the poor in our congregations.

ARTICLE XVI. We shall not interfere in cases which, according to law, ought to come before our civil magistrates, and in all respects submit to the laws of our country.

ARTICLE XVII. If any person in the congregation should have a complaint against his minister, he is to make it known to the church council and wardens, and if these officers are unable to bring the difficulty to an amicable settlement, they are bound forthwith to acquaint the president with the circumstances by a written communication, who is then to take the matter in hand.

ARTICLE XVIII. All the families of our united evangelical congregations bind ourselves solemnly to attend regularly divine service agreeable to our duty; to labor earnestly for the propagation of our holy religion; frequently to attend the means of grace; to avoid sectarianism as much as possible; and to walk carefully according to the prescription of pure doctrine.

ARTICLE XIX. Our united zealous endeavor shall be directed to promote the welfare of our

Church, the extension of the religion of Jesus, as well as of our Zion; and with the adoption of this discipline we make a beginning of this endeavor. May God further grant his richest blessing.

ARTICLE XX. Should it hereafter be considered necessary, after due reflection, to change, abrogate, or disannul any of these Articles of Discipline, or add anything to the same by the Church assembled in Directory, such resolution shall be added as a lawful by-law to these regulations, and which member soever shall wilfully resist these rules, and will in nowise agree to the same, cannot find fault with the Church to which he has hitherto belonged, nor with the Directory, if he shall be deprived of the benefits and claims to either.

Acted and unanimously resolved and confirmed by the Directory, August 8th, 1788; which we, who have been present at this Church meeting, confirm with our seals and subscription of our names.

NAMES OF MINISTERS AND THEIR SEALS.

FRIEDERICH DASER, A.M., *President pro tem.* [L.S.]
CHRISTIAN THEUS. [L.S.]
J. G. BAMBERG. [L.S.]
FRIEDERICH AUGUST WALLBERG. [L.S.]
CARL FRIEDERICH FROELICH. [L.S.]

NAMES AND SEALS OF THE DEPUTIES.

Philip Berghoch.	[L.S.]
Johann George Koeller.	[L.S.]
Peter Michler.	[L.S.]
Johannes Gartmann.	[L.S.]
George Gortmann.	[L.S.]
Jacob Buchmann.	[L.S.]
Leonhard B. Buch.	[L.S.]
Johannes Schwaigart.	[L.S.]
John Jacob Stiefel.	[L.S.]
Johann Philip Zauerwein.	[L.S.]
Matthias Sen.	[L.S.]
Christopher Schlagel.	[L.S.]
Heinrich Koch.	[L.S.]
Johann Balthaser Mark.	[L.S.]

Proceedings of the Corpus Evangelicum in South Carolina.

On the 13th of November, 1787, the undersigned ministers assembled themselves in Zion's Church, on Twelve-mile Creek, after due notice had been given, and united themselves from that day into a ministerial society. The constitution proposed by Rev. Mr. Wallberg was laid before the meeting and adopted, and Frederick Daser was chosen Senior of the ministry, and appointed the second Sunday of January, 1788, as the day on which they would again meet at the same place, to take into consideration the various petitions signed by different German Protestant congregations, and further to regulate the affairs of their society. In confirmation whereof the ministers signed their names.

Friederich Daser, Christian Theus, John George Bamberg, M. Carl Binnicher, Friederich August Wallberg, Friederich Joseph Wallern, Carl Friederich Froelich.

Actum, January 8th, 1788.—The undersigned ministers assembled as members of the Ministerium in Zion's Church, on Twelve-mile Creek. Fred. Aug. Wallberg was unanimously elected Secretary, and all the Evangelical Lutheran ministers were sworn on the Symbolical Books. The subscription of the petition for incorporation of the different congregations was laid before the Ministerium. Bethel Church and the new congregation of St. Martin's wished to have more time for consideration of the subject.

Resolved, That the President should inform the members by a circular of the time of our next session.

Signed by Revs. Daser, Wallberg, Bamberg, Froelich, and Theus.

Actum, January 9th, 1788.—Rev. Messrs. Wallberg and Bamberg moved that the subscriptions of Bethel Church and of the new St. Martin's Church should be added to the subscriptions of the other churches, and laid before the General Assembly of this State, which motion was approved and accepted by Rev. Senior Daser.

As it had been mentioned the preceding day that Mr. Bamberg had for some time performed ecclesiastical duties, and had received a call as minister from several congregations, and as it was known to the Ministerium that he had studied theology but had never been ordained, and as he had petitioned for an examination and ordination, it was

Resolved, That the Rev. President and Secretary examine Mr. Bamberg this day; and he, the said Bamberg, being approved of in said examination, was this day ordained in Zion's Church, in the presence of a numerous audience and his church officers.

FREDH. AUG. WALLBERG,
Secretary.

Actum, *Sandy Run*, *August 12th*, *1788.*—Revs. Messrs. Senior Daser, Theus, Bamberg, and Wallberg assembled in Salem Church at Sandy Run, with the deputies of the respective congregations. It was

Resolved, That Bethlehem Church should henceforth be known under the name of "The German Reformed Church at Fust's Ford."

The act of incorporation passed by the General Assembly of this State was read; and the Church regulations or discipline proposed by President Daser was likewise read and adopted in its nineteen articles, signed and sealed.

Resolved, To hold the next session in Zion's Church, January 14th, 1789.

Actum, *January 19th*, *1789.*—Revs. President Daser, Theus, Bamberg, Wallern, and Secretary Wallberg met in Zion's Church.

After prayer and sermon, the conference was

opened. The Church regulations, as adopted, signed, and sealed, were read once more without opposition.

Next session is to be held in Salem Church, Sandy Run, on the second Wednesday in the month of August. Pastor Wallern was appointed to preach on said occasion.

Rev. Senior Daser was again unanimously chosen President, and Wallberg, Secretary. George Hook was appointed President of the lay members of the Directory.

Notice of the Translator.—The records of the succeeding sessions of the Directory are partly torn, and partly so badly written that it is impossible to arrange them in any kind of order.

The Directory seems to have met as late as the year 1794; at least, so far the records go which I have seen.

Signed, ERNEST L. HAZELIUS,
Principal of the Theological Seminary, Lexington, S. C.

The seven German ministers of the Gospel who formed this Corpus Evangelicum were located as follows:

Rev. Frederick Daser, A.M., at St. Matthew's Church, Orangeburg District, South Carolina. He was a Lutheran minister.

Rev. Christian Theus, on the west side of the Congaree River, eight miles below Columbia, South Carolina. He was a German Reformed minister.

Rev. John George Bamberg labored until 1798 in

Lexington District, South Carolina, and was pastor of Zion's Church, as the records of that church indicate, when he resigned and located himself in Barnwell District, South Carolina, where he remained to the close of his life. He was a Lutheran minister, and died during the year 1800.

Rev. Frederick August Wallberg labored among the churches in Lexington District before Bamberg's time of service, probably about the time the Corpus Evangelicum was organized. He was a Lutheran minister, and is supposed to have lived in the Fork of the Saluda and Broad Rivers to the close of his life.

Rev. Carl Friederich Froelich, according to J. C. Hope's statement, was a German Reformed minister, but where he lived and labored is not known.

Rev. Frederick Joseph Wallern was the pastor of the churches in Newberry District, South Carolina. He was a Lutheran minister, and died about the year 1816.

Rev. M. Carl Binnicher, according to J. C. Hope's statement, was a Lutheran minister, but where he labored is not positively known. It is presumed, however, that he was the pastor of the Hard Labor Creek congregation, Abbeville District, South Carolina, and probably also served the church on Slippery Creek, Ninety-six District.

From the constitution and proceedings of this Corpus Evangelicum we learn many interesting facts, namely:

1. That the Lutheran ministers in South Carolina at that time held the Symbolical Books of the

Lutheran Church in very high esteem, the records say: "All the Evangelical Lutheran ministers were sworn upon the Symbolical Books;" that is, they were sworn to teach and preach its doctrines.

2. They were likewise churchly in conducting public worship, &c., as is manifested by their observance of all the festivals of the Lutheran Church, catechetical instruction, confirmation, and opposition to the inroads made upon the Church by the surrounding sects.

3. They still adhered to the ancient custom of wearing the gown, both in "public and private," in the discharge of all the duties of the ministerial office.

4. They were very strict in the enforcement of discipline, both among the ministers and lay members; and made provision for the support of the poor in their midst.

5. Parochial schools likewise claimed the attention of this body; and the keeping of church records was made the duty both of the pastor and secretary of each congregation.

Section 5. The act of incorporation of the fifteen German churches in the interior of South Carolina.

No. 1414. An Act for Incorporating divers Religious Societies therein named.

Whereas, by the constitution of this State, passed the nineteenth day of March, one thousand seven hundred and seventy-eight, it is declared that all denominations of Christian Protestants in this

State shall enjoy equal religious and civil privileges; and that whenever fifteen or more male persons, not under twenty-one years of age, professing the Christian Protestant religion, agree to unite themselves in a society for the purpose of religious worship, they shall (on complying with the terms thereinafter mentioned), be constituted a church, and be esteemed and regarded in law, as of the established religion of this State, and on petition to the legislature shall be entitled to be incorporated and to equal privileges; and that every society of Christians so formed shall give themselves a name or denomination by which they shall be called or known in law.

And whereas, the name of "Hopewell," in the Long Cane settlement, in the county of Abbeville and State aforesaid; and the Presbyterian congregation or society of Christian Protestants of "Indian Town," in Georgetown District; and also the several congregations and societies of Christian Protestants, styling themselves by the general appellation of "The Ecclesiastical Union of the several German Protestant congregations in the back part of the State of South Carolina;" and by the particular names of:

"The Frederician Church, on Cattel's Creek;"
"The German Calvinistic Church of St. John, on the Fourhole;"
"The German Lutheran Church of St. Matthew, in Amelia Township;"
"The German Lutheran Church of Salem, on Sandy Run;"
"The German Lutheran Church of Mt. Zion, on Twelve-mile Creek;"

"The German Lutheran Church of Bethel, on High Hill Creek;"
"The German Lutheran Church of St. Peter, on Eighteen-mile Creek;"
"The German Lutheran Church of St. Martin;"
"The German Lutheran Church of Bethlehem, on Forest's (Fust's) Ford;"
"The German Protestant Church of Bethany, on Green Creek;"
"The German Protestant Church of Appii Forum, Cedar Creek;"
"The German Protestant Church dedicated to Queen Charlotte, on Slippery Creek;"
"The German Lutheran Church of St. George, on Hard Labor Creek;"
"The German Lutheran Church of St. Jacob, on Wateree Creek;"
"The German Protestant Church of St. George, on Indian Field Swamp;"

have petitioned the legislature of this State, praying to be incorporated, and setting forth that they have severally complied with the terms required by the constitution as preparatory thereunto, and the allegations in the said petitions appearing to be true.

I. *Be it therefore enacted*, by the honorable, the Senate and the House of Representatives, now met and sitting in General Assembly, and by the authority of the same, That the several and respective societies hereinbefore mentioned, and the several persons who now are, or shall hereafter become members of the said societies, respectively, and their successors, officers, and members of each of the said societies, shall be, and they are hereby declared, respectively, to be a body corporate, in law, in deed, and in name, by the respective names and styles of: (Here follows a repetition of the names of all the churches above-mentioned.) And by their said respective names shall, severally, have perpetual succession of officers and members, and a common seal, with power to change, alter, break, and make new the same, as often as they, the said corporations, shall severally judge expedient; and each and every of the said corporations respectively are hereby vested with all the powers, privileges, and advantages which are specified and expressed in "the Act for incorporating divers religious societies therein named," passed the twenty-sixth day of March, one thousand seven hundred and eighty-four.

II. *And be it further enacted*, by the authority aforesaid, That this act shall be deemed and taken as a public act, and notice shall be taken thereof in all courts of justice and elsewhere in this State; and the same may be given in evidence on the trial of any issue or cause, without being specially pleaded.

In the Senate, Friday, the twenty-ninth of February, in the year of our Lord one thousand seven hundred and eighty-eight, and in the twelfth year of the independence of the United States of America.

JOHN LLOYD,
President of the Senate.

JOHN JULIUS PRINGLE,
Speaker of the House of Representatives.

1. The question now arises: Were there any other German churches in South Carolina besides these

fifteen, incorporated by the above act of the legislature, and the Lutheran Church in Charleston?

With the single exception of the German Reformed St. John's Church on the Congaree River, of which Rev. Theus was the pastor at one time, there is no knowledge of any other German Church in the State at that time; but why it was not incorporated, or what had become of it, is not known. It has now long since ceased to exist.

2. Of these fifteen German Churches nine were Lutheran; seven of these Lutheran Churches are in existence at the present day, the other two are, St. Martin's, of which no record can be found in any of the minutes of Lutheran synods; and St. George's Church on Hard Labor Creek, Abbeville District, which had already ceased to exist in 1811, according to the missionary report of Rev. R. J. Miller.

3. The other six churches are: (*a.*) The Frederician Church on Cattel's Creek, which was located in Orangeburg District. According to Drs. Jamieson's and Shecut's statement in the Appendix of Ramsay's History of South Carolina, this church was erected in 1778, and named after Andrew Frederick, "who was its principal founder;" it is called by them a Presbyterian Church, but this is an error; it was doubtless a German Reformed Church. It has long since ceased to exist.

(*b.*) The German Calvinistic Church of St. John, on the Fourhole Creek, was also located in Orangeburg District, which has likewise ceased to exist. There are four Lutheran Churches now in that part of Orangeburg County: St. Matthew's, Mt. Lebanon, Pine Grove, and Trinity, which have, doubtless, absorbed the principal part of the descendants of these two German Reformed Churches, whilst others have connected themselves with other denominations.

(*c.*) The German Protestant Church of Bethany on Green Creek cannot be located by the writer, nor are any traces of it to be found at the present time; if, as is supposed, it was located in Newberry District, its material must have been absorbed by the Lutheran Church or other denominations.

(*d.*) The German Protestant Church of Appii Forum, on Cedar Creek, was located in Richland District, near the Fairfield line. Its history has already been given. The congregation and its house of worship are long since no more, and the material has been absorbed in the Methodist Church.

(*e.*) The German Protestant Church, dedicated to Queen Charlotte, on Slippery Creek, Ninety-six District, had its location either in Abbeville or Edgefield District, which comprise part of the territory of what was then known as Ninety-six District. This church has likewise long since passed out of existence.

(*f.*) The German Protestant Church of St. George, on Indian Field Swamp, was located in Barnwell District, fifty miles from Charleston, is known no more under that name. There are two Lutheran Churches in that vicinity at the present time.

4. If these fifteen German Churches comprised the entire German element in the interior of South Carolina in the year 1788, then, as a matter of course, all other Lutheran Churches, not mentioned in this act of incorporation, must have been organized at a subsequent period. This fact will enable any future writer on the subject to unravel their history the more readily.

Section 6. Arrival of Revs. Bernhardt, Storch and Roschen in North Carolina, A.D. 1787 and 1788.

In the year 1787 Rev. Nussmann's heart was gladdened in being permitted to welcome another laborer into the mission field of the Lutheran Church in North Carolina. This was the Rev. Christian Eberhard Bernhardt, a native of Stuttgard, in the kingdom of Würtemberg. He was ordained in his native country, and came to America in the year 1786. He landed at Savannah, and then proceeded to Ebenezer, Georgia, where he remained twelve months. In 1787 he went to Rowan County, N. C., and labored among the churches there one year, doubtless in that part of the county east of the Yadkin River, now known as Davidson County. In 1788 he took charge of the congregations in Stokes and Forsythe Counties, which had been organized and frequently visited by Rev. Nussmann; here Rev. Bernhardt was married, but the records do not mention the name of his wife. One year later he removed to Guilford County, where he remained to the close of the year 1800, when he accepted the call to become the pastor of Zion's and several other Lutheran churches in Lexington District, S. C. This account has been furnished by his daughter-in-law, the widow of the late Rev. David Bernhardt.

In September, 1788, Rev. Nussmann, the faithful pioneer and father of the Lutheran Church in North Carolina, was permitted to grasp the hand of another brother in the ministry, who was sent to his assistance by the Helmstaedt Mission Society, namely: the Rev. Carl August Gottlieb Storch, whose early history is best described by himself in his manuscript journal, an extract of which has been translated and published in the Evangelical Review, vol. viii, pp. 398–404. However, we will let Rev. Storch speak for himself, simply giving his remarks an English translation.

"I, Carl August Gottlieb Storch, was born in Helmstaedt, Duchy of Brunswick, June 16th, 1764; my father's name was George Friederich Storch, a native of the city of Danneberg and merchant in Helmstaedt: my mother's name was Von Asseburg. In the year 1779 I was confirmed by Rev. Abbot* Velthusen, after which I went three years to the high school of Helmstaedt, when I was declared by the Director, Professor Windeburg, fitted to enter the University, and in the year 1782, I became a student of the University of Helmstaedt. Having devoted myself three years to theological sciences, I was recommended in

* The word "Abbot" is the title of an office.

1785 by Rev. Abbot Velthusen to the tutorship of a young nobleman, Von Hodenberg, who resided with Major Von Scheither in Gisthorn, where I remained only one year, because the young nobleman, Von Hodenberg, was elected to the position of page in Hanover; whereupon I became the teacher of Mr. Friese's children, a merchant of Fresenhede, near Bremen. Having remained there two years, I received the call and order from Rev. Abbot Velthusen to go as a pastor to North Carolina, whereupon I was examined and ordained to the ministry, and journeyed in May, 1788, from Germany, and arrived in America about the end of June of the same year. God be praised that he has thus far wonderfully and paternally led me, and safely preserved me in the midst of dangers. I selected my first residence in Salisbury, and commenced to board with Lewis Beard on the 8th of November, 1788."

On another page of his journal, Rev. Storch makes the following record: "April 16th, 1788. I left Fresenhede and journeyed to North Carolina, in North America. The cause of my making this distant and dangerous journey was as follows: Rev. Adolph Nussmann, who was sent as a minister from Germany to North Carolina in the year 1773, and who is still living, greatly desired Rev. Abbot Velthusen to send him several assistant ministers, when Rev. Velthusen selected and persuaded me to undertake this journey. Upon the ducal consent and command I was examined by the five Helmstaedt professors, and ordained as a minister for North Carolina by Abbot Velthusen. All the expenses of my journey were paid, and, upon request, I received the written assurance from my ruler of the land, that, if I should return after a few years, I should still receive my promotion. Under those circumstances, and in reliance upon God, I went to sea on the 4th of May, 1788, and arrived safely in America, landing in Baltimore on the 27th of June of the same year. The whole journey lasted seven weeks and five days. In Baltimore I met with a kind and friendly reception, and after having enjoyed a delightful stay of six weeks in that city, I journeyed by water to Charleston in six days. In Charleston I remained fourteen days, purchased a horse for eleven pounds sterling, and rode to Rev. Nussmann's residence, making a circuit of about 300 English miles, and arrived there at the beginning of the month of September, 1788. Rev. Nussmann serves a congregation at Buffalo Creek. After having recruited myself, we made arrangements with the congregations that desired to have me as their pastor. Three congregations elected and called me, namely: the one in Salisbury, where I first took up my residence; the second, named Organ Church, on Second Creek, ten miles from Salisbury; and the third, Pine Church, which, however, I had to resign, and now only serve two congregations, Salisbury and Organ Church, which have promised me in writing £80 North Carolina currency, paper money; the funeral sermons and marriages are paid extra, usually with one dollar.

I commenced my ministry on the twenty-third Sunday after Trinity, and at Salisbury the Sunday following. On the 7th of January, 1789, I commenced to preach in the Irish settlement once every month, for which I am promised £13 or £14 North Carolina currency."

The high esteem in which Rev. Storch was held in his native country can best be seen from the account given by Rev. Dr. Velthusen, in one of the Helmstaedt Reports, of the ordination and subsequent departure of Rev. Storch to North Carolina. Dr. Velthusen says:

"On the 12th day of March, 1788, the candidate, Carl August Gottlieb Storch, was ordained, under the highest ducal patronage, to the gospel ministry as an assistant preacher for North Carolina. The ordination address has been published under the title, 'Address and Prayer at the Consecration of Mr. Carl A. G. Storch as an Evangelical Assistant Preacher for North Carolina, &c. One and a half sheets, to be had at the book-store of our publications.'

"He has been sent away with the most gracious assurances and best wishes of his Fatherland, that should he, in the lapse of several years, have good occasion to return to the same, after having faithfully discharged his official duties among our brethren in the faith in that country, he may find an open situation as teacher in his Fatherland.

"He was born in Helmstaedt, and was educated under our immediate auspices. During the years which he spent as tutor, we received repeated assurances of his capacity and fidelity as a teacher from those who had opportunity to observe him daily, and had also heard him preach, where he is still held in gracious remembrance. In addition to that, at an appointed examination, conducted in the strictest manner, we have found him well prepared and fitted for his office, and the public evidences of his capacity for preaching and catechizing which he has rendered have given cause of universal satisfaction. The family in which he last served as tutor were very unwilling to part with him; and after having taken his departure from us on his way to America, he returned to this friendly family, in order that he might be in the vicinity of Bremen, and await the sailing of the vessel which is to take him to Baltimore. It will now wholly depend on the affectionate reception which our brethren in the faith in America, and the citizens generally, especially in North Carolina, will bestow upon him, in what manner we shall hereafter aid them in their necessary church affairs."

A few months after the arrival of Rev. Storch came the Rev. Arnold Roschen, who was likewise sent to North Carolina by the Helmstaedt Mission Society. He was a native of the city of Bremen, educated by the Rev. Pastor Nicolai, of that city—that is, as is supposed, under his auspices; and, on the eve of his departure to America, married a lady of Bremen, doubtless with the view that he might become permanently settled, and be contented in his new home.

All these facts are gathered from the Helmstaedt Reports, in which there is found also a published letter, which Rev. Roschen wrote to his friend and preceptor, Rev. Nicolai, giving him an account of his journey to America, kind and hospitable reception at Charleston, and safe arrival in his field of labor in that part of Rowan County, now known as Davidson County. Rev. Roschen writes as follows:

"North Carolina, Rowan County, near Abbot's Creek; in the midst of the forests of North America, sixty-six miles from the Blue Ridge Mountains, eighteen miles from Salem; from April 29th to June 21st, 1789.

"Our journey was a fortunate one, although it lasted twelve weeks from shore to shore. With the exception of two heavy showers in the Channel, which soon passed over, we did not have a single storm upon our long journey by sea; on the contrary, the weather was as good as our friends wished for us at our departure. True, sea-sickness did often and long inconvenience us, but not in such a manner, as that we have to complain greatly concerning it. The want of good water and of necessary refreshments was the hardest to bear. After the New World came to our view—a joy which cannot be described with words—the wind became very unpropitious to us. The great number of vessels that were gathered around us made the crossing along the coast very dangerous; and here we would have been lost without hope, when we thought that we had overcome all difficulties, had not Providence miraculously saved us. After a few days we arrived safely over the bar—a sand-bank which incloses the ship-channel, and in which there are but three openings where a vessel can enter, but which do not permit an entrance without the aid of a pilot. Here a new and glorious prospect awaited us. Life and commotion, a coming together and crossing of so many kinds of vessels, on all sides the loud and resounding song of the sailors, a lovely day, the view of Charleston, the islands that lay around us, the trees which had not yet shed their foliage, the negroes and their apparel, the language—in short, everything that we saw here, and particularly the long-wished-for termination of our journey by sea—awakened within us impressions and feelings which we had never experienced before. On the same evening, November 28th, 1788, we were already brought to shore, and entered into the house of a German; but we did not remain there long. The merchant, Mr. Gäbel (a native of Bremen, who had also kindly entertained our Storch, and had in various ways offered his hand to our (mission) institute, says Dr. Velthusen), heard that same evening of our arrival, sent a friend to us with reproaches, that we had passed the house of our countryman, and desired us to move into his dwelling immediately, if we wished to be regarded as his friends. He offered us several rooms, received us in a noble manner, and spoke to us very obligingly. At the same time he commanded his negroes to look upon us as their masters, so that we wanted for nothing.

"I found an upright friend in Rev. Mr. Faber, the German minister, who treated me, during the ten weeks that we had to remain here, in such a manner, as any one could have desired under the circumstances. He besought me to conduct Divine service with him, and to preach whenever it would be agreeable to me. In this manner I preached here about five times. Upon the whole, I must acknowledge that all the Germans endeavored to make the place, which is in itself a very charming one, as agreeable to us as possible, although the obligations became very costly to us; for everything, even the smallest article, is very dear here, so much so that I and my wife could live very well in my native city on the amount that has to be expended here for extras.

"At length the wagons, sent by our congregations, came for my things, and horses for us to ride—for every person rides here—and we two began our journey of 300 North Carolina miles on horseback, which was at first very fatiguing. It was very hard for me to leave Charleston; I had many opportunities there of becoming profitably associated, and I found at times very noble friends, whose magnanimity astonished me. At the first moment of my stay there, I was delighted at the banishment of all ceremonies, which among us are regarded so sacredly. Besides that, we heard such dreadful reports of the people where my congregations are situated, which, however, God be praised! arose from the fact, that in

Charleston the citizens are as badly informed as in Germany concerning this country.

"We were accompanied several miles on our journey by our friends; our way then went through a great part of South to North Carolina. This overland journey lasted fourteen days, and was very wearisome, as may be readily supposed. Sometimes we slept at night at a plantation, where we were friendly received and kindly treated; at other times we lodged with a new settler, where seven or eight people rested in the same room beside us, among whom, at times, were sick and dying persons, and our repose became very unpleasant; then again we slept under a tree; and sometimes under a wagon and in the rain; nevertheless, we had generally very pleasant weather.

"We passed through three American towns, which, on account of the small number of houses, would scarcely be considered by us as villages. Among these was Camden, which is very handsomely built, containing about thirty houses, and is distant about 150 miles from Charleston, where we lodged for the night with a German from Hamburg, named Schütt, whose brother lives in Charleston and is in good circumstances.

"At length we arrived in Salisbury, where Pastor Storch resides, whom I especially esteem and love as a friend, and who rendered me very important services, where we were as kindly received as we could have expected. Upon the first intelligence of our arrival, the deacons of one of the nearest of my congregations, together with some wealthy planters residing there, came to the town to welcome us. The people here know nothing of compliments, but express their opinions in a manner that indicates good thinking faculties. They informed us that we would not find a dwelling-house as yet prepared for us, because, upon consultation, it was thought best to wait until my arrival, so that I could myself direct the building of the same. And now the whole train moved along, increased by Pastor Storch's accompanying us, until we came to the place appointed for me, situated on Abbot's Creek, a small stream that empties itself about twelve miles distant into the Yadkin River. A deacon of my central congregation took us to his home, where we remained several months, until we moved to our own plantation of two hundred acres of land, which we have purchased advantageously, assisted by several upright planters of this place; we were advised to take this step by Pastor Nussmann, who came to meet us in Salisbury, in which advice Rev. Storch also joined.

"As soon as we arrived, the deacons out of three congregations came and visited us. A fourth congregation, which is now almost the largest, also placed itself under my ministry. So now I am the pastor of four churches. The people from all parts of the country brought us abundantly flour, corn, hams, sausages, dried fruit, chickens, turkeys, geese, &c., so much so, that there has been scarcely any necessity to spend one farthing for our housekeeping up to this time."

According to these statements, it may be seen that the Lord of the vineyard had now five laborers in the Lutheran Church in North Carolina, namely, Revs. Nussmann, Arndt, Bernhardt, Storch, and Roschen, and they were "workmen that needed not to be ashamed," for they were all talented men, and filled with the spirit of their Master; besides, they were men of the most profound learning; even Arndt had received an excellent education, although he came to this country in the capacity of a school teacher, and all had been brought up in the most refined society, and might have been an acquisition and an honor to any college or university in the land; but because they were Germans, and spoke a foreign language, little was ever known of them by the general inhabitants of the State; however, they were so much the better known, and the more highly esteemed by the people among whom they lived, and for whose spiritual welfare they labored.

Section 7. The Helmstaedt Mission Society—Letters from Revs. Nussmann, Storch, and Roschen, published in the Helmstaedt Reports, indicating the condition of the Lutheran Church in North Carolina during the years 1788 and 1789.

The Lutheran Church is at present tolerably familiar with the titles of two extensive German publications, denominated "The Halle Reports" and "The Urlsperger Reports;" however, it is not generally known that a similar work, although not so extensive, and therefore, perhaps, more readable, entitled "The Helmstaedt Reports," to which frequent allusion has been made, had likewise been published for the purpose of imparting information to European readers, concerning the state of some of our Lutheran mission stations in America.

The missionary spirit in the Lutheran Church was engendered more than two centuries ago, and soon after the close of the Thirty Years' War. Various mission societies have been formed in Europe, under a variety of appellations, but all having the same object in view, that of spreading the knowledge and benefits of the Christian religion in foreign lands. The different mission fields appear to have been properly apportioned and selected by the numerous societies over all Protestant Europe.

Among the various fields of labor of our pious German forefathers, America was not forgotten, and the Lutheran Church in Europe was foremost in the ranks in her efforts to provide for the spiritual welfare of her people on this continent and its adjacent islands. Not only were faithful and self-sacrificing missionaries sent, their salaries paid them by charitable donations of Christians in the Fatherland, but also churches, school-houses, and sometimes orphan asylums were both erected and supported by these munificent contributions. Books of worship and devotion, as well as of education and instruction, were sent gratuitously in great numbers to our forefathers in America.

In point of time the Swedish Delaware-River Mission was the first enterprise of this kind; its object was the planting of the Lutheran Church systematically and firmly in America, not mentioning the Danish Lutheran mission in Greenland, and the different missions on some of the islands along the Atlantic coast of America.

Next in order was the Ebenezer Mission in Georgia, with which we are tolerably familiar, and the extensive minute reports of its missionaries, which were sent to the parent society in Augsburg, and cover about six thousand quarto pages of printed matter, were all published by the Rev. Dr. Urlsperger, and thus originated "The Urlsperger Reports."

Then the University and Orphan House at Halle, institutions founded by the celebrated August Herrmann Francke, sent missionaries to another vacant field farther north, which claimed their attention, and the Rev. H. M. Muhlenberg, D.D. and others were sent to Pennsylvania, who likewise transmitted the reports of their labors to the parent Mission Society, and which were all published under the title of "The Halle" or "The Pennsylvania Reports."

However, between Pennsylvania and Georgia there was a large territory still unoccupied, and, at a later period, the Professors of the Julius Charles University, in the city of Helmstaedt, Duchy of Brunswick, became interested in this field, midway between the two American missions established by Halle and Augsburg, and on this wise was North Carolina selected and regarded as a hopeful locality for still farther missionary operations, and the Rev. John Caspar Velthusen, D.D., Professor of Theology in the above-mentioned university, with his associates, sent missionaries, upon the earnest call of Rev. Nussmann, to labor among the Germans in North Carolina. The reports which these missionaries sent to the parent society in Helmstaedt, were also published, and were denominated "The Helmstaedt or North Carolina Reports," which, until recently, were no longer known to exist.

From an article in one of these published reports, we are informed that "up to the present time (March 13th, 1788), the net proceeds of donations and funds advanced upon the publication of our (their) seven advertised books of instruction, amount already to 1238 rix-dollars, 13 groschen, and 8 pfennigs." This was the beginning of a treasury for the welfare of the North Carolina mission field; in other of the reports, acknowledgments of additional donations, and the names of the donors occur. Dr. Velthusen goes on to state:

"For nearly a year past it appeared that we would not be able to carry out our purpose in so short a time, namely, the sending of well-qualified preachers to North Carolina." (Here follows what has been stated already in another section.) "Our spirits were likewise revived by the statement of several other trustworthy friends, who had been in Virginia, as well as to the borders of North

Carolina, and who were unanimous in praising the Christian willingness of our evangelical brethren in the faith in that country to provide liberally for those preachers sent to them, so that they need want for nothing, provided they were in any way worthy of their confidence."

In the following pages of this narrative Dr. Velthusen mentions the names and acts of kindness of several friends of the mission enterprise who resided in New York, Baltimore and Virginia; besides, the delay of the publication of several works for the benefit of the mission, occasioned by the call and removal of Prof. Klügel to Halle; the names and character of the works intended for publication; the delay of the publication of a geographical work until the reception of more recent information from Charleston; list of donors to the mission cause in which the Professors had embarked, &c.; the whole of which is dated and signed by them as follows:

"Helmstaedt, at the Ducal Brunswick-Lüneburg Julius-Charles University, March 13th, 1788.

"J. C. Velthusen, Professor of Theology, and Abbot.

"H. P. C. Hencke, Professor of Theology, and Abbot.

"L. Crell, Professor of Medical Science and Philosophical Mineralogy and Mining.

"G. S. Klügel, Professor of Philosophy and Mathematics.

"P. J. Bruns, Professor of the History of Philosophy and Literature."

A Letter from Rev. A. Nussmann to Rev. Dr. Velthusen.

NORTH CAROLINA, MECKLENBURG COUNTY,
BUFFALO CREEK, November 12th, 1788.

HONORABLE ABBOT, MY BEST FRIEND:

The indications of Providence develop themselves more and more visibly in this religious work, so that God's finger is made manifest here in the work for the welfare of his people. In Charleston a warm interest is taken in our affairs. Rev. Mr. Faber is an active man. Rev. Storch's sickness gave me much uneasiness and sorrow, for I love him on account of his learning, virtue, spirit and friendship, which had already commenced in Germany. All persons who see and hear him, love and honor him. But even in this respect has God helped us,—Rev. Storch is again restored; and may God preserve his health in future, so that whether I live or die, my expectations concerning him may be realized.

A change has taken place concerning his call to the congregation in Guilford County; Providence has directed otherwise. Storch felt at that time so feeble, that he believed himself to be unable to make the long journey on horseback, which was necessary to reach his field of labor. Besides, he would have then been one hundred miles distant from me, and in a wilderness where no messenger can be obtained. These difficulties were at once removed by God. A call was extended to him from three vacant congregations, Salisbury, Pine Church and Second Creek, with the written assurance of a salary of £110, and in a few days afterwards £14 more from a congregation seven miles distant from Salisbury, which he will have to serve during the week-day. These congregations, through their deacons, promised to pay the freight on his things, which will be about two Spanish dollars for every 100 pounds, but they could not pay his traveling expenses from Baltimore to Charleston. It is a hard matter to take everything out of the pocket of a private man, in a country where the congregation have as yet nothing of their own.

A book printing establishment would be of the greatest benefit to religion, and which could readily obtain assistance here, if we only had the type. The capital necessary for such an establishment could not only be kept up, but also improved, for there is no German printing office from Georgia to Maryland, and not even a good English one in North Carolina. If we only had one, then we could suit ourselves to circumstances, and print those publications immediately, which are the most necessary; the transportation from Germany is so slow, and the want in a new country so urgent, that one dare not wait long to meet this want.

An organ is also necessary, as it must be our chief concern to reinstate church music. In the last sixteen years I have had an oversight of several hundred square miles, partly by personal visits and partly through reliable intelligence, and I have found that in proportion to the music, which the people were able to conduct, congregations spring up, increase, flourish, decay, fall into ruin. An improvement, therefore, must be made; fifty copies of an excellent singing-book, judiciously scattered in schools and families, would soon secure its adoption as a school and family singing-book; afterwards it would come into general use through the country.

The 370 rix-dollars should, according to the intent of the donors, be a permanent investment for the benefit of religion, principally in the congregations from Rocky River to Salisbury. This would be satisfactory to all, and would re-establish and preserve peace and quietude. God, who has so often and visibly aided us in these matters, and brought forth great results out of small things; who has always arranged matters differently to what I had imagined, but always better than my expectations, will also help here, and through his wisdom direct everything in such a manner, so that the four philanthropists, your assistants, in connection with all those upright persons who have aided the good cause, may experience joy in their work.

I am, &c.,

Your most devoted friend,

ADOLPH NUSSMANN.

Report of Rev. C. A. G. Storch, dated May 28th, 1789.

This report was sent to the Helmstaedt Mission Society, from which Dr. Velthusen makes the following extracts.

"Rev. Storch, as well as Rev. Roschen, are both

satisfied in the midst of their congregations. Rev. S. mentions, that of his three congregations, Organ Church, on Second Creek, is the strongest, and consists of eighty-seven families. He praises the people, who treat him with love and respect, and supply him with the necessaries of life." (Here the salary, &c., is again stated, much the same as in Nussmann's report.) "His congregation is building a house for him, and have offered him a loan for the purpose of purchasing a plantation, without which one cannot succeed there. He still lives in Salisbury, where an academy has been established, in which there are some students, who receive instruction in Hebrew from him. In addition to that duty, he has also established a small German school, so that the youth may accustom themselves to a purer German language. He expects to confirm about fifty children next harvest season. He says that Rev. Roschen is likewise treated with love and respect; that he has four congregations, and receives from them about £100, current paper money; that he resides about eighteen miles from him, on the other side of a broad river; has already purchased a plantation, and is accustoming himself well to the climate and mode of living in that country."

Report of Rev. Arnold Roschen.

"In my middle congregation I have confirmed twenty-four persons; in the congregation situated towards the Yadkin River I confirmed twelve, and in the others I have this duty yet before me." (Here follows a lengthy description of the customary funeral ceremonies.) "Marriages are here performed in two modes; the one, according to the rules of the Church, requires to be announced three times; the other is managed as follows: The groom gets a certificate from Salisbury, rides, accompanied by his friends, with his bride to the minister, or, if there is none in the place, to the magistrate, where the marriage takes place. The first questions of the minister are, Whether he has taken his bride without her parents' knowledge?—this occurs frequently—and, Whether the parents have given their consent? If any one has stolen his bride, and has a license from Salisbury, then the objections of the parents avail nothing. Upon the whole, in this free country, a son, whenever he has arrived at his twenty-first year, and a daughter, as soon as she is eighteen years old, is no longer under the parents' control. Persons generally marry very young, because they need not be much concerned for the future. He that will work, can soon have a plantation; and poor people are not to be met here at all. A person can often meet with families that have thirteen to fourteen children, nearly all living. I myself am acquainted with a planter here, who has had a family of twenty-three children, born of one mother, and who, with the exception of two, are all living and well.

"My catechumens, whom I have instructed three days in every week for seven weeks, consist partly of married persons, some of them as old as thirty years, and young persons from sixteen to twenty years of age. Among other things, I advise them not to intermarry with persons of other nationalities, because such mixed marriages are generally unhappy, and sometimes occasion murder and homicide, and because the English in these regions belong to no religious denomination, and do not permit their children to be baptized, nor send them to school.

"Rev. Storch and I recently passed by the court-house in Salisbury, at the moment when a man was standing in the pillory. A German called to us to stop awhile, and see how the Americans punish rogues and thieves. Upon my asking him, 'The criminal is certainly not a German?' I received the literally true reply, 'Never has a German stood in the pillory in Salisbury; nor has ever a German been hung in this place.'

"Most persons are well satisfied with their plantations in this country. I recently visited a member of my congregation, and inquired of him how he was getting along. To which he replied, 'Were we to complain, God would have to punish us. We have need of nothing, and possess a large surplus above our wants. We are enjoying good health, and everything is in good order on our plantations; and since we are possessed of such an abundance so soon after the war, we must certainly become wealthy if God continues to give us peace.'

"So far as my situation as planter is concerned,

I can say nothing else than that I am very fortunate and happy, and it would cost me a great struggle on this account, as well as that I am beloved and respected as pastor by my congregation, to exchange my present location with any other. I pray God, that he would not separate Storch and myself, for he is now also beginning to feel satisfied. Not long ago, when I had service in my upper congregation, I was surrounded by the elders and deacons, who besought me never to leave them. A certain Colonel declared, that he would never again be connected with the church, if I were to move away. I can assure you that I will not abandon these congregations so easily as persons in Germany doubtless imagine. We ministers are treated with a respect, which is shown to no other person. There is no difference in rank acknowledged here, and yet no one has ever spoken with me, who did not hold his hat in his hand. I must say the same of Storch; he is treated with such love and respect by his congregations, as few ministers in Germany are treated.

"At first Storch, in his hypochondria, looked upon all things in a false light; besides, his arrival in America was unpropitious" (that is, he was laid upon a bed of sickness soon after his arrival in North Carolina); "now he speaks differently. Nussmann, who is a good and upright man, lives upon his plantation in very moderate circumstances. Arndt, formerly a catechet, now a preacher, possesses two fine plantations, is wealthy, and edifies his people by his life and conduct. We all preach in black clothes and collar, but mostly without a gown, and oftentimes in our overcoat, during bad weather in winter.

"I endeavor to make the Divine service as impressive as possible, and suitable to the occasion, but as simple as I can. I dare not make my discourse shorter than three-quarters of an hour, because there are members, who have to ride eighteen miles to church, and in each church there is service only once every four weeks. Baptisms take place after the sermon, and in the presence of the whole congregation. Whenever the communion is administered on Sunday, the preparatory service takes place on Friday or Saturday preceding. Nothing is known here of private confession."

This interesting report of Rev. Roschen is quite lengthy, and has been somewhat abridged, because it alludes to customs that would require a lengthy explanation, before they would be properly understood by the general reader, and because some things are reported of his own personal affairs, which would not be interesting to any one at the present time.

Rev. Dr. Velthusen yet adds, that a letter had arrived from Mr. Gäbel in Charleston, South Carolina, fourteen days ago, corroborating the above church intelligence. Mr. Gäbel, who is on a visit to Bremen, writes, that he had left Nussmann well and hearty in Charleston (doubtless Rev. Nussmann was on a visit there at the time); that Storch has no inclination to return to Germany, and assures us that Roschen is well satisfied, and that he will have good profit in a few years from the tract of land which he purchased there. Mr. Gäbel likewise states, that in his journey through Georgia he met with the pastor at Ebenezer, Rev. Mr. Bergmann, and found him in a situation in which he may be well satisfied.

Section 8. Further Intelligence from St. John's and Organ Churches; and a Ministerial Assembly in North Carolina called to Ordain the Rev. Robert Johnson Miller.

Extract from the old German (St. John's) Church-book.—"January 16th, 1790, the church council held a meeting, when the following members were present: Paul Barringer, Peter Quillmann, George Meissenheimer, Daniel Jarrett, Matthew Meyer, Nicholas Reitenhauer, Jacob Fegert, Andreas Stauch, Ulrich Dürr, Jacob Bast, and the pastor, Adolph Nussmann. Paul Barringer, Sr., was chosen chairman of the council. The object of the meeting was to promote a greater degree of union and true sincerity in matters of religion, both in schools and churches.

"It was resolved, that the doors of the church shall no longer be closed before the commencement of the Lord's day services; but as soon as one-half of the congregation shall have been assembled, the doors shall then be opened, and at ten o'clock the services of the sanctuary shall commence; and those persons who shall be guilty of making disturbance during worship shall be reported to the magistrate. The services shall also commence in future without any further calling in of those persons who remain outside.

"*Resolved*, That at the celebration of the Lord's Supper, alms shall be gathered at the doors. The members of the congregation are furthermore requested to celebrate their marriages in the church, at which time of rejoicing they and their benevolent guests are desired to contribute alms to the church, and to lay their mites upon the altar, as is customary in many places in our Evangelical Church.

"*Resolved*, That whenever slanderous reports are circulated, which might cause dissensions in the church, they shall be made known to our President, Paul Barringer, who shall investigate the matter, and shall decide in such a way, as shall best promote the interests of true religion and the church.

"*Resolved*, That persons bringing their children to the church to be baptized, must make the fact known before service, name the sponsors, the day of the child's birth, the names of the parents, so that it may be recorded in the church-book."

Pastor Storch commenced his labors at Organ Church, October 26th, 1788; and in Salisbury on the Sunday following, November 2d, being the 23d and 24th Sundays after Trinity. A very concise constitution was introduced and adopted on the following New Year's Day, 1789, which, however, contains nothing of special interest to the general reader, except that it indicates how much our forefathers felt and labored for the order, discipline and consequent welfare of their congregations.

Organ Church alone promised their pastor an annual salary of £40, North Carolina currency, and the number of those members, who subscribed this amount, and undersigned the new constitution, amounted to seventy-eight persons.

In the year 1791, the present massive and, as was then considered, large and commodious stone church was erected, having large galleries on each side, except where the pulpit stands; and an organ, excellent in its day, built by one of the members, Mr. Steigerwalt, was placed in the centre of the long gallery, and opposite the pulpit. The pulpit, as a matter of course, was goblet-shaped, with a sounding-board overhead, and has but recently been removed when the church was repaired. Those time-honored relics are fast passing away by the encroachments of our novelty-seeking age.

The first *English* Lutheran preacher in North Carolina was the Rev. Robert Johnson Miller, who was a Scotchman by birth, a native of Baldovia, Angusshire, near Dundee, born July 11th, 1758, the third son of George and Margaret Miller. His parents designed him to study for the ministry, and for this purpose sent him to the Dundee classical school. After he had completed his education there, and before he entered the ministry, he migrated to America, and arrived in Charlestown, Massachusetts, A.D. 1774. His brother, an East and West India merchant of that place, had invited him from Scotland to reside with him, with whom he labored as an assistant in his business for some time.

It now happened that his adopted country became involved in the Revolutionary struggle, when he at once declared himself a friend of liberty, and as soon as General Greene passed through Boston with his army, young Miller enlisted as a Revolutionary soldier. He was engaged in the battles of Long Island, where he received a flesh wound in the face, of Brandywine, White Plains, and the siege of Valley Forge; but God preserved his life in all these engagements, as he had a more glorious work in store for him. With the army he traveled to the South, where he remained after peace was declared and the army disbanded.

He now remembered his duty to God, his former vows, and his preparation for the ministry, and applied for license to preach the Gospel in connection with the Methodist Episcopal Church, as the minutes of the Methodist Conference plainly indicate; and thus authorized, he commenced preaching in the western counties of North Carolina, traveling often one hundred miles to meet his appointments.

Although licensed to preach by the Methodist Episcopal Conference, yet not having the authority to administer the sacraments, his people of White Haven Church, in Lincoln County, sent a petition to the Lutheran pastors of Cabarrus and Rowan Counties, with high recommendations, praying that he might be ordained by them, which was accordingly done at St. John's Church, Cabarrus County, on the 20th of May, 1794. The ordination certificate is still extant, although much mutilated, and inasmuch as it contains some interesting historical facts, it is here inserted:

"To all whom it may concern, greeting:

"*Whereas*, A great number of Christian people in Lincoln County have formed themselves into a society by the name of White Haven Church, and also having formed a vestry: We, the subscribers, having been urged by the pressing call from the said Church to ordain a minister for the good of their children, and for the enjoyment of ye gospel ordinances among them, from us, the ministers of the Lutheran Church in North Carolina, have solemnly ordained," (here much of the certificate is torn away and lost) "according to ye infallible word of God, administer ye sacraments, and to have ye care of souls; he always being obliged to obey ye Rules, ordinances and customs of ye Christian Society, called ye Protestant Episcopal Church in America. Given under our hands and seals, North Carolina, Cabarrus County, May 20th, 1794.

"Signed by Adolphus Nussmann, Senior, Johann Gottfriedt Arendt, Arnold Roschen, Christopher Bernhardt, and Charles Storch."

On the reverse side of this certificate the Lutheran ministers gave their reasons why they had ordained a man who was attached to the Episcopal Church as a minister of that denomination.

As all the Lutheran ministers were present at the ordination of Rev. R. J. Miller, there must have been a synodical or conferential meeting of some kind held at that time, as such *actus ministeriales* are performed generally on those occasions. This conclusion is substantiated by the fact that Miller went to St. John's Church with the view to be examined and ordained, in accordance with the petition of his congregation; and Rev. Nussmann's name is signed to the certificate of ordination as *Senior*, an office honorably conferred by such a body at that time. It is, therefore, but reasonable to conclude that the first ecclesiastical assembly of the Lutheran Church in North Carolina was held in St. John's Church, Cabarrus County, in the month of May, 1794, and that the first minister ordained by that Lutheran Ministerium was the Rev. R. J. Miller.

Section 9. Death of Revs. Nussmann and Martin—Resignation of Rev. John Charles Faber—Removal of Rev. Bernhardt to South Carolina—Return of Rev. Roschen to Germany—Arrival of Revs. Paul and Philip Henkel.

Rev. Nussmann's labors in North Carolina extended over a period of more than twenty years, remaining faithfully at his post until God called him to his rest. He was the pioneer minister of the Lutheran Church in the State, and commenced his labors among his people in the days of their colonial hardships and trials; he had been with them through all the devastating influences of a most sanguinary war; he had seen them rise again to comparative comfort and prosperity under the new government; he had ministered to them in all circumstances of life, and had himself experienced many trials and afflictions through which he was called to pass. All denominations of Christians, that had ever heard of him, mention his name with honor and praise. "Caruther's Life of Rev. David Caldwell, D.D.," a Presbyterian work, speaks of Nussmann as having "labored faithfully in poverty and privations." Dr. Velthusen, in the Helmstaedt Reports, says: "The intelligence which I have received from strangers concerning Nussmann, of which there is not the slightest intimation to be found in his own letters, informs us, that his faithfulness in his ministerial office is so great, that he places his temporal welfare and the care of his children's worldly prosperity too far in the background, and is more earnestly concerned for the building up of the Church, than for the success of his planting interests."

During his ministry he had suffered many privations, as he had never received an adequate support for himself and family; and during the Revolutionary War, he was often in despair of his life on account of his liberal principles. At one time he was obliged to secrete himself in the tall undergrowth along the banks of a small stream near his house, in order to escape the fury of the Tories, who had prowled about destroying valuable lives, and robbing persons of their property and daily bread. The Helmstaedt Mission Society sent him a selection of valuable books for his library, and other publications to be disposed of for his benefit, but it is doubtful whether he realized much from the sale of them. It is known, that some of these books were donated by him to indigent persons.

An anecdote is related of him by Christopher Melchor, Esq., that on one occasion, when he received but one dollar for a marriage fee, and some person remarked, that the sum was rather a small one, he good-humoredly remarked: "It is small if the wife proves to be a good one, but if otherwise, it is sufficiently large."

Shortly after Rev. Nussmann came to this country, he was united in marriage to Barbara Layrle, a daughter of Christopher Layrle, one of the deputies sent to Germany to bring pastors and teachers to North Carolina; with her he lived in blissful harmony, and was the father of several sons and daughters, none of whom are now living; but his grandchildren and descendants to the fifth generation are still to be met with in Central North Carolina, respected by all who are acquainted with them.

Pastor Nussmann had for some time been afflicted with a cancer on his neck, and it became evident that it would terminate in his death, yet he bore his affliction meekly and with Christian fortitude, when on the 3d of November, 1794, his family and friends were called to witness the departure of a faithful husband, father and pastor. It was a severe loss to his congregation; he was their first pastor, and had labored long and faithfully for them; and how they would now be supplied with the means of grace, was a question not easily answered. His memory is still cherished by the members of St. John's Church, who have placed a new marble tombstone at the head of his grave; the former one, an ancient-looking blue stone slab, upon which time had done its work, is now safely and sacredly deposited in St. John's Church, and still bears the following German inscription: "Christus ist mein Leben, Sterben ist mein Gewinn. Das Andenken der Gerechten bleibet im Segen. Hier ruhen die Gebeine des treuen Predigers, Adolph Nussmann, in Deutschland geboren, im August, 1739, gestorben den 3ten November, 1794" ("For me to live is Christ, to die is gain. The memory of the righteous is blessed. Here repose the remains of the faithful preacher, Adolphus Nussmann, born in Germany, August, 1739, died November 3d, 1794.") He was aged 55 years, 3 months, and some days.

Besides having labored in Cabarrus County, he also performed missionary duty in several German settlements in the northern part of North Carolina, as before stated. The following record is taken from the minutes of the North Carolina Synod of 1831: "The Rev. Mr. Nussmann, weak as he was, established two congregations in Surry, now Stokes County, and instructed and confirmed old and young; these churches have not yet died out." More could not be said to his praise than, that he lived the life of a pious and useful Christian, and died in the triumphs of that Gospel, which he faithfully preached.

A few months after Nussmann's death, God called another and once active laborer in the Lutheran Church in the Carolinas to his rest; this was the Rev. John Nicholas Martin, who had become aged and infirm, and was no longer able to perform any active duties of the gospel ministry, but who still took a deep interest in the welfare of the Church. "He was born at Zweibrücken (Deux-Ponts), in Rhenish Bavaria, and emigrated to North America about the middle of the eighteenth century. He was then a married man with several children. The colony, after some delay, settled in Anson County, near South Carolina. From this point Rev. Martin, with the larger portion of his congregation, removed to a district between the Broad and Saluda Rivers," but labored mostly in Charleston, as pastor of St. John's Church, where he finally made his permanent home on a farm located about a mile from the city; "there he closed his honored and useful life, July 27th, 1795." His descendants are numerous, the most of whom are still attached to the Lutheran Church, and are devoted members of the same.

In the year 1800, the Lutheran Church in Charleston became vacant by the resignation of Rev. John Charles Faber, on account of the failure of his health. According to Ramsay's History of South Carolina, vol. ii, p. 23, reprinted edition, Rev. Faber's successor was Rev. Matthew Frederic, but no such name occurs in any of the records of the

Church now accessible, and it is exceedingly doubtful whether Dr. Ramsay's statement is correct. The statement of the vestry of that church, made a few years ago, and extracted from the old church-book, is as follows: "Rev. Mr. Pogson officiated on Sundays for a short time, and on his retiring, Mr. Faber consented to serve the church as far as his strength would allow." No other minister's name is mentioned until Mr. Faber's successor, the younger Faber, is introduced in the narrative as the regular pastor. The vacancy continued five years.

At the close of the year 1800, Rev. C. E. Bernhardt received and accepted the call as pastor of the Saluda charge, in Lexington District, South Carolina, to which place he removed with his family from Guilford County, North Carolina; by this removal another vacancy was created in the Lutheran Church of that State. But this was not the only charge which suffered in this manner; the Rev. Arnold Roschen, who was, at first, so well satisfied with his field of labor, and had no other thought but that of continuing there the remainder of his life, now changed his mind, when his heart yearned for his Fatherland, and he returned to Germany about the year 1800; however, his place was soon occupied by the arrival of Rev. Paul Henkel, whose name occurs in the Halle Reports as a catechet laboring in Virginia, but who was afterwards ordained by the Ministerium of Pennsylvania.

In the year 1801, the Rev. Philip Henkel, a son

of Rev. Paul Henkel, came to North Carolina, and took charge of the Guilford pastorate, made vacant by the removal of Rev. Bernhardt to South Carolina. It is stated in the Helmstaedt Reports, that a third minister was to have been sent by Helmstaedt Mission Society to North Carolina; he is spoken of as "a candidate of a noble heart and excellent attainments," but for some reason or other he never came to America.

Section 10. St. John's Church, Cabarrus County, N. C., after Rev. Nussmann's death—Report of Rev. Storch to Dr. Velthusen—Decline of the German Reformed Church in South Carolina.

After the death of Pastor Nussmann, St John's Church remained vacant for two years, after which time it was supplied temporarily one year with the labors of Rev. Storch, so his journal informs us, and in 1797 the Rev. Adam Nicholas Marcard, who had been laboring in the vicinity, at Cold Water Creek, a newly organized church, became the pastor of St. John's Church, and labored there nearly three years, and then also removed to South Carolina. It must be said to his credit, that the records of the church during his time were neatly made by himself, being both ample and well arranged.

As no other pastor could be obtained, Rev. Storch took charge of this congregation, and served it in connection with his other churches.

He was a faithful laborer, and introduced many wholesome reforms, but his health failed him, and recommended that the congregation elect another pastor, when they called the Rev. John Henkel, from Virginia, who accepted the call in 1803, and was on the point of moving to North Carolina, when God called him from time to eternity. There was now no other alternative left but for Rev. Storch to continue his labors among this people, and he remained their pastor until the year 1821, laboring as faithfully as his health would permit.

The condition of the Lutheran Church in North Carolina at this time is reported in a letter of Rev. Storch to Rev. Dr. Velthusen, dated "Salisbury, N. C., February 25th, 1803," and published in one of the Doctor's works. Pastor Storch writes:

"It is now nearly three years that I live in very sad circumstances; not only have I suffered during this time from various severe attacks of sickness, which had brought my body near to death, but likewise from an apparently incurable disease of the eyes, which seems to baffle all medical skill, and made it impossible for me either to read or write. I am, however, quite restored from my sickness of last fall, a disease similar to yellow fever, and which rages in this entire vicinity with great mortality. I now feel tolerably strong, and my eyes are somewhat better; nevertheless, according to the opinion of the physician, I need not expect any permanent restoration of my health in this climate. However, we have an eternity before us, where we will be always well.

"The present condition of this country is remarkable, both in a political and religious aspect. Party spirit is risen to a fearful height. Infidelity prevails to a great extent, both among the higher and lower classes of society.

"I still serve my old congregations, and I continue to preach the doctrines of Jesus Christ, the crucified, in simplicity, and have happily experienced the power of his grace upon myself and others. The prevalence of infidelity, the contempt of the best of all religions, its usages and servants, the increase of irreligion and crime, as remarked, have occasioned me many sad hours. Nevertheless I have found consolation and courage in the thought:

'So long as Christ protects His Church,
May hell its rage continue;'

and I held fast to my faith, convinced that truth and religion will at last mightily raise up their head and prevail.

"The congregations at the Catawba River are without a preacher. The faithful brother, Ahrend, has become totally blind. It is a sad calamity for that good man and the churches. The Buffalo Creek congregation (St. John's) is likewise unprovided for; however, it has at present the hope of obtaining the services of a brother of Paul Henkel, the successor of our Roschen. Rev. Bernhardt has left his situation in Guilford, and is now serving for the past two years several congregations in South Carolina. The congregations in Guilford County are now served by a son of Rev. Paul Henkel. Rev. Magister Faber has resigned his pastoral office in Charleston some three years ago; the congregation has extended a call to me, connected with very favorable offers; but I could not accept it. Mr. Faber continues to preach for them as long as the congregation has no other pastor. I am rejoiced that Pastor Roschen has again been appointed to a charge (in Germany), and I heartily wish that, with enduring health, he may long continue to be useful to the Church."

During this period the German Reformed Church in South Carolina commenced to decline; all the old ministers had departed this life, and no new pastors were obtained to take charge of the vacant churches. The Rev. A. Loretz, from North Carolina, and perhaps some others, visited these congregations about once or twice a year, preached, and administered the sacraments; but as the journey always embraced several hundred miles, and was made with much difficulty at that time, these visits became less frequent from time to time, until they ceased entirely, and the denomination became extinct in that State; the members were at length absorbed by other professions of faith, a large proportion of which connected themselves with the Lutheran Church, particularly where the houses of worship were held jointly by Lutheran and German Reformed congregations.

Section 11. The great religious revival of the years 1800 and 1801, which swept over the United States; reports of Rev. Storch and Henkel concerning it.

On the subject of revivals the opinion of the Lutheran Church of America has been, and is still, divided, both as to whether such revivals are right or wrong in themselves, and again, among those who favor these revivals, as to the proper mode of conducting them.

These revivals of religion, that is to say, what is generally understood by that name, so far as the Lutheran Church is concerned, are purely an American feature, ingrafted upon a portion of the Lutheran Church in this country, and has nothing in common with what is called "*Pietism*" in Germany.

At this late period of time, and with an experience of more than half a century, the Church cannot be regarded an uninformed stranger to this "new measure;" the opinion of all our ministers and members is now generally confirmed as to the effects of these revivals.

Not desiring to discuss the merits of this revival question at this point of the history of our Church in the Carolinas, because it would be out of place in point of time, revivals not having been then introduced in our churches, it is, nevertheless, peculiarly interesting to read what our forefathers thought of them more than seventy years ago, when the great revival of 1800 and 1801 swept over this entire country, and the subject was presented to their minds for the first time.

Rev. Storch writes: "By the side of this pestilence (infidelity), there prevails now, for over a year, a something, I know not what to name it, and I should not like to say *Fanaticism.* Christians of every denomination assemble themselves in the forest, numbering four, six and sometimes ten thousand persons; they erect tents, sing, pray and preach, day and night, for five, six and eight days. I have been an eye-witness to scenes in such large assemblies, which I cannot explain. I beheld young and old, feeble and strong, white and black, in short, people of every age, position and circumstances, as though they were struck by lightning, speechless and motionless; and, when they had somewhat recovered, they could be heard shrieking bitterly, and supplicating God for mercy and grace.

"After they had thus spent three, and many even more, hours, they rose up, praised God, and commenced to pray in such a manner, as they never were wont to do, exhorting sinners to come to Jesus, &c. Many of those, who were thus exercised, were ungodly persons before, and we can now discover a remarkable change in them. Even deists have been brought to confess Christ in this way. Thus this thing continues even to this hour.

"Opinions are various in regard to it; many, even ministers, denominate it the work of the devil; others again would explain it in a natural way, or in accordance with some physical law; whilst others look upon it as the work of God. Please give me your opinion and explanation. This thing has occasioned me no little uneasiness. In our German congregations nothing of this kind has yet been manifested. Besides that, it is not known to me that something like it has taken place in Germany; but in England and Ireland there are similar occurrences. The inclosed published accounts will, therefore, not be uninteresting to you; the facts are like those which I have seen myself. The authors of these accounts are generally respectable men and worthy of belief."

This account of Rev. Storch, dated February 25th, 1803, was sent to Rev. Dr. Velthusen in Germany, who published it in his "Maurerey und Christenthum Gegeneinanderuebergestellt," vol. i, pp. 64–70.

In the German minutes of a Virginia Conference, held in 1806, in the new Roeder's Church, in Rockingham County, Rev. Paul Henkel writes on this subject as follows:

"Towards the close of the year 1801, there occurred a mighty waking up of religion among the English people in Guilford and Orange Counties, which caused our German people to understand the true worth of the gospel. Both the pastors and their people were surprised, for it appeared exceedingly strange to those, who were well acquainted with the order of salvation, that true conversion should consist in such a way as declared by these people; that true faith should originate in such sermons, which caused such corporeal convulsions, such representations of the devil, death and hell; the fearful and awful expressions of lightning, thunder, hail, fire and brimstone against the sinner deprived many of their senses, and prostrated them in fainting fits.

"As the like proceedings were upheld and defended by so many English preachers, and as many had declared, that by means of such workings they had received the true and reliable witness of the pardon of their sins and of the new birth, many of us hesitated to contradict such proceedings, although they were thought so contrary to the doctrines of the gospel. Many passages of Scripture were pointed out as opposed to these outward manifestations; but many good-meaning persons defended them as scriptural, whereupon the important question arose among them: 'Must we not also experience the same thing in order to be saved?' The people became anxious and concerned, were much affected and distressed, pressed upon their pastors to decide this matter for them, who were unwilling to do this without due consideration and the fullest assurance.

"The German ministers were at first divided in their opinions on this subject; nevertheless, it drove them to more intimate communion with each other in their official acts, and they had thus the opportunity to investigate this matter more closely. The Lutheran pastors (of North Carolina) formed themselves into a Conference (Synod), in which they and the lay delegates transacted the usual business of the Church as in other States. Each pastor concluded that he would not bear the name of an evangelical minister in vain; consequently the Gospel was preached industriously and earnestly.

"The two young pastors, Revs. Dieffenbach and Henkel, were surrounded by the fire. Many assaults were made upon them and their congregations. But they always stood in good understanding with each other, and unitedly taught the same doctrine, consequently their congregations were edified on both sides. Better order was obtained among the youth; however, the churches greatly lamented that Rev. Philip Henkel felt constrained to leave them. Rev. R. J. Miller, an English Lutheran minister, preaches the gospel orderly, with effect, earnestness and due consideration. He was also much assailed in his teachings by those who sought to excite the people to these extraordinary manifestations of body. Having been ordained by our German brethren, he stands in regular connection with them, and always defends the doctrines of the Lutheran Church in a rational and acceptable manner."

The Rev. Dieffenbach, alluded to in the above report, was a minister of the German Reformed Church.

Section 12. Organization of the Evangelical Lutheran Synod of North Carolina, A.D. 1803.

It is not known precisely at what time the Helmstaedt Mission Society either became disbanded, or ceased to labor for the welfare of the mission field in North Carolina. In the year 1788, Professor Klügel was called from the University of Helmstaedt to a professorship in the University of Halle. In 1790 we find Rev. Dr. Velthusen a resident of Rostock, as *Oberkirchenrath* in the Grand Duchy of Mecklenburg, an office similar to that of superintendent or bishop; and also Professor of Theology in the same place. Dr. Velthusen, nevertheless, continued to labor in the interest of the Lutheran Church in North Carolina, after his removal to Rostock; but the impression is, that owing to these, and perhaps other changes, the Helmstaedt Mission Society ceased to exist, and the Lutheran churches in the State were necessitated to struggle on unaided by the parent Church in Europe. Correspondence was continued for some time between Rev. Storch and Dr. Velthusen as late as 1803, which is proved by a published letter of Rev. Storch, and inserted in the preceding section; but the fact, that it was published in one of Dr. Velthusen's individual works, and not in a Helmstaedt Report, indicates that the Society was then no more.

Rev. Dr. Velthusen was a most learned man and a voluminous writer. He was raised to high positions in the Lutheran Church in Germany.

We find, that even in Horne's Introduction, a work placed in the hands of every English theological student, Dr. Velthusen's name occurs as one of the authorities referred to and consulted by Dr. Horne.

The North Carolina Lutheran ministry, having now no dependence upon which they could rely other than their own efforts, and having been reinforced by a number of ministers in that field, but chiefly, on account of the anxiety of inquiring souls and the distracted state of the Church, caused by the breaking out of the revival of 1801, resolved to labor more unitedly and in an organized capacity, and hence originated the North Carolina Synod or Conference, for so were Synods then sometimes denominated by our German ministers. This Conference or Synod stood under no jurisdiction of any other or higher ecclesiastical body, but had the power to exercise sole jurisdiction for itself from its commencement; "in which," says Rev. Paul Henkel in 1806, "they and the lay delegates transacted the usual business of the Church as in other States."

The Lutheran Church in North Carolina felt the necessity of organizing a Synod, in order to labor for its continuance and future prosperity, for there was no Lutheran Synod in all the Southern States. The Pennsylvania Synod, which is the oldest Lutheran Synod in America, never extended its jurisdiction farther south than Virginia. All the Lutheran churches south of that State, had been either under the care of a mission society in

Germany, or stood in an independent position. The organization of the Corpus Ecclesiasticum in South Carolina was the only previous attempt to bring the German congregations under the care of an organized ecclesiastical union, but had ceased to exist several years before the North Carolina Synod was formed. Hence the Lutheran ministry in North Carolina were impressed with the necessity and advantage of concentrated and organized labor for the welfare of the Church in a synodical body.

In the address to the congregations, published in the first minutes of the North Carolina Synod, the following excellent thoughts occur: "That which you herewith receive for your perusal and contemplation is to show you what we, your teachers and delegates in Conference assembled, have considered, resolved, and shall endeavor to introduce as rules of order for the welfare of our Church and the furtherance of true godliness. In this we have acted according to our best understanding. Ye yourselves will know, that it is necessary, if the Christian Church is to be perpetuated, that order must be preserved both among the ministers and in the congregations. Dear brethren, we look to you to assist us in this noble undertaking. God's work calls for help; the condition of our Church and people calls for help; the condition of thousands, both of old and young, calls for help; and shall this call of God and the cry of so many immortal souls not be heard at all, or heard in vain? We have no fear of it, but are assured that your heart and mind will be united with us in so praiseworthy an undertaking, so that the instructions and quickening influence of the Gospel may be brought to many thousands of souls, who have hitherto been necessarily deprived of the same." Signed by Robert J. Miller, Carl Storch, Paulus Henkel, Christopher Bernhardt, Philip Henkel, Ludwig Markert.

The first session of the North Carolina Synod was held in the town of Salisbury, on Monday, May 2d, 1803. On the preceding Saturday and Sunday, the ministers held Divine service and administered the holy communion to a large assembly in Pine (Union) Church, four miles from Salisbury.

The names of the ministers present at that first Synod were: Rev. Gottfried Arndt, of Lincoln County; Rev. Robert J. Miller, of the same county; Rev. Carl A. G. Storch, near Salisbury; Rev. Paul Henkel, from Abbot's Creek, Rowan (Davidson) County. These ministers, with a number of elders and deacons from most of the congregations as lay representatives, formed the North Carolina Synod, which is the oldest Lutheran Synod in the Southern States, and the third Synod in America in point of time, the Pennsylvania and New York Synods having preceded it in their organization.

CHAPTER IV.

HISTORY OF THE LUTHERAN CHURCH IN THE CAROLINAS CONTINUED, FROM THE ORGANIZATION OF THE NORTH CAROLINA SYNOD, A.D. 1803, TO THE FORMATION OF THE FIRST LUTHERAN GENERAL SYNOD IN AMERICA, A.D. 1820, EMBRACING A PERIOD OF SEVENTEEN YEARS.

Section 1. Condition of the Lutheran Church in South Carolina in the year 1803.

WE now come to the dark period of the Lutheran Church in South Carolina, a period frequently spoken of and greatly lamented by the aged ministers and laymen of our Church in the presence of the writer some twenty or more years ago, when such men as Revs. Michael Rauch and George Haltiwanger, Sr., were still living, whose memory is yet fondly cherished in the Church.

All the early pastors, who came from the Fatherland, were dead. Revs. Martin, Daser, Theus, Hochheimer, Froelich, Bamberg, Friederichs, Wallberg, and others were gathered to their fathers, and, with the single exception of the sending of pastors to the Lutheran Church in Charleston, no reinforcement of ministers came any longer from Germany to South Carolina, and the German congregations were generally fast going to destruction. Proselyting sects were only too industriously engaged in gathering the scattered members of our churches into their fold, and some once flourishing German congregations became irretrievably lost to the Church of their fathers. The only survivor of the Corpus Evangelicum was the Rev. Frederick Joseph Wallern in Newberry District. Here and there exhorters arose in the various vacant congregations, but they were men of very limited education, though zealous and active, and, with their restricted influence, they could do but little more than preserve a spark of vitality in a few scattering churches, which were glad enough to be served with such ministrations as these exhorters could bestow upon them.

A brief review of the condition of the several pastoral charges in South Carolina will manifest the truth of the above statement, and will indicate how sad and mournful was the state of the Lutheran Church at that time, and as far as the German Reformed Church is concerned, it had then almost ceased to exist.

St. John's Church in Charleston was vacant at this time; the Rev. J. C. Faber was still living, but his health had declined, and was therefore necessitated to resign his charge, merely serving it as a temporary supply, and as far as his strength would allow, until some other pastor could be obtained. The congregation extended a pressing call to Rev. Storch of North Carolina, which he, however, was obliged to decline, on account of his own feeble health and the wants of the Church in that State. "In February, 1805, the Rev. M. T. Charles Faber, a younger brother of the former pastor, arrived from Bremen, and became the pastor of this church. He resigned in 1811, and soon afterwards died of the yellow fever. Ministers from other denominations were now engaged for a term of six months only, according to a rule of the church, and the Rev. Mr. Spieren, the Rev. Mr. Darnielle, the Rev. Mr. Best, the Rev. Mr. Hanckel, and the Rev. Mr. Mills, all ministers of the Episcopal Church, at different periods supplied the congregation. They received the same remuneration as if they had been stated ministers."

The Lutheran churches in Barnwell District were likewise in a sad condition, as about this time, A.D. 1803 or 4, their beloved and efficient pastor, the Rev. J. G. Bamberg, departed this life, and they engaged the services of a certain John Henry Graff, a native of Saxony, who had been ordained to the gospel ministry in 1800, by the Rev. Mr. Wallern of Newberry District. Graff continued to "work at his trade, being a shoemaker, to support his family," and, as might be expected, accomplished very little good, except that the churches did not become entirely extinct.

St. Matthew's Church or pastorate, in Orangeburg District, fared very little better; the Rev. J. P. Franklow, who said, that he had obtained license to preach and baptize from the bishop of the Episcopal Church residing in Charleston, in the year

1798, but who was afterwards licensed by the North Carolina Synod in 1812, and subsequently ordained by the same body at its next session, served this charge from 1799 to 1814, but whether he administered the Lord's Supper, previous to his licensure and ordination by the North Carolina Synod, is not known.

The Sandy Run Church had no pastor at all at this time, but was visited by Revs. Franklow and Bernhardt; the latter officiated there only every recurring fifth Sunday in the month, consequently this congregation enjoyed the services of a regularly ordained ministry only four times a year, for a long period of time, and had gone down to such an extent, that it was necessary to reorganize the congregation on the 29th of December, 1811.

The Lutheran congregations, located on both sides of the Saluda River in Lexington District, were more fortunate in securing the services of a succession of pastors. A year or so after the resignation of the Rev. J. G. Bamberg, who removed to Barnwell District in 1798, the Rev. John Nicholas Marcard, who came from St. John's Church in Cabarrus County, North Carolina, became the pastor of the Saluda charge, but he did not labor long in that portion of the Lord's vineyard; whether he died or moved away is not known. At the close of the year 1800, the Rev. C. E. Bernhardt, from Guilford County, North Carolina, became the pastor of the Saluda churches, and labored there to the close of his life. He died August 27th, 1809. He had charge of four congregations: Zion's, Bethel, St. Peter's, and Salem Church on Hollow Creek. He was buried near his residence, about one mile distant from the present St. Michael's Church; no tombstone, but some dogwood trees mark the spot, where repose the remains of this faithful servant of God. These churches have always continued in a prosperous state to the present time, one of which, Zion's, had an organ to assist in the musical part of divine worship, as the records indicate, which is, perhaps, still remaining in the church, but not now in use. In 1805, the organ was put in repair by a gentleman from Ninety-six District, who was paid for his services by an amount raised by subscription. In 1797, the congregation petitioned the State legislature to grant them the privilege of establishing a public ferry on the Saluda River, "for the convenience and use of the church members on the Sabbath-day, when they attend divine service; and for passengers, in order to receive funds for the support of the church in paying the minister's salary, &c., as the funds were not adequate to the wants of the church, for the property consisted only in land, and the members were too poor to defray the ordinary church expenses." "In April 25th, 1802, a subscription was taken to complete the church, that is, to lath and plaster it, to wainscot the pews and window shutters, and to paint the outside of the church." The above is an extract from the church-book.

Rev. R. J. Miller, in his missionary report, under date of November 19th, 1811, speaks very highly of the Saluda congregations, as follows: "From Hollow Creek Church, called Salem, I preached through all the German congregations in the neighborhood until the 28th. It is a pleasure to labor here; the people love the Gospel of Jesus and his servants."

Rev. Wallern labored as pastor in Newberry District, and a Rev. Mr. Winckhouse, who afterwards preached occasionally in the Saluda charge, made vacant by the death of Rev. C. E. Bernhardt, was also a resident of the same District; but when he commenced and ended his labors in Newberry is not known to the writer. By means of the labors of Revs. Wallern and Winckhouse the Newberry churches were preserved from annihilation, although Rev. Wallern was a worldly-minded man, and attended industriously to his planting and other worldly interests, as is still reported of him, and at which the Rev. R. J. Miller hints, when he said in his missionary report: "I went to the Lutheran minister, Wallern; found him about his farming business; conversed that evening and the following day much with him on the state of the Church, of religion, and on other subjects, and found him a man acquainted with the world."

The German congregations in Abbeville District had a sad history at this time. St. George's Lutheran Church on Hard Labor Creek was also visited by Rev. R. J. Miller in his missionary tour in 1811, and the following is his report concerning this church:

"Sunday, November 10th. I preached in a German meeting-house on Hard Labor Creek, where my appointments were to commence; here was formerly a Lutheran congregation, but no remains of it are now to be found; here the Methodists and Baptists have pulled each other out of the pulpit. Every person seemed very attentive; here is full proof of the necessity of missionary preaching. The former Lutheran minister became a Methodist."

The other German congregation in this District, incorporated under the title of "The Charlotte Church, on Slippery Creek, Ninety-six District," has no other now known history, except that of its incorporation by the State legislature.

When we consider all these facts, relating to the condition of the Lutheran Church in South Carolina at that time, and gathered from the reports of the then living witnesses, we need not be astonished that a number of the German congregations in that State became entirely extinct; but the greater wonder is, that so many of those congregations struggled on and continued to live through that dark and trying period. The few charges that were blessed with the continued and faithful services of the Gospel ministry were preserved in a flourishing condition, proving fully, that nothing but the faithful and proper administration of the word and the sacraments can preserve the Church, and promote its welfare.

Section 2. Henkel's Report on the Condition of the Lutheran Church in North Carolina in the year 1806.

From the German minutes of a Virginia Conference, held in the New Roeder's Church, in Rockingham County, A.D. 1806, and published by the Rev. Paul Henkel, we gather the following interesting account of the condition of all the Lutheran congregations in the State of North Carolina at that time. Rev. Henkel writes:

"As soon as the Germans had located themselves in different parts of North Carolina, they became concerned about the regular administration of Church worship and ordinances in their midst. They soon erected houses of worship according to their ability, which were generally the joint property of both the Lutheran and German Reformed Christians.

"In that region, which lies partly in Orange and partly in Guilford Counties, there are three Lutheran and three Reformed churches, besides one other joint-church, named Frieden's, which is served in connection with the others. Since the year 1801, Rev. Henry Dieffenbach has served the Reformed churches, and in the same year Rev. Philip Henkel was called to serve as Lutheran pastor, who remained there until 1806, when he accepted a call to an enlarged field of labor in Lincoln County.

"In Rowan County (now Davidson) on Abbot's

Creek, we find three joint and one Lutheran church on the Sandhills. These were served by the Rev. Paul Henkel from the year 1800 to 1805, when he was necessitated to resign this charge, on account of the failure of his own and his family's health; he therefore introduced the Rev. Ludwig Markert as candidate preacher into these congregations, which he was himself compelled to leave.

"In the vicinity of Salisbury, Rowan County, there are three strong Lutheran congregations, which have been served by the Rev. Charles Storch for nearly twenty years; but under many disadvantages on account of the frequent and severe attacks of fever, which prostrated his energies for the last ten years, and which apparently had several times brought him near to the grave. His numerous official duties lay often heavy upon him on account of his ill-health, especially the administration of the Lord's Supper to two hundred and fifty communicants at one time, so that his feeble powers of body were always exhausted after having served all these people. Some twenty years past, there was a tolerably strong German congregation in Salisbury; they had erected a comfortable church for themselves, but as the German people and their language were changed into English, the German worship soon became extinct.

"Near Buffalo Creek, Cabarrus County, we find one of the strongest German Lutheran churches in the whole State; however, since the death of their former pastor, Rev. Adolph Nussmann, which occurred some twelve years ago, the congregation has suffered much, as it is now served by Rev. Storch, who moved a little nearer to this congregation. In the year 1803, the Rev. John Henkel had been unanimously chosen as the pastor of this church, and consented to serve them; he made the necessary arrangements to move his family from Virginia, but whilst the people were waiting for the intelligence when they should send for him, they received the message that the Lord had called him to his home. This was sad news, not only to the congregation, but likewise to the remaining ministers in the State, who lamented the want of so many faithful laborers in the Lord's vineyard. The few sermons Rev. H. preached, whilst on a visit to that church, will long be remembered. It is rejoicing to know, that this people are now blessed with the labors of so faithful a pastor.

"About eighteen miles from Salisbury there is another church, which was built by the Germans as a joint house of worship, but as they are so much intermingled with English settlers, this German congregation will also become extinct. Many English residents had become members of this church. During the visits of Rev. Paul Henkel in the fall season, from 1785 to 1789, many adult and aged persons were baptized, instructed and confirmed, and thus a very strong congregation was gathered. Much experimental Christianity was supposed to exist here; however, hopeful as appearances were outwardly, they were nevertheless of short duration; many tore themselves away from the church, and were divided into different singular persuasions. The Germans became degenerated, lead disorderly lives with these other settlers, so that at this time a perfect Babel exists; foolish pride and many vices prevail. The few remaining upright souls are constrained to weep in silence over this desolation.

"In Lincoln County there are eight or nine congregations, several of which are quite large. All these have erected joint houses of worship. The Lutheran congregations were served by the Rev. Gottfried Arndt for twenty years. Before that time he had labored in the vicinity of Salisbury, and even at that time he often traveled among these churches, and performed official duties, as far as his circumstances would permit. He labored faithfully in his calling over the whole State, wherever he could find German brethren. For the last four years he became unfitted for his calling, as he met with the misfortune of losing his eyesight entirely. He is at present quite an aged man, and were it not for his misfortune, he might still serve in his holy calling. The greater number of his former congregations are now served by Rev. Philip Henkel.

"In Burke County there are also a number of Germans, among whom, as yet, no church has been built. Rev. Arndt preached there several times, so also did the Rev. Paul Henkel, in the German and English languages, during his visit through that county in 1787. In May, 1804, he made another visit among this people in company with the German Reformed minister, Rev. Jacob Laros. It was their intention to preach several days in each congregation, but in this they were hindered by the many rains and consequent high waters, so that each of them could preach but two sermons.

"In Wilkes County may be found a small German flock in the wilderness, surrounded by human beings, who know of nothing so little as of the true way of salvation, and who in their own opinions are wiser than the Bible itself. These often persecuted the members of this little flock. Rev. Paul Henkel visited them twice whilst he was still living in North Carolina. During his last visit in 1805, he instructed and confirmed their youth, and administered the Lord's Supper. He informed them that he had reason to believe that the Lord was in their midst. As it concerns the spiritual condition of this church, it may be truly said that here, as elsewhere, many having neglected to embrace their opportunity, are still strangers to that work of grace, which they should experience in their hearts; there are others again to be found, who are enlightened by something better than their own blind reason, who seek the salvation of their souls not in works, but in the merits of their Savior, and who strive with all their hearts to become the followers of Jesus. In this place not so many learned and feeling sermons have been preached as in other congregations, nevertheless, many became savingly acquainted with the doctrines of the gospel from their own experience. The labors of traveling ministers had awakened attention to the word; serious impressions deeply affected their hearts, which resulted in much good, and enabled many to declare the things they had experienced in their own hearts.

"The two German Reformed preachers, Revs. Jacob Christman and Jacob Laros, who, for the last two years, had labored in the State of Ohio, were, at the time above mentioned, residing in Guilford County. As soon as Rev. J. Christman was ordained, he labored in various localities and performed many journeys. He was peculiarly fitted to impart private instruction in families, which duty he performed industriously. Rev. J. Laros, who did not labor so extensively, was more successful among children and youth in schools and catechetical instruction; he was always very edifying in his sermons, and his exemplary walk was an ornament to his official duties." (Here follows the lengthy report on the revival of 1801, which has been given in the 11th section of the preceding chapter.)

"The Evangelical Brethren, that is, the Moravians, have five German and one English church in this State. Their pastors preach the gospel with exemplary order and propriety; they are always friendly in their deportment towards all other orderly pastors. Among these brethren may be found many members, who are well acquainted with true godliness and experimental Christianity."

Section 3. Extract from the First Minutes of the North Carolina Synod, from A.D. 1803 to 1810.

Immediately upon the organization of the Synod of North Carolina, a new life appears to have been infused into the Lutheran Church in the Carolinas; the various scattered congregations were now brought into a closer relationship with each other, a uniform church discipline was introduced with good and wholesome effect, arrangements were made to supply all the vacant congregations with the means of grace, and the scattered members were visited by missionaries appointed by Synod, who organized new congregations wherever it was practicable. However, the want of ministers of the Gospel was still very great, and in order to supply this demand, pious laymen were licensed as catechets, who afterwards became candidates for the ministry; in this way originated the licensure system, and the preparation of pious young men for the ministry by receiving private instruction from some of the older ministers; this arrangement afterwards received the name of "the home student system." The most urgent necessity demanded this departure from the rule of the Lutheran Church in the Fatherland, where an education at the University was necessary, before any one could be admitted to the gospel ministry, and where a candidate was ordained as soon as he had received a call as pastor of a church, without having to pass through a state of licensed probation.

All the Lutheran ministers residing in South Carolina connected themselves with the newly organized North Carolina Synod, with the exception of Rev. Faber, in Charleston, who doubtless could not attend this or any other Synod, on account of the want of public conveyances at that time, and the great distance from the place where the Synod usually met; also the Rev. F. J. Wallern, who continued to remain in an independent and isolated position as long as he lived; what his motives were for so doing is not stated in the reports of the Synod's missionary, who visited Rev. Wallern and his congregations in 1811.

Rev. C. E. Bernhardt, who labored in Lexington District, connected himself at once with the North Carolina Synod, and labored in great harmony with his brethren to the close of his life. Rev. J. P. Franklow also attended the meetings of Synod, and was licensed by that body at its spring session of 1812, and ordained the same year at its fall session. Rev. Godfrey Dreher was presented to that body as a candidate for the ministry, October 23d, 1810, when he was licensed, and was afterwards ordained in South Carolina in 1812, by a committee appointed by Synod for that purpose. From all accounts he is still living, being now in the sixty-second year of his ministry, although no longer able to perform any official duty.

Revs. Michael Rauch and J. Y. Meetze appeared before Synod at a later date; they were both licensed October 19th, 1812, at Lau's Church, Guilford County. Rev. Rauch was ordained April 28th, 1819, at St. John's Church, Cabarrus County; but Rev. Meetze was not ordained until 1822, when by the order of Synod he received his ordination in South Carolina. All these Lutheran ministers, residing in South Carolina, continued their connection with the North Carolina Synod until 1824, at which time the Synod of South Carolina was organized.

At the first session of the North Carolina Synod, held in Salisbury, May 2d, 1803, very little business was transacted. The Synod was then simply organized, and a resolution was passed, at the suggestion of Rev. Arndt, that Rev. Paul Henkel should visit Rev. Arndt's charge in Lincoln County the following August, in order to perform the necessary official duties, to which Rev. Arndt could not attend, owing to the loss of his eyesight and his feeble health. Rev. Henkel attended to this duty.

The second session of Synod was held at Lincolnton, N. C., October 17th, 1803, when a constitution was adopted, consisting of nine articles. They are much the same as are generally adopted by all Lutheran Synods. The fourth article requires candidates of the ministry "to understand the order of the Latin language, and so much of Greek as to be able to understand the New Testament." Rev. J. G. Arndt was President, and Rev. R. J. Miller was Secretary of this synodical convention.

The third session of Synod was held at Abbot's

Creek Church, in Davidson County, October 21st, 1804. Rev. Paul Henkel was elected President, and Rev. Miller, Secretary. Very little business was transacted at this session of Synod, because nearly all the ministers were unfitted for duty on account of sickness. It was resolved that a special conference be held at Pine Church, Rowan County, the following April, for the purpose of ordaining Rev. Philip Henkel. John Michael Rueckert and Ludwig Markert were licensed as catechets. The next session of Synod was held at Organ Church, Rowan County, October 20th, 1806. Rev. Storch was chosen President, and Rev. Bernhardt, Secretary.

There appears to have been no meeting of Synod during the years 1807 and 1808, doubtless prevented by the prevailing sickness during the fall season.

In the year 1809, August 7th, the Synod was convened in Guilford County, at which meeting some additional articles were added to the constitution. The officers of Synod were, Rev. Charles A. Storch, President, and Rev. Ludwig Markert, Secretary.

On the 22d of October, 1810, the Synod convened at Organ Church, at which time a considerable amount of business was transacted. The Rev. C. A. Storch was re-elected President, and Rev. Gottlieb Schober was elected Secretary. At this meeting there were ten ministers present, and the names of the lay delegates were published for the first time. Rev. G. Schober was ordained to the gospel ministry; he was a member of the Moravian Church, and continued in connection with that Church to the close of his life, nevertheless, he became a Lutheran minister, and was pastor of several Lutheran congregations in the vicinity of Salem, N. C., where he resided, and served those congregations during his life. Revs. Storch, Miller and Philip Henkel officiated at his ordination.

"On motion of Rev. Philip Henkel, it was resolved that, inasmuch as awakenings arise in our days by means of three days' preaching, and the like is to be wished among our brethren in the faith, a trial of such preaching be made, with the proviso, that three ministers of our connection hold those meetings, to which also ministers of the Moravian and Reformed Churches, whether German or English, be welcomed; at each of these meetings the communion is to be administered." The time was then appointed when these meetings were to be held in each pastoral charge.

Rev. R. J. Miller was appointed as a traveling missionary for the Synod, with the power to organize new congregations, and to take up collections for this object.

It was also resolved, that Revs. Storch and Schober prepare a pastoral letter to the various churches in connection with this Synod, and that it be appended to the minutes.

The candidates, Revs. Jacob Scherer and Godfrey Dreher, were then licensed to the ministry, and the catechets, J. M. Rueckert and Jacob Krieson, had their limited licenses renewed.

The names of all the congregations belonging to the Synod, with their pastors, lay readers, elders and deacons, are appended to the minutes; the names of these churches are as follows:

Rev. Storch's pastorate: Zion's or Organ; Buffalo Creek or St. John's; Irish Settlement, now Luther Chapel; Pine, now Union; Crooked Creek; and Bear Creek, now Bethel.

Rev. Markert's pastorate: Pilgrim's; Beck's; Schweiszguth (Swicegood), now Sandy Creek; Lau's; Frieden's; Graves, now St. Paul's, Alamance County. Richland Church was supplied by Jacob Krieson as catechet or lay reader.

Rev. Schober's pastorate: Muddy Creek; and Dutchman's Creek.

Rev. Philip Henkel's pastorate: St. John's; Old Church; School-house Church; Kasner's; Lebanon; Emanuel's; Hebron; and Zion's; all in Lincoln County.

"*Various congregations in South Carolina*, which connected themselves with our Synod:" Bethel Church, on High Hill Creek; St. Peter's; Zion's; and a Reformed Church, of which Henry Kuhn, Samuel Bockman, and Henry Schull were the elders.

A synodial seal was also adopted with certain devices, bearing the words "Pax vobis" and "Sigil. Minist. Evang. Luth. in Carolia Sept. et Stat. vicin." A lengthy explanation of the devices and a translation of the Latin words as quoted above are given in the minutes.

Then follows the admonitory pastoral letter as adopted by the Synod, and prepared by Revs. Storch and Schober.

Section 4. Missionary tours of Revs. Miller, Franklow and Scherer.

In order that a correct knowledge might be obtained concerning the condition of the scattered Lutheran congregations and settlements in South Carolina, Virginia, Tennessee and Ohio, the Synod of North Carolina sent several exploring missionaries into these States, with instructions to preach the gospel, administer the sacraments, and otherwise to encourage and build up the dispersed members of the Lutheran Church in their most holy faith. From the published reports of these missionaries most valuable information is obtained, affording us a portraiture of the condition of the Lutheran Church in those States at that time.

The Rev. Robert Johnson Miller was the first one of these missionaries sent by Synod to explore the field; he started upon his first tour June 18th, 1811, passing through Wilkes, Surry and Stokes Counties, N. C., into Virginia. And, although the State of Virginia is not embraced in the history of the Lutheran Church in the Carolinas, nevertheless, a few extracts from Rev. Miller's journal of his tour into Virginia and return through

Tennessee may still be acceptable. Rev. Miller states: "I departed from my home in Burke County on the 18th day of June, 1811, in confidence of the protection of God, preached twice in Wilkes County, as often in Surry, four times in Stokes, and mostly to large, serious and attentive congregations, particularly in Germantown. In the first forty-two miles of my journey in Virginia, I found only one small Methodist meeting-house, and heard of no settled minister of any denomination. From the 27th to the 30th I traveled through much spiritual wilderness, where all denominations live dispersed, their youth being without any religious instruction, and found three families whose parents had been Lutherans.

"Sunday, July 2d. I met preacher Meyer with his numerous congregation, and preached to attentive and serious people; their teacher (pastor) is not appointed or ordained by the Pennsylvania Lutheran Ministerium, yet he administers all the sacraments; I warned him and his flock against such conduct. He informed me that he attended six congregations, each of which consisted of from 25 to 30 families.

"In New Market I preached three times to large and serious congregations, and at my departure Dr. Solomon Henkel, in whose house I baptized two children, and his brother Ambrose presented me with 200 small English catechisms to be given to the poor and ignorant, which order I afterwards faithfully executed. After having crossed the Shenandoah Mountain, I met with

Moses Henkel, who is a Methodist preacher, and a brother of our Rev. Paul Henkel.

"On the 2d of August, after having passed the rough Alleghany Mountain, I found in the neighborhood of Lewisburg a Lutheran congregation, who are attended by the Rev. Mr. Flohr, from Wythe County, three times a year. Excepting a small congregation on Jackson's Fork of James River, there are but few Lutheran families in Monroe County, and all are without Christian instruction. In this whole territory, including the South Branch of the Potomac, and the counties of Pendleton, Bath, Greenbriar, Monroe, Montgomery and Wythe, there is but one Lutheran minister. Aug. 11th. I arrived at Rev. Mr. Flohr's in Wythe County; he attends six congregations; further up New River there is another numerous but divided congregation, where, minister and justice, Stanger resides.

"From here I went by way of Abingdon into Sullivan County, Tennessee, where I found some German congregations, who are attended by Rev. Mr. Smith; before his arrival here they were attended by Rev. Mr. Sink, now gone to Kentucky; I preached in all congregations and in other places, particularly in Blountsville. Aug. 31st. I met with Rev. Smith, who has been now ordained by our Synod, and found him an honest, upright man; both he and his congregations were glad of the opportunity to be connected with our Ministerium; I visited as many of Mr. Smith's congregations as possible, partly accompanied by him, and on the

11th of October, after having preached at Cove Creek to a large and attentive congregation, I separated from Rev. Mr. Smith and the good people, wishing them spirit, life, fidelity and zeal, especially in the instruction of their youth, so that the future race might not be more bewildered, and departed on my homeward journey, where I arrived in safety, after an absence of three months."

The next tour the Rev. Mr. Miller made into the State of South Carolina. He says in his journal: "The second part of my journey I began on the 4th of November, 1811, and spent the first evening about twenty-five miles from home. When I came to Rutherfordton, my appointment to preach had not been made. From thence I rode, crossing Broad and Green Rivers, through a thinly settled country to Spartanburg, South Carolina. Saturday, 9th, I arrived at Mr. Robert Smith's, on Hard Labor Creek, where my appointments were to commence, and preached on Sunday in a German meeting-house." (This part of the journal is omitted, having been given on a preceding page.)

"On the 13th I preached fourteen miles from Savannah River to a serious congregation, chiefly Presbyterians. Farther up on Little Saluda River, which I passed the next day at a dangerous ford, there is a considerable number of our people, whom I did not see. Throughout this whole country no attention is paid to the religious instruction of youth, except among the Presbyterians. In such a condition of things there can, of course, be but very little vital religion among the people.

"On the 19th, after sermon in Hallow Creek Church, called Salem, I became acquainted with a poor man calling himself a preacher, but to all appearance destitute of the spirit and temper of a Christian, as well as of every qualification to preach. I gave him some advice, but received very little thanks. From hence I preached in all the German congregations throughout the neighborhood until the 28th. It is a pleasure to labor here; the people love the gospel of Jesus and his servants.

"About forty miles south of this place, I arrived at one of the first settled congregations in all these quarters (St. Matthew's, Orangeburg District); visited their teacher, Mr. Franklow; found the congregation much decayed, but it might be revived and increased if it could be supplied with a minister of talents and grace. They have been attended for several years past by Mr. Franklow, who, as he says, had received license from the Bishop of the Church of England to baptize.

"On my return to the Saluda River I preached, December 1st, in the oldest German church in this vicinity to a large and very serious congregation, and found the people very desirous to place themselves under the care of our Synod.

"On the 4th, after having preached, I arrived again at Brother John Dreher's. This man has exerted himself for some years past, in the absence of a settled minister, to keep the light of the gospel burning. He had divinely pious books printed at his own expense, spreads them for a low price among the people, and an evident blessing rests upon his exertions. On Friday, the 6th, I went to the Lutheran minister, Wallern, found him about his farming business, conversed that evening and the following day much with him on the state of the Church, of religion, and on other subjects, and found him a man acquainted with the world. Sunday, the 8th, I preached in his church. He accompanied me also the following day to a funeral, where I addressed the people on the subject of death and preparation; he preached from Ps. 37 : 18. On the following day I preached to a small but, to all appearance, serious people, and therewith finished my missionary tour for this year.

"I have to observe that in the counties of Botetourt, Augusta and Rockingham, in Virginia, an itinerant minister, qualified to preach both in the German and English, would be of great benefit, and I have no doubt that he would have great success in bringing back many of those, who have been obliged to leave the Church for the want of a minister qualified to administer her ordinances to them. The people there are much in want of such a minister, and a circuit could be formed on that plan, that would work beneficially. Another itinerant minister, qualified as above, to travel from Broad River westward near to the Savannah River, and southward near to Charleston, would be employed equally as useful, and there is no doubt but that the people would cheerfully contribute what would be sufficient for a decent support. Oh! that the Lord would give us three or four young ministers, endowed with grace and talents, and gifted to preach in both languages, much could then be done for his Church. The congregations there now are sensibly mouldering away for the want of such preachers. Among the old Germans there is a standing still; their youth learn and speak English; if a teacher speaks German, it is to them like the sound of the church-bell. But the affair is the Lord's.

"On my whole tour I have baptized this year two adults and sixty children, preached sixty-seven times, traveled three thousand miles, and received $70.44 for my support, without asking for a cent in any way, and arrived home in health and safety. Honor, thanks and praise be to the Lord."

On page 11 of the minutes of the North Carolina Synod for 1812, the following record may be found: "The Rev. Mr. Franklow was hereupon requested to make one or more visits in a part of South Carolina called Saltketcher, there to inquire into the situation of the residue of our members, who formerly had a well-regulated congregation, and report the result of his inquiries to the next Synod."

This duty Rev. Franklow performed faithfully, and reported at length, which report was greatly abbreviated and inserted in the minutes; but the original document having been found some twelve years ago among Rev. G. Shober's papers, in a garret of one of his grandchildren in Salem, North Carolina, it is now presented, and reads as follows:

"Sunday, March 28th, 1813. I set out on my journey from my church after Divine service, and arrived in the evening at Mr. Moss', on Edisto River. Here I made an appointment to preach in a new Methodist meeting-house on my return on Thursday, April 8th. The next day I crossed the Little Saltketcher through a long swamp and deep water, and came in the evening to Mr. Shobert, a church-warden of St. Bartholomew's Church. I made my appointment to preach in this church on Friday, April 2d, and on Sunday and Monday following at St. Nicholas Church, and again at St. Bartholomew's on my return on Tuesday, April 6th.

"March 31st. To-day I was introduced to several members of the church, when I was informed that they had a minister, who had lived and preached nine years among them, named John Henry Graff, a native of Saxony, in Germany, and who labored there ever since the death of Rev. Mr. Bamberg. Graff was ordained by the Rev. Mr. Wallern to the ministry of the Gospel. For two years the members of St. Bartholomew's Church had not employed Graff any longer as their pastor, and in St. Nicholas Church his time expires in three weeks. I found that the minister and people were opposed to each other, and upon inquiry as to the cause of this division, I was informed that Mr. Graff could not speak the English language so as to be understood, and that his sermons were three and four hours long; that he had no energy and life in his discourse; that he spoke too low to be heard distinctly; in short, that they would engage him no longer as their pastor. Mr. Shobert desired me to go and see him, which I had intended to do.

"April 1st. I visited Mr. Graff, and stayed several hours with him. I found him at home, expecting to see me, from the report of some of his neighbors that a strange minister was come to visit him and the congregations. He received me in a friendly manner, and I found him well informed in religion and the Scriptures. He told me of the dislike which his congregations had against him, which he said proceeded from the family in which his daughter had married, who was then a widow, and now they were maliciously affected towards him. He showed me his letter of ordination, signed by Rev. Mr. Wallern and church-wardens, dated September, 1800. He works at his trade, being a shoemaker, to support his family.

"April 2d. I went to St. Bartholomew's Church, which is in sight of their minister's house, and preached in the German and English languages to a small but attentive congregation, one of whom, Mr. Copel, asked me to baptize a child for him on my return next Tuesday. I was surprised, and told him I did not wish to do it, as they had a minister; to which he replied, that Graff was no longer their minister, as he had not been engaged in that church these two years, and that if I would not baptize his child, Mr. Graff should not do it. The next day I crossed the Big Saltketcher at Rivers' Ford, nearly three-quarters of a mile wide, and very deep, and arrived at Mr. Jacob Hardee's, one of the wardens of St. Nicholas Church. He has a mill, and by that means most of the people were informed that divine service would be performed the next day.

"Sunday, April 4th. I went to St. Nicholas and preached to a serious congregation; the people were very attentive, both to the German and English discourses. After service I published, as I had promised, that the Lord's Supper would be administered on Easter Sunday by their minister, but not one offered to give in their names, and wished that I should administer it to them on that day; to which I replied that it was impossible, as I had two appointments to fill, one at Sandy Run next Sunday, and at my own church on Easter Day. They then begged me to visit them again, and administer the sacraments, as Mr. Graff was not worthy to administer any sacrament. I told them that, if possible, I would pay them another visit in the fall, and would make my appointments by letter before I came. On Monday I preached again at St. Nicholas, to a tolerably full congregation, part of the members having been prevented from attending on account of the session of Barnwell court, which commenced this day. The people complained that whilst Mr. Graff lived among them, no other minister would come to be their pastor.

"Tuesday, April 6th. After having crossed Broxton's Ford in a canoe, and swimming my horse, I arrived yesterday at my old lodging-place, Mr. Shobert's. I went to-day to St. Bartholomew's Church, where I met Mr. Graff, who promised to preach in English after my discourse. He informed me that a neighbor of his baptized children without license or authority, and that the people employed him in preference to Mr. Graff's attending upon this duty. After my discourse Mr. Graff preached in the German instead of the English language, although it was contrary to his promise and the people's expressed desire. After service I baptized Mr. Copel's child, rather than suffer it to be baptized by an improper person. Here I took my leave of this people, exhorting them to reconciliation and unity with their minister. They answered that this could not be, but that they were now as lost sheep without a shepherd; that they went to hear the word of God among the Methodists and Baptists, but would not join them, as they wished to keep to the religion of their fathers. They hoped that some good minister would soon be their pastor, and begged me to state their condition before the Lutheran Synod, and that they would appoint me or some other minister to visit them again.

"April 7th. I went to Mr. Moss with the hope of filling my appointment at the Edisto Methodist Meeting-house, when I was informed that they objected to me, on account of my being a Lutheran minister. The next day I went to Sandy Run, in accordance with my promise, where I met Revs. Dreher and Henkel. We preached to a numerous assembly; and on Sunday friend Dreher and I administered the Lord's Supper to many communicants in the presence of a large assembly. I arrived at home, thanks to God, safe and well, and found my family in good health, although my horse could scarcely carry me home."

Rev. Jacob Scherer's missionary tour was made within the State of Ohio, where a great number of families, who had emigrated from North Carolina, were then residing, and for whose spiritual welfare the Synod of North Carolina was much concerned.

Rev. Scherer accompanied Rev. Miller into Virginia, who then made a second tour through that State, in 1813, as far down the Shenandoah Valley as Winchester, and whose lengthy report is published in the minutes of that year. In Pendleton County, Revs. Scherer and Miller separated from each other, each one taking his journey as prescribed by Synod.

Rev. Scherer writes: "On the 4th of June I parted from Rev. Miller, and taking Mr. Gobel with me, we journeyed westwardly towards the State of Ohio, passing through Tiger's Valley, a region of great spiritual darkness. Proselyting is carried on extensively here, and some of the Germans have united themselves with the Baptists and Methodists, but very few heathens have become Christians.

"From Clarksburg we went to Marietta, where

we crossed the Ohio River, and passing New Lan caster we came to Dayton on the 17th of June. On this route I baptized seven children and one adult.

"On the following Sunday I preached twice among the Germans, who are mostly from North Carolina, and intend building a church, desiring to have a preacher from that State." (The first English Lutheran Church of Dayton, Ohio, was organized and established at a subsequent period by a minister from North Carolina, the Rev. D. P. Rosenmiller, so the writer was informed on his visit to that city in 1868.) "From here I visited my uncle, Christian Scherer, in which neighborhood I preached four days, from the 24th to the 27th, to large congregations; baptized five children. The spiritual condition of Ohio is dark; people of all denominations are intermixed, and although they have many preachers among them, there appears to be a want of such, who have sound doctrine and are of good repute.

"On the 29th of June we left the State of Ohio, and proceeded on our homeward journey, and arrived on the 7th of July in Powell's Valley, where I preached and baptized seventeen children. The people complained with tears of their desolate situation, urgently beseeching us to send them a minister. There are many families here from North Carolina, and several congregations could be formed; the people are willing to build houses of worship. We promised them that they should be visited, and their children instructed and confirmed. On the 9th I preached in Grassy Valley, and the next day arrived at Rev. Smith's, who accompanied me from the 13th to the 19th, for here Mr. Gobel left me. In one place twenty-five children requested to be instructed and confirmed, and other persons subscribed their names to form a congregation.

"On the 20th I formed another congregation in the Fork of the Holstein, and eleven young people desired to be instructed. On the 21st I preached in Rossler's Church; the congregation with joy placed itself under our Synod, and nine persons requested to be confirmed. The next day I preached in Buler's Church, where a Mr. Zink officiates, who said that he had been once in Pennsylvania, when Rev. Mr. Helmuth and Smith had given him license, but that it had long since expired, and still he persuaded the people that he had a right to act as a minister.

"Sunday, the 25th, I preached in a new church on the Middle Fork of the Holstein, in Washington County, Virginia, where a small congregation was formed; thirteen persons gave in their names for instruction; the Rev. Mr. Flohr promised to instruct them. On the North Fork of the Holstein there is another desolate congregation, which had never yet been visited. Here I found an ignorant man preaching and baptizing without the least ceremony; he takes up the children, pours water on them, and says nothing, and yet the poor ignorant people know no better, but acknowledge him as a minister.

"On the 28th I arrived at Rev. Mr. Flohr's, by whose loving and brotherly treatment, condescending and spiritual conversation, I was exceedingly comforted—I was delighted. From here I journeyed homewards, having traveled in all 1617 miles, preached 50 times, baptized 72 children and one adult, and in connection with Brother Miller, and partly alone, 13 congregations were formed, consisting of 1175 members, and 215 persons requested to be instructed in the doctrines of Christ."

Section 5. Emigration from North Carolina to several new States and Territories.

At what time the exodus from North Carolina to other States and Territories commenced cannot now be precisely stated. Before the Revolutionary War, very few English and German settlers had crossed the Alleghany Mountains from any portion of the Atlantic slope, and during the progress of the war, as a matter of course, emigration to the West was impossible. Now allowing the inhabitants of the United States several years' time to recover from the effects of the war, and the dangers of travel through sparsely settled countries and among hostile Indian tribes gradually subsiding, this westward emigration scarcely commenced until the beginning of the present century, and most probably not until after the purchase of the Western territory by the United States from the government of France, under Napoleon I, in 1803, usually called "The Louisiana Purchase."

Thousands of German families, as well as American citizens, induced by the flattering reports of the fertility of the lands in the West, and the advantageous offers made to settlers to secure for themselves a home almost "without money and without price," sold their paternal possessions in North Carolina, and migrated to Tennessee, Kentucky, Ohio, Indiana, Illinois and other States and Territories. The Synod of North Carolina, feeling concerned for the spiritual welfare of its former children, and hearing their continued call for the bread of life, sent missionaries to these settlers to visit them, who, themselves becoming enamored with the flattering advantages and prospects of these "new countries," likewise soon became classed among the new settlers. In this manner were Lutheran congregations formed in Ohio, Indiana and Illinois, composed almost entirely of North Carolinians; and whilst this was a decided advantage to the West, it was, on the other hand, a fearful drain upon the strength of the Lutheran Church in "the old North State."

In many instances the German Lutheran settlers in the West became so scattered, that it was found impracticable to continue their connection with the Church of their fathers, and thus were they absorbed by other denominations, and lost to the Lutheran Church. Concerning all this, a recent correspondent to "The Lutheran and Missionary" expresses himself as follows: "Instead of (the Lutheran Church in North Carolina) being strengthened by immigration into it, it has suffered greatly by emigration from it. For forty (and more) years large numbers of Lutherans have each year gone westward. They and their descendants are found in nearly all the Western States. Some of these have been gathered into congregations in their new homes; but the great majority have been lost, not only to the Church in North Carolina, but to the Lutheran Church. Some congregations, once large and flourishing, have been almost destroyed by it. A very large proportion of the young men of the Church of the State have gone entirely beyond her reach. She has not only been weakened by these losses, but discouraged."

In South Carolina the Lutheran Church also lost heavily in the number of her membership by emigration to other States, but not at this early period of her history. Numbers moved away at a later date, and formed colonies in Georgia, Florida, Alabama, Mississippi and Texas, many of whom are still true to the Church of their fathers, whilst others again have connected themselves with other denominations.

Section 6. Additional Extracts from the Minutes of the North Carolina Synod from 1811 to 1815, exhibiting the Rapid Increase of its Influence, the Extension of its Borders, and its Great Want of Ministers.

The meeting of Synod of 1811 was not well attended, hence very little business was transacted. A special meeting of Synod was therefore held in April, 1812, at which time the Synod numbered twelve ministers, including the licentiates; nine congregations in Tennessee, under the pastoral care of Rev. C. Z. H. Smith, connected themselves with the Synod at this meeting; the names of these churches were, Zion's and Roller's, in Sullivan County; Brownsboro and (name not mentioned), in Washington County; Patterson, Sinking Spring and Cove Creek, in Green County; Lonax and Thomas, in Knox and Blount Counties. "A petition from South Carolina, signed by 18 Reformed and 13 Lutherans, was read, praying that Synod should ordain William Hauk as a German Reformed minister, but this Synod, after due consideration, concluded that they could not consistently do anything in the matter."

The parochial reports, ranging from two to twenty-four years, and which had never been handed in before, sum up as follows: 26 congregations, 2071 confirmations, 100 adult baptisms; infant baptisms and communicants were not reported; besides these are the reports of only five of the ministers whose congregations were all located in North Carolina.

"It was resolved that Sunday-schools should be publicly recommended from the pulpit in all our congregations."

A written plan, embracing ten articles, was presented to Synod for the purpose "of establishing schools for our poor children," to be supported by voluntary donations from the members of the Church; in which schools the German and English languages were to be taught. It was also unanimously declared, that Luther's Smaller Catechism "must remain the foundation of instruction;" also the catechisms printed by Ambrose Henkel & Co., were recommended for general adoption.

"A fervent wish being expressed to enter into a nearer and more cordial connection with the brethren professing our faith in Pennsylvania, a letter of the year 1807, addressed to our Ministerium from the Ministerium of Pennsylvania, was read. We felt sorry that, because in said and the succeeding year no full Synod had been assembled, the same was mislaid, and the receipt thereof never acknowledged, nor has the letter been answered. Revs. Storch and Shober were hereupon appointed in the name of this Synod to answer the said letter, and to send them, at the same time, a copy of the principal transactions of this and the last Synod, together with the most memorable matter of Rev. Miller's missionary tour."

Rev. Mr. Storch was commissioned to prepare a liturgy, and lay the same before the next Synod.

On the 18th October, 1812, the regular session of Synod was held. President, Rev. R. J. Miller, and Rev. G. Shober, Secretary. Rev. Jacob Sherer was ordained at this meeting. A letter from Rev. J. G. Schmucker, of York, Pa., was read, acknowledging the receipt of the friendly letter from the North Carolina Synod, by the Ministerium of Pennsylvania, and informing the Synod that their President, Rev. Mr. Helmuth, was requested to reply to the same.

The following condensed missionary report of Rev. Philip Henkel is inserted in the minutes: "I served as missionary preacher from the 11th of May to the 7th of August; traveled 1534 miles, preached 50 times, baptized 115 children and 4 adults, and administered the Lord's Supper 4 times, in all to 45 communicants. I found in the States of North Carolina, Tennessee, and Virginia, many deserted congregations, and they everywhere pray that preachers be sent them."

Two new congregations, organized by Rev. Shober, named Hopewell and Bethlehem, were received in connection with the Synod; so also was the Sandy Run congregation in South Carolina, under the pastoral care of Rev. Godfrey Dreher.

The Synod of 1813 convened in Pilgrim's Church, Davidson County, N. C., in October; it was well attended by ministers and lay delegates, and the minutes contain fifty-two pages of closely printed matter, made up principally of sermons and the missionary journals of Revs. Miller and

Scherer. Rev. Storch was elected President, and Rev. Shober, Secretary. Revs. David Henkel, J. P. Schmucker, and Daniel Moser, were licensed to the ministry. Four congregations in Shenandoah and Rockingham Counties, Virginia, named Hoxbiehl, Solomon's, Rider's and Paul's Churches, were received in connection with the Synod.

"Rev. Scherer also gave information that fifteen congregations, which he had visited last summer, and of which some were newly formed by Rev. Miller and himself, desired to be admitted to our association, and to be placed under the care of our ministry; and they were, with thanks to our gracious Lord, accepted, which resolution was, however, accompanied with this deep sigh: O! had we more faithful servants of the Lord! In these fifteen congregations there are 1323 souls desirous to be waited on with the word, and out of that number 241 have given in their names, requesting to be catechized and confirmed." Whereupon it was resolved to petition the Moravian Church for one or more ministers to labor in connection with the Synod, to supply the "want of able laborers in the vineyard of the Lord, entrusted to the Synod."

On the 16th of October, 1814, the Synod convened at Organ Church, Rowan County, N. C. At this meeting there were eighteen ministers present, twelve of whom were licentiates. The officers of the preceding year were re-elected. It was resolved that, inasmuch as the Pennsylvania Synod had concluded to publish a liturgy, no further steps be taken to prepare one by this Synod, hoping to be united with that Synod in the introduction of its liturgy in our congregations.

The congregations in Tennessee having lost their minister, Rev. Mr. Smith, by death, during the past year, Rev. Philip Henkel consented to become their pastor.

A difficulty arose with catechet Michael Mackin, who insisted that prayer would not be answered unless performed in a kneeling posture, and who introduced that position in prayer in the congregations where he exhorted; he being absent from Synod, Rev. Storch was appointed to examine him, and if still unwilling to conform to the established rules of the Church, to withhold his license from him.

A circular from the Lutheran congregation in Charleston, S. C., was presented, earnestly beseeching the Synod to send them a minister capable of preaching in the German and English languages. The Synod regretted that none could be found among them to labor in this hopeful field, and resolved to send that congregation a friendly letter, with the promise that if deemed necessary, it should be visited the following spring.

The following congregations were received in connection with the Synod: St. Michael's and Paul's (Rall's), Lexington District, S. C. One congregation in Newberry District, S. C., of which Michael and Peter Rickard, Andrew Wecker, and Martin Kinard, were elders; and Coldwater Church, in Cabarrus County, N. C.

In accordance with a written communication

from brother John Dreher, of South Carolina, and upon his desire, it was—

"*Resolved*, That negro slaves be instructed in our holy religion, and be received into our Church as members; and that congregations should make proper arrangements in their houses of worship to give the slaves also the opportunity to hear the Gospel. It was also—

"*Resolved*, That all our ministers unite themselves to labor against the pernicious influence and consequences of dancing, and seek to prevent it in every possible way.

"*Resolved*, That a special conference be held on the third Sunday after Easter, in St. Michael's Church, Lexington District, S. C."

An appendix to the minutes contains the correspondence as ordered by Synod at its last meeting, between the Synod's committee, Revs. Storch and Shober, and Bishop Van Vleck, of the Moravian Church, on the subject of obtaining a supply of ministers from that Church. And although the Bishop's letter was a very friendly one, yet he regretted exceedingly, that at that time, no minister of their Church could be spared.

October 15th, 1815, the Synod convened in the Lutheran Church in Lincolnton, N. C., but on account of sickness, few ministers were present.

Resolved, That no minister has a right to leave his congregations and labor in another field whenever he deems it advisable, without informing the elders and deacons of his intention some time beforehand, and the matter be brought before Synod for final decision.

A congregation at McCobbin's Creek, Mecklenburg County, N. C., was received in connection with Synod. Quite a number of petitions from three congregations in Fairfield County, Ohio, from Washington County, Indiana, then still a territory, from Sevier County, Tennessee, were presented, petitioning Synod for ministers of the gospel, but which could only be partially or occasionally supplied with the means of grace by a visiting minister.

Two congregations in Iredell County, N. C., named New Pearth (now St. Michael's) and Christ Churches, were taken into connection with the Synod. The other transactions of this meeting of Synod are of no special interest.

Section 7. Origin and History of several new Congregations established in North and South Carolina.

From the extracts of the minutes of the North Carolina Synod, as given in the preceding section, it may be readily perceived that the Synod was not only a necessity to the Lutheran Church in the two Carolinas, but also to the same Church in other States; its influence extended itself into Virginia and Tennessee, and even into other and more distant States. Congregations placed themselves under its care in such numbers as to distress the members of Synod to know how to make provision for the spiritual wants of all these churches.

Not only hundreds, but thousands were added to the number of its communing membership in an almost incredibly short period of time. In addition to that, a number of new congregations were organized in its immediate territory, likewise claiming the attention and care of Synod.

God certainly gave the Synod a large field to occupy, and that was the time when it should have taken immediate steps to establish a classical and theological school for the education of young men to the ministry; and it would have been well, if some of the older and more educated ministers had abandoned their congregations, if necessary, but particularly their private interests, such as farming, &c., had conscientiously taken this matter in hand themselves, and would have gone at once as professors into the lecture-room. At first a log hut might have been built for this purpose in almost any locality; this would have sufficed for a beginning, until a more convenient and stately edifice could have been erected, and at a place where it might have been made more successful. True, a few years later, an effort was made in Tennessee to establish such an institution, but it, of necessity, became a failure, as shall be shown hereafter, for want of proper encouragement and good management.

The new congregations that were formed in North and South Carolina are the following:

1. *Bethel Church, Stanly County, N. C.*, which is more commonly known as "Bear Creek Church," on account of its contiguity to that stream. It was

at this time a unitedly Lutheran and Reformed congregation, and its Lutheran members mostly belonged previously to St. John's Church, Cabarrus County. About the year 1804 divine worship was held in Christopher Layerle's barn for two or three years, who donated one hundred acres of well-timbered land to the newly organized congregation; the male members then went to work in felling the trees, squaring the logs, and piling them up in true colonial style, until the new church edifice was sufficiently elevated for having the roof placed upon it, and other necessary work done to it. The following extract is a translation from its church-book: "We erected this church on the 19th and 20th of March, 1806, in the western part of Montgomery (Stanly) County, which was quickly brought under roof, and was made so far comfortable that on the following 25th of May, Whitsunday, service was held in it for the first time by Rev. George Boger (a German Reformed minister), who was our pastor at that time."

The church was afterwards completed at a cost of about $300, and presented a very respectable and comfortabe appearance. A petition for aid was then drawn up by Theophilus Lotter, their school-teacher, and was sent to the Lutheran congregation in Charleston, S. C., who were moved to present this infant enterprise with three boxes of window glass, which was received with thankfulness, duly recorded with their church-book, and accordingly appropriated for the purpose intended.

This same church building is still standing in

all its early strength of architecture, and may resist the encroachments of time for many years to come.

The congregation was for a long time deprived of the services of a regular Lutheran pastor, but was frequently visited by Revs. Storch and J. W. Meyer; and was received into connection with the Synod in the year 1810.

2. *Coldwater Creek Church, Cabarrus County, N. C.*, now St. James' Church, Concord, N. C. The early records of this congregation have all been destroyed by the ravages of those enemies to ancient documents, the rats and mice, who have appropriated the leaves of the records of this church to their own comfort. Audubon, the ornithologist, was served once in the same manner, when his earliest portfolio leaves were all ruined; however, he could replace what had cost him three years' toil to gather together, by once more shouldering his knapsack and gun, and returning to the fields and forests for a renewed supply. But there is no such remedy for the seeker after historical facts; when once the early records are destroyed and lost, no efforts can reproduce them; diligent inquiry and search was made to obtain at least a portion of the records of this church, but all in vain, the work of destruction was done effectually.

Coldwater Church was at one time the oldest German religious organization in Western North Carolina; it had a pastor even before the Rev. A. Nussmann came to America in 1773; this pastor was the Rev. Mr. Suther, a German Reformed minister, some of whose descendants are still living in Concord, N. C., and are worthy members of the Lutheran Church there.

In Wheeler's History of North Carolina, vol. ii, p. 11, the following record in Governor Tryon's journal occurs: "Sunday, August 21st, 1768. Heard Mr. Luther, a Dutch minister, preach." This is a very brief record, but it contains much information, when all the circumstances connected with it are considered. *Firstly*, the place was near Major Phifer's residence, Mecklenburg (now Cabarrus) County, where Governor Tryon with his suite lodged from the 19th to the 22d of August. *Secondly*, the church was a German one, called "Dutch" according to the common parlance of that day, and was none other than the Coldwater Church, which was then the nearest German church to Major Phifer's residence. *Thirdly*, the minister's name was Suther, and not Luther, which is undoubtedly a mistake of the copyist of the Governor's journal, or of the printer, inasmuch as the letter "S," in writing, so nearly resembles the letter "L;" for no minister with the name "Luther" ever resided in that vicinity, and it is known that the Rev. Mr. Suther was the minister of that church about that time. *Fourthly*, the time dates the existence of the Coldwater Church as far back as 1768.

Now whether the Lutherans had, at that time, a common right in the property of that church with the German Reformed is not known. Thirty years later a Lutheran minister occasionally preached there, at least in performing funeral services in that church, as may be seen from the records of St. John's church-book. This minister was the Rev. A. N. Marcard, then the pastor of St. John's Church.

In the minutes of the North Carolina Synod mention is first made of this church in the year 1814, when it was received in connection with the Synod, giving the names of Philip Cress and Michael Winecoff as its church officers, and it is exceedingly probable that its organization as a Lutheran congregation, worshiping with the German Reformed, dates back only to about that time. In the year 1843, under the pastoral care of Rev. W. G. Harter, the Lutheran congregation withdrew from the Coldwater Church, and erected their own house of worship in the town of Concord, adopting the name of St. James' Church, where it continues to exist to the present day.

3. *St. Michael's Church, Lexington District, South Carolina.*—This congregation is likewise comparatively a new organization, and its church edifice is better known as "The Blue Church."

The congregation originated in the following manner: A number of members of Bethel Church, on High Hill Creek, were desirous of hearing the Word of God in the English language, which innovation being met with much opposition, the friends of English preaching withdrew and worshiped for a time in a schoolhouse, but afterwards secured a portion of land by gift or otherwise, and erected their own church. A number of members from old Zion's Church also soon connected themselves with the new enterprise. The Rev. Godfrey Dreher became their first pastor, and their first communion was held in the church on the fifth Sunday in June, 1814. It was admitted into connection with the North Carolina Synod, October 18th of the same year. Its elders and deacons at that time were: John Wise, John Dreher, Samuel Wingard, and Thomas Shuler, whose names are mentioned in the minutes of the Synod.

According to a resolution of the North Carolina Synod, a special Conference was held in this church, at which Conference the Revs. Storch, Miller and Shober, from North Carolina, were present. The Lord's day services were held in Bethel Church, April 29th, 1816, "when Rev. Charles A. Stork opened public worship by preaching from John 3:14, 15, and the Rev. R. J. Miller in the English language from Matt. 21:43. During the first sermon, the Rev. G. Dreher and Candidate M. Rauch addressed the English visitors out of doors, and during the second, the Rev. G. Shober addressed an assembly of negroes near the church on the subject of Christianity, and afterwards preached a sermon in the church from Matt. 13: 25, in the German language. It is hoped that among that great concourse of people, who listened attentively during the long service, some precious seed fell on good ground. It was then thought advisable that the meeting of Conference should be held at St. Michael's Church at nine o'clock, Monday morning." The above extract is taken from the printed minutes of that special Conference, and is herein inserted, because this was the first ecclesiastical meeting of the *Lutheran* Church held in this State. The conventions of the Corpus Ecclesiasticum preceded it some twenty-nine years, but it was a German Reformed as well as a Lutheran body.

The object of holding this Conference was to adjust certain difficulties, that had arisen and disturbed the Lutheran Church in South Carolina, in reference to the baptism of the children of unworthy church members and of non-professors of religion. The decision arrived at was, that the children of all such members, who were not expelled from the Church, could be presented by their own parents for baptism, and that the children of all others were likewise to be baptized, provided worthy members of the Church acted as sponsors, and presented them to the altar. Another vexed question had reference to the colored population, namely: 1. When should they be baptized and confirmed? 2. Should they afterwards be immediately admitted to the communion or remain awhile in a state of probation? 3. Should they belong to the same church with their masters, or be at liberty to select a church for themselves? 4. Should they bring their own children to baptism themselves? 5. The marriage relation was recognized and strictly enforced. A resolution was then also passed, requesting Synod to publish in the minutes of every year the list of its authorized and recognized ministers.

4. *St. Michael's Church, Iredell County, North Carolina.*—The German citizens of Iredell County came originally from Rowan and Cabarrus Counties. All the productive and available lands in these two counties had been preoccupied by their forefathers, whose descendants were, therefore, compelled to go westward, and many of them occupied lands in Iredell that were still vacant, or purchased farms from the original Scotch-Irish settlers.

This influx of a German population occurred about the close of the last or commencement of the present century, and owing to the peculiarities of their settlement here, many of them are intermarried with the original Scotch-Irish colonists, and nearly all are more or less scattered over the whole of that country, and some of them are of necessity located rather remotely from their own house of worship.

The Rev. R. J. Miller was the first Lutheran minister who gathered the German settlers in Iredell County into a congregation, A.D. 1815. This fact is ascertained from the church records, as well as from the minutes of the Synod of 1815, when that congregation was admitted under the name of "New Pearth." The church land was donated by Mr. Daniel Walcher, and was given as joint property for the use of both the Lutheran and Episcopal denominations, and was so continued as a union house of worship for several years, when the Episcopalians withdrew and erected their own church a few miles distant from St. Michael's

Church, leaving the Lutheran congregation the sole possessor of that property.

The church edifice has since been considerably enlarged, and is located on a pleasant site near the public road leading from Charlotte to Statesville, and recently the "Atlantic, Tennessee and Ohio Railroad" has been located very near to this church and its graveyard. Rev. Mr. Miller continued to labor here for six years, when he voluntarily disconnected himself from the Lutheran Church, in 1821. It was in this congregation that the Rev. Simeon W. Harkey, D.D. and his brothers, who are also in the ministry, were born and reared up for enlarged usefulness in the Lutheran Church. Dr. Harkey was for a time President of Illinois State University; many interesting circumstances of his early life are still related by his former schoolmates and early associates. St. Michael's Church has lost heavily by the removal of many of its members, principally to the State of Illinois.

5. *McCobbin's Creek Church, Mecklenburg County, N. C.*, is also mentioned in the minutes of the North Carolina Synod, as having been received into its connection in 1815. Of its history nothing is known to the writer; it is probable, that this is the present "Morning Star Church" in that county, and now connected with the Tennessee Synod. There are, doubtless, other new Lutheran congregations which were organized in other parts of the Carolinas at or before this time, but as they are not mentioned in the minutes of the Synod,

and no other records are at hand, nothing can be said concerning them.

Section 8. Continued History of several of the older Lutheran Congregations in the Carolinas.

The Lutheran Church in the interior of South Carolina was beginning to present a more hopeful appearance; much good was accomplished by the labors of its young ministers, who had recently been licensed or ordained by the North Carolina Synod; the Synod itself was also exerting a wholesome influence upon those churches in South Carolina that were connected with it. In Newberry District the Rev. F. J. Wallern was still laboring, but he and his congregations remained isolated and uninfluenced by synodical counsel and authority, consequently no improvement was manifested in their condition; one congregation, however, placed itself under the care of Synod in 1814, whose elders' and deacons' names have been mentioned, yet it is not stated who was its pastor at that time.

Soon after the death of Rev. C. E. Bernhardt, in 1809, the churches in Lexington District, on both sides of the Saluda River, were served by the Rev. Godfrey Dreher, who was licensed by the North Carolina Synod in 1810, and labored there for a number of years, having still the charge of Zion's, St. Peter's, and other more recently organized congregations, as late as 1848, at about which time he resigned. The Rev. J. Y. Meetze also resided and preached in this District, serving several congregations; and after the year 1814, the Rev. J. P. Franklow, who resigned his charge in Orangeburg District, likewise labored in Lexington, so that the congregations in this District were for the time well supplied with ministerial labor.

The Sandy Run congregation was supplied once a month with the means of grace by Revs. Dreher, Franklow and Rauch, from and after the year 1812; Rev. Franklow, however, soon afterwards resigned; whether Rev. Rauch continued to preach there any length of time is not stated, but Rev. Dreher remained the pastor of that church until the close of the year 1821.

The St. Matthew's charge in Orangeburg District was supplied with a pastor in the Rev. J. P. Franklow, who remained in office in that charge until 1814, when he resigned, and Rev. M. Rauch became his successor. By resolution of the North Carolina Synod, he also took the oversight of the two congregations in Barnwell District.

The Lutheran church in Charleston was vacant from the year 1811, but was supplied with the means of grace, six months at a time, by several Episcopal clergymen, until the Rev. John Bachman, from the State of New York, became the pastor in January, 1815. Of his arrival in Charleston and of his pastoral labors more will be stated in the next section.

The various churches in Lincoln County, N. C., were served with the pastoral labors of Revs. R.

J. Miller, David Henkel and Daniel Moser; the latter became the successor of Rev. Philip Henkel, who had resigned and accepted the call to the Tennessee congregations, made vacant by the death of Rev. C. Z. H. Smith.

The two congregations in Cabarrus County were supplied by the Rev. C. A. G. Storch; St. John's Church was served as a part of his regular charge, whilst the Coldwater congregation received occasional visits from him. The other now existing congregations in this county were not organized at that time.

In Rowan County Rev. Storch was laboring still at Organ Church, in the bounds of which he then resided; it is probable that he also served Savage's or Sewits' Church, now called Lutheran Chapel; but the Union or Pine Church he had resigned, and the Rev. J. W. Meyer became its pastor.

St. John's Church, in Salisbury, was at this time still vacant; it had become a neglected field, and, according to the provisions in the title granted by Mr. Beard, the Episcopalians occupied the church, since they had no house of worship of their own, and the few remaining Lutherans worshiped with them.

The churches in Davidson County were served faithfully by their pastor, Rev. Lewis Markert, from 1805 to 1816, when he removed to the State of Indiana, where he continued to labor until the Lord called him home, November 22d, 1850. After the removal of Rev. Markert, and at the request of the vacant congregations, the Synod, in

1816, appointed Rev. G. Shober to supply two of the churches of that charge, whilst the remaining two were placed under the care of Rev. J. W. Meyer. In 1817, Catechet Daniel Walcher was sent by Synod to labor in these vacant churches, where he remained until 1821, when he removed to Pendleton County, Virginia.

In the year 1810, the Rev. Jacob Scherer became the pastor of the churches in Guilford and Orange Counties, which had been vacant about four years, but through the energetic and faithful labors of Rev. Scherer's ministry, this charge became one of the most promising in the State. His catechetical instructions were specially blessed. At one time a certain young man came to him and declared that "he would not for the whole world have been without these instructions, for by means of them he had found what was worth more than the world to him." The Rev. Jacob Grieson was licensed to preach the gospel in 1810, and labored as an assistant pastor with Rev. Scherer, accomplishing much good, and was always willing and prepared to lighten the burdens and labors of the regular pastor in that extensive charge.

The congregations in Forsythe County, near Salem, N. C., were greatly built up by the efficient labors of their first pastor, the Rev. Gottlieb Schober, who commenced his ministry there in 1810, and continued in charge of these churches to the close of his life, June 27th, 1838.

Section 9. Arrival of Rev. John Bachman as Pastor of St. John's Lutheran Church in Charleston, S. C., and his Report on the State of the Country and of the Condition of the Lutheran Church in America in the year 1815.

At last we have reached that period in the history of the Lutheran Church in the Carolinas which comes within the range of still living witnesses, one of whom is the Rev. John Bachman, D.D., LL.D., now in his eighty-third year, and in the fifty-eighth year of his ministry in Charleston, S. C., as pastor of St. John's Lutheran Church; and though no longer able to preach the gospel, he still manifests the liveliest interest in the welfare and prosperity in the Lutheran Church, both in his own Synod and in America; and has but recently (March 28th, 1872) been permitted, in a reclining posture, to participate in the dedication of St. Matthew's German Lutheran Church of Charleston.

It is not designed to give a sketch of Dr. Bachman's life and ministry in this section of this work, as it would require more than a few pages, and belongs properly to biographical literature; besides, it would bring at once the history of Lutheranism in Charleston to its present date, and disarrange the entire plan of this work. Rev. Dr. Bachman's name, life and labors will now accompany and be included in the history of the Lutheran Church in the Carolinas to the present day, as he is inseparably connected with it as one of its most useful and prominent ministers.

On Sunday, January 10th, 1858, Dr. Bachman preached an anniversary sermon to his congregation, on the occasion of his having then been forty-three years their pastor. This sermon has been published, and furnishes the Church the most interesting incidents in his life and ministry, besides embracing a report on the state of the country and of the condition of the Lutheran Church in America in the year 1815. Truly that was the day of small things to the Lutheran Church in this country, when her ministry numbered not quite one hundred, and there were still but three Synods in the United States,—the New York, the Pennsylvania, and the North Carolina Synods.

The following extracts are taken from Dr. Bachman's anniversary sermon:

"On the 10th of January, 1815, I arrived in this city for the purpose of taking charge of this congregation. A meeting of the vestry of the church took place on the 12th, two days afterwards, and the charge of the congregation was, in due form, committed to my trust. This day, then, is the forty-third anniversary of my arrival to engage in the ministry in this city.

"On the 10th, the day of my arrival, I attended the first funeral service, which was performed by another clergyman, who had previously been engaged, and on the 16th I performed the first baptismal service.

"*My Antecedents.*

"I was licensed by the Lutheran Synod of New York in 1813, having previously been elected pastor of three congregations in the vicinity of my own neighborhood, in the county of Rensselaer, N. Y., where I would have gladly spent the remainder of my days, among the friends and relatives of my boyhood and early youth. A hemorrhage of the lungs, however, of which I had been attacked whilst at college, was making a fearful inroad on my health, and I was advised by my physicians to seek relief in a more southern climate. A call had been sent from this congregation to the President of the Synod of New York, Dr. Quitman, with a request that he should recommend some clergyman who might be adapted to this field of labor. He was the father of the present General Quitman, and was regarded as one of the most learned and eloquent men of his day. He and my ever faithful friend, Dr. Mayer, of Philadelphia, proposed my name to this congregation. They immediately sent me a call to become their pastor. After consultation with my family and congregation, they reluctantly gave me leave of absence for nine months, during which time the hope was expressed that my health would be sufficiently restored to enable me to resume my ministerial labors among them. As the Lutheran Church had scarcely an existence in our Southern States, and as we had no Synod here, an extra meeting of the Synod of New York was convened in December, 1814, at Rhinebeck, Dutchess County, the place of my nativity, for the purpose of ordaining me. The ordination services were performed by Dr. Quitman and the other officers of the Synod in the Lutheran church at Rhinebeck, where I had been baptized in infancy. Without returning home, I proceeded on my way to this city.

"*The State of our Country.*

"We were in the midst of a three years' war with the most powerful of foreign nations. Fearful battles had occurred on our Northern frontiers, on the ocean and on the lakes. The traces of devastation and death were visible in the half-covered graves along the highway between Baltimore and Washington. The blackened walls of the Capitol at Washington, and the waste and destruction in every part of the city, presented an awful picture of the horrors of war. On my arrival here I found our citizens working on the lines of defence thrown around the landside of our city—even ladies went there with hoes and spades to cheer the citizen soldiers by their presence, their countenance and example, and I too joined, at least in form, for it was our common country that was to be defended. In the meantime the battle of New Orleans had been fought, on the 8th of January, and a treaty of peace had been signed at Ghent;

but these important events were not known until some time afterwards. The war had fallen heavily on our Southern people. The principal staple of our commerce, cotton, had for several years, during the embargo and war, been sold at a mere nominal value, and was stored away in various depositories in King Street. Our city was then only a village compared with its present growth, and the grass was growing in our most public streets. Men had the necessaries of life, and these were cheap; but all the means of enterprise and all the avenues to wealth were closed up. Fortunately men were driven to the necessity of manufacturing their necessary articles, and they were compelled to deny themselves luxuries; they studied economy, and hence there was not much suffering among our people from any want of the necessaries of life. But the constant dread of invasion, the sufferings and dangers to which our friends who were in the army and at sea were constantly exposed, kept the minds of our citizens in an unsettled and feverish state. The means of traveling were very different from what they are now in the days of steamers and railroads. The roads were almost impassable; as an evidence of this, I would state that with the exception of a Sabbath on which I preached for Dr. Mayer, of Philadelphia, I came in the regular stage line, which traveled day and night, and arrived at Charleston on the morning of the twenty-ninth day after leaving Dutchess County, which is a hundred miles north of the city of New York.

In the meantime our vehicles were either broken or overturned eight times on the journey.

" *The State of the Lutheran Church in America at the time of my Arrival at the South.*

"The Lutheran Church in America was at a very low ebb. There were only three Synods, one in New York, composed of seven ministers; one in Pennsylvania, which in point of numbers was considerably larger; and a small Synod in North Carolina." (In the North Carolina Synod there were, October 17th, 1814, the last meeting of Synod previous to Dr. Bachman's arrival, nine ordained ministers and eleven licentiates, twenty ministers in all.) "Our ministers, with very few exceptions, performed service exclusively in the German language. This was a great error, inasmuch as it excluded from the Church the descendants of Lutherans, who had by education and association adopted the language of the country. Our doctrines were not objectionable to them, but they could not understand the language in which they were promulgated. Thus the progress of the Church was greatly retarded in consequence of the bigoted attachment of our ancestors, and especially their clergy, to a foreign language. Since the introduction of the English language into our ministrations the Church has made rapid progress.

" *The State of our Church in Charleston, South Carolina, and in the other Southern States.*

"When I arrived here the congregation worshiped in a small wooden church, situated in the rear of the present church; it was an antiquated building of a peculiar construction, resembling some of the old churches in the rural districts of Germany. The congregation was composed of Germans, who, during the stormy season of the Revolution, had been the strenuous advocates and defenders of the rights of their adopted country.

"The services continued for many years to be conducted in the German language. The Rev. Mr. Faber, the younger of two brothers, who were pastors of this congregation, introduced the service in the English language. After his death, there was for several years no minister of the Lutheran Church presiding over this congregation. I have scarcely a doubt that the congregation was preserved from total annihilation through the pious zeal and devotion of the venerable Jacob Sass, who, for a long series of years, was the president of the vestry, and who was one of the purest and best men with whom it has been my privilege ever to associate.

"It does not become me to speak of my own labors in this congregation; suffice it to say, that I feel how imperfect are the best efforts of man, and wherever there has been any success, let us ascribe all the praise and glory to God, to whom they legitimately belong. Men are but the instruments in His hands, and He, the Master, often gives the blessing whilst the servant is unworthy.

"For many years the Germans of our city formed a part of this congregation; I preached for them in the German language, at first, once a month, and for some years afterwards, occasionally in the evenings. For nearly twenty years I preached three sermons on each Sabbath. I now feel convinced from experience that this labor is beyond the capacity of most constitutions, especially in our debilitating climate. In the autumn of 1837, my health and strength failed me. My congregation, feeling a deep interest in the preservation of my life and the restoration of my enfeebled health, unanimously requested me to remove for a season from my field of labor. I left my home and people in 1838, believing that I looked upon the land of my nativity for the last time, and that I was destined to breathe my last breath among strangers in a foreign land. I was absent eight months, during which time I wandered nearly over all Europe, and was received with a sympathy, kindness, and untiring hospitality that have left deep traces of gratitude on my heart. I returned in January, 1839, with health partially restored. For a few years, until my health was re-established, this congregation engaged an assistant minister.

"I cannot here withhold from you the candid admission that the establishment of our Church in the South was a source of greater anxiety to my mind than even the prosperity of my own congregation. I came as a pioneer in our holy cause. For several years I held my membership with the Synod of New York. We had very few materials in the South from which the Church could be built up; no emigrants from abroad.

"There were Lutherans in Lexington and Orangeburg Districts, but they were almost destitute of the means of grace. There had been a church in Savannah, erected before the Revolution, that belonged to the Lutherans, but it was burnt down in 1797. This congregation contributed $500 towards rebuilding it; no congregation was, however, subsequently organized, and the small building was occupied as a Sunday-school by another denomination. They were visited, a congregation was organized from the materials which could be collected, and a clergyman, who had been raised up in this congregation, became their pastor. They have now a new church and a flourishing congregation. Ebenezer was also visited. The pastor there, who seemed not aware that Lutheranism had any existence in the South, had taken a license in another Church. He soon became a co-worker with us, and they have now two pastors and several churches in the neighborhood. We at length began to discuss the propriety of forming a Synod in our State. We had no theological school, we had but three or four pastors who were able to perform duty, and the few Lutherans that remained were either poor or in very moderate circumstances.

"On my first arrival here I became a member

of the German Friendly Society, which was then composed of nearly one hundred members; these have all passed away, and I am now the oldest member. Of the few communicants I found in this church at my arrival, one only is now alive. The vestrymen, whose names were signed to my call, were: Jacob Sass, President; Abraham Markley, John Strohecker, Henry Horlbeck, Jacob Strobel, J. E. Schirmer, Benjamin A. Markley, Jacob Eckhardt, Sr., and John Strobel. Wardens: J. M. Hoff, C. C. Philips, Adolph Beckman, and Anthony A. Pelzer. All these have gone to their account.

"Of the committee of twenty-one who, in 1815, reported on the expediency of building this church, all are dead. Of the pastors who occupied the pulpits of our city on my arrival, not one is now living. Of the managers of the Bible Society, who met me in 1815, I only am left, and of its members I am the oldest on their record. At our first confirmation in 1816, of sixty-four persons, who were then dedicated to God, nine only are now alive.

"I have given you a very brief and imperfect sketch of the days that are past in my long ministry. Time will not permit me to enter into any details; they would fill volumes. Little now remains of that thread of life, which has been spun out in the midst of you. I would not wish to recall that life, unless it could be spent in greater usefulness to you and to others, and I trust, through the mercy of that Savior who died for a fallen world, I will be prepared to resign it cheerfully into the hands of that God who gave it, whenever He shall see fit to call me hence. This congregation was the only one of which I have had charge since my ordination. To all invitations from other sources in the Church and seats of learning—offering higher pecuniary advantages—I did not hesitate a moment in giving a negative reply."

Such matter in Rev. Dr. Bachman's sermon, which was not strictly of a historical character, or which had been quoted in other parts of this book, in its proper chronological position, has been omitted; other historical data, brought out in the Doctor's discourse, but referring to a later period, will find their place in some of the succeeding chapters.

Section 10. The Ordination Question, and Opposition to the Licensure of Candidates for the Ministry.

The principal transactions of the North Carolina Synod during the year 1816, were certain reports and resolutions on the question of ordination, which were occasioned as follows:

In consequence of the great want of ministers, and in order to preserve harmony and uniformity with the Pennsylvania Synod, the licensure system was adopted also by the Synod of North Carolina. This system is altogether an American feature, so far as the Lutheran Church is concerned, and arose entirely on account of the great paucity and want of ministers of the gospel in this country.

The various Lutheran congregations which had been organized in America, besought the different Synods to furnish them preachers or pastors; but what could the Synods do towards answering these numerous and repeated calls made upon them? Few ministers came or were sent from Germany, and no university or college had as yet been established for the education of candidates for the ministry by the Lutheran Church in this country; it was, therefore, thought expedient to license persons who could exhort and catechize, to take charge of these vacant churches, at the same time making it the duty of the ordained ministers residing in the vicinity to administer the sacraments as frequently as possible in those congregations. These exhorters were called catechets. A course of study was prescribed for them in Latin, Greek and theology, to be studied privately or with some of the older ministers; as soon as they stood a fair examination, they were advanced in their ministerial standing and received license, to be renewed every year, to administer all the ordinances of the Church. They were called candidates, and were obliged to continue their studies, report their ministerial acts to Synod, bring a written sermon annually for examination, and, whenever they passed a good examination on their studies, character and ministerial usefulness, were solemnly ordained to the gospel ministry. They were then called pastors, enjoying all the privileges of the older ministers. This arrangement was regarded as an educational one, and not as having established different grades or orders of the ministry.

There now arose in Lincoln County, N. C. a great opposition to this system, because the candidates were authorized to perform all ministerial acts without having been previously ordained; a long statement, covering more than three pages of the minutes of Synod for 1816, is devoted to this subject, from which the following extracts are made:

"Upon the adoption of the report (on the licensure of a number of candidates), a sad opposition manifested itself from Lincoln County, and, under the pretext that disturbances had been caused in said county by the impression that it was antichristian for any one to administer the sacraments without ordination, it was vehemently insisted upon that the candidates be ordained." Here follows a lengthy statement of the reasons why the Synod adopted and continued the licensure system, namely: that it had been a blessing to the Church, and that the Synod wished to conform also in this particular usage to the long-established practice of their brethren in Pennsylvania. The report of the Pennsylvania Synod on this subject, as found in its minutes of 1814, is also given, which report reads as follows:

"Upon motion, the ordained ministers were called upon to express their opinion on the question proposed by the (North) Carolina Ministerium, namely, '*Have candidates the right to perform the Actus Ministeriales without a previous laying on of hands?*'

Some expressed their opinions verbally, others in writing. It was unanimously—

"*Resolved*, That, according to the testimony of the Bible and the history of the Church, a written authority is equally as valid as the imposition of hands, that our ministerial arrangement is not in opposition to the principles of the Evangelical Lutheran Church, and that, therefore, licensed candidates can perform all Actus Ministeriales with a good conscience." The Secretary of the North Carolina Synod adds yet this remark to the above resolution of the Pennsylvania Synod: "At this Synod twenty-two ordained ministers and twenty-nine candidates were present, and all were agreed on this subject; their resolutions and opinions were sent to us in writing in 1814; we should, therefore, be uniform in practice, and one or two otherwise thinking individuals among us should yield that much from motives of love.

"All, however, was of no avail; therefore, upon motion of Rev. Shober, it was resolved to make the following alteration for one year only: that if the present candidates can pass through their this year's examination, their license be handed them publicly before the congregation, after having affirmatively answered that they would observe all what the Bible and the Augsburg Confession requires of a minister, and that in the name of the Church a blessing be pronounced upon them with imposition of hands.

"The President (Rev. Mr. Storch), protested openly against this innovation; the resolution was, nevertheless, adopted. And, inasmuch as the President could not conscientiously perform this ceremony, he requested Rev. Shober to attend to this duty for him." A fear is also expressed in the minutes, that all this would eventually cause a division in the Church.

At the next meeting of Synod, in 1817, the subject came up again, and was finally disposed of by vote, Rev. R. J. Miller being the only one who voted in the negative, namely, against the licensure of candidates.

From all this we can also arrive at the number of Lutheran ministers in the United States in 1814. The Pennsylvania Synod, 51 present, probably only a few absent at that meeting; the New York Synod, 7; and the North Carolina Synod, 21; Total, 79. Suppose we allow 6 absentees to the Pennsylvania Synod, then we have 85 Lutheran ministers in 1814 in this country. This number also agrees with the statement made by Rev. Dr. Hazelius, in an inaugural address.

Section 11. The Literary Institution in Tennessee for the Education of Ministers; and the Publication by authority of the North Carolina Synod of a book called "Luther."

In East Tennessee Lutheranism was spreading rapidly; three new congregations, named Union, Hopeful and Lick Creek, were organized, and connected themselves with the Synod in 1817;

and in this State, where a few years ago there was but one minister, the Rev. C. Z. H. Smith, there were now four laborers, namely, Revs. Philip Henkel, Jacob Zink, Adam Miller and Joseph E. Bell; the last mentioned was a good classical scholar, and was received as a catechet in 1816, in accordance with his own request, and because he could not be present at Synod that year; the next year, however, being present, he was regularly licensed as a candidate.

In 1817, Revs. Philip Henkel and Jos. E. Bell, commenced a classical and theological seminary on their own responsibility, at which the Synod was greatly rejoiced, for it was high time that something was done in that direction. A report on this institution, and the action of the Synod in reference to it, are here presented.

"Rev. Philip Henkel reported, that in Green County, in the State of Tennessee, a seminary, on a small scale, was established under his and Rev. Bell's supervision, in which theology, the Greek, Latin, German and English languages are taught, and in which Rev. Bell is the principal teacher. In accordance with a report, said seminary was received with joy under the counsel and aid of Synod, with the confident expectation that this small beginning, by the help of God, located in so healthy and cheap a region of country, this institution, so long and earnestly desired, may prosper in such a manner, that many well-qualified ministers and missionaries may be educated as preachers of the glorious Gospel of Jesus in all parts of the world, who will be prepared to give to every man a reason of the hope that is in them. Thousands of the present and future generations will then thank both those who have been instructed in that institution, as well as those who have contributed their gifts for the support of this new enterprise, &c.

"A letter was also read to Synod from Rev. Mr. Bachman, pastor in Charleston, South Carolina, in which he expresses his joy and desire to labor in harmony with us, and greatly desires to see that a seminary for the education of ministers be established, and that his congregation would gladly contribute towards the support of the enterprise; furthermore, that the New York Ministerium, to which he belongs, would willingly aid us with missionaries, and that he regrets that, at this season of the year, he cannot be present with us.

"The reading of this letter was listened to with much rejoicing; and as the time for the meeting of Synod is now changed, we hope to have the pleasure, through Rev. Bachman, to become more intimately acquainted with the New York Ministerium."

Arrangements were also made to take up collections the following May in all the congregations for the support of the seminary in Tennessee.

It is sad to relate that this institution was short-lived, because it was remotely located, and therefore did not properly come under the influence of Synod; also, because the leading men of Synod did not take hold of it themselves. They were very willing to extend their counsel, sympathy and aid, when others did the work in establishing it; but that is not the proper way to build up an institution, which requires the entire wisdom and energy of all the members of Synod.

But the principal cause of the failure of this institution at *that* time was the division which arose in the Lutheran Church in the South in 1819. After the year 1820, nothing more of importance is known of this seminary in Tennessee.

From the minutes of Synod for 1819 the information is received that $246.75 was sent from South Carolina in aid of this institution, out of which Rev. Bachman's congregation had contributed $221.75.

Concerning Rev. Shober's book, familiarly entitled, "Luther," and published by authority of Synod, the following action was taken. In 1816, on motion of Rev. Philip Henkel, it was resolved that the secretary, Rev. Shober, compile all the rules adopted by this Synod, and publish them in the English language, inasmuch as our Church is very little known among the English inhabitants.

In accordance with this resolution, the Secretary prepared and laid before Synod in 1817, "A manuscript compilation entitled: Comprehensive Account of the Rise and Progress of the Reformation of the Christian Church by Dr. Martin Luther, actually begun on the 31st day of October, A.D. 1517; together with views of his character and doctrine, extracted from his books; and how the Church, established by him, arrived and progressed in North America; as also the Constitution and Rules of that Church in North Carolina and adjoining States as existing in October, 1817."

"On motion, a committee, consisting of the Rev. R. J. Miller, Philip Henkel and Joseph E. Bell, was appointed to examine the same." A few days afterward the committee reported: "That they had examined said manuscript, and do highly approve of its contents, and recommend it to be published, believing that it will have a beneficial effect throughout our congregations, and give succinct information to other Christians what the Lutheran Church is."

"The Synod unanimously adopted said report, and directed the treasurer to have 1500 copies printed." The proceeds of the sale of this book were to be applied to the Tennessee Seminary and other synodial objects.

The contents of this book are: a history of the Reformation, a history of the Lutheran Church "transplanted to America," particularly in North Carolina and other Southern States; the Augsburg Confession; Constitution and Rules adopted by the North Carolina Synod; extracts from Luther's writings; and some concluding remarks.

The character of the book appears on some of its pages to be soundly Lutheran; on other pages compromising and unionistic. The tenth and eleventh articles of the Augsburg Confession are not passed by without a comment, in the shape of a foot-note, weakening their force, and making them agreeable to all denominations. In the "Conclusion" the following remarks occur: "I have attentively examined the doctrine of the Episcopalian Church, read many excellent authors of the Presbyterians, know the Methodist doctrine from their book, 'Portraiture of Methodism,' and am acquainted with the Baptist doctrine, so far as that they admit and adore Jesus the Savior. Among all those classes, who worship Jesus as a God, I see nothing of importance to prevent a cordial union; and how happy would it be if all the Churches could unite, and send deputies to a general meeting of all denominations," &c., &c.

This full account of the action of Synod in reference to this book, and this full description of it, have been given for very good reasons, which are briefly as follows:

Firstly, inasmuch as the Synod authorized the secretary to write this book, had it examined by a committee, had adopted it without a dissenting voice, had it published at the expense of Synod, had it afterwards scattered in its congregations, and generally circulated, the conclusion, therefore, is natural, that the Synod was perfectly satisfied with its contents, that the sentiments therein expressed were the sentiments of Synod at that time, and that all its ministers were united in the faith as therein exhibited.

Secondly, inasmuch as Revs. Philip Henkel and J. E. Bell composed two-thirds of the committee to examine this book, and reported favorably, "*highly approving of its contents*," branding the eleventh article of the Augsburg Confession as "conciliatory" to the Roman Catholics, but no longer observed; that their faith and opinions in regard to those doctrines and usages were in harmony at that time with those of Rev. Shober, its author.

Thirdly, inasmuch as Revs. David Henkel, Philip Henkel and others of the then future Tennessee Synod circulated this book by sale, up to the time of their withdrawal from the North Carolina Synod, it is but reasonable to conclude, that doctrinal differences did not, *at first,* cause the division in the Church in the years 1819 and 1820.

In short, the fact is apparent that all the members of Synod, with many of their forefathers before them, both in America and in the greater part of Germany, had gradually departed from the pure faith as confessed by the Reformers.

Section 12. The Convention which was called for the purpose of organizing a General Synod.

On the 19th of October, 1817, the Synod of North Carolina convened at Pilgrim's Church, Davidson County, N. C.

At this synodical meeting it was resolved that, owing to the prevalence of sickness during the fall season, the time when the meetings of Synod had been generally held, the Synod hereafter shall be convened on Trinity Sunday of each year. This time of meeting was "*firmly fixed*" (vest gesetzt). It was also resolved that the next meeting of Synod shall take place on Trinity Sunday of 1819; consequently there was no meeting of Synod held in 1818, since that year's Trinity Sunday occurred only about seven months after the last meeting of Synod; the next meeting was therefore postponed to Trinity Sunday of 1819.

This arrangement became the occasion of a threefold difficulty, namely: nineteen months without a meeting of Synod was too long a time to intervene for the welfare of the Church; many evils might have been prevented had a meeting of Synod taken place in 1818. Too many important interests were intrusted to its care, and the Synod should have heeded the warning contained in Matt. 13 : 25. Then again, the call from the Pennsylvania Synod to consult with that body, during its session in Baltimore on Trinity Sunday of 1819, about the propriety of organizing a General Synod, presented another difficulty, conflicting with the time of the meeting of the North Carolina Synod, and occasioned no little trouble to arrange this matter properly. The third difficulty will become apparent in the next section of this book.

In compliance with the call of the Pennsylvania Synod, the North Carolina Synod was convened six weeks before the time appointed, on the second Sunday after Easter, as the following statement in the English minutes of Synod of 1819 fully explains.

"The cause of changing the time of meeting of the Synod from Trinity Sunday to this day was explained, namely: that at the last Synod of the Lutheran ministry in Pennslvania, a general desire was expressed, if possible, to effect a more intimate union with all the Synods of our Church in the United States; which was officially communicated by the officers of their Ministerium to our secretary, and in private letters from other reverend sources. This information was then communicated to ministers of our Synod, and particularly to our reverend president, and all such who, in the vicinity, could be informed thereof, united in opinion, that towards a union of our Church in this extensive country all possible assistance ought to be rendered on our part. But as the Synod of Pennsylvania and adjacent States was this year to meet in Baltimore on Trinity Sunday, and the officers of their last Synod had invited us to send a deputy or deputies to the same; the consideration whether this Synod would send deputies could not be postponed to the same day, and for that reason this meeting was called at this time. And after the said letters from the reverend secretary, Endress, of Lancaster, and the reverend president, Lochman, were read, this Synod unanimously approved of our present meeting.

"It was further unanimously agreed that our reverend president, with the consent of two or three ordained ministers residing in his vicinity, is authorized to call a Synod, and to make other orders and regulations which will not admit of delay; and which should be valid until the succeeding meeting of the Synod."

This would have all been well enough, if the matter which claimed their earlier attention had been urgent; also if the time of the meeting of Synod had not been "firmly fixed."

That the question, concerning the establishment of a General Synod, did not require speedy action at that time is evident from the fact, that the meeting in Baltimore in 1819 was simply an annual meeting of the Pennsylvania Synod; where the question was to be discussed as to the *propriety* of organizing a General Synod; it was certainly injudicious haste on the part of the North Carolina Synod to disarrange its own Church affairs, merely to send a deputy to a meeting of the Pennsylvania Synod; at which meeting no steps could possibly be taken, except to discuss the question and call for a convention of delegates from all the Synods. The North Carolina Synod should have had more respect for its own legislation at its last meeting, and let "firmly fixed" remain so, until reconsidered and changed at a regular meeting of Synod.

"After deliberating on the manner how a desirable union of the whole Church might best be effected, it appeared unnecessary to send more than one deputy at the beginning of an attempt towards a union; because if one deputy of each now existing Synod was elected, they could form a constitution of our general Church, which would then be laid before the different Synods for acceptance.

"According to this view, our secretary, Gottlieb Shober, was elected to attend the Synod at Baltimore, and, in the name of this Synod, endeavor to effect such a desirable union.

"*Resolved*, that if he accedes to a constitution for the purpose of uniting our whole Church, and that constitution be in accordance with his instructions received from this Synod, it be adopted by us; but if such constitution be not in accordance with his instructions, the same must first be communicated to our next Synod; and only then, if adopted, can it be binding upon us.

"A committee to form instructions for our deputy was appointed, namely: the Revs. Robert Johnson Miller, Jacob Scherer, and Mr. Jonas Abernathy." The committee afterwards reported, and the "instructions were considered, paragraph after paragraph, amended, and then unanimously approved." These instructions were not published in the minutes. Rev. Shober attended the meeting of the Pennsylvania Synod in Baltimore, and labored with a committee of said Synod in preparing a plan for the organization of a General Synod; this plan was published for general distribution among all the ministers and delegates of the several Lutheran Synods in the United States, a copy of which is found reprinted in the minutes of the Tennessee Synod of 1820, from which it is seen that Rev. Shober was the *only delegate* that appeared upon the floor of the Pennsylvania Synod from other Lutheran Synods.

The next step, that was taken for the organization of the General Synod, was the convention of delegates from the several Synods in October, 1820, at Hagerstown, Maryland, at which convention a constitution was adopted for the government of the future General Synod. At this convention four Synods were represented, namely: The Pennsylvania, the North Carolina, the New York and the Maryland-Virginia Synod. The Ohio Synod at first adopted the proposed "Plan" of the Pennsylvania Synod, but afterwards reconsidered its action, and withdrew from the enterprise; the Tennessee Synod never became connected with the General Synod. The North Carolina Synod elected Revs. R. J. Miller, Peter Schmucker and Mr. John B. Harry as deputies to the convention at Hagerstown, Maryland.

The first session of the General Synod was held in October, 1821, in Fredericktown, Maryland. Delegates present from the North Carolina Synod were Revs. G. Shober and D. Scherer.

Section 13. The First Rupture in the Lutheran Church in America, and the subsequent formation of the Tennessee Synod, A.D. 1819 and 1820.

It may be seen from the preceding sections, that dissensions were beginning to arise in the Lutheran Church in the Carolinas. This state of things might have been expected, when ministers from other denominations, still holding fast to their un-Lutheran principles, were admitted as members of the Synod; and when no theological seminary was established, in which the future ministers might be trained alike in the doctrines and usages of the

Lutheran Church. Doctrinal differences were at first not very apparent, except on the ordination question; however, it was perceptible, as early as 1816, that everything was tending towards a disruption, and that only some occasion or circumstance was wanting to produce it.

This event was not long delayed, for in the year 1819 the Synod of North Carolina held its sessions six weeks earlier than the appointed time, which, with the transactions of that meeting of Synod, furnished the occasion to rend the Church asunder.

The persons who became the leaders in this division were Rev. Gottlieb Shober, on the part of the North Carolina Synod, and Rev. David Henkel, on the part of the withdrawing party, that afterwards formed the Tennessee Synod.

Rev. Shober was a man of decided opinions, unyielding in everything which he considered right, as may be seen from a sketch of his life in the Evangelical Review, vol. viii, pp. 412–414; "with a mind that knew no dissimulation, a lofty independence, an ardent temper, and a character decidedly affirmative, he frequently experienced difficulties, and encountered points other than pleasant, in his pilgrimage through life, and which a disposition more pliant could have averted." "The lineaments of his countenance gave indications of a strong and active mind." "He was one of the most active defenders of (the) General Synod, as he had also been prominent among its early founders." But Rev. Shober was no Lutheran, he was a member of the Moravian Church, and never disconnected himself from communion with the same; he lived and died as a member of that Church. This information the writer received from his own daughter, the widow of Bishop Herrman. He merely served the Lutheran Church in the capacity of one of its ministers, being the pastor of several neglected Lutheran congregations in the vicinity of his place of residence, Salem, N. C. It may be readily perceived that no compromise could be expected on his part, in the difficulties which distracted the Lutheran Church at that time.

Firm as was the Rev. G. Shober, he found his equal, in that respect, in Rev. David Henkel, who, though a young man then, was equally as decided and unyielding in his opinions. He was a hard student and well educated, not only in the German and English languages, but also in Latin, Greek, Hebrew and Theology, all of which he had principally acquired by private study and close application. He was the best informed candidate for the ministry the North Carolina Synod had at that time, and wielded even then a considerable influence in the Church. It is not to be supposed that he would readily yield his opinions to others, or permit himself to be led about at the will of even those who were older than himself, when he believed his cause to be just. In him the Tennessee Synod had a champion who could not be easily overcome. He had a mind that was clear, active and penetrating; he was quick in discerning an advantage, and not slow in making use of it.

These characteristics are gathered principally from his own writings.

The difficulty was at first a personal one, and, as admitted by the North Carolina Synod (English minutes of 1820, p. 6), "errors had been committed on both sides;" but it soon took a wider range; a strong opposition was created to the formation of the General Synod, and, in the heat of controversy, doctrinal differences between the two opposing parties became manifest, which widened the breach already existing, and all attempts at reconciliation during the meeting of the North Carolina Synod, which convened in Lincolnton, N. C., May 28th, 1820, proved unavailing.

On the 17th of July of the same year, Revs. Jacob Zink, Paul Henkel, Adam Miller, Philip Henkel and George Easterly, with delegates from the Tennessee congregations, met in Solomon's Church, Cove Creek, Green County, Tennessee, and organized the Tennessee Synod. Rev. David Henkel could not attend this meeting, but acknowledged himself a member of the new organization. The separation between the two contending parties was now fully effected, and both Synods labored industriously in their own selected spheres of usefulness; not, however, without considerable opposition to each other, and the publication of controversy.

Although divisions in the Church are always to be dreaded, and, except in cases of doctrinal differences, always to be avoided, nevertheless, when they do occur, they sometimes effect good in vitalizing dormant energies, and in re-establishing the pure faith of the Gospel. Such was the case in this division; it increased the number of ministers, it provided for the wants of so many neglected congregations, it made ministers and laymen all the more energetic, zealous and faithful in the discharge of their duties, and it resulted in an enlarged increase in the strength of the Church.

But God made use of this division in the Church in accomplishing a special purpose for the welfare of the Lutheran Church in America:

Firstly, In attracting attention once more to the pure doctrines of the Lutheran Church, as confessed by the early Reformers, and in awakening inquiry into those truths, which the symbols of the Lutheran Church exhibited. So gradual and yet so sure were the departures from the confessed faith of the Church, as well as the assimilation to the teachings and practices of other denominations, that for a long time it awakened no alarm, and but a learned few had any idea of what the faith of the Lutheran Church was; admirers of Luther there were in abundance, even among other denominations, but very few knew anything of the secret which made Luther the conscientious, fearless and zealous man that he was. Multitudes admired Luther's energy and labors, but they knew little of the faith which actuated his labors, and of the doctrines upon which that faith was based. Had they known it and experienced it themselves, more would have been accomplished at that time in the Lutheran Church in America, and divisions would not have occurred; then also there would have been less manifest desire to unite all denominations into one Church, but a stronger desire to advance the interests of that Church, to which God has given a peculiar field of labor.

Secondly, By means of this division the symbols of the Lutheran Church were translated into the English language. This was a want that had long been felt, but before that time no one possessed the patience and energy to apply himself to the task. There was an abundance of anxious desire manifested by some to make the Lutheran Church in America an English, as well as a German Church, but no anxiety manifested itself to anglicize the faith of the Lutheran Church, that is, to translate its confessions and theology into the English language. All honor then to the Tennessee Synod for undertaking this work, which has accomplished more in preserving the faith of our fathers in this country than any similar undertaking in the English language.

Thirdly, The Lutheran Church in America has had its publication boards and societies in abundance, which have doubtless accomplished a good work; but the oldest establishment of the kind is the one in New Market, Virginia, which dates its existence as far back, at least, as 1810, for the minutes of the North Carolina Synod were printed there at that time. It was established by the Henkel family, and has continued under their management to this day; at the time of the division in the Lutheran Church in North Carolina, it came at once into the service of the Tennessee Synod, and has issued more truly Lutheran theological works in an English dress than any similar institution in the world. We may well say, "What hath God wrought?" How imperceptible have been his purposes! How brightly they shine forth now!

CHAPTER V.

FROM THE ORGANIZATION OF THE TENNESSEE SYNOD TO THE ESTABLISHMENT OF THE THEOLOGICAL SEMINARY AT LEXINGTON, SOUTH CAROLINA, A.D. 1833.

Section 1. A Glimpse into the History of some of the older Congregations.

St. John's Lutheran Church, Charleston, S. C.—Nothing contributes more to the prosperity of a congregation than the voice and presence of a living and faithful ministry; the want of an efficient and useful pastor for the short time of only one year is of incalculable injury to any church, not that the building up of a congregation is the work of man, but that Christ has so ordained, that pastors should watch over and "feed the flock of God." Disarrange the relationship between pastor and people, and no promise is given that a congregation will be blessed. The voice of a living ministry must be heard; the faith of a people is built up by the preached word and the administered sacraments.

This was also exemplified in the Lutheran Church in Charleston. Before the arrival of their pastor, the Rev. John Bachman, in 1815, the congregation had greatly declined, but from that time it commenced to improve, and soon enjoyed a high state of prosperity. Their new pastor possessed the confidence of his people and of the community at large, and was peculiarly fitted for the work intrusted into his hands.

The "small wooden church erected in colonial times," soon became filled with devout worshipers, and became too small to accommodate the growing congregation. "The commanding attainments, and the attractive geniality and social habits of the new pastor, won so rapidly the admiration and esteem of his good people and the public, that the erection and dedication of the present handsome temple became almost at once a matter of necessity.

"A committee of twenty-one was appointed to inquire into the expediency of building a new church, who reported favorably, and in July, 1815, Mr. F. Wesner's contract for the wood work of the edifice, and Mr. J. F. H. Horlbeck's for the brick work, were accepted. The new building was dedicated on Sunday, January 8th, 1818, by the Rev. John Bachman."

God blessed the labors of his servant, and made him a shining light in the Church, laboring in harmony with his brethren, and accomplishing much good. A few years after his arrival in Charleston, Rev. Bachman connected himself by marriage with the family of a former and greatly beloved pastor of this congregation, the Rev. J. N. Martin, whose son's daughter became the new pastor's partner in joy and sorrow, and thus were the past and present happily linked together, and all circumstances, together with the pastor's unremitting and appreciated labors, contributed to the growth and prosperity of the congregation.

St. John's Church, Salisbury, N. C.—In the year 1818, whilst the Episcopalians were worshiping in this church, they made the proposition to erect a new frame church, the old log building being greatly out of repair. The members of the Lutheran Church agreed to this proposal, and also aided in the building of the new house of worship.

However, this arrangement gave rise to serious difficulties; as soon as the new church was completed, the question of its dedication arose, and the Lutherans were fearful that, if the church would be consecrated by a bishop of the Episcopal Church, they would forfeit their right and title in the property. And thus it was, whilst the Lutherans claimed the land on which the church stood, the Episcopalians claimed the building. Whose then was the church? Who had the right to worship there? These questions seriously agitated the minds and feelings of both parties; but before any very decisive hostile steps were taken, and in order to effect a compromise, the Lutherans agreed to purchase the interest in the building to which the Episcopalians laid claim, gave their bond in the meantime for the amount agreed upon, and afterwards raised the funds by subscription to liquidate the debt.

In August, 1822, the President of the North Carolina Synod, Rev. G. Shober, sent a written communication to the members of the Lutheran Church in Salisbury, which was publicly read to them. It is herewith inserted in order to show the sad state of this congregation at that time.

"RESPECTED FRIENDS, MEMBERS OF THE LUTHERAN CHURCH BY BIRTHRIGHT OR OTHERWISE:

"Being appointed by the Lutheran Church in our last Synod, President of the same for one year, I regard it as being part of my duty during the recess of the Synod, to have a constant eye towards the preservation of the same in all its rights, privileges and possessions, and to encourage the revival of former congregations.

"I am convinced, by the reading of the deed of conveyance from Mr. Beard, deceased, to our Church, for a lot of ground, near or in Salisbury, where the church now stands, that we have an undoubted right for the same; that there was, for many years, regular service performed by the Rev. Senior Stork, is well known, and it only abated on account of his disability to attend. It is my opinion that we, as a Church, are acting disrespectfully to the donor of the lot and to his heirs, who, by that deed, are expressly charged to protect us in the right and privileges of the same, and that it is a dereliction of duty in the members of our Church not to preserve the lot and burying-ground, particularly for the interment of the heirs of the donor, and members of our Church and their descendants, and also from being a general burying-ground.

"I therefore beg leave to advise you *now* to elect elders and trustees, whose duty it is, according to law, to preserve the property of the church as trustees (particularly if the heirs of the donor decline acting as such), and also to give to them the necessary authority to regulate all external things according to the constitution and rules of our Church.

"I beg leave further to propose that if you agree to revive a congregation according to our rules, by appointing elders and trustees, to appoint a time when the church can be dedicated by our ministry and according to our form of worship, when two or three ministers of our Church will attend for that purpose; other preachers may also be invited to attend and to preach the word, all for the purpose of causing a revival of true religion for our department of the Church of Christ, by whose Spirit alone it can through the word be effected. But it is to be observed that only such Lutheran ministers as are in union with our

Synod, and such who bring and show credentials of being duly appointed in other States, can be admitted. The standing of each minister must be inquired into by the elders, who have the power to admit or refuse.

"In expectation that the Lord will bless your exertions for the revival of the congregation of the Lutheran Church,

"I remain, your humble servant,

"G. SHOBER."

This communication, sent by Rev. Shober to the remaining Lutherans of Salisbury, had the desired effect of once more rousing and encouraging them to action. On the 20th of September, 1822, the following articles, drawn up by Hon. Charles Fisher, member of Congress, for the purpose of reorganizing the old Lutheran congregation, were sent around to the citizens of Salisbury for their signature:

"*Salisbury Lutheran Church.*

"We, the subscribers, believing that the cause of religion will be promoted by re-establishing the Lutheran congregation which formerly existed in the town of Salisbury, and believing, moreover, that it is a sacred duty we owe to the memories of our fathers and predecessors no longer to suffer the church and the graveyard where their bodies are at rest to lie in neglect and disregard, do hereby agree to unite our names and efforts to the purpose of reviving the congregation, keeping the graveyard in decent order, and for other purposes properly connected with a work of the kind. We further agree to meet at the church on such day as may be fixed upon for the purpose of consulting together upon such subjects as may be connected with the establishment and prosperity of the congregation.

"Dated and signed by

John Beard, Sr.,	John H. Swink,
Charles Fisher,	Bernhardt Kreiter,
Daniel Cress,	Lewis Utzmann,
Peter Crider,	H. Allemong,
John Trexler,	M. Bruner,
John Beard, Jr.,	John Allbright,
Peter H. Swink,	Henry Swinkwag."
Moses Brown,	

Through the efforts of Mr. John Beard, Sr., the devoted friend and firm member of the Lutheran Church at that time, funds were collected for the purpose of inclosing the graveyard, which had long been neglected.

For some time no regular pastor could be obtained, and the energies of the members again lay dormant until the year 1825, when brighter prospects dawned upon this neglected congregation, and once more revived the hopes of its members. A meeting of a respectable number of the citizens of Salisbury and its vicinity was held in the church on the 3d of September, 1825, for the purpose of adopting measures to reorganize a Lutheran congregation; John Beard, Sr., was called to the chair, and Charles Fisher appointed Secretary.

"After due deliberation as to the best method of accomplishing the object of the meeting, it was unanimously resolved, that a committee of two persons be appointed to draft an instrument of writing, and offer the same for the signature of such persons in the town of Salisbury and its vicinity as are disposed to aid in the formation of a Lutheran congregation in this place, either by becoming members of said congregation, or supporters thereof. Messrs. John Beard and James Brown were accordingly appointed to compose said committee.

"It was further resolved, that a committee, consisting of George Vogler and Robert Mull, be and are hereby appointed to offer a subscription list to the good people of Salisbury and vicinity for the support of a Lutheran clergyman for preaching part of his time for one year in the town of Salisbury. The meeting then adjourned to meet again the following Monday.

"CHARLES FISHER,
"Secretary.

"At a subsequent meeting George Vogler was appointed treasurer, and Henry C. Kern recording secretary of this society. It was also resolved that a Bible be purchased and deposited in the church, to be the property of the same forever. The church council elected at this meeting were: Elders: Messrs. John Beard, Sr., George Vogler, Moses Brown. Deacons: Messrs. Nathan Brown, George Fraley, and Henry C. Kern."

In the year 1826, the Rev. John Reck, having received and accepted the call tendered him, became the pastor of this church; the number of communicants at that time was but fourteen, which, however, steadily increased under the faithful ministrations of their pastor, who was greatly beloved by the people, and through his zeal and energy accomplished much for his Master's kingdom.

The condition of this church under Rev. Reck's ministry in 1827 is stated in the minutes of the North Carolina Synod, as follows: "In Salisbury, where eighteen months ago there was no regularly organized Lutheran congregation, there are now thirty members in full communion; and by the active measures of several respectable persons, a large and commodious church has been purchased, and a subscription raised to pay for it. In this place a lecture meeting is held once a week, which is generally well attended, and not unfrequently the utmost solemnity pervades the audience. The people are liberal and attentive to the cause of benevolence, and assist in supporting Bible, missionary, and other religious societies."

Thus might this church have been greatly increased in strength, energy, and usefulness, but Rev. J. Reck, after having been its pastor for five years, felt it his duty to resign and return to Maryland, and after this time the congregation had such a continued and rapid succession of ministers, besides having been at times also unsupplied with the stated means of grace, as to be unable to command the influence which the regular ministrations of a permanent pastor might have given it.

St. John's Church, Cabarrus County, N. C.—In the last account of this church, it was seen that the Rev. C. A. G. Stork was the pastor of this congregation, but his health having become too feeble to attend to the wants of so many churches, he introduced the Rev. Daniel Scherer as his successor. During a communion season in the spring of 1821, when a large class of catechumens, numbering seventy-seven persons, were confirmed, their aged pastor being present, but too feeble to stand during the ceremony, called all his catechumens to him, and gave them and the other members and friends of the church his last farewell. So affecting was the scene, that the whole of that vast assembly were moved to tears, and long has the serious lesson been remembered, which their aged pastor addressed to them at that time, whilst he held out his hand to each, and gave them his parting blessing.

Rev. Daniel Scherer proved himself to have been likewise a faithful pastor. He was much beloved by his people, and remained nearly ten years among them; however, during his ministry and for some time previous, a large number of persons from St. John's and other Lutheran churches in North Carolina settled themselves in Illinois Territory, and their pastor's heart followed them to the wild prairies of their newly-adopted country, and he soon cast his lot among them, and labored there for their spiritual good.

Organ Church, Rowan County, North Carolina.— As Rev. Stork was the pastor of this congregation as well as that of St. John's, it had much the same history at this time. Rev. Daniel Scherer also became his successor here some two years afterwards. Thirty-five years did Rev. Stork labor in this church, and with great success. It was the first congregation he served, and the last he resigned. He lived in favor with God and man; his example and usefulness are still felt, and his memory is cherished with affection by all who knew him. During this period he baptized 1500 children, and confirmed 1300 young people in Organ Church alone, and probably as many more in the other churches under his charge.

At length the feeble state of his health compelled him to resign this church also in 1823. His successor labored here likewise with much success, and had at one time probably the largest class of catechumens, numbering 83 persons, that were confirmed in this church, during a session of the North Carolina Synod at this place, in which ceremony their aged pastor took the deepest interest.

Rev. Scherer labored but six years in this congregation. As he had the oversight of so many churches, he thought it advisable to resign some portion of his charge into the hands of another minister, in order to do justice to the cause of Christ, and Rev. Jacob Kaempfer became his successor in 1829.

Section 2. Fraternal Union of the North Carolina Synod with the Protestant Episcopal Convention of North Carolina.

The first step taken in this direction was Rev. Robert J. Miller's attendance upon the Episcopal Convention held in Raleigh, April 28th, 1821. His object was to connect himself fully with the Episcopal Church, to which he really belonged, having been ordained by the Lutheran ministers of North Carolina in 1794 as an Episcopal minister, and was the pastor of an Episcopal congregation, White Haven Church, in Lincoln County, but because there was no Episcopal diocese at that time in the State, he was admitted as a member of the Lutheran North Carolina Synod at its organization in 1803.

From the journal of the Episcopal North Carolina Convention of 1818, the following item of intelligence is taken: "Previously to November, 1816, there was no Episcopal clergyman in this State, and but one congregation in which the worship of our Church was performed." That having been the condition of the Episcopal Church at that period, Rev. Miller felt it his duty to form a temporary connection with the Lutheran Church, and continued to labor for her welfare twenty-seven years, when in 1821 he severed that connection, and was ordained in Raleigh to deacon's and priest's orders in the Episcopal ministry in one day. Whilst in attendance at said Convention, Rev. Miller proposed to effect, "as far as practicable, intercourse and union between the Episcopalians and some of the Lutheran congregations." His proposition was referred to the Committee on the State of the Church, who afterwards reported as follows:

"A very interesting communication has this session been laid before the committee, on the subject of a union between that truly respectable denomination, the Lutherans, and our Church. To carry this measure into effect, the committee propose the following resolution:

"*Resolved*, That a committee, consisting of three persons, two clerical and one lay member, be appointed to meet the Synod of the Lutheran Church, to consider and agree upon such terms of union as may tend to the mutual advantage and welfare of both Churches, not inconsistent with the constitution and canons of this Church, or the Protestant Episcopal Church in the United States.

"The Convention then proceeded to take into consideration the resolution proposed by the committee, when it was adopted, and the Rev. Adam Empie, Rev. G. T. Bedell, and Duncan Cameron, Esq., were appointed a committee to attend the Lutheran Synod, and to carry the resolution into effect."

On the 17th of June, 1821, the Lutheran North Carolina Synod met in Lau's Church, Guilford County, and from its minutes the following is quoted:

"The President now reported that the Rev. R.

J. Miller, who had labored for many years as one of our ministers, had been ordained by the Bishop of the Episcopal Church as a priest at a convention of that Church. That he had always regarded himself as belonging to that Church, but because the Episcopal Church had no existence at that time in this State, he had himself ordained by our ministry, with the understanding that he still belonged to the Episcopal Church. But as the said Church had now reorganized itself (in this State), he had united himself with it, and thus disconnected himself from our Synod, as was allowed him at his ordination by our ministers. Rev. Miller then made a short address before Synod and the congregation then assembled, in which he distinctly explained his position, so that no one should be able to say that he had apostatized from our Synod, since he had been ordained by our Ministerium as a minister of the Episcopal Church. He then promised that he would still aid and stand by us as much and as far as lay in his power.

"With this explanation the whole matter was well understood by the entire assembly, and was deemed perfectly satisfactory. Whereupon it was resolved that the president tend to Rev. Miller our sincere thanks, in the name of the Synod, for the faithful services he had hitherto rendered our Church. This was immediately done in a feeling manner.

"After this a letter was read from Rev. Bishop Moore, addressed to our Synod, in which he reported to us, that a committee was appointed by their Convention to attend our Synod, with the view of making an effort towards a more intimate union between our respective bodies, whereupon the members of that committee presented themselves, and submitted their credentials. Their names are, Revs. Adam Empie, G. T. Bedell, and Duncan Cameron, Esq. They were all affectionately received, and the following committee was appointed by our Synod to confer with our visiting brethren what possibly might be done towards a more intimate union, namely: Revs. G. Shober, Michael Rauch, and Henry Ratz, Esq." The next day the following report was submitted and adopted:

"The committee of the Protestant Episcopal Church of North Carolina, and the committee on the part of the Lutheran Synod of North Carolina and adjacent States, having conferred on the subject of their respective appointments, have agreed on the following articles:

"I. *Resolved*, That we deem it expedient and desirable that the Lutheran Synod and the Protestant Episcopal Church of North Carolina should be united together in the closest bonds of friendship.

"II. *Resolved*, That for this purpose we will mutually make such concessions as may not be inconsistent with the rules and regulations of our respective Churches, for the purpose of promoting a friendly intercourse.

"III. *Resolved*, That the Convention of the Protestant Episcopal Church may send a delegation of one or more persons to the annual Synod of the Lutheran Church, which person or persons shall be entitled to an honorary seat in that body, and to the privilege of expressing their opinions and voting in all cases except when a division is called for; in which case they shall not vote.

"IV. *Resolved*, That the Lutheran Synod may, in like manner, send a deputation to the Convention of the Protestant Episcopal Church, who in all respects shall be entitled to the same privileges.

"V. *Resolved*, That *all the ministers* of the Lutheran Church in union with the Synod shall be entitled to honorary seats in the Convention of the Protestant Episcopal Church; and the clergymen of the said last-mentioned Church shall, in like manner, be entitled to honorary seats in the Synod of the Lutheran Church.

"The committee respectfully recommend to the Convention of the Protestant Episcopal Church, and to the Synod of the Lutheran Church the adoption of the foregoing resolutions.

"G. Shober,
"Michael Rauch,
"Henry Ratz,
"Committee of the Lutheran Synod.

"A. Empie,
"Duncan Cameron,
"Committee of the Protestant Episcopal Church."

The report was adopted by Synod, and the following persons were elected to attend the next

Convention of the Episcopal Church: Revs. G. Shober, Jacob Scherer, and Henry Ratz, Esq.

At the next Convention of the Episcopal Church, held in Raleigh, April 18th, 1822, the following action was taken in reference to this matter.

"The Rt. Rev. President of the Convention then read a letter from the Rev. Mr. Shober on the same subject, after which it was moved that the report be received, which was unanimously agreed to; it was then

"*Resolved*, that the Secretary be required to address a letter to the President of the Lutheran Synod, informing him of the unanimous adoption of the above report.

"The following delegation to the Lutheran Synod was then appointed: Rev. Messrs. Miller, Davis, and Wright, of the clergy; Messrs. Alexander Caldcleugh, Duncan Cameron, and Dr. F. J. Hill, of the laity."

At the next meeting of the North Carolina Synod, three of the above delegation, "the Rev. R. J. Miller, the Rev. R. Davis, and Alexander Caldcleugh, Esq., appeared, were welcomed, and took their seats with us.

"On information that the Protestant Episcopal Church will hold their next annual Convention for North Carolina in Salisbury, on the second Thursday after Easter, in the year 1823, the following persons were elected to attend the same, and there represent the Synod, namely: the Rev. G. Shober, the Rev. Daniel Scherer, General Paul Barringer, and Colonel Ratz." All of these delegates appeared at said Convention and attended its sessions.

After the year 1823 nothing more appears concerning the fraternal relations of these two ecclesiastical bodies, although this "bond of friendship" does not appear to have been revoked, nevertheless, the interchange of delegates, being attended with some difficulty in those days of traveling by private conveyance, fell practically into disuse.

Section 3. Rev. John Bachman's labors in Savannah and Ebenezer, Georgia.

Although a sketch of the Lutheran Church in the State of Georgia does not strictly belong to the history of the same Church in the Carolinas, nevertheless, as one of the Lutheran ministers of South Carolina visited Georgia, with the view of reorganizing and infusing new life into several long-established Lutheran congregations of that State, it is but proper that an account of his efficient labors in this direction should not be passed by unnoticed.

Rev. Bachman having been informed that at one time two Lutheran congregations had been established in Georgia, at Ebenezer and Savannah, by the Salzburgers, who commenced emigrating to Georgia in 1733, and arrived there in March, 1734, he felt a desire to become more intimately acquainted with the condition of those churches.

During one of the winter months of 1823–4, Rev. Bachman journeyed to Savannah "as a pioneer in our holy cause," and discovered that a Lutheran church had been erected in that city some time before the Revolutionary War, but that it was burnt down in 1797. The congregation in Charleston, S. C., had contributed $500 towards rebuilding it, but nothing was done towards keeping up the congregation; it had no pastor, and became gradually disorganized; the small building, erected as a Lutheran church, "was occupied as a Sunday-school by another denomination," "and had been sequestered for many years." The prospects were certainly not bright, and a few more years of neglect would have extinguished the name of Lutheranism in Savannah. Rev. Bachman's visit was not one moment too soon; by means of his well-directed and energetic labors "a congregation was organized from the materials which could be collected," and, "about a month after this event," Rev. S. A. Mealy "came to reside in Savannah," as the pastor of that congregation. He was "a clergyman who had been raised up in" the Lutheran Church in Charleston, and received his theological training from Rev. Bachman, whom he acknowledged as his "spiritual father." From that time forward the Lutheran congregation in Savannah commenced to prosper, under the efficient labors of a succession of pastors, two of whom, Revs. Mealy and Karn, have been called to their rest.

Rev. Bachman having completed his labors in

Savannah, now also "determined to extend his visit to Ebenezer," for he had learned that, though a Lutheran congregation still existed in that place, its "aged pastor was fast sinking into the grave." This pastor was "the Rev. John E. Bergman, a native of Germany, and the learned and exemplary minister of this church for the long period of thirty-six years." He had a son, who had devoted himself to the work of the Gospel ministry, named Rev. Christopher F. Bergman, "who had received a classical education, and had carefully attended to his theological studies, under the care of his revered and excellent parent, and was well qualified for the ministry;" but not being "aware that Lutheranism had any existence in the South," he had taken "license to preach the Gospel under the auspices of the Presbyterian Church."

"This was the source of the most unfeigned regret, both to his father and his father's congregation. The latter was fully aware, that from the increasing age and infirmities of their venerable and esteemed pastor, they would soon have to resign him to the grave, and their eyes were directed without hesitation to the son as his successor. This wish was extremely natural. The son had been educated for the ministry, and was possessed of the most exemplary piety; and having been born and raised in their neighborhood, and under their own immediate eye, he would be as a son to the aged, and a brother to the younger parishioners. This fondly cherished hope, however, was nearly crushed, when an event of Providence occurred, which brightened the scene around them."

This event was the opportune arrival of Rev. John Bachman on a visit to Ebenezer. His discerning mind soon penetrated the difficulty under which the younger Bergman labored, and "was made the instrument, in the hands of God, of giving a new direction to Rev. C. F. Bergman's theological views, of securing his belief in the doctrines, and his attachment to the institutions of our beloved Church, and of cheering the last hours of a venerable servant of Jesus Christ."

Too much cannot be said in praise of Rev. Bachman's judicious labors in Ebenezer. The elder Bergman had probably not seen the face of a Lutheran minister for a number of years; how it must have brightened his last hours of life to have Rev. Bachman standing at his bedside ere he departed this life, and to welcome him as God's instrument in leading his son back to the Church of his fathers. He could now die in peace, for his eyes had seen what he no longer expected to see on earth. And what a blessing was this visit to the Ebenezer congregation also; it was not only saved to the Lutheran Church, but it was also provided with a Lutheran pastor, and he the one whom the members preferred above all others.

It is necessary yet to add, that the Rev. C. F. Bergman attended the meeting of the newly organized Synod of South Carolina, held in St. John's Church, Lexington District, November 18th, 1824, where he "was solemnly ordained to the Gospel ministry by the Rev. Messrs. Bachman, Hersher, and Dreher."

All these items of intelligence, concerning Rev. Bachman's labors in Georgia, have been mainly derived from Rev. Mealy's "Funeral Sermon occasioned by the death of Rev. C. F. Bergman," published in Savannah, A.D. 1832.

Section 4. Organization of the Lutheran Synod of South Carolina, A.D. 1824.

The time had now arrived, when the number of ministers made it possible, and the wants of the Church made it necessary, to organize a Lutheran Synod in South Carolina; accordingly, "on the 14th day of January, 1824, the following clergymen of the Evangelical Lutheran Church met at St. Michael's Church, Lexington District, S. C., with the intention of organizing a Synod for South Carolina and adjacent States, namely: Revs. John P. Franklow, John Y. Meetze, Godfrey Dreher, Michael Rauch, Jacob Moser, all residing in Lexington District, and Rev. Samuel Hersher from Orangeburg District, S. C."

These ministers were members of the North Carolina Synod; those residing in Lexington District have already been introduced to the reader. The Rev. Samuel Hersher had become connected with that Synod only since 1822; he was a student of Rev. Mr. Meierhöffer, of Rockingham County, Virginia, and recommended by him as worthy to become a member of Synod. He was accordingly examined, licensed, and sent by the North Carolina Synod to labor in the vacant congregations of Orangeburg District, S. C.

After due consideration, the ministers present unanimously resolved, "that the situation and wants of the Evangelical Lutheran churches in 'South Carolina' require that a Synod be now organized."

Rev. G. Dreher was then elected President, and Rev. S. Hersher, Secretary. The first item of business was the ordination of Rev. S. Hersher. Five lay delegates now handed in their certificates, and were admitted as members of Synod.

Rev. John C. A. Schönberg, a licentiate of the Pennsylvania Synod, presented his license with the request to have it renewed, which was accordingly done on the next day.

"On motion, it was resolved, that the Augsburg Confession of Faith be the point of union in our Church.

"It was resolved, that the Revs. G. Dreher, S. Hersher, and M. Rauch be nominated a committee, for the purpose of entering into a friendly correspondence with the North Carolina Synod."

On the 18th of November of the same year, the South Carolina Synod met at St. John's Church, Lexington District, at which meeting eight Lutheran ministers were present, and two, Revs. Franklow and Mealy, were absent. Revs. Bachman, Bergman, and Mealy were added to the list of members of Synod, and nine lay delegates were admitted as representatives from the various congregations.

It was reported to Synod that Rev. Jacob Moser had been ordained by the committee appointed by Synod, on the 4th of April; and that on the 20th of May, Revs. Dreher, Franklow, and Hersher had ordained the Rev. Stephen A. Mealy. Rev. C. F. Bergman was ordained at this meeting of Synod. The New York English Lutheran Hymn book was recommended to be introduced by the ministers into their churches.

The most interesting item of information, contained in the minutes of that synodical meeting, is the report of the committee on the "State of the Church," which is as follows:

"There are in the State of South Carolina twenty-four Evangelical Lutheran churches, and in the State of Georgia, two. Of those in South Carolina, one is in Charleston, under the care of Rev. J. Bachman, having 275 communicants. Three under the care of Rev. S. Hersher, having 380 members. Six under the care of Revs. J. Y. Meetze, J. P. Franklow, and G. Dreher, having 260 members. Four under the care of Rev. M. Rauch, having 380 members. Four under the care of Rev. J. Moser, having 136 members.

"Of those in the State of Georgia, one is in Savannah, under the care of Rev. S. A. Mealy, having 35 families. One at Ebenezer, under the care of Rev. C. F. Bergman, having 130 members. Six churches are vacant in South Carolina, and two or more congregations might be formed in the

State, if Lutheran clergymen could be obtained. The number of communicants in our churches has considerably increased, and that, on the whole, there are some flattering prospects in our Church."

The committee lamented "that whilst the harvest is plenteous, the laborers are few."

Section 5. Removals to the West, and Missionary Labors of the North Carolina Synod in Illinois and other States.

Allusion has already been made to the vast emigration from the State of North Carolina to other new States and Territories. This drain upon the strength of the Lutheran Church in North Carolina continued for many successive years; colonies from St. John's Church, Cabarrus County, and from the neighboring congregations, may be found in most of the Northwestern States, as well as in Tennessee, Missouri, and Arkansas. By means of this extensive colonizing in new countries, the labors and influence of the early pastors in North Carolina are felt over a much greater extent of country than what is included in the boundaries of the congregations they served.

For a long time those Western colonies were destitute of the means of grace; they naturally looked to the Synod of North Carolina, under whose fostering care they had been brought up in the Church of their fathers, to be supplied with pastors.

At a meeting of the Synod in 1825 an urgent call came from Union County, Illinois, signed by forty-three persons, for a pastor or missionary who would be able to preach in the German and English languages, establish schools, and labor for the welfare of the Church. They furthermore declared, that if their spiritual wants be not soon supplied, the consequences to them and their children would be very injurious.

The letter was read in open Synod, and the Secretary was required to write to those congregations in Illinois. Rev. Wm. Jenkins was then requested to visit those people, and a resolution was passed to send a letter to Rev. Samuel Schmucker, beseeching him, if it be possible, to have a missionary sent to that State.

In the minutes of the Synod of 1827, the Committee on Letters and Petitions presented the following:

"No. 11 contains a petition from three congregations in Union County, Illinois, in which they give a mournful description of their destitute condition; pray that they may be visited by the Rev. Jacob Scherer, and, if he cannot comply with this their request, that the Synod would send them another, and promise to give him an adequate support. Your committee would recommend these congregations to the particular notice of this Synod, for if they are not soon supplied with a minister, they will be dispersed."

Whereupon it was

"*Resolved*, That, as it is impracticable for the

Rev. J. Scherer to visit those petitioning congregations in Illinois, the Rev. John C. A. Schönberg visit them immediately, and, if practicable, to locate among them; and that he receive ten dollars out of the synodical treasury to defray the necessary traveling expenses to Illinois."

The Rev. Mr. Schönberg accepted this appointment of Synod, and moved to Illinois in 1827, and thus the North Carolina Synod has the honor of sending the pioneer missionary of the Lutheran Church to that State. Rev. Schönberg labored there for several years, and continued his connection with the North Carolina Synod, when, in 1829, he wrote a letter to Synod, stating "that in consequence of indisposition he has been necessitated to resign his churches in Illinois."

About the close of the year 1831, the Rev. Daniel Scherer, the successor of Rev. Storch as pastor of St. John's Church, Cabarrus County, N. C., felt it to be his duty to remove to Illinois, and succeeded Rev. Schönberg as pastor of the Lutheran congregations in Union County, Illinois. In 1833 he wrote a letter to Synod, "containing the pleasing information of his success in forming a congregation in Hillsboro, Illinois, consisting of thirty-five communing members."

Professor Haverstick, of Philadelphia, who visited Rev. D. Scherer and his congregations in 1835, during his exploring missionary tour in the West, having been sent by the Pennsylvania Synod, speaks of the untiring labors of Rev. Scherer in the most exalted terms, mentions that he frequently travels 150 miles from home on horseback, in order to minister to the spiritual wants of such colonies as are not included in his own immediate charge, and this of necessity, inasmuch as he was the *only* resident Lutheran minister at that time in the entire State of Illinois. Rev. Scherer labored faithfully in that State to the close of his life, April 4th, 1852, and may justly be considered the father of the Lutheran Church in Illinois.

Rev. Wm. Jenkins, who became connected with the North Carolina Synod in 1824, upon the recommendation of Rev. D. F. Schäffer, President of the Maryland Synod, was sent the following September to the State of Tennessee, and labored in the Lutheran congregations at Duck River, "where he was received with joy, and kindly treated." He formed additional congregations in Franklin and Lincoln Counties, and reports having found a large settlement of Lutherans at Faugunder Creek, near Jackson, who were anxious to obtain a pastor. He further states: "Since last Synod I have traveled 3000 miles on horseback, preached 175 times, baptized 84 children and 14 adults, admitted to church membership 34 persons, and had 8 funerals." All these congregations were admitted under the care of the North Carolina Synod in 1825, and Rev. Wm. Jenkins was acknowledged as their pastor, having located himself in Bedford County, Tennessee, serving ten congregations, where he was still laboring as a member of the North Carolina Synod as late as 1835, when he connected himself with some other Synod, but did not remove from Tennessee until 1854, when he became the pastor of the Lovettsville charge, in Loudon County, Virginia.

Shortly after the year 1811, when Rev. R. J. Miller was first sent on an exploring missionary tour through the State of Virginia, all those Lutheran congregations, situated in the southwestern part of Virginia, with their pastors, connected themselves, with but few exceptions, with the North Carolina Synod; so intimately were those churches united with that Synod, that five of its annual sessions were held in the State of Virginia.

Much missionary labor was devoted to that field and with good results. Originally this territory was connected with the Pennsylvania Synod, and the Rev. Mr. Flohr was the first regular minister who labored there, but its contiguity to North Carolina brought it under the influence of the Synod of that State, which arrangement was continued until the year 1842, when the Synod of Western Virginia was formed.

Section 6. Rapid Progress of the South Carolina Synod, and the Missionary Labors of Revs. Scheck, Schwartz, and W. D. Strobel.

As soon as the South Carolina Synod was organized it commenced to increase, and its influence was extended rapidly; all the strength of the Lutheran

Church in that State and Georgia became concentrated, and the affairs of Synod were managed with wisdom and prudence. A desire was manifested at once to labor earnestly and faithfully for the welfare of the Church, and everywhere success attended the efforts of its ministers.

However, as there were still many vacant congregations in the bounds of Synod, at its second session, in 1825, it was—

"*Resolved*, That the Secretary of this Synod be requested to write to the different Northern Synods, and endeavor to ascertain whether it may not be practicable to obtain well-educated Lutheran ministers to supply our vacant churches, or to labor as missionaries within the bounds of this Synod."

This appeal was not made in vain. The next year the Rev. C. B. Wessells, a licentiate from the State of New York, commenced his labors in South Carolina. He opened a school at Leesville, Lexington District, and preached occasionally; but "he soon gave evidence of mental derangement," and returned to the North. In 1827, the Rev. John D. Scheck arrived from Maryland, and labored as the first missionary in the bounds of the Synod.

From Rev. Bachman's congregation in Charleston, three useful and well-educated young men entered the ministerial ranks, the Revs. S. A. Mealy, J. G. Schwartz and W. D. Strobel, and from the interior congregations the Synod received three additional ministers in the Revs. J. Wingard,

J. C. Hope and Daniel Dreher. In this manner was the Synod greatly increased.

The Rev. J. D. Scheck was employed by Synod to make a missionary tour through the State for the purpose of organizing new congregations, and also to visit the vacant churches as much as possible. He commenced his labors June 2d, 1827, and the following extract from his journal was presented by the committee:

"He labored one week at Amelia, preaching every day: he represents those people as being wealthy and respectable, and possessing the largest church of any denomination in this part of the country. After having preached at Sandy Run and at Nazareth Churches, he labored at Lexington Court-house. Near North Edisto River he found a number of Lutherans who are very destitute of spiritual privileges, and have not heard a sermon from any of our ministers for three years, yet none have left our Church, though solicited to do so. They are now building a house of worship.

"Mr. Scheck also visited Edgefield, where he found many of our people who have not been visited for many years by any of our ministers. He represents their condition as truly deplorable, but says that they are now building a church, and expect to hear preaching from some of our ministers. Sunday, July 1st, he preached in Long Church, where also the people were very desirous of obtaining a Lutheran minister. On Monday, at Wise's school-house (Newberry); here he found the people very destitute; but there are many persons who would be members of our Church immediately, if supplied with preaching. They are both able and willing to build a place of worship and support a minister.

"On Thursday, Mr. S. preached in the settlements of G. Egner to fine congregations, who hear the word but once in three weeks from any denomination. Many of our people here are wealthy, and desirous of obtaining a minister among them. They have already commenced the building of a church. On the 15th and 17th he preached in the two churches in Barnwell District, both of which are in a destitute condition, and have been so for five years. Some of the people have united themselves to other societies; they have resolved to bring their destitute situation to our view, and request us to send our ministers to preach to them occasionally.

"The neighborhood of Myers, Rhinehardt's, Wise's, Peterbaugh and Egner's are entirely destitute of the means of grace, and are loudly calling upon us in the words of the man of Macedonia, Come over and help us."

February 11th, 1828, the Rev. J. G. Schwartz was employed as a missionary, and the following interesting items are taken from his report:

"I first visited a few Lutherans east of Broad River, in the upper part of Richland District, who occasionally hear preaching from the Rev. Mr. Dreher. The people of this neighborhood are principally descendants of members of our Church. From this I passed over into Newberry, and preached twice in Mount Pleasant Church, owned in part by Lutherans. There is here a fine congregation, and the people appear favorably disposed towards our Church. A neat and commodious building was about to be erected for the exclusive use of Mr. Scheck. He can preach there, however, but once a month.

"From this I passed into Spartanburg, and preached at the residence of a member of our Church; the house was full, and the people remarkably attentive. Some of the Lutherans here have attached themselves to other denominations, in consequence of the absence of their own. Six miles beyond the village I preached at the residence of a gentleman who had been brought up to the Lutheran Church. He informed me of several families who, from similar circumstances with himself, had connected themselves with other societies. I next preached at Spartanburg Court-house, where also there is a great call for regular preaching. The day after, I preached at the house of a Lutheran family below the village.

"On Good Friday I preached at Sandy Run Church. This place is common as a house of worship to Lutherans, Baptists and Methodists. Rev. Mr. Wingard has the care of the Lutherans, and ministers to them once a month. I subsequently passed through Chester, York, Lancaster, Chesterfield, Darlington, Sumter and Orangeburg, and preached wherever I had an opportunity. From all that has come to my knowledge, I have no hesitation in saying, that twelve or fourteen Lutheran ministers could find abundant employment in this State. Descendants of Germans are to be found in almost every part of the country, and here I might deplore that prejudice which has so fatally operated, and in some places does still operate upon the minds of those who continue to minister to their people in the German language. I know it has been in part a matter of necessity; but had those who removed from Germany to this country endeavored to introduce the language of their adopted country, our Church might now, in all probability, nearly be equal to the united churches of other denominations."

During the greater part of the year 1830, the Rev. W. D. Strobel was engaged as a missionary, and his labors were blessed wtth practical results. Several important congregations were organized, and the vacant churches greatly revived and strengthened. He reports as follows:

"Immediately after receiving my appointment in Savannah, I made it my business to visit the congregations designated for my care in the minutes of the Synod, to wit: St. Nicholas, St. Bartholomew's, and Erwin's, at the Saltketchers; Mount Calvary in Edgefield; Brandenburg's, in Orangeburg. In addition to these, I took under my care Nazareth, Lexington Court-house, Platt Springs, all in Lexington District. In all these stations I have kept up regular appointments during the year, with the exception of Erwin's, where I considered, after preaching some time, that there was no prospect of success.

"I have encouraged the congregations to meet at their churches on the Lord's day, and have engaged their elders in reading sermons and other religious exercises. During the year we have succeeded in building a church at Brandenburg's, to be known by the name of Shiloh. A large church is in a state of forwardness at Lexington Courthouse, and that at Nazareth will soon be completed. From the vicinity of so many members of our Church, we expect that Lexington Courthouse will become one of the most important stations."

The above reports from Revs. Scheck, Schwartz and Strobel have been very much abbreviated, and only that much as has reference to the history of the Church has been given as literally as possible.

Section 7. Death of Rev. Charles A. G. Storch, in 1831, and arrival of other Lutheran Ministers in North Carolina.

It is, as a matter of course, not expected to give a lengthy obituary notice of every departed Lutheran minister who labored in North or South Carolina, but when such a prominent servant of God as the Rev. Charles Augustus Gottlieb Storch is called by death to his long rest, it creates a void that is not soon filled, and a wound so deep, however long the event may be expected, which is not healed in a short period of time. The last link which bound the past with the present in the establishment of Lutheranism in North Carolina was now broken, and Rev. Storch descended to his grave sadly lamented by all the members of his entire pastoral charge, and his loss was deeply deplored by the whole Synod, of which he was one of the early founders. He went to his grave with the highest honors upon his hoary head, as one of the fathers of the Lutheran Church in North Carolina.

A notice of the funeral occasion of Rev. Storch, in one of the secular papers, says: "The deep and unrestrained emotions of the assembly of his spiritual children at the grave of their departed friend evinced the magnitude of their loss, and the extent of his worth."

From the minutes of the North Carolina Synod, giving a lengthy account of his life and labors, the following extract is made:

"He enjoyed the love of all his dear congregations; he refused sundry lucrative situations to other cities out of love to his flock; and as soon as a Synod of the Lutheran Church was formed in North Carolina, he was annually elected President, whenever he could be present, and his nearly thirty-seven years' service will remain in blessed memory. Since a few years his sickness, which often kept him in bed, compelled him to give up his congregations, but he always participated in the happiness and woe of the Church and his former flock by praises, prayer, sighing and temporal assistance. The last days of his life were very painful, until his friend, Jesus, whom he loved, took him to his eternal rest on the 27th of March, 1831, where all weakness and trouble are buried under his feet.

"Two funeral discourses were delivered at Synod in remembrance of our venerable and lately departed father, Charles A. Storch, to a numerous and attentive audience. The German discourse was on John 12 : 36, by the Rev. G. Shober; the English by the Rev. D. P. Rosenmiller, on John 20 : 17."

The following extract is taken from Dr. Hazelius' History of the American Lutheran Church, pp. 224–226:

"The Church suffered a great loss in the departure of Rev. C. A. G. Storch. His missionary tours in South Carolina are still held in grateful remembrance by many, who through his instrumentality were first brought from darkness to light, and from the kingdom of Satan to the living God. As a man of science he was highly esteemed by all who knew him in that respect. As a minister of the Gospel, he richly possessed the rare talent to create a deep interest for his subject in the well-informed, while he was fully understood by persons of no education. As friend, husband, and father, his remembrance will be cherished, blessed, and honored, so long as one friend and one child lives, to feel what he was to them in these capacities in life.

"During the last six years of his earthly existence, bodily infirmities prevented him from attending the services of the house of God, but still he cheerfully embraced every opportunity to counsel and comfort the afflicted. His last illness continued for nine weeks, and he frequently gave, both to his family and visiting friends, the assurance of his firm hope of eternal life, and of his desire that true piety and the religion of the heart might become general among mankind, and especially that these blessings might be universal in the churches to whom he had administered the word of life. He departed full of faith and hope in his Redeemer."

In the Evangelical Review, vol. viii, pp. 402 and 403, the following additional facts are stated:

"He was familiar with the Hebrew, Greek and Latin, and it is said he could converse fluently in five or six different languages. Such was his thirst for knowledge that he kept pace with the improvements of the age, and was constantly adding to his stores of information. His mind was active and discriminating, and so well disciplined that he had no difficulty in grasping any subject that claimed his attention. It is said his library was large and valuable, embracing quite a number of distinguished German authors. Many of these he bequeathed to our Theological Seminary at Gettysburg, of which he was elected one of the first directors, and in whose prosperity he always manifested a deep interest. The most of his books are, however, in the possession of North Carolina College, at Mount Pleasant, Cabarrus County, N. C.

"Rev. Samuel Rothrock, who succeeded him in

one of his churches, writes: 'Mr. Storch was truly a man of God! Many are yet living who formerly sat under his preaching, in whose hearts he is sacredly embalmed, and who still cherish for him the most profound respect.'"

The following inscription is engraved upon the tablet in the adjoining God's acre of Organ Church, which marks the spot where this useful servant of the Lord was laid down to rest: "Sacred to the memory of the Rev. Charles A. G. Storch, Pastor of the Evangelical Lutheran Church; who was born on the 16th day of June, A.D. 1764, and departed this life on the 27th day of March, 1831. Aged 66 years, 9 months and 11 days."

In addition to those pastors laboring in Virginia and retaining their connection with the North Carolina Synod, namely, Revs. Jacob Scherer and Daniel J. Hauer, who removed from North Carolina to that State, and Revs. Martin Walther, Andrew Seechrist and John P. Cline, the Synod received a considerable accession to its ministerial ranks in Revs. Henry Graeber, Jacob Kaempfer, William Artz and David P. Rosenmiller, all of whom became connected with the Synod in 1828.

"Rev. Henry Graeber was for a number of years a member of the Lutheran Synod of Maryland and Virginia, and lately accepted a call to Lincoln County, N. C., where he preaches to six congregations. The people there are generally liberal in supporting the Gospel. As an evidence of this, a certain individual made a donation of fifty acres of land to be appropriated as a parsonage, and a commodious house was built on it by the congregation, where Rev. Mr. Graeber now lives."

The Revs. Artz, Kaempfer, and Rosenmiller were three young men, who had completed their theological course of studies at the Seminary at Gettysburg, Pennsylvania, and came to labor in North Carolina upon the recommendation of Professor S. S. Schmucker. They were admitted at once as members of the Synod. Rev. Artz took charge of the vacant congregations in Guilford County; their pastor, Rev. Jacob Scherer, having removed to Virginia. Rev. Rosenmiller located himself in Lexington, the seat of justice in Davidson County, where he opened a classical school, and attended to the duties of pastor among several of the churches in the county, and the one lately established in the village. Rev. Kaempfer became the pastor of Organ Church and some of the other contiguous congregations, made vacant by the removal of their pastor, Rev. Daniel Scherer, to the State of Illinois.

Section 8. Principal Transactions of the Tennessee Synod, from 1820 to 1833.

The name of this Synod would indicate that its labors were confined to the State of Tennessee; such is, however, not the case, as that Synod, like some other Lutheran Synods in this country, has many congregations in the States adjoining. Some of these churches are located in North and South

Carolina, and hence the history of the Tennessee Synod also belongs properly to the history of the Lutheran Church in the Carolinas.

As stated before, the Tennessee Synod was organized July 17th, 1820; at that meeting the German language was made the business language of Synod, and all its transactions were to be printed in German.

All articles of faith and practice, as well as all books used in public worship, are to be arranged according to the doctrines of the Holy Scriptures and the Augsburg Confession.

Two ranks of the ministerial office were acknowledged, namely, Pastor and Deacon, both of which requiring a separate ordination by the imposition of hands. Only the pastors had the right to perform all ministerial acts; the deacons could catechize, read a sermon to a congregation, bury the dead, exhort, and, in case of necessity, baptize, provided no pastor can be obtained.

Each congregation had the right to send a delegate to Synod, but the number of the lay-delegates' votes was limited to the number of ministers present at Synod.

At the fifth session of Synod, Rev. Nehemiah Bonham, of Tazewell County, Virginia, an English Lutheran minister, with his congregations, was admitted as a member of Synod. Rev. Bonham became an active worker in the Lord's vineyard, and accomplished much good.

In 1825 the minutes of Synod were printed also in the English language. At that same meeting "a memorial, subscribed by nine persons," was handed in, "in which the Synod is requested to make another attempt to effect a union with the ministers of the North Carolina Synod; yet so, that the genuine Lutheran doctrine be not thereby suppressed."

November 27th, 1825, Rev. Paul Henkel departed this life at New Market, Virginia. He had been in the ministry forty-four years, and, at the time of his decease, had arrived at an advanced age of life.

During the seventh session of the Synod, the following action was taken in reference to the difficulty respecting the English language. "As several members of this body do not understand the German language, and yet do not desire to form a separate Synod, it was, therefore,

"*Resolved*, that David Henkel should act as interpreter to them; furthermore, that the business of Synod shall be transacted in the German language during the first three days, afterwards the English language shall be used."

At the ninth session a new constitution was adopted, and appended to the printed minutes. Rev. David Forrester was ordained at this session to the office of a pastor, and several students of theology were received under the care of Synod.

From the minutes of 1829, it is manifest that the Synod was extending its bounds and influence, and through the labors of Rev. Bonham, Lutheranism became known in Habersham and Carroll Counties, Georgia. Rev. John L. Morkert, from

Ohio, attached himself to the Synod, and Rev. John N. Stirewalt was ordained to the pastoral office. A vote of thanks was presented to Dr. Solomon Henkel "for his extra and benevolent services he has rendered this body from time to time, in printing" the transactions, &c., of Synod.

In 1831 the Rev. William C. Rankin, a licentiate of the Presbyterian Church, and in good standing, as seen from the records of Union Presbytery, East Tennessee, having adopted the principles of the Lutheran Church, and desiring to become one of its ministers, was examined by a committee, and recommended for ordination. "He was first admitted to full membership of the Lutheran Church by the rite of confirmation, and after having taken the solemn vows of a minister, he was ordained as pastor with prayer and imposition of hands."

The same day Rev. Henry Goodman was ordained as deacon. During this year, on the 15th of June, Rev. David Henkel departed this life, aged thirty-six years, one month, and eleven days. His remains were interred at St. John's Church, Lincoln County, N. C. As a youth of seventeen years he commenced to preach the gospel; he delivered his first sermon, November 1, 1812, at St. Peter's Church, in South Carolina. "He was a diligent student, and searched deep into the truths of divine revelation." He was the author of nine different publications, the most of which are of a theological character. He was asked on his deathbed whether he remained steadfast in the doctrine he preached, to which he replied in the affirmative, and that he had no fear of death. "His last words were: 'O Lord Jesus—thou Son of God—receive my spirit.'" He left a wife and seven children to mourn his loss.

During the years 1832 and 1833, nothing of any special interest was transacted at Synod, except the ordination of Rev. H. Goodman to the pastoral office, and the withdrawal of Rev. W. C. Rankin from Synod; whether he connected himself with some other ecclesiastical body is not stated.

Appended to the minutes there is an obituary notice of Rev. Philip Henkel, who departed this life October 9th, 1833, aged fifty-four years and seventeen days. His remains were interred at Richland Church, Randolph County, N. C. He was one of the first founders of the Lutheran Tennessee Synod, and was thirty-three years and three months in the ministerial office.

Section 9. Establishment of a Theological Seminary in South Carolina, under the Professorship of Rev. John G. Schwartz, A.D. 1830.

The first steps taken towards the establishment of a Theological Seminary by the South Carolina Synod, were sundry resolutions passed at the meeting of Synod held in Savannah, Georgia, November 20th, 1829, and are as follows:

"The several resolutions already mentioned, as having reference to the establishment of a Theological Seminary, within the bounds of this Synod, were now taken up, and after mature discussion, *unanimously adopted.*

"*Resolved*, That this Synod regard the establishment of a theological seminary under the auspices of this judicatory, and within its bounds, as highly calculated to advance the interests of our Church, and as an object worthy of attention.

"*Resolved, therefore*, That we direct our efforts forthwith to the erection of a fund, to be hereafter devoted to the establishment and support of such a seminary.

"*Resolved, also*, That a committee, to consist of *twenty*, be now appointed, who shall be authorized to receive any donations which may be presented or legacies which may be bequeathed towards the erection of such a fund.

(Here follow the names of the members of that committee.)

"*Resolved, moreover*, That this committee act until the ensuing session of this Synod. That the chairman of the committee report at the next annual meeting, whether any and what donations have been received, and that a similar committee be appointed from year to year."

The next year fully decided the fate of the proposed institution. The President of the Synod, Rev. J. Bachman, opened the subject in his annual address to Synod, as follows:

"Although by the blessing of God our Church under the direction of this Synod is evidently on the increase, yet there still continues a lamentable want of ministers. Our congregations are enlarging, and new ones are forming from year to year, yet the number of our ministers is not proportionably on the increase; and such are the calls for their services, that although some of our ministers attend to from four to seven congregations, it is feared that there will be some churches left but very partially supplied during the coming year. There are also petitions from Georgia and Alabama for missionaries, to which it is feared we can only respond by our wishes and our prayers. We have applied to our sister Synods in vain for aid. So wide a sphere is opened to them in the North and West, that they have no ministers to send us; and it is believed that our only permanent dependence, under the blessing of God, will be upon pious individuals who will hereafter be educated for our Church, who are natives of the States within the bounds of our Synod, and who are attached to our institutions, and accustomed to our climate.

"Let us bring the means of a theological education within the reach of our pious young men, and we may be assured that they will profit by these advantages. And I come now to recommend with all the earnestness I am capable of, and imploring Almighty God for his blessing on our humble exertions, the institution and support of a Theological Seminary. Hitherto I have had many anxieties on this subject, and great doubts of our success. I feared that in attempting too much we might entirely fail. But Providence seems to have removed the greatest obstacles to the establishment of such an institution. Our people have become united and zealous in the cause, and evince a liberality which, until now, we had no reason to expect. A proposition has emanated from them to subscribe a hundred dollars each, payable in four and five years, which would enable persons even in moderate circumstances to render their efficient aid to our contemplated institution. The success in obtaining subscriptions, thus far, is quite encouraging. The clergy of our denomination, although in most instances they receive but a very inadequate support, express their views of the importance of such an institution to our Southern Church in a desire to share with their people the burden of expense. This united zeal and perseverance will, we confidently hope, enable us at the next meeting of our Synod to report that ten thousand dollars have been pledged—a sum sufficient to enable our institution to go into successful operation; and although it would have but an humble origin, yet fostered by our liberality, our watchfulness, and our sincere and fervent prayers, we may, under the blessing of heaven, look forward to a long train of signal blessings upon our Church."

In addition to this address, Rev. Bachman also brought the subject before Synod in his discourse, which is likewise appended to the minutes of that year, and although an exceedingly interesting document, it is much too lengthy to be inserted here. It had the good effect of awakening the minds of the people generally on the importance of establishing the proposed Theological Seminary, and it accomplished good results even after the adjournment of Synod.

The chairman of the committee to receive donations, &c., for this object, reported that by the 1st of January next, "$3000 will have been subscribed."

The Synod then adopted the following series of resolutions:

"*Whereas*, The committee appointed at the last meeting of this Synod for the purpose of raising a fund for the support of a Theological Seminary, have made considerable progress in obtaining contributions; and whereas, there is a prospect of having a sufficient fund collected in a short time;

"*Resolved*, That in humble reliance on the Divine blessing, we now establish a Theological Seminary, to be conducted under the auspices of this Synod, and that we, by this resolusion, do consecrate our efforts to Him, who is the great Head of the Church, the Shepherd and Bishop of souls—God over all, blessed forever.

"*Resolved*, That as a course of preparatory study may be necessary for many theological students, and in order to the defraying of the expenses of a Theological Institution, we have connected with it a classical academy, under the superintendence of the Professor of Theology, and that this academy be open to all males over ten years of age."

The other resolutions refer to the appointment of a board of ten directors, the election of a treasurer, when the board is to be elected, the election of a Professor of Theology, &c.

"Mr. Henry Muller was elected Treasurer, and the Rev. J. G. Schwartz was unanimously chosen Professor of Theology."

Concerning Rev. Schwartz's election, and his fitness for the office, Rev. Bachman says:

"It was necessary that a professor to the institution should be elected, and that he should enter at once upon the discharge of his duties. Every eye among the clergy and laity was immediately directed to Mr. Schwartz. They knew his education, his talents and piety. Although but twenty-three years of age, he had made the best use of his short life. There were few better Greek and Latin scholars in our country; he had attended considerably to the Hebrew language; he was proficient in the French, and he was studiously directing his attention to the German, and read and translated that language with considerable ease. He had made an equal proficiency in the other sciences. In theology he was probably as well read as any young man of his age. He had attentively read all the most important writings on the subject; and although he preferred the doctrines of our Church to all others, yet his soul was the seat of Christian liberality, and it should be spoken to his praise, that although surrounded by Christians of other denominations, yet he never gave them offence, and they generally attended with satisfaction and improvement on his ministrations. The objections to his youth were every day removing. He received a unanimous vote as Professor of Theology. After the election there was a pause of many minutes, when he arose to address us. For a time his feelings almost prevented the power of utterance. He at length proceeded to thank us for our favorable opinion; stated his sense of his incapacity to discharge the duties of the station to which he had been appointed; pointed out its difficulties, but signified his willingness to undertake it by the help of God, and entreated our prayers and intercessions, and those of all Christians in his behalf. The youth of the individual—the occasion—the importance of the subject, and the feeling and eloquent address, melted the whole audience into tears, and I am sure that few who were then present will ever forget that impressive scene.

"He had entered the Junior Class of the South Carolina College in the autumn of 1824, and graduated in 1826, having throughout his collegiate course conducted himself with such propriety, that he was greatly beloved by the members of his class. He received a high honor when he graduated, and a letter from one of the professors stated—'He is not only among the best scholars, but one of the very best young men that graduated here for many years past.'"

The permanent location of the Theological Seminary was postponed to some future time; however, as Professor Schwartz had taken charge of several congregations in Newberry District, which he was unwilling to resign until another year had expired, he gave notice "that for the year 1831 his residence will be in Newberry District, with

Colonel John Eigleberger, about ten miles below Newberry Court-house, and that he will be prepared, by the first Monday in February, to receive as theological students such persons, as shall have been approved by the standing committee of the Board of Directors.

"Boarding, inclusive of washing, &c., will be furnished at seventy dollars per annum."

The Seminary of Theology opened with very flattering prospects; so many students became connected with it, that Professor Schwartz expressed his fears in a letter to Rev. J. Bachman, that if many more would come, they could not be accommodated: and of their character he further states: "All the young men now with me are promising—and if their hearts be right in the sight of God, I have no doubt they will prove a blessing to our Church. The heart is known, however, only to God—we can judge only by the outward appearance; but did I think that any of these students were deficient in proper views of religion and of the ministerial office, I should feel it my bounden duty to advise them at once not to enter this institution. I dread the idea of being instrumental in educating any one for the holy office of the ministry, who through a want of personal religion may bring disgrace upon our sacred calling."

Section 10. New Churches erected in South Carolina; and the early death of Revs. Wingard, Schwartz, Bergman, and Daniel Dreher.

1. *Mount Calvary Church*, Edgefield District, was dedicated by the Rev. Messrs. Schwartz and W. D. Strobel, on the 21st of February, 1830. The congregation at that time numbered twenty-four communicants.

2. *St. Paul's*, a fine new church in Newberry District, was dedicated on the third Sunday in June, 1830, by the Rev. Messrs. Rauch and Schwartz. A revived state of religion had been visible for some time past, and soon after the dedication of the church thirty-seven persons were added at one time by confirmation.

3. *Shiloh Church*, in the fork of the two Edisto Rivers, and in the neighborhood of Mr. Brandenburg, was completed this year, and on the second Sabbath in January, 1831, it was dedicated; it contained at the time a membership of but fifteen communicants.

4. *Ebenezer Church*, in the city of Columbia, a neat brick edifice, located in an extensive lot, with an ample God's-acre for the repose of the dead, was completed this year, and dedicated the 28th of November, 1830. This congregation was gathered together and organized by Rev. Jacob Wingard, who manifested great zeal and good management in this laudable enterprise. The congregation being small, and the membership generally in lim-

ited circumstances, the church edifice was erected principally through the munificence of Mr. Henry Muller, Sr., of Platt Springs, Lexington District, S. C. In February, 1865, it became a prey to the flames of the burning of Columbia by the Northern army, under General Sherman; but has since been rebuilt by funds, donated partly by Lutheran congregations and individuals at the North.

St. Stephen's Church, at Lexington Court-house, a frame building, with ample accommodations, was erected this year, but not completed until the fall of 1831, when on the fifth Sunday in October it was dedicated to the service of Almighty God. Being located in a town where the Lutheran element largely predominates, it has the prospect of becoming a flourishing church. It was likewise burnt down during the late war.

6. During the year 1831, "the *Church in the Sandhills* was also dedicated."

7. "The *Church at Hollow Creek* is said to be nearly completed, and will be opened for worship in the course of a month."

8. "A new church in Barnwell District, near the Saltketchers, is also being erected, and is in a considerable state of forwardness."

The above are quotations from the president's report to Synod in 1831.

God was visibly blessing the South Carolina Synod in enlarging its sphere of influence and usefulness, in the increase of its members and congregations; but there is also a shady side to that picture—God visited the Synod by the removal of a number of useful ministers of the Gospel by the strong hand of death; they were taken away when yet in their years of youthful strength and vigor, when the Church had centred great hopes in them, and they gave promise of a long life of service in the Lord's vineyard.

Rev. Jacob Wingard was the son of Samuel Wingard, and a young man of much promise; of him the Rev. J. Bachman, President of Synod, remarks in his report of 1831: "Mr. Wingard had but recently returned from the Theological Institution at Gettysburg, where he had been highly respected for his talents, his piety, and worth. But his friends beheld with anxiety and sorrow that his constitution, which had never been strong, had been attacked by an insidious disease; but trusting to that heavenly physician, who is able to restore health and vigor to the diseased frame and cheer the drooping hopes of man, we still looked forward to the time when his recovery would restore him to usefulness in the Church, and by our advice he was solemnly ordained and set apart to the work of the ministry. But on the 14th day of January last, the God whom he loved to serve, and in whose cause he had spent the whole of his short life, summoned him away. Mr. Wingard was a young man of uncommon attainments, considering the disadvantages under which he had labored in his youth, for the want of a systematic education. He was in most cases his own instructor; every leisure hour that could be spared from those occupations in which he was necessarily engaged was devoted to books; and all his reading and study had for its object the promotion of his Savior's religion. For this object he left his peaceful home, and devoted himself to solitude and study in a distant part of our land. Here he was attacked by a disease, which he bore with Christian resignation. When he was summoned away, he appeared still at the post of duty, and meekly resigned himself to the will of God, trusting through the mercy of his Savior for the salvation of his soul, and the joys of heaven."

With Rev. Prof. John G. Schwartz the reader is already well acquainted. He commenced his labors as the first regular Professor of Theology in connection with the Lutheran Church in the Carolinas, early in February, 1831, under the most flattering prospects, and with the high hopes of the Church centred upon him; but these hopes were destined to a speedy disappointment; in less than seven months Prof. Schwartz was numbered with the dead.

The following brief sketch of his life is furnished by Rev. Dr. Hazelius in his "American Lutheran Church:"

"The Rev. John G. Schwartz was born in Charleston, S. C., in the year 1807, where he also received the preliminary part of his education. Afterwards he became an alumnus of the South Carolina College, at Columbia, where he graduated with distinguished honor in December, 1826. On his return to Charleston he commenced the study of theology under the direction of the Rev.

Mr. Bachman. In 1828 he was elected Junior Professor of Languages in the Charleston College. But desirous of serving the Lord as a minister of the Gospel, he freely surrendered his present advantages, as well as his fair temporal prospects of the future, and engaged as a missionary among the destitute churches in the interior of South Carolina.

"His labors were eminently blessed, and our brother enjoyed the full confidence of the members of his churches. But his career was to be short; for wise purposes, to us unknown, the Lord called his young servant away in the midst of his useful labors. In the summer of 1831 he was seized with a violent fever, which at first appearance seemed to yield to the influence of medicine, but returning with increased severity, put relief beyond the power of human means, and on the 26th of August it terminated his valuable life, having just reached the 24th year of his age."

From a funeral discourse, occasioned by the death of Rev. J. G. Schwartz, and delivered by the Rev. Mr. Bachman, the following testimony of the character and worth of Prof. Schwartz is obtained:

"Should it be asked what was the peculiar trait in the character of Mr. Schwartz, I would say that it was a solemn determination conscientiously to discharge his duty to his God. For this he left his peaceful home and the friends of his youth, and retired into a sickly part of our county; and from thence he wrote: 'Here in the woods of

Carolina I suspect my lot is cast—here I shall live, and here I shall die. To be instrumental in doing good and enlarging the Redeemer's kingdom is all I ask.'

"That a man who was so devoted to the duties of the Christian should possess the amiable graces of benevolence, we cannot wonder. He felt it his duty to exert all his powers to do good to the bodies and souls of men. The great maxim, no man liveth to himself, was engraven on his mind. Without profession or show, he engaged in and ardently devoted himself to every work of benevolence.

"The shock given to the people among whom he lived by this event was unusual, and the calamity was heightened by its bereaving them of their fondest hopes. A gentleman who attended the funeral writes: 'No tongue can express, no pen can describe the feelings of the people on this melancholy occasion. The remains of our dearly beloved friend were interred this morning in Bethlehem churchyard; the largest concourse of people that were ever assembled in this country attended the funeral. The sad looks, the loud sobs and the tears shed on this mournful occasion, amply testified the high esteem in which he was held by all, rich and poor, old and young, white and black—pardon me for introducing the word black, but I must say, that even the poor Africans sympathized and sorrowed, saying, "Dear Mr. Schwartz."' Three of the ministers of our Church officiated at his funeral, and all bore testimony, that never had an individual departed in that community who was more beloved, or whose loss was more sincerely lamented than was that of our departed friend."

The next victim in the ministerial ranks of the South Carolina Synod, which death claimed as his own, was the Rev. C. F. Bergman, who, though laboring in Ebenezer, Georgia, was ordained by, and labored in connection with, the South Carolina Synod, and maintained his official relationship with the Lutheran Church in the Carolinas to the close of his life. It is therefore proper that an account of his life, labors and death be here inserted, which is furnished by Rev. S. A. Mealy in his funeral discourse, preached to Rev. Bergman's congregation at Ebenezer, occasioned by the death of their beloved pastor:

"The Rev. Christopher F. Bergman was born at Ebenezer, Georgia, on the 7th of January, 1793. His father, the Rev. John E. Bergman, a native of Germany, and the learned and exemplary minister of this church for the long period of thirty-six years, had the exclusive care of the education of the subject of our present recollections. He may, indeed, with the utmost truth, be said to have been trained up from youth to manhood in his own father's study.

"The general deportment of our friend was grave, and his very appearance forbade the rude approach of impertinent curiosity. One who saw him for the first time, would have thought him, perhaps, inaccessible and austere. But the same individual, upon a closer acquaintance, would have perceived his error, and found himself in the presence of gravity indeed, but a gravity most delicately softened by every generous virtue and amiable emotion. His outward bearing to others was affable, but unobtrusive. He was almost always cheerful, but never trifling. I have often seen his countenance lighted up with a smile among his friends, but distorted with laughter, never. His feelings, though cautious in their display, were constitutionally warm; and his affection for those whom he loved, ardent. In all the social relations of life, as a man—as a citizen—a husband—a parent—a master—a neighbor, and a friend—those who best knew him will bear me out in the assertion that he reflected honor upon the age in which he lived, and may be safely imitated, without any qualification whatsoever, by those whom he has left behind him.

"And what he was to this people, as the affectionate pastor, there are none of you will ever forget. How this 'good man, who was over you in the Lord,' preached to you—how he consoled you in the hour of sorrow—how he dried your tears in the season of affliction—how he prayed beside your sick-beds—how sincerely he loved you, and how faithfully he admonished you—is well known to all of this congregation, and shall be known to assembled worlds in the great day of judgment, when pastors and their charges shall meet again.

"I inquired whether, if it was the Divine will, he would not wish to be spared a little longer to his dear family and congregation. He said nothing for a considerable space, till I began to think he had not heard my question. At length he replied, 'If it is the divine will, I would rather go now. I feel that for me to depart and to be with Christ is far better. I think I can truly say, "for me to live is Christ, and to die is gain."' I observed, 'Then you are not afraid to die?' He said, 'No!' 'You have no doubts of your acceptance with God, through our great Mediator?' He replied, 'None. Blessed be the God and Father of my Lord Jesus Christ, I have no doubts.'

"While I was engaged in prayer, he held one of my hands clasped in both his own, and distinctly though feebly repeated almost every word after me, and concluded the prayer for me with the usual Amen. He then lay composed for some time, when at length he warmly pressed my hand and said, louder than he had yet spoken, 'Farewell.' He now repeated that triumphant hymn,

> 'Cease, fond nature, cease thy strife,
> And let me languish into life.'

"These were among the last words he used. At a quarter before three, A.M., on the 26th of March, 1832, he ceased to breathe, and was gathered to his rest in peace."

On the 14th of August, 1832, God called another young laborer to his early rest. Of him, Dr. Hazelius writes:

"The Rev. Daniel Dreher, son of Mr. John Dreher, of Lexington District, enjoyed the advantages of the advice and instruction of pious parents during his childhood and years of his youth, and by that instrumentality the Lord directed him early to the knowledge of his sinful nature, the need of a Savior, and to Jesus, the friend of repenting sinners, whose merits he embraced, through faith in application to his own soul. Having found Jesus precious, and the rock on which he had built the house of his hope, he became anxious to recommend him also unto others. Having given some attention to the study of divinity under the direction of his elder brother, the Rev. Godfrey Dreher, he was received by Synod as licentiate. He was an acceptable and zealous preacher, and his remembrance is cherished by all who enjoyed his acquaintance. He departed in hope of eternal life."

Thus was the Synod of South Carolina sorely smitten at that time, and the Church bereft of some of its most promising laborers. In view of these severe afflictions, the President of Synod, Rev. John Bachman, in his address to Synod, thus expresses himself:

"Let our past afflictions teach us humility, an increase of zeal and an humble trust and confidence in the protection and mercy of God; and as the hour of the night is darkest which precedes the rising morn, and as the day is often calmest which succeeds the violence of the tempest, so these visitations of heaven, like the calamities which befell the Church of old, may be followed by a long train of mercies and blessings to our beloved Zion. But whilst we rely for future success and prosperity on the blessings of heaven, let us in the meantime do all that lies in our power to promote its best interests."

Section 11. Founding of the Theological Seminary at Lexington, S. C., and Arrival of Rev. E. L. Hazelius, D.D., as Professor of Theology.

The fund necessary for the endowment of a professorship in the Theological Seminary was constantly increasing, and at the meeting of the South Carolina Synod of 1831, "liberal offers were made by several persons for the location of the Seminary in their respective neighborhoods.

"After much interesting discussion had been elicited, in which several, both of the clerical and lay members, took an animated part, the following resolutions were finally adopted:

"*Resolved*, That the location of our Theological Seminary be deferred till the next meeting of Synod; and that during the recess of the Synod the Board of Directors ascertain which of any two places selected will hold out the greatest inducements for the establishment of our Seminary in that place.

"*Resolved*, That Lexington Village and Sandy Run, the latter comprising a circuit of from one to two miles from the church, be the places designated in the above resolution."

At the next meeting of Synod, held in St. Matthew's Church, Orangeburg District, the question of locating the Seminary was finally disposed of by the reading of the proposals made by the above-mentioned two places, which were as follows:

"Lexington Village, in money and other property,	$5287
Sandy Run, " "	4000
Excess in favor of Lexington Village, . . .	$1287"

And the passing of the following resolution:

"*Resolved*, That since Lexington Village holds out the greatest inducements, our Theological Seminary shall be located in that place."

In reference to the Seminary, it was also

"*Resolved*, That the sincere thanks of this Synod be returned to our friends and the members of our Church for their very generous subscriptions to our Theological Seminary.

"*Resolved*, That it be enjoined on all our ministers to bring the subject of our Theological Seminary to the view of their respective congregations, and to impress upon them the necessity of using their most strenuous exertions to promote its best interests.

"*Resolved*, That the Rev. Godfrey Dreher and Mr. Henry Muller be appointed by this Synod as their agents, to solicit donations and subscriptions to our Theological Seminary, and that they report to this Synod at its next meeting."

Mrs. Mariana Chisolm, of Charleston, S. C., presented to the Synod, for the use of the Seminary, a large Bible and hymnbook, "accompanied with her earnest prayer that the institution may be instrumental in furnishing the now destitute churches with many pious and able ministers of the Lutheran faith." Whereupon the Synod

"*Resolved*, That the thanks of this Synod be returned to Mrs. Mariana Chisolm for her very acceptable present of a valuable Bible and Lutheran hymn and prayer book for the use of our Seminary."

During the year 1833 the necessary buildings were erected near Lexington Court-House, both for recitation rooms and a dwelling for the theological Professor; and at the same time the Board of Directors elected Rev. Dr. E. L. Hazelius, of Gettysburg, Pennsylvania, Professor of Theology; and the Rev. Washington Muller, a graduate of South Carolina College, Principal of the Classical Academy.

Rev. Dr. Hazelius was a native of Silesia, in the kingdom of Prussia; in early life he was connected with the Moravian Church; and, having "received his collegiate education in Saxony and Prussia, he subsequently graduated in the Moravian Theological Seminary at Niesky, in 1797. He arrived in America in 1800," and was for a time the classical teacher at Nazareth, Pennsylvania, a Moravian institution of learning, where one of his pupils was the future Bishop Van Vleck. In 1809 he was ordained by the New York Ministerium a minister of the Lutheran Church. In 1815 he was elected Professor of Theology at Hartwick Seminary, New York, "where he remained a faithful and successful instructor until 1830, when he removed to Gettysburg Seminary," as one of its professors.

In the fall of 1833, he became located at Lexington, S. C., where he remained in the service of his Master for nearly twenty years, to the close of his life.

In the synodical address of Rev. J. Bachman, he was kindly and heartily welcomed as Professor of Theology and as a member of the South Carolina Synod in the following terms:

"It is a source of no small gratification to me to be permitted to welcome among us our brother and friend, the recently elected Professor of Theology in our Seminary. He has come, we hope and believe, to spend the remainder of an active and a useful life in the midst of us. He has brought along with him those talents which God gave him—that learning which a life devoted to study has enabled him to acquire—and that experience, zeal, and fidelity which caused him to be respected, and rendered him eminently useful, in all those valuable institutions over which he was heretofore called to preside. His unanimous election to this responsible office—the pleasure which we all felt on hearing of his acceptance of the appointment—the sacrifices he has made to come among us—are all so many loud calls upon us to perform our part of the contract with liberal and cheerful hearts. Let us co-operate with him in all those regulations which are calculated to promote the best interests of the institution, and let us give to that institution our united efforts and our fervent prayers."

Both the Theological Seminary and the Classical Academy went into operation on the first Monday of January, 1834, and both commenced with very favorable prospects; a number of young men enrolled themselves as students of theology, whilst the local and other patrons of the classical department were quite numerous.

In the inaugural address of Rev. Dr. Hazelius, in which he impresses his audience with the necessity of a theological training for ministers of the gospel, the following are the closing remarks: "Brethren! Benefactors of this institution! I am aware your satisfaction at the success which has crowned your efforts, your labors, and your expense, is great, and you regret not having attempted, though few in number, what in other sections of our country, large legacies, the contributions of strangers, and the united efforts of several Synods only could accomplish. To you the Lutheran Church of South Carolina and the adjacent States is largely indebted; and though no monuments of marble may hereafter point out to posterity what you have done for the Church, your latest posterity will bless your memory, and the Searcher of the heart will reward you.

"We have the proud consciousness of knowing that we all have entertained and do now entertain no other view, no other aim in the establishment of this Seminary than the enlargement of the Redeemer's kingdom, and there is no doubt, if our institutions remain faithful to this principle, and faithful in the application of the means intrusted to us by our brethren for the benefit of the Seminary, and also in the instruction of our young brethren, if we never stoop to mean intrigue and management, but act with a single eye to the glory of God, and with candor towards man, the blessing of Almighty God will accompany this institution; it will prove a benefit to the Church, and its blessings will descend to the latest generations."

CHAPTER VI.

HISTORY OF THE LUTHERAN CHURCH IN THE CAROLINAS CONTINUED, TO THE CLOSE OF THE YEAR 1850.

Section 1. Condition of the Lutheran Church in North and South Carolina in 1834.

During the three years which intervened between 1831 and 1834, very few changes occurred in the North Carolina Synod; the Rev. John T. Tabler, a student from Gettysburg, became connected with the Synod, and labored as pastor in Salisbury, but he remained there only one year, after which he removed to Virginia.

In 1832, the Rev. Henry Graeber resigned his charge in Lincoln County, and became the pastor of St. John's and Organ Churches, which had become vacant by the removal of Revs. D. Scherer and J. Kaempfer. In 1833, the Rev. Samuel Rothrock, having completed his studies at Gettysburg, returned to North Carolina, was licensed by Synod, and labored as missionary in several vacant churches for a short time, after which he became the pastor of Salisbury and Union Churches. The following year the Rev. Daniel Jenkins became connected with the North Carolina Synod; he came from "the State of Maryland, about the beginning of November, 1833, and expressing a desire to serve our Church in this Southern section as a missionary," was licensed by the President of Synod "to preach in our destitute churches until the next session of the Ministerium."

The congregations in Lincoln County, having had no regular pastor of the North Carolina Synod since the removal of Rev. Graeber from their midst, and having been only occasionally visited by missionaries and other members of Synod, became eventually connected with the Tennessee Synod.

Concerning the state of the Church in 1834, the President of Synod reports: "The events of the past synodical year have become, in some measure, more encouraging than they have been for several years before. Those churches in our connection that could be regularly supplied, had not only a considerable increase since our last annual meeting, but are also generally in a prosperous condition. The gospel has been faithfully preached, and the holy ordinances regularly administered. There are still a goodly number of small but respectable congregations that are vacant, which, if they could be supplied with ministers, would add considerable strength to this weak but evangelical member of the Lutheran household of faith. Prospects have also appeared during the last year, of forming several new congregations."

During the year 1834 the Tennessee Synod had no meeting, caused by the absence of so many ministers. The next year the Synod met at Blue Spring Church, Green County, Tennessee, at which meeting the Rev. William Hancher, Daniel S. Schulfeld, Christian G. Reitzel and Samuel C. Parmer, were ordained to the office of deacon. At that time the Revs. Daniel Moser, Adam Miller, Jr., and Jacob Casner were laboring in Lincoln County, N. C.; the Rev. H. Goodman, in Iredell County, N. C.; the Rev. C. G. Reitzel, in Guilford County, N. C.; and Rev. J. N. Stirewalt, in Rowan County, N. C. The other twelve ministers of the Tennessee Synod had charges in other States outside of the Carolinas.

During this year, on the third Sunday in August, a new Lutheran Synod was organized in the State of Indiana, with which the three ministers of the Tennessee Synod, who resided in Indiana, doubtless connected themselves. They besought their brethren of the parent Synod not to regard this movement as "a separation or schism," but rather as a means of "strengthening" the Church.

In the South Carolina Synod no changes of importance occurred during the year 1834. "The Theological Seminary located at Lexington," says the President of Synod, in his annual report, "has thus far fully equalled our most sanguine expectations." Nine young men formed the first class of students of theology, namely, F. F. Harris, J. P. Ring, D. Bernhardt, E. A. Bolles, E. Hawkins, W. Berly, H. Stoudenmyre, L. Bedenbaugh and P. A. Strobel. Valuable additions to the library of the Seminary were presented by Messrs. Henry Muller, Sr., of Platt Springs, Thomas Purse, of Savannah, and the congregation of Ebenezer, Georgia.

In December, 1833, the Missionary Committee of the Synod employed the Rev. P. Rizer, "who arrived at Lexington, S. C., from the State and Synod of Maryland," as a traveling missionary in the States of Georgia and Alabama. "He met with a very cordial reception from many Lutherans who had emigrated from Carolina, and found them still attached to the doctrines and usages of our Church." In Monroeville, at Flatt Creek, and at Bogue-Chitto Creek, in the State of Alabama, the prospects for the immediate organization of Lutheran churches was so flattering, and the demand for a pastor so urgent, that on the return of Rev. Rizer, one of the theological students, Mr. F. F. Harris, was licensed, and sent at once to these people as their pastor. At the meeting of

Synod in 1834, he was ordained as the pastor of this hopeful charge in Alabama, and remained in that State eight years, when he removed to Ohio. He was succeeded by Revs. Daily and Stoudenmyre, but nothing is now known of these churches, and no Lutheran minister is at present laboring in that portion of Alabama.

The President of Synod, Rev. J. Bachman, in his annual report, urges upon the members of Synod the importance and necessity of catechetical instruction, stating: "The mind of man requires *instruction* as well as *excitement*, and in all our ministrations we should be cautious to enlighten the understanding, and to enable our hearers to give a reason for the hope that is in them."

Section 2. Rev. Daniel Jenkins' Revivals in North Carolina—Commissioners sent by the South Carolina Synod to the North Carolina Synod, with Proposals in Behalf of the Lexington Theological Seminary—Death of Rev. Gottlieb Shober.

The revival system or "new measures," as it was then called, was not introduced into the North Carolina Synod to its full extent until the year 1835, when the Rev. Daniel Jenkins, from Maryland, introduced it in his congregations. It created considerable opposition both among the clergy and laity of the Lutheran Church in North Carolina. The subject was debated at Synod, and the Ministerium passed the following resolutions:

"*Resolved*, That we countenance no distinction between those Christians who are separately prayed for in public, and those who retire into their chambers for devotion.

"*Resolved*, That if any licentiate should depreciate religious instruction of youth by way of catechization, or otherwise, he can never be ordained."

At no period of time has the North Carolina Synod abandoned catechetical instruction, although in some few congregations this old-established "good rule of our Church" fell into disuse. Frequently the "new measures" accomplished more harm than good; and, to use a paradoxical expression often quoted, several churches were "revived to death." The system finally culminated into regular camp meetings; but from that time forward it commenced to decline, and the ruins of the temporary little cabins, denominated "tents," and of the covered sheds for preaching to large assemblies, denominated "arbors," may still be seen in some places, but they are no longer used for the purpose originally intended.

In the year 1836, Rev. Dr. Hazelius and Mr. Henry Muller attended the meeting of the North Carolina Synod. They came as commissioners sent by the Synod of South Carolina for the purpose of conferring with the members of the North Carolina Synod, "as to the possibility and mutual advantage of a union of effort in the support and patronage of the Seminary at Lexington."

The commissioners made the following proposals:

"1. The Synod of South Carolina will allow that of North Carolina such share in the government of the institution established at Lexington, as their portion of the funds shall equitably entitle them to.

"2. The students from North Carolina that enter the Seminary, shall be entitled to free tuition, as well as the students from South Carolina.

"3. The fund collected by our brethren from North Carolina shall remain under the control of the Synod of North Carolina, and only its yearly proceeds made over to the treasurer of our Seminary."

The Synod of North Carolina having "attentively heard" the proposition of the South Carolina Synod's commissioners, unanimously—

"*Resolved*, To appoint two delegates, one clerical and one lay delegate, to meet the Synod of South Carolina at its next session in November, with instructions from this body to unite our efforts with our brethren in South Carolina, in the support of their Seminary."

The delegates elected by ballot were Rev. Wm. Artz and Col. John Smith; alternates, Rev. H. Graeber and Moses L. Brown.

Arrangements were then made for the creation of a fund for the support of the Seminary at Lexington, S. C. The committee were also instructed "to adhere strictly to the propositions made by the commissioners of the South Carolina Synod, and to make no agreement to raise a larger sum of money than can be obtained."

At the succeeding meeting of the South Carolina Synod, Rev. Wm. Artz, delegate from the North Carolina Synod, being present, the above propositions were confirmed, with a few additional provisos, one of which was, "That the right be conceded to the Synods respectively to rescind this agreement, and annul the obligations growing out of it, whenever in the opinion of either body such a dissolution is advisable."

On the 27th of June, 1838, the Rev. Gottlieb Shober "departed this life, after being confined for one day only, although for some years past his bodily health and native vigor of mind had been rapidly declining. At his death he was in the eighty-second year of his age. His life was spent in untired activity and useful labors until old age admonished him to seek retirement." In memory of his death, the North Carolina Synod passed the following resolutions:

"*Resolved*, That this Synod has heard with deep regret of the death of the Rev. Gottlieb Shober, who has, for many years, been an efficient and useful member of this body.

"*Resolved*, That this Synod will ever cherish with grateful remembrance, the active zeal and eminent services of *Father Shober*."

A lengthy memoir of Rev. Shober is contained in the Evangelical Review, vol. viii, pp. 404–415, from which we learn that he was a native of Bethlehem, Pennsylvania, and, "at the time of his death, was the only survivor of those who had commenced the building of the town of Salem, N. C."

"In the spring of 1810, in company with Rev. Mr. Storch, he visited South Carolina, during which occasion he preached his first sermon." He was a member of the North Carolina Synod for a period of twenty-eight years.

Section 3. Increase of Lutheran Ministers in the Carolinas—Establishment of New Congregations—Visit of Rev. Dr. Bachman to Europe.

The influence of the Theological Seminary at Lexington, S. C., was now beginning to be felt in the Lutheran Church in the Carolinas; both the North and South Carolina Synods received from it large additions to the number of their ministers, and in other Southern States a number of its graduates were called to labor. It supplied a greatly and long felt want of the Lutheran Church in the South.

During the five years preceding the meeting of the North Carolina Synod in 1840, the following additions were made to its clerical roll:

1. Rev. Edwin A. Bolles, a graduate of the Lexington, S. C., Theological Seminary, was licensed by the South Carolina Synod in 1835, and became the pastor of the Lutheran church in Salisbury, N. C., where he, however, remained but a short time, and removed to Ebenezer, Georgia. He is laboring at present in South Carolina, as State Agent for the American Bible Society.

2. Rev. Benjamin Arey, from the Theological Seminary of Gettysburg, Pennsylvania, licensed by the North Carolina Synod in 1836, became at

first located in Davidson County, and labored in various charges in the bounds of Synod, but finally located himself permanently in Iredell County, N. C.

3. Rev. John Swicegood, licensed at the same time, made his permanent home in Davidson County, but frequently labored in the counties adjoining. He departed this life September 9th, 1870, in the full triumphs of a Gospel faith.

4. Rev. Elijah Hawkins, a graduate of the Seminary at Lexington, S. C., became connected with the Synod in 1837, and labored in Wythe County, Virginia, to the close of a most useful life.

5. Rev. Philip A. Strobel, likewise connected himself with the North Carolina Synod in 1837, having graduated at Lexington, S. C., in 1836; he labored for a short time as agent for the Seminary, and then located himself in Concord, N. C. He did good service in the North Carolina Synod in establishing several new churches, and remained in Concord four years, when he returned to South Carolina.

6. Rev. Jacob Crim, from the Lexington Seminary, attached himself to the North Carolina Synod in 1838, and labored successively in Davidson, Rowan and Davie Counties. In 1869 he removed to the State of Texas, where he shortly afterwards was called to his rest.

7. Rev. John J. Greever, a "student of the Gettysburg Theological Seminary," was licensed by the North Carolina Synod in 1840; he labors

still in Wythe County, Virginia, where he was first located.

8. Rev. N. Aldrich, a "student of divinity of the Episcopal Church at Bristol College, Pennsylvania," was licensed by the North Carolina Synod in 1840, remained only a few months at Concord, N. C., when he removed to Savannah, Georgia, and became the successor of Rev. S. A. Mealy, as pastor of the Lutheran church in that city. He is the present pastor of St. Mark's Lutheran Church, in Charlotte, N. C.

9. Rev. Gideon Scherer, "a student of the Theological Seminary at Lexington, S. C.," was licensed by the North Carolina Synod in 1840, and located himself in Wythe County, Virginia.

In the South Carolina Synod the increase in the number of ministers was still greater, and it was not long before all the vacant charges were supplied with the regular ministrations of the word and sacraments.

In the year 1831, before the Theological Seminary went into full operation, four ministers were licensed by the South Carolina Synod, whose names have not yet been mentioned, namely: Revs. Herrman Aull, William Hotchkiss, George Haltiwanger, Sr., and Robert Cloy. Rev. Aull lived, labored and died in Newberry District, S. C. Rev. Haltiwanger became the pastor of St. Matthew's Church in Orangeburg District, S. C., and labored with great acceptance and usefulness in various parts of South Carolina to the close of his life, April 18th, 1849. Rev. Cloy labored in Barnwell District, S. C.; he died May 4th, 1853.

From 1835 to 1840, the following additional names were added to the ministerial roll of the South Carolina Synod:

1. Rev. James P. Ring, a graduate of the Lexington Theological Seminary, was licensed by the South Carolina Synod in 1835, and devoted his life to teaching. He was Professor of a classical institution in the city of Augusta, Georgia, at which place he died, April 12th, 1852.

2. Rev. David Bernhardt, was the son of Rev. C. E. Bernhardt, whose history has been given in a previous chapter. The son became a student and graduate of the Theological Seminary at Lexington, and was licensed by Synod, A.D. 1835. He had charge of St. Matthew's Church, Orangeburg District, and Sandy Run Church, Lexington District, S. C., up to the close of his life, April 13th, 1843.

3. Rev. Levi Bedenbaugh, a student of Lexington Seminary, was licensed at the same time. His principal field of operations has been Coweta County, Georgia, where he is still laboring.

4. Rev. David Hungerpeler, was licensed in 1836, and died April 20th, 1840. He labored in Barnwell District, S. C.

5. Rev. William Berly, a graduate of the Lexington Seminary, was licensed in 1836, labored for a time in Newberry District, S. C., was elected the second Professor of the Theological Seminary at Lexington in 1850, whereupon he removed to

Lexington Court-House in 1851, where he is still residing, laboring as pastor there.

6. Rev. William G. Harter, also a graduate of the Lexington Seminary, was licensed in 1837, labored in the States of South Carolina, North Carolina and Kentucky; he was called to his rest July 31st, 1864.

7. Rev. H. Stoudenmyer was licensed in 1838, and labored for a time in the State of Alabama.

8. Rev. S. R. Sheppard, a student of the Lexington Seminary, was licensed in 1838, labored for some time in Edgefield District, S. C., removed to the State of Mississippi in 1853, where he recently departed this life.

9. Rev. J. Kleckly was licensed in 1839, and labored in the State of Georgia, where he died a few years ago.

10. Rev. William H. Smith, of the State of Maryland, was elected assistant pastor to Rev. John Bachman, D.D., in 1839, was ordained by the South Carolina Synod April 24th, 1839, remained three years, and returned to the North.

11. Rev. S. Bouknight, licensed in 1840; he labors principally in Lexington District, S. C.

12. Rev. J. P. Margart, a graduate of the Seminary at Lexington, licensed in 1840, labored in Orangeburg, Newberry and Lexington Districts, S. C., removed to Alabama in 1862, where he still resides, making strong efforts to build up the Lutheran Church in that State.

13. Rev. George Haltiwanger, Jr., a student of the Lexington Theological Seminary, was licensed

in 1840, labored in Lexington District, S. C., until 1849, when he became the pastor of the Ebenezer charge in Georgia, where he labored to the close of his life; he died on the 10th of February, 1862.

14. "Rev. C. B. Thuemmel, formerly of the Synod of New York," took charge of the classical school connected with the Theological Seminary at Lexington, S. C., in 1841; he labored in that capacity three years, when he returned to the North.

15. Rev. J. Daily was licensed in 1840, and labored in Alabama.

Other ministers were licensed by the South Carolina Synod during this period, but as their names have been mentioned in connection with the North Carolina Synod, it is not necessary to insert them here again.

The Tennessee Synod was likewise blessed with a considerable addition to her ministerial strength, during the five years preceding the year 1840, as follows:

1. Rev. Abel J. Brown, was ordained a deacon in 1836, labored for several years in Lincoln County, N. C., but made his home finally in Tennessee, where he is still doing good service in his Master's vineyard.

2. Rev. Jacob Killian was ordained a deacon at the same time, and labored in Augusta County, Va., where he departed this life July 5th, 1871.

3. Rev. Jonathan R. Moser was likewise ordained to the deacon's office in 1836, labored a number of years in Lincoln County, N. C., but

finally moved to Missouri, where he is still residing.

4. Rev. Henry Wetzel, was ordained deacon in 1837, is still laboring in Virginia.

5. Rev. Adam S. Link was ordained at the same time, but afterwards moved to Ohio, where he died, March 30th, 1862.

6. Rev. Jacob Stirewalt was likewise ordained deacon in 1837; he became pastor in New Market, Va., where he labored to the close of his life; he died August 26th, 1869, in his 67th year.

7. Rev. Albert J. Fox was ordained deacon in 1837, labored successively in North Carolina, Tennessee, and Alabama, but since 1855 has been residing near Lincolnton, N. C., where he is still laboring in the Lord's vineyard.

The following new congregations were organized and new church edifices erected in the Carolinas during the five years preceding 1840.

1. *Luther's Church*, in Rowan County, N. C., is first mentioned by that name in the minutes of 1830, but at what time the congregation was organized is not stated. The Rev. Jacob Kaempfer was its pastor in 1830.

2. *St. Enoch's Church*, in Rowan County, N. C., is a colony from the Sewitz's or Luther Chapel congregation, and was organized in 1836; it is not stated when their church edifice was erected; it was dedicated at some time during the fall of 1839.

3. *St. Paul's Church*, in Rowan County, N. C., is first mentioned in 1837, under the name of

Holdshouser's Church, with Rev. S. Rothrock as its pastor. A new brick church has been recently erected and was dedicated July 21st, 1872.

4. *St. Stephen's Church*, Cabarrus County, N. C., was organized in 1837 by the Rev. P. A. Strobel, who was its first pastor. It was received under the care of the North Carolina Synod in 1838.

5. *St. Matthew's Church*, Rowan County, N. C., sent a communication to the North Carolina Synod in 1838, "stating that they have regularly organized themselves into a congregation, and pray to be received under the care of Synod; also, that they have chosen the Rev. B. Arey as their pastor."

6. *St. Matthew's congregation*, in Davie County, N. C., is first mentioned in 1839 in the minutes of the North Carolina Synod, when forty-three persons in that locality petitioned the Synod to send them a minister "to break unto them the bread of eternal truth, to baptize their children, and instruct their youth."

Two new church edifices were erected in old-established congregations during the year 1839, namely: St. Paul's Church, Orange (now Alamance) County, N. C., which was dedicated on the third Sunday in September, 1839; and Luther Chapel, in Rowan County, N. C., which was dedicated about the same time.

7. *St. Paul's Church*, Iredell County, N. C., and the above-named *St. Matthew's Church*, in Davie County, N. C., are mentioned in the minutes of

the North Carolina Synod of 1840, as having "been regularly organized during the last synodical year," and were received, in 1840, under the care of Synod.

In the bounds of the South Carolina Synod the following churches were added to the strength of the Synod.

1. *St. Andrew's Church*, Lexington District, S. C., was organized in 1835, and during the same year their church edifice was erected and dedicated. In 1835, they petitioned Synod for the pastoral labors of Rev. L. Bedenbaugh, but from the minutes of 1836 it appears that Rev. M. Rauch was their first pastor.

2. *Mount Zion Church*, Newberry District, S. C., having been organized under the pastoral care of Rev. J. Moser, their church edifice was dedicated on the fifth Sunday in August, 1840.

3. *Good Hope Church*, at Cloud's Creek, Edgefield District, S. C., having been organized some time in 1839, their newly-erected church edifice was dedicated on the 19th of April, 1840. Their first pastor was the Rev. R. Cloy; it was received under the care of Synod in 1840.

The labors of Rev. John Bachman, D.D., LL.D., having been for many years very arduous, inasmuch as he was necessitated to preach three times every Sunday for the long period of twenty years, and frequently both in the English and German languages, his being the only Lutheran church in Charleston, S. C., at that time; besides, having also devoted much of his time to natural science, he and the renowned naturalist, J. J. Audubon, being associated together in preparing for the press "The Quadrupeds of America," his health at length became impaired, and, at the repeated solicitations of his congregation, to whom his life and labors were exceedingly valuable, he left his home on a visit to Europe, in 1838, believing that he looked upon the shores of his native land for the last time. He was absent eight months, and was received everywhere on his transatlantic tour with "sympathy, kindness, and untiring hospitality." He "returned in January, 1839, with health partially restored," and his congregation engaged the Rev. William H. Smith, of Maryland, as an assistant minister for a few years, until his health was re-established, when, in 1842, he once more assumed the entire charge of the pastoral duties of his church.

Section 4. Settlement of North-Germans in Southern cities. Organization and Early History of St. Matthew's German Evangelical-Lutheran Church, Charleston, S. C.

Many years had now elapsed since the tide of German emigration to North and South Carolina had entirely ceased. The dependence for the increase of the Lutheran Church in those States rested mainly upon the descendants of the early settlers. However, about the year 1835, emigration from North Germany found its way also to Southern cities, and every fall new emigrants from that portion of the Fatherland continued to arrive.

The largest number of these settlers located themselves in Charleston, S. C., but many have found homes in Wilmington, N. C., Savannah, Georgia, and other Southern cities. They are mostly natives of Hanover, Oldenburg, Holstein, Mecklenburg, and the once free cities of Hamburg and Bremen, although a number of emigrants from other German states may be found among them.

These North Germans are regarded as the direct descendants of those Saxon nations which conquered ancient Britain, a portion of whom, after the Saxon conquest, located themselves permanently in England. That this is a fact established beyond dispute may be readily learned from the pages of history, and easily perceived from the contiguity of those North-German countries to England, their maritime character, and their language. It may not be generally known, that the North Germans speak two languages, the high German, which is the written language, taught at school and preached from the pulpit, and the low German (Platdeutsch), which is the original language of the ancient North Saxons, still spoken and generally used in those countries, and bears a remarkable resemblance to the present pure English or Anglo-Saxon language. Hence, North Germans generally find no difficulty in acquiring a knowledge of the English language soon after their arrival in this country, and learn to pronounce it correctly with remarkable facility.

As the North Germans are natives of maritime States, they prefer mercantile to agricultural pursuits, and hence they are generally found engaged in mercantile employments in our Southern cities, though not entirely confined to that kind of life.

Captain H. Wieting, a name familiar to all our North-German citizens in the Southern States, and his vessels, the "Johann Friederich," and the barque "Copernicus," of which successively he was commander, usually arrived, for some length of time, once a year in Charleston, S. C., filled with German passengers, who expected to make their future home in the South.

These German settlers, by means of their economy, good management, and excellent business talents, have acquired considerable property, and control a large portion of the commercial and other interests in the cities and towns where they reside.

The Lutheran faith being the prevailing religion in North Germany, although German Reformed and Roman Catholics may likewise be found there, these immigrants are generally members of the Lutheran Church, and, upon their arrival in this country, usually attach themselves immediately to Lutheran congregations.

Rev. E. L. Hazelius, D.D., President of the South Carolina Synod, in his annual report of 1839, speaks of the first attempt of the native German citizens of Charleston, S. C., in establishing a second, and altogether German, Lutheran Church, in the following manner:

"A desire having been expressed by a considerable number of German citizens of Charleston, to have the Gospel preached to them in the language of their Fatherland, meetings of the Germans were held during my stay in the city and afterwards, for the purpose of making the necessary arrangements; and I have since learned that articles of a Church union were drawn up and adopted; that $500 had been collected, and about as much had been subscribed for the salary of a German preacher. I endeavored to encourage these friends to proceed in the good cause."

In the Charleston Courier may be found an account of the next steps that were taken in this direction.

"On the 3d day of December, A.D. 1840, the first German congregation was organized in this city, with the following founders: John A. Wagener, George Caulier, C. Heide, F. Mehrtens, F. Hilgen, J. Hürkamp, W. H. Hoops, J. Haesloop, J. Stelling, Geo. Rieke, J. H. Ostendorff, J. Schröder, J. Kleinbeck, C. Gerdts, J. Bauman, and L. F. Behling. The congregation so formed soon made arrangements for the erection of a place of worship."

They adopted a constitution for their government on the 9th of December, 1840, and soon afterwards purchased a lot on the corner of Hasell and Anson Streets, on which they erected a brick church edifice. In the election of officers, Col.

John A. Wagener was chosen their first President. In the month of October, 1841, the cornerstone of this (St. Matthew's) church was laid, at which time the congregation already numbered two hundred and twenty-five members. Their first pastor was the Rev. F. Becher, who had been, up to that time, a minister of the German Reformed Church, but connected himself with the South Carolina Synod in 1841, after having taken charge of this new German Lutheran congregation.

However, the Rev. Mr. Becher did not remain long in Charleston. In 1842 the Rev. F. W. Heemsoth took charge of the congregation, and on the 22d of June of the same year, the new church was dedicated, and the newly elected pastor duly installed. "Rev. Mr. Heemsoth served the congregation until 1848, when he resigned and returned to his native country, where he now resides," and is the beloved pastor of a large Lutheran church in Germany.

Section 5. Formation of the Western Virginia Synod, and Death of Rev. Henry Graeber.

It would not be proper to notice the formation of the Synod of Western Virginia in the history of the Lutheran Church in the Carolinas, were it not for the fact, that the territory of the Synod of Western Virginia was, for a long period of time, embraced in the limits of the North Carolina Synod, which watched over the interests of the

Lutheran Church in Western Virginia with a mother's tender care, supplying that field with missionaries at first, and afterwards with pastors.

But the time had now arrived, when the old mother Synod was to be confined within the limits of the State from which she derived her name; all her ecclesiastical operations were henceforth to be devoted to North Carolina alone. The interests of the Church demanded that the brethren in Southwestern Virginia were to form a Synod for themselves, and the sequel has proved that this was a step taken in the right direction, for it has developed the energies of that portion of the Lutheran Church in a most remarkable manner, both in missionary and educational enterprises.

Accordingly, on the 20th of September, 1841, a convention was held in Wythe County, Virginia, for the purpose of taking the preliminary steps towards the formation of a Synod, and on the 21st of May, 1842, "the ministers residing in Western Virginia, with their lay delegates, assembled in Zion's Church, Floyd County, Virginia." The ministers, who registered their names as members of the newly formed Synod, were: Revs. Jacob Scherer, Samuel Sayford, Elijah Hawkins, John J. Greever, Gideon Scherer and Stephen Rudy. The officers of Synod then elected were: Rev. Jacob Scherer, President; Rev. Elijah Hawkins, Secretary; and Mr. Joseph Brown, Treasurer. The strength of Synod then reported was, fifteen congregations and seven hundred and seventy-eight communicants.

From the Synod of North Carolina, established in the year 1803, and which at one time embraced a large scope of territory, the following Synods have gone out, and are still doing good service in the vineyard of the Lord:

The Tennessee Synod, organized A.D. 1820.

The South Carolina Synod, organized A.D. 1824.

The Western Virginia Synod, organized A.D. 1842.

From these again the following additional Synods have been formed: The Georgia Synod, the Mississippi Synod, the Holston Synod, and the Concordia Synod. The Lutheran Church in the West, and particularly in Illinois, was also cradled and nourished in its infancy by the North Carolina Synod.

The Rev. Henry Graeber, who at one time wielded a considerable influence in the North Carolina Synod, and who, on account of his sterling virtues and power of his native intellect, as well as by his energy of character, accomplished much good, was now called to his rest, while yet in the strength of his years, and in the height of his usefulness. After a short illness he unexpectedly departed this life, September 11th, 1843. The President of Synod, Rev. Wm. Artz, gives us the following account of this sad event, connected with a brief memoir of Rev. Graeber's life:

"When the names of the members of our ministerial association shall be called, and every one present shall take his seat, the place of our worthy and beloved brother, the Rev. Henry Graeber, will be vacant. How sad! How unexpected! He has ceased from his labors in the vineyard of the Lord on earth, and has entered the rest above, to reap the eternal reward which Jesus has promised to all his faithful servants.

'His conflicts with his busy foes
For evermore shall cease,
None shall his happiness oppose,
Nor interrupt his peace.
But bright rewards shall recompense
His faithful service here,
And perfect love shall banish thence
Each gloomy doubt and fear.'

"Our worthy brother, the Rev. Henry Graeber, was born of Christian parents in the State of Pennsylvania, in the year of our Lord 1793, the 28th of January. He prosecuted the study of divinity chiefly under the able and pious instructions of the Rev. Messrs. Melsheimer and Lochman. He obtained license to preach the Gospel from the Synod of Pennsylvania, on the 7th of June, in the year 1818, and was shortly afterwards set apart to this holy work by the imposition of hands and prayer. Nine years of his ministerial life he spent as pastor of several congregations in Frederick County, Maryland, and the remaining sixteen years were spent in several congregations in Lincoln, Rowan, and Cabarrus Counties, in the bounds of our Synod, of which he was an efficient member, and in which he repeatedly filled with honor the highest offices. He was a liberal supporter of benevolent institutions, and a warm and decided friend of an enlightened and educated ministry.

He was himself an able and faithful minister of the New Testament, rightly dividing the word of eternal truth, and giving to both saints and sinners their portion in due season. And I need not add, in the presence of those who knew him long, and who knew him well, that through the course of his ministerial life, he uniformly adorned the doctrines which he preached by zeal, fidelity, firmness, and charity, and all those virtues that are so essential to the character of the Christian minister. He died of nervous fever on the 11th of September last, in the 51st year of his age. While his ashes sleep in the peaceful tomb, may his memory be cherished by us with fraternal affection."

His body lies entombed in the Organ Church graveyard, not far distant from the place where repose the remains of Rev. C. A. G. Storch, and where at this time the bodies of four Lutheran ministers sleep until the morning of the resurrection.

The following epitaph has been inscribed on the marble slab which covers his mortal remains:

"Sacred to the memory of the Rev. Henry Graeber, who was born on the 28th of January, 1793; and departed this life on the 11th of September, 1843. Aged 50 years, 7 months, and 13 days.

'The Gospel was his joy and song,
E'en to his latest breath;
The truth he had proclaimed so long,
Was his support in death.
The grave is now his favored spot,
To sleep in Jesus blessed,
There, where the wicked trouble not,
He laid his head to rest.' "

Section 6. Endowment of a Second Professorship in the Theological Seminary at Lexington, S. C.—Memoir of Henry Muller, Sr.

The educational interests of the Lutheran Church in the Carolinas had now become so greatly developed, that it became necessary to endow an additional professorship for the Theological Seminary at Lexington, S. C. Provision had been made for several years past to have a classical Professor connected with the Seminary, and the Rev. Washington Muller, Rev. C. B. Thuemmel, and Mr. S. E. Caughman had each successively been appointed to this position by the Board of Directors, and had acted in that capacity; but for want of a permanent endowment of this professorship, the arrangement was subjected to repeated interruption.

The discussion of this matter, as well as that of the location of the Seminary, during the year 1848, in the columns of the Lutheran Observer, brought the subject prominently before the Church, and at the next meeting of the South Carolina Synod, held at Sandy Run Church, in Lexington District, the President of Synod recommended "the appointment of a special committee to investigate and report upon this whole subject."

The committee appointed in accordance with the recommendation of the President were: Revs. John Bachman, D.D., John F. W. Leppard and J. B. Anthony, of the clergy; and Messrs. George

M. Fulmer, John C. Geiger and John Rauch, of the laity, who gave the matter a thorough and prayerful consideration, closing their lengthy report as follows:

"In the midst of our anxious and prayerful deliberations, a providential and thrilling scene presented itself, that gave a presentiment of God's favor and our prospect of success. One of our benevolent lay members, whose untiring zeal and liberality has ever kept him far in advance of all our other benefactors, and whose praise is in all the churches, rose to present to this object the sum of $4000, on condition that individuals from the various portions of our Church should pledge themselves to make up a similar amount, to be appropriated to the same benevolent object. From that moment we regarded the work as done. We have only to say to ourselves, to our brethren, the ministers, delegates, and members of our churches, 'go,' and in proportion to your circumstances, 'do ye likewise,' and the object of our anxious solicitude and ardent prayers will be accomplished. We have been purchased by the blood of Christ—let us evidence our gratitude by contributing to send the light of salvation to those for whom he died.

"The Church demands these small pecuniary sacrifices—let us say to our people and to the world, we esteem it an honor and a privilege to respond to her call. Here, in the presence of the Living God, surrounded by the ministers, and fathers, and representatives of our beloved Church, let us resolve that ere we separate for our distant homes, nay, ere yon sun shall set, ere another night shall intervene to awaken the feelings of selfishness, or throw a shadow of doubt over the bright picture of Christian benevolence which is now before us, let us resolve in the strength, the fear, and love, and in imitation of our benevolent Master, whose office on earth was to go about doing good, that this work shall be consummated. Let us resolve with the pious men of old: 'O Jerusalem, if I forget thee, let my right hand forget her cunning. If I do not remember thee, let my tongue cleave to the roof of my mouth, if I remember not Jerusalem, my chief joy.'"

(Signed)

JOHN BACHMAN,	GEORGE M. FULMER,
JOHN F. W. LEPPARD,	JOHN C. GEIGER,
J. B. ANTHONY,	JOHN RAUCH.

This stirring appeal had the desired effect—the inspiration of a sense of this new duty and of love to the Church pervaded the whole assembly, and before the Synod closed that memorable day's session, the required sum was pledged, secured, and afterwards paid in as the instalments became due. An additional sum of $3223 was subsequently added to this fund, through a seven months' agency of Rev. G. D. Bernheim, who was employed by the Board of Directors for this purpose.

The following resolution of thanks to Mr. Henry Muller, Sr., was then adopted:

"*Resolved*, That the thanks of this Synod be presented to our venerable and esteemed friend and benefactor, Henry Muller, Sr., for his many labors and sacrifices in behalf of our Theological Seminary, and the various interests of the Church, for his generous contributions from year to year, and for his liberal donation to the Seminary, at our present session, of $4000."

Mr. Muller's benefactions toward this object did not cease with that donation; at his own expense he had a dwelling erected, costing about $2000, for the use of the second Professor, and donated it to the Synod, so that this new enterprise for the welfare of the Church could go into operation forthwith.

No one can speak too highly of Mr. Henry Muller's humble and devoted christianity, and of his never-failing and munificent acts of benevolence. Not only did the Theological Seminary receive a very large share of his benefactions, but churches, Sunday-schools, ministers of the Gospel, indigent students of theology, and many other persons were assisted by him with amounts in proportion to their necessities. Never in traveling over seventeen States of our Union has the author seen Mr. Muller's equal in every respect; such members are a blessing to any Church.

The amount of his wealth was not enormous; many there are in almost any Synod, who possess as much property, and even more than he did. Besides, Mr. Muller had a large family of children, to whom he gave all the advantages of a most liberal education; but he had also a large heart, beaming with the love of Christ, and regarding himself merely as a steward, he was ready to aid any and every worthy object that was presented to him.

As a just tribute to his memory, the following account of his life will not be uninteresting:

Ernest Henry David Muller was born in the Kingdom of Saxony, November 20th, 1774, and was left an orphan at the early age of five or six years. He was brought up in the city of Bremen as a merchant, and came with his brother to America, December 16th, 1805, being then in his thirty-first year. He located himself at Granby, in Lexington District, and engaged in merchandising, but afterwards moved his place of business to Sandy Run. He was married to a Miss Geiger, a descendant of the early German settlers of Saxe-Gotha Township, Lexington District, and resided near Platt Springs. He was the father of eleven children, five sons and six daughters, nine of whom survived him. He departed this life in great peace on the 12th of October, 1850, aged 75 years, 10 months and 22 days.

"In him," says the President of Synod, "the Church has lost one of its most ardent lovers, the institution at Lexington one of its warmest friends, and the Board of Directors one of its most active and useful members."

The following preamble and resolutions were adopted by Synod in memory of this mournful event:

"WHEREAS, It has pleased the kind Disposer of all human events to remove from the endearments of his family and friends—from the sphere of active duty in society, and his labors of love in the Church—the late Henry Muller, the Treasurer of our Seminary; and whereas it is a pious duty to cherish the memory and record for the imitation of posterity the virtues of the benevolent and pious, be it therefore—

"1. *Resolved*, That this Synod will cherish the memory of our deceased brother, whose whole life was an exhibition of those virtues which emphatically characterize the just man. That they feel grateful for the untiring zeal, industry and accuracy with which he performed the duties of Treasurer of the Seminary, from the time when the institution was first organized until the day of his death—and that we will ever bear in remembrance his acts of munificence, by which we were enabled to establish a second professorship in the Seminary, and those deeds of charity which characterized his whole life, which rendered him an ornament to the Christian Church while living, and which will embalm his memory in the hearts of pious men of all denominations after his removal from the earth.

"2. *Resolved*, That this Synod will use their utmost efforts to promote the best interests of those institutions in our Church which our deceased brother so strenuously labored to cherish and advance; and that we feel thankful to the great Head of the Church that we have enjoyed the benefit of being stimulated by so noble an example, who, although dead, still speaketh to us of the high and holy duty of Christian beneficence.

"3. *Resolved*, That this Synod secure to the family of the deceased Henry Muller, and their descendants, one scholarship for the Seminary, as long as the institution continues to exist.

"4. *Resolved*, That this Synod express their sympathy and condolence with the bereaved family of the deceased; that the Secretary transmit a copy of these resolutions to the bereaved widow and mourning family of the deceased, and that they be published in our minutes and in the Lutheran Observer."

Section 7. Colony of German Settlers at Walhalla, S. C.—Additional New Congregations organized —The Mississippi and Texas Missions.

The number of German settlers in Charleston, S. C., having increased rapidly within the past few years, it was deemed advisable to locate a German colony somewhere in the interior of the State. Accordingly, about the year 1850, a land company was formed among the Germans residing in Charleston, through the energetic labors of Col. John A. Wagener, a public-spirited and enterprising German, and a large body of land was purchased in Pickens District, S. C., of Col. Gresham and others.

The land was admirably located, being in the mountain regions of Carolina, exceedingly fertile and well adapted for the cultivation of all the necessary cereals, fruits and vegetables, with an abundant supply of excellent water, free from the heat of less elevated latitudes, and possessing a most salubrious climate, making this settlement a most desirable summer retreat for strangers from the low country. A town was soon laid out, and received the ancient German name, *Walhalla*, and the remaining land was divided into farms and sold to German settlers. So rapidly did the population in the new settlement increase, that Walhalla has become a place of importance, even to native American citizens. It has, of course, a Lutheran church, for nearly all the original settlers are of that faith. This church was erected in 1855, under the pastoral care of Rev. C. F. Bansemer; it was built with a spire 112 feet in height; but there are three churches of other denominations likewise located in the town. Newberry College, the literary institution of the Lutheran Synod of South Carolina, has been recently removed to Walhalla, all of which, with its Female Seminary, its trade and its abundant railroad facilities, will make Walhalla eventually one of the largest inland towns in the mountain districts of Carolina. It numbers now about 1500 inhabitants, and has recently become the county seat of Oconee County, a newly-formed judicial section of the State.

In North Carolina, under the ministry of Rev. W. G. Harter, a new Lutheran church was erected in the town of Concord, and the Lutheran portion of the old Coldwater Creek congregation transplanted thither, receiving the name *St. James* at the day of its dedication, which event occurred on the 6th of April, 1843. The dedication sermon was preached by Rev. Henry Graeber from the text Luke 14 : 23: "Compel them to come in, that my house may be filled."

In the year 1850, a new congregation was organized in Rowan County, N. C., "seven miles from Salisbury, on the Beattie's Ford Road, with twenty-two members," under the ministry of Rev. B. N. Hopkins. It afterwards received the name of Salem Church. In the town of Newton, Catawba County, a new mission church was established during the same year.

The Church in North Carolina under the care of the Tennessee Synod became also greatly enlarged, but it is impossible to particularize the organization of new congregations, inasmuch as these items are not reported in the minutes of that time.

"On the fourth Sabbath in May," 1842, "a new Lutheran church by the name of *Corinth*, in the District of Edgefield, S. C., was dedicated to the service of the triune God. The dedicatory sermon was preached by Rev. G. Haltiwanger, Sr., and a sermon by Rev. Wm. Berly on the doctrines, government and usages of the Lutheran Church in this country. Rev. Messrs. Aull and Leppard were present on the occasion, and rendered their appropriate share of service."

In 1843, under the ministry of Rev. G. H. Brown, a new Lutheran congregation was organized and a church erected in Newberry District, S. C., receiving the name of *Beth-Eden*. It was dedicated on the second Sunday in September; the ministers present on that occasion were Revs. J. C. Hope, H. Aull and the pastor in charge.

"Another church building was erected by the St. Matthew's congregation, to be a branch of the old church, which was dedicated to the service of the triune God on Sunday, the 26th of March, 1843. Brethren in attendance—pastor in charge and Brother Sheppard. This constitutes one of the three churches connected with St. Matthews," in Orangeburg District, S. C.

St. David's Church, in Lexington District, S. C., was organized and received in connection with the South Carolina Synod in 1845.

In 1849 three new churches were dedicated for newly-organized Lutheran congregations in South Carolina, namely, one located on the Monk's Corner Road, St. Matthew's Parish, Orangeburg District, on the first Sunday in June. It is presumed that this is the church called "*Trinity Church.*"

Macedonia Church, in Lexington District, was dedicated on the fourth Sunday in September by Rev. Mr. Berly.

Another church, near Leesville, S. C., was consecrated on the fourth Sunday in October by Revs. S. Bouknight, S. R. Sheppard and J. B. Lowman.

The Mississippi mission was commenced by the Synod of South Carolina in the year 1846, when the Rev. G. H. Brown resigned his pleasant Beth-

Eden charge, and from conscientious convictions of duty felt himself called to labor for the Church in that promising field, where Lutheran colonists from North and South Carolina had located themselves. The new missionary enterprise was not a mere experiment, for, "after many discouragements and severe trials," it became eminently successful; the Lord blessed the labors of his faithful servant, the Rev. Mr. Brown, who had not been long in Mississippi when he called for more laborers, and in 1847, the Rev. James D. Stingley came to his assistance, who was soon followed by the Revs. S. R. Sheppard, C. D. Austin and J. T. Warner. A Synod was formed in that State in 1855, and the Lutheran Church in Mississippi, after having overcome many difficulties, appears at present to be in a prosperous condition. The Revs. Brown, Stingley and Sheppard have all been called to their final rest and reward, but their works still follow them.

In the year 1850, the South Carolina Synod sent the Rev. George F. Guebner as a missionary to the State of Texas, who, at first, traveled over a considerable portion of its territory, organizing congregations, but finally located himself in the city of Galveston. Rev. Guebner remained there but a few years, when his health failed him, and he removed to one of the Northwestern States, residing, a few years ago, in the State of Indiana, and being in connection with the Evangelical Union of the West. The Texas mission, however, is not a failure; ministers from Germany located themselves there soon afterwards, and in considerable numbers, who now have a flourishing Synod in that State.

Section 8. State of the Lutheran Church in the Carolinas, in the year 1850.

During the twenty-five or thirty years preceding the year 1850, the Lutheran Church in North and South Carolina made rapid progress in almost every respect, and without any material addition to her strength by foreign immigration, yea, even with a constant drain upon her strength by the removal of many of her members to the West. Nor has she ever made any effort to propagate her doctrines legitimately among those of no ecclesiastical connection, but rather shrank from all public notoriety, modestly laboring for the good of those, whom God had specially committed to her care; she has, notwithstanding, accomplished an amount of good fully equal to the talent intrusted to her keeping. God has upheld her by His own right hand, and preserved her for a work and purpose that will glorify His name; and, judging from the past, will make her future still more prosperous.

In 1820, when the Tennessee Synod was organized, only five ministers became connected with it; and in 1850 the number had increased to twenty-eight ministers, and, had not other Synods been formed, with which some of its ministers became connected, the increase on its clerical roll would have been much larger.

The principal additions to its number of ministers since 1840, were Revs. John Roth and Joel W. Hull, who were ordained as deacons, December 13th, 1841; Rev. Dennis D. Swaney, ordained as deacon in 1842; Revs. Jesse R. Peterson, Polycarp C. Henkel, Jacob M. Schaeffer, who were ordained to the office of deacon, October 5th, 1843; Revs. J. M. Wagner, Timothy Moser, ordained to the same office, October 10th, 1844; Revs. James K. Hancher, Thomas Crouse, ordained as deacons in 1845; Rev. Adam Efird, ordained as above in 1847; Rev. D. M. Henkel, ordained October 5th, 1848; Revs. Socrates Henkel, D. Efird, J. B. Emmert, and James Fleenor, ordained to the deacon's office in 1850. Of these, Revs. Hull, Peterson, P. C. Henkel, T. Moser, T. Crouse, A. Efird, and D. Efird, were laboring in North Carolina in 1850. The Efird brothers soon afterwards removed to South Carolina, and Rev. J. M. Wagner subsequently labored several years in North Carolina. Rev. Adam Efird has since departed this life, September 13th, 1870.

The North Carolina Synod was likewise largely increased by an addition of ministerial strength, but the number of its ministers became greatly reduced in 1842, by the organization of the Western Virginia Synod, at which time the North Carolina Synod became restricted within the limits of its own proper State boundary, whilst at the same time, nearly one-half of the strength of the Lutheran Church in North Carolina is embraced in the Tennessee Synod.

The ministers who connected themselves with the North Carolina Synod since 1840, were the following:

Rev. John D. Scheck, of the South Carolina Synod, who became the pastor successively of the Salisbury, St. John's, Cabarrus County, and the Alamance pastorates. During his ministry, and in 1845, the large brick St. John's Church, in Cabarrus County, was erected, and was dedicated August 22d, 1846. Its dimensions are eighty by fifty-five feet, and is at present the fifth house of worship, which has been built for this congregation, since the first settlement of Germans on Buffalo Creek, and was considered at the time the largest and most commodious house of worship in Western North Carolina.

Rev. William G. Harter, also from the South Carolina Synod, became the pastor of the Concord Church, whose history has already been mentioned.

Rev. Joseph A. Linn, a student both at Lexington, South Carolina, and Gettysburg, Pennsylvania, and licensed in 1844, became the pastor of the Gold Hill charge, in Rowan County, where he was much beloved, and generally useful to the Lutheran Church in North Carolina. His death was a sad one: returning home on Sunday from one of his churches, he was thrown from his horse, which fractured his head, and he expired the following Wednesday, March 16th, 1864.

Rev. J. B. Anthony was received by the North

Carolina Synod May 6th, 1844, and labored some twenty years in the bounds of the North and South Carolina Synods, but is at present residing in the State of Pennsylvania, as pastor of the York Sulphur Springs charge.

Revs. Fink, Coffman, and Hopkins were added to the list of ministers successively in 1847, 1848, and 1849, but their names had soon to be stricken from the roll.

Rev. Levi C. Groseclose, a student from Lexington, S. C., and Gettysburg, Pennsylvania, was licensed in 1849 by the West Virginia Synod, and has been doing good service in the North Carolina Synod since 1850, being at present the pastor of the St. John's charge in Cabarrus County, N. C.

The Synod of South Carolina manifested at this time a more rapid growth and a greater degree of prosperity than either the North Carolina or Tennessee Synods; this was owing to its Theological Seminary and extensive missionary operations outside of the limits of the State. In 1824 this Synod was organized with seven ministers, and in 1849 it had forty-six ordained and licensed ministers on its clerical roll; however, this number has since been reduced by the formation of the Mississippi and Georgia Synods.

During the ten years preceding the year 1850, the following ministers were added to the clerical strength of the South Carolina Synod:

Rev. John F. W. Leppard, who was licensed November 30th, 1841, was the pastor of St. Stephen's Church, Lexington Court-House, and Sandy Run

Church. He was adjunct Professor of Theology at the Lexington Seminary during the years 1848 and 1849; he was an eloquent preacher, and a man greatly beloved, but departed this life, February 13th, 1852.

Rev. P. Kistler was licensed at the same time, and labored successively in South and North Carolina. He has connected himself with another denomination.

Rev. C. F. Bansemer entered the ministry, February 20th, 1842; was for several years pastor of the Lutheran Church in Walhalla, S. C., and President of North Carolina College, at Mt. Pleasant, N. C., in 1867 and 1868.

Rev. F. W. Heemsoth was received as a member of Synod in 1842; was pastor of the German Lutheran Church in Charleston, S. C., but returned to Germany in 1848.

Rev. Elias B. Hort was licensed in 1842; became the pastor of the Lutheran Church in Columbia, S. C., where he remained in office to the close of his life. He died January 15th, 1863.

Rev. George H. Brown's history has been given; he was licensed in 1842.

Revs. George R. Haigler and *James H. Bailey* were licensed November 11th, 1845. The former labored for a time in St. Matthew's Parish, Orangeburg District, after which he removed to Alabama. The latter is still doing good service in Lexington County, S. C.

Rev. L. Müller, admitted as a member of Synod in 1848. He is still the pastor of St. Matthew's

German Lutheran Church in Charleston, S. C. His congregation has recently built a large and magnificent church edifice, which was dedicated March 28th, 1872.

Revs. E. Elmore, Eph. Kieffer, J. B. Lowman, B. N. Hopkins and Ephraim Dufford, were licensed November 24th, 1848. Revs. Elmore and Kieffer labored in Georgia; Revs. Lowman and Dufford are still laboring in South Carolina.

Rev. A. J. Karn became the pastor of the Lutheran Church at Savannah, Georgia, in 1848, and connected himself with the South Carolina Synod the next year. "He died December 19th, 1860, in Chicago, Illinois, aged forty years."

Revs. George F. Guebner, G. D. Bernheim, Mark Posey, C. D. Austin, E. Caughman, A. W. Lindler, D. Sheely and S. W. Bedenbaugh, were admitted to the ministry November 14th, 1849, all of whom are still living except Rev. Posey, who died at Franconia, Alabama, August 26th, 1852. Revs. Caughman, Lindler and Sheely are still laboring in South Carolina; Rev. Bedenbaugh in Georgia. The history of the others has already been furnished, all of whom are still actively engaged in the work of the ministry.

Section 9. Concluding Remarks.

In order to understand the age in which we live, it is important and necessary that we should carefully study the history of the past. The various and succeeding epochs of the world are not a number of disjointed parts rudely thrown together, which might as well have happened at some other time, but a successive course of events all occurring "when the fulness of time was come."

The present is a development of the past; it is the child of a parent that has stamped upon it many of the characteristics and manifestations of the past. And as individuals are possessed of virtues and faults, so is every age in which man lives an intermixture of excellencies and errors, which the study of history enables us to discover, so that we may walk in the light of the one, and studiously avoid the other.

In ecclesiastical affairs it is equally important and even more necessary diligently to study the history of the past, inasmuch as an error committed in the Church invariably leads to eternally fatal consequences. And that departures and errors have occurred in the Church is well known; these should be ever kept in view, like so many pillars of salt, with "Remember Lot's wife" inscribed upon them, so as to apprise us of our dangers, and point out to us the path of safety.

We can become wiser than our forefathers, only when we have mastered their knowledge and experience, and add our own thereto; but never by obliterating the past, and starting upon a career in the world, unprepared to meet and avoid its dangers, and unfitted to take advantage of the opportunities it offers us.

As the Lutheran Church professes to be, and is,

in intimate connection with the past, let her not unwisely assume the character and put on the garb of infancy, casting away her priceless history and experience, and starting upon a voyage on the ocean of life without compass, rudder, anchor, or chart.

These thoughts apply equally as well to the local history of the Lutheran Church. Here in America, yes in every Province or State, events have occurred which have had their influence upon her character, and which it is our duty to know and to study. Had there been no departures either in faith or practice, there would never have been any divisions; this is a truth which ecclesiastical history teaches us on almost every page. It was once thought wise and praiseworthy to cast aside the shackles of the past, by which the Lutheran Church was believed to have been enslaved, and start her upon a new career with improved doctrines, altered forms of worship and a new cultus; but events have proved, that nothing has been gained by this departure, but rather—that thereby she "was wounded in the house of her friends."

It is needless now to conceal the divisions that are apparent in the Lutheran Church in the Carolinas, as well as in America—they do exist; and all our lamentations, &c., cannot heal them; they are the legitimate developments of the past; let us rather study them in the light of past experience, in order that we may discover the mistakes then made, which prepared the way for such divisions, and endeavor to heal them at their very root. Let us no longer make the attempt "to agree to disagree," but honestly ask for the old paths, diligently study "the faith once delivered to the saints," so that we may intelligently and "earnestly contend for it;" let us in this way seek to become united in faith and practice, not from motives of policy, but as an honest conviction of duty.

May then also this history of the Lutheran Church in the Carolinas inspire our people and their ministers with a greater respect for their time-honored Church, and build upon the foundation which their forefathers in the days of the Reformers have laid, and do this with such a zeal and energy, as proceeds only from a conscientious conviction of duty; then indeed will their labor be productive both of the dissemination of the pure doctrines of God's word, and of the glory of God in the advancement of our Savior's kingdom on earth. The fact, that inquiry has been awakened in regard to these things in the Lutheran Church both in Europe and in every section in America, is a hopeful indication of her future healthy development, and of her increased activity and prosperity.

"Thou shalt arise and have mercy upon Zion: for the time to favor her, yea, the set time, is come. For thy servants take pleasure in her stones, and favor the dust thereof." Psalm 102 : 13 and 14.

THE END.